NEW RESEARCH ON KNOWLEDGE MANAGEMENT APPLICATIONS AND LESSON LEARNED

Edited by **Huei-Tse Hou**

New Research on Knowledge Management Applications and Lesson Learned
Edited by Huei-Tse Hou

Published by InTech

Janeza Trdine 9, 51000 Rijeka, Croatia

Publishing Process Manager Anja Filipovic

Technical Editor Teodora Smiljanic

Cover Designer InTech Design Team

Additional hard copies can be obtained from orders@intechopen.com

New Research on Knowledge Management Applications and Lesson Learned,
Edited by Huei-Tse Hou
p. cm.
ISBN 978-953-51-0073-7

For EU product safety concerns:
IN TECH d.o.o., Prolaz Marije Krucifikse Kozulić 3, 51000 Rijeka, Croatia,
info@intechopen.com or visit our website at intechopen.com.

Meet the editor

Dr Huei-Tse Hou is an Assistant Professor of Graduate Institute of Applied Science and Technology, National Taiwan University of Science and Technology, Taiwan. He has received the Ta-You Wu Memorial Award (Young Outstanding Researcher Award) (Year 2010) by the National Science Council, Taiwan. His research interest focuses on knowledge management/sharing, e-Learning behavioral pattern analysis, e-Learning system development, and game-based learning systems. Professor Hou has published many academic papers in famous SSCI indexed journals such as *Computers in Human Behavior*, *Computers & Education*, *Educational Technology & Society*, *British Journal of Educational Technology*, and *Interactive Learning Environments*.

Contents

Preface

In a highly interactive Internet environment, the research issues in knowledge management vary based on the development of new technology and modes of interaction in the knowledge community. Due to the development of mobile and Web 2.0 technology, knowledge transfer, storage and retrieval have become much more rapid. The technologies and methods continue to get more and more diverse. At the same time, the types of online communities with high levels of interaction become more and more multi-dimensional. To optimize organizational performance and further promote knowledge innovation and knowledge management in organizations, new and expanded strategies for sharing knowledge within and between knowledge communities are required.

In recent years, there have been more and more new and interesting findings regarding theories, methods, and models in the research field of knowledge management. There are also innovative technologies and tools in knowledge management technology. It is worth noting that the technologies, tools, and models in technology have been applied to more fields (e.g., education and digital learning) as technology and management concepts have continued to develop. These trends speak to the importance of studies of knowledge management, and the studies expand their influence on more multidisciplinary applications. New research issues in knowledge management await researchers. A comprehensive understanding of these novel research issues will assist with the academic development and practical applications in the field of knowledge management.

Therefore, this book aims to introduce readers to the recent research topics in knowledge management, it is titled "New Research on Knowledge Management Applications and Lesson Learned" and includes 14 chapters. The book focuses on introducing the applications of KM technologies and methods to all kinds of fields. It also shares the practical experiences, effectiveness, and limitations of such application.

I expect this book to provide relevant information about new research trends in comprehensive and novel knowledge management studies. This information will serve as an important resource for researchers, teachers and students, and will further scholarly work and the development of practices in the knowledge management field.

Prof. Huei-Tse Hou
Graduate Institute of Applied Science and Technology
National Taiwan University of Science and Technology
Taiwan

1

How Industrial Clusters and Regional Innovation Systems Impact the Knowledge Innovation Within the Taiwanese Science-Based Parks Firms?

Han Chao Chang[1], Chung Lin Tsai[2*] and Steven Henderson[3]
[1]*Instrument Technology Research Center, National Applied Research Laboratories (NARL)*
[2]*Department of Finance, Chang Jung Christian University*
[3]*Solent Business School, Southampton Solent University*
[1,2]*Taiwan*
[3]*U.K.*

1. Introduction

The international competitiveness of science and technology has gradually become more intense in the light of its rapid development and the era of globalization. Governments around the world share a general consensus on seeking national economic progress and reinforcing comprehensive national strengths based on science and technology development. Since the 1970s, western economies have strategically established science-based parks at special regions for developing of cutting-edge technology. This strategy seemed to be adopted in Taiwan, and enabled Taiwan to mark its position in the global computer and optoelectronics industries. For example, Hsinchu Science-based Industrial Park (HSIP, located in northern Taiwan) owns the most integrated and complete industrial chain in the semiconductor field, and it offers a strong industrial model the semiconductor industry. In addition, the campus manufacturers are not only the key original equipment manufacturers for global computer and optoelectronics products, but also the main engines of Taiwan's foreign exchange reserve. Beside the semiconductor, the industries that locate in Taiwan Science-based Industrial Parks, such as liquid crystal display, light emitting diode and green energy seek to develop a globally competitive supply chain.

According to the 2007-2008 Global Competitiveness Report published by the 2009 World Economic Forum (WEF), Taiwan has again taken first place worldwide in the "state of cluster development" index, after integrated effecting the upstream and downstream resources of IT and opto-electronics industry within the Science-based Industrial Park. Its score of 5.7 points (out of a possible 7 points) shows an increase of 0.18 points from 5.52 points the previous year, indicative of its outstanding industrial clusters of Taiwanese Science-based Parks.

In Taiwan, the National Science Council (NSC) of the Executive Yuan (executive branch of the Taiwan) is the highest Taiwan government agency responsible for promoting the

* Corresponding Author

development of science and technology, it is also the administration to establish Hsinchu Science-based Industrial Park (HSIP, located in northern Taiwan), TaiChung Science-based Industrial Park (CSIP, located in central Taiwan), and the Tainan Science-based Industrial Park (TSIP, located in southern Taiwan). Basing on the 2009 annual report of NSC, comparing to other countries, the impact from global financial tsunami was slight to campus manufacturers. These campus manufacturers still contributed 1,586 billion of turnover in 2009 therein the turnover was 951.8 billion NT dollars at the latter half of year, this amount was higher 16.2% when comparing to the corresponding period of 2008 (Table 1). When the turnover was analyzed by the industrial categories, the IC industry devoted 802.5 billion, the Optoelectronics industry also contributed 643.1 billion, and these two industries occupied 91.2% of total turnover at 2009 (Table 2).

In addition, from 1975 to the end of 2009, the Science Park Administration of National Science Council approved the establishment of factories to be constructed by 720 firms in campus. When analyzing by the industrial categories, some 224 firms were in the IC field – the largest category ratified. Second were the 172 firms from the Opto-Electronics industry with 106 Precision Machinery firms (Table 3) being the forth highest category. The campus manufacturers within Taiwanese Science-based Park also offered employment opportunities and boosted the regional economy. There were 200632 campus employees by 2009, with growth 0.6% from the previous year (Table 4). In addition, the current year's graduate from nearby universities such as National Chiao Tung University and National Tsing Hua University are provide substantial numbers of recruits for HSIP (Fig 1).

Location	year	Jan.	Feb.	Mar.	April	May	June	July	Aug.	Sep.	Oct.	Nov.	Dec.	Total
HSIP	2008	101	81.1	91.3	92.1	31.1	94.8	91.6	90.9	85.4	80.1	52	54.6	1,008
	2009	42.5	49.8	56.1	67.6	66.9	77.5	81.3	85.6	88.2	85.8	82.3	99.9	88.4
CSIP	2008	28	27	28.6	28.1	27.3	28.5	27.9	26.5	24.1	19.7	11.9	8.6	286
	2009	8.6	10.4	13.2	16.3	18	20.8	21.6	25.3	27.7	26.4	25.8	27.1	241.2
TSIP	2008	53.6	46.3	51.4	52.6	48.5	49.1	47.3	46.9	52	43.7	29.7	26.4	547.5
	2009	21.2	23.4	30.4	35	35.2	41	42.2	43.4	47.5	46.1	45.4	50.2	461.0
SUM	2008	182.6	154.4	171.3	172.8	168.9	172.4	166.8	164.3	161.5	143.5	93.6	89.6	1,842
	2009	72.3	83.6	99.7	118.9	120.1	139.3	145.1	154.3	163.4	158.3	153.5	177.2	1,586

Unit: Billion NT

Table 1. Turnovers from Taiwan Science-based Industrial Park at 2008 and 2009

	2008				2009				Growth Rate (%)
Industry	HSIP	CSIP	TSIP	Total	HSIP	CSIP	TSIP	Total	
IC	704	55.1	162.9	922	601.4	50.9	150.2	802.5	-13.0
Opto-Electronics	176.3	223.4	353	752.7	174.3	183.1	285.7	643.1	-14.6
Computer & Accessories	77.6	0.1	1.4	79.1	62.4	0.2	0.8	63.4	-19.8
Precision Machinery	11.1	6.7	22	39.8	11.6	6	15.6	33.2	-16.6
Telecommunications	32.4	0	2.4	34.8	27.1	0	2	29.1	-16.4
Biotechnology	3.9	0.1	3.7	7.7	4.3	0.2	4.7	9.2	19.5
Others	2.7	0.8	2.1	5.6	2.4	0.8	2	5.2	-7.1
SUM	1008	286.2	547.5	1841.7	883.5	241.2	461	1585.7	-13.9

Unit: Billion NT

Table 2. Compare the turnovers between 2008 and 2009 by Industry

Industry	HSIP	CSIP	TSIP	Total	Percentage (%)
IC	204	9	11	224	31.1
Opto-Electronics	97	30	45	172	23.9
Computer & Accessories	51	4	3	58	8.1
Precision Machinery	28	33	45	106	14.7
Telecommunications	46	1	12	59	8.2
Biotechnology	33	15	31	79	11.0
Others	5	8	9	22	3.1
SUM	464	100	156	720	100.0
Percentage (%)	64.4	21.7	13.9	100.0	

Unit: amounts of factory

Table 3. Turnovers at 2009 by the amounts of factory

Location	2008	2009	Growth rate (%)
HSIP	130,577	132,161	1.2
CSIP	20,736	19,845	-4.3
TSIP	48,136	48,626	1.0
Total	199,449	200,632	0.6

Unit: number of employee

Table 4. Comparing the number of employees in Taiwan Science-based Industrial Park between 2008 and 2009

Fig. 1. Geographical position of Hsinchu Science-based Industrial Park

On the other hand, under the continuous progress of the economy, industries in Taiwan have gradually moved from being manufacturing-oriented to investment-oriented. The new capabilities and advantages from these science parks have always been considered an important link to investment development in industrial technology policies. Innovation can strengthen the flexibility of organisations and adaptation towards the environment (Geroski 1994). It is widely held that developing an excellent knowledge innovation capability is unavoidable for enterprises in adapting to globalization and the highly dynamic competitive market environment, making this an important area for research in academia (Shane and Ulrich 2004).

Afuah (1998) suggested that although innovation introduces and applies new products and processes, the important thing is for firms to connect the innovation with market demands in order to achieve a favorable performance. Theories of successful innovation have always stressed the strategic behavior and alliances of firms, as well as the interaction between research institutes, universities, and other institutions (Freeman 1987; Lundvall 1992). According to James (2002), innovation activities have evident regional differences and their effects in various regions are diverse, perhaps resulting from dissimilarities in methods and weights attached to composite elements.

In Taiwan, government and agencies at all levels and regions seek to stimulate innovation, and consequently innovation policy is located at the centre of policies for promoting regional and national economic development. At the regional level, clusters and regional innovation systems have been looked upon as policy frameworks or models for the implementation of long-term, development strategies that facilitate learning-based processes of innovation, change, and improvement (Asheim 2001; Asheim and Isaksen 2002; Cooke 1998). Fernandez-Ribas and Shapira (2009) also argue that policy formulation for regional innovation systems must consider multiple impacts; the systemic measures of innovation must tally enterprise objectives with policy formulation. Meanwhile, Fernandez-Ribas and Shapira (2009) provided an interesting theory; that if either the regional or public policy was integrated into the innovation system, these policies could directly influence the behavior and strategy making for innovation partnerships while at the same time indirectly influencing the knowledge innovation capability of enterprises.

Thus, this study will investigate the impact of the knowledge innovation capability, industrial clusters, and regional innovation systems on operational efficiency by examining the cases of the Hsinchu Science-based Industrial Park (HSIP, located in northern Taiwan) (Fig. 1), TaiChung Science-based Industrial Park (CSIP, located in central Taiwan), and the Tainan Science-based Industrial Park (TSIP, located in southern Taiwan). Findings from this study should inform policy for developing countries when plotting for Science-based Industrial Parks to create either clusters or regional innovation systems, and give recommendations to the campus manufacturers concerning the innovation operations.

2. Literature review

2.1 Knowledge innovation capability

Gilbert and Cordey-Hayes (1996) took an organisational viewpoint and classified knowledge into instrumental knowledge and developmental knowledge. Instrumental knowledge means the basic knowledge is owned to complete a task including the operational procedures and related process. Developmental knowledge means the knowledge is raised above the level of operational knowledge such as technological innovation and commercialization. Schulz (2001) thought the organisation-oriented knowledge may be influenced by various properties, which cannot be sufficiently described by tacit knowledge and explicit. He proposed three groups - technological knowledge, marketing knowledge and strategic knowledge - to supplement the coverage. Technological knowledge relates to the information system, and engineering and R&D jobs; marketing knowledge relates to the market, advertisement and product delivering, and strategic knowledge includes the acts of government, competitors, suppliers and policy issues.

Therefore, to be able to meet the expressed and potential needs of customers, firms must be able to not only use existing knowledge, technology, and capability; more importantly, they must possess knowledge innovation capability. Cervantes (1997) pointed out that given the competitive conditions in the global economy, knowledge innovation capability is a determining factor in the ability of firms and countries to adapt to new constraints and take advantage of new opportunities. Knowledge innovation capability not only involves individual proposals and implementations, but involves the commitment and support of the entire organization.

Benn and Danny (2001) considered knowledge innovation capability in organizational procedures as the capacity to integrate key abilities and business resources to introduce innovation successfully. From a dynamic perspective, knowledge innovation capability in organizations can also be defined as continuously transforming knowledge and ideas into new products, processes and systems to achieve benefits for firms and their shareholders. The essence of innovation is to recreate frontiers according to the distinctive visions or missions of firms. Once individuals in the firms make a commitment towards this vision of innovation, they will naturally participate actively in the innovation of new knowledge, term as the organizational knowledge innovation capability. Adler and Shenbar (1990) defined knowledge innovation capability as the ability to develop and respond and identified its four dimensions: (1) ability to develop new products that meet market needs; (2) ability to apply appropriate process technologies to producing these new products; (3) ability to develop and adopt these new products and process technologies to satisfy future needs; and (4) ability to respond to related technology activities and unexpected activities created by competitors. From this definition, it can be observed that the aim of knowledge innovation capability is to apply a set of appropriate process technologies to producing new products that meet market needs and at the same time, to be able to respond to unexpected technology activities and competitive conditions. In other words, knowledge innovation capability not only resolves present problems relating to products and processes of enterprises, but must also be able to respond to changes in the external environment.

Several researchers consider that knowledge innovation capability plays a key role in introducing competitive strategies. The differentiation that should ensure that product ranges are more diversified than those of competitors and provide consumers with product and service choices in order to maintain long-term competitive advantages (Cho and Pucik 2005; Damanpour 1996; Jayanthi and Sinha 1998). Drucker (1994) suggested developing a superior knowledge innovation capability as an important market strategy. That is, firms transform competitive threats derived from changes in the environment into profits in the face of highly uncertain market environments. The study of Tidd and his colleagues (1997) concluded that firms with a high degree of knowledge innovation capability are on average twice as profitable as other firms.

Various researchers have offered different views on the categories of knowledge innovation capability. Moore (2004) distinguished knowledge innovation capability into disruptive, applicative, product, process, marketing, structural, and business model capabilities as he connected these with the market development life cycle. In a study on high-tech firms in Taiwan, Chuang (2005) categorized technological innovation as product and process innovations and administrative innovation as staff's innovation, marketing innovation, and organization structure innovation. Tsai and his members (2001) believed knowledge innovation capability must be the administrative innovation of business activities such as planning, organization, employment, leadership, and control and technological innovation of products, processes and facilities obtained by firms from the outside and produced within. In addition a China study group, Lin and colleagues (2004) proposed that aside from the technical aspect of products and processes, innovation must also refer to changes or breakthroughs in administrative procedures and management skills.

Therefore, on the basis of these distinctions and classifications, this study seeks to discriminate between technology innovation and knowledge innovation, two innovation capabilities with direct correlation with business decisions of firms and their knowledge innovation capability.

2.2 Industrial clusters

Clusters encompass an array of linked industries and other entities important to competition. These task-oriented clusters include suppliers of specialized inputs such as components, machinery and services, and providers of specialized infrastructure (Asheim 2007). The term 'industrial cluster' refers to the firms and institutions in close proximity to each other in a particular field and area maintaining an interactive relationship, influencing and supporting each other, where production efficiency is achieved and externalities are created through a fine division of labor. From this, small firms are also able to achieve economies of scale in production as enjoyed by large firms; and at the same time these production networks encourage mutual learning and collaborative innovation as well as forming more flexible production systems (Porter 1998; Rosenfeld 1997; Swann and Prevezer 1996).

Hu (2007) thought while scholars discuss the cluster effect within Science-based Industrial Park, the initial concept "cluster economy" should be reviewed. In Hu's article, the "cluster economy" emphasizes that external economies and economies of scale produced from the proximity of firms within an area reduce production and transaction costs through the sharing of infrastructures, technology, labor, and resources. Thus, external economies and reduction of transaction costs are the main factors driving industrial clustering. Aside from these economic reasons, much literature has also stressed the importance of social and culture factors. Clusters are formed when actors or communities possessing innovation and management capabilities exchange uncodified knowledge which results from the need to frequently interact face-to-face in order to solve technology and management problems during industrial development in an environment where collaborative relationships among firms. These collaborative relationships occur when local firms having common development goals, common views, values, norms, and support; and social structures supporting local industry development termed as institutional thickness (Amin and Thrift 1995; Storper and Salais 1997) exist. Some scholars also believe clusters result from the coincidence of several events. Once specialized clusters are formed, external economies of scale are generated while promoting or maintaining the sources of external economies like the labor market, specialized suppliers, and technology spillovers (Boschma and Lambooy 1999; Cooke 1998).

Furman and Porter (2002) indicated that industrial clusters are advantageous for industrial innovation. The competitive pressures and market opportunities experienced by geographically proximate firms within the cluster are more visible and the rapid flow of information and human resources is beneficial to introducing industry knowledge spillovers and strengthening the advantage of industrial innovation. Isaksen's (2005) analysis, based on results from a European comparative cluster survey, showed that regional resources and collaboration are of major importance in stimulating economic activity within clusters. Moreover, within regional clusters, firms can benefit from agglomeration economies and spillover effects stimulated, for example, through labor force training or mobility, paid access to market information, collaborative relationships with nearby research institutions, or the exchange of tacit knowledge (Shapira 2008).

Porter (1998) argued that inter-firm competition is the greatest motivation for innovation. As a result of competition, firms monitor each other and reproduce products and processes of nearby firms gained from learning, while exerting efforts to improve and aiming to surpass their competitors. Under this competitive environment, several firms observe, learn from and imitate each other, striving to identify any innovation that will give them a lead over competitors, and help them to achieve overall innovation and learning. Porter integrated these elements to develop the competitive diamond model. For this model, four forces that drive cluster development of firms were identified: (1) factor conditions, which are production inputs such as labor, capital, natural resources, specialized resources and physical, administrative, information, and technological infrastructures; (2) demand conditions, which refers to the highly sophisticated and demanding domestic consumers; (3) related and supporting industries, which refers to the numerous viable local suppliers and support firms or industries; and (4) firm strategies and rivalry of firms. These are strengthened and integrated by governments to promote development of local industrial clusters. Science-based Industrial Parks in Taiwan have followed this trend in their development.

With regards to measuring the effects of industrial clusters, Anderson (1994) outlined three types of industrial clusters The first category of industrial clusters is buyer-supplier relationships. This industrial cluster is characterized by collaborative vertical relationships of upstream suppliers and downstream buyers. Many scholars have acknowledged its importance as value chain cluster (Anderson 1994; Brenner 2005; Fester and Bergman 1999; Porter 1998) comprised of suppliers of materials, related industries, locations, and customers. In many senses it can be regarded as critical, since innovation carries much additional technical, production and marketing cost, it is essential that a well integrated value chain eliminates cost drivers to restore a profitable margin to the innovator. Under the second category, competitor and collaborator relationships, industrial clusters are formed from firms producing identical or similar products and services. Here, relationships exist because competitors frequently share information concerning products and production processes to innovate opportunities in the market (Anderson 1994; Fester and Bergman 2000; Kim 2003). The third type refers to shared-resource relationships. Here, industrial clusters are referred to as social entities composed of firms within a region where various resources such as technology, knowledge, stock of product, infrastructure, and place are shared (Anderson 1994; Morosini 2004; Porter 1998; Rosenfeld 2002). From these, this study focused on three categories for evaluating industrial clusters: value chain clusters, competition clusters, and shared-resource clusters.

2.3 Regional innovation systems

The concept of the regional innovation system is relatively new, having first appeared in the early 1990s (Asheim and Isaksen 1997; Cooke 1992, 1998, 2001). The regional innovation system (RIS) is defined in more general terms as, "the institutional infrastructure supporting innovation within the production structure of a region" (Asheim and Coenen 2005). Cooke and Morgan (1998) viewed regional innovation systems as a concept of systems. They defined RIS as a system in which firms and other organisations systematically engaged in interactive learning through an institutional milieu, characterized by embeddedness.

With this definition, three aspects require more explanation: first, "interactive learning" refers to the interactive processes by which knowledge is combined and made into collective asset of different actors within the product system; second, "milieu" regarded as an open, territorialized complex, which involves rules, standards, values, and human and material resources; and third, "embeddedness" includes all of the economic and knowledge processes created and reproduced inside and outside firms. After undergoing social interaction, these different forms of creation and production processes arrive at a hard-to-copy state (Maskell and Malmberg 1999). From the 1990s onwards, regional innovations have become an important policy tool and have been operated successful in developed countries. Through the systematic promotion and application of localized learning processes, several countries and areas have thus been referred to as innovative economies.

In the analytical framework for regional innovation, strategic policy measures are formulated based primarily on concentrating resources, improving local business environment, and strengthening convenient connections of firms within the RIS in order to intensify business capability and performance and regional competitiveness. Innovation within an RIS is a process dependent on the gradually evolving factors within and outside the firm. This not only relies on the knowledge assets and systems created by firms, but also includes interactive patterns among firms and with their environment. An innovation environment can be regarded as a network of actors and a reservoir where firms which engage in interactive learning transform into agglomeration economies (Asheim 2007).

Cooke and colleagues (1997) believed that firms clustered in an innovative region possess characteristics of learning and innovation systems: (1) a formal or informal network of relationships, such as with customers, suppliers, and collaborators, serving as part of a firm; (2) knowledge centers, such as universities, research institutes, cooperative research organisations, and technology transfer intermediaries; and (3) governance structure of private business associations, chambers and public economic development, training and promotion intermediaries and government departments.

From the perspective of researchers, discussion on RIS focuses on technology, people, and money and the main actors include firms, research institutes, the financial sector, and governments (Sternberg 1996). Fukugawa (2008) pointed out that it is important for regional innovation policymakers to design incentive mechanisms for knowledge transfer according to the characteristics of the regional innovation systems.

Development of certain regional innovation systems has been spontaneous, such as Emilia-Romagna in Italy where there is no major participation of national or the provincial governments; and instead experience in industrial novelty was adopted as strategic guideposts. Some others, such as Northern Italy, developed through the network of firms, associations, and locally-organized design and technology transfer centers. Wales in the United Kingdom was intended as a catalyst by government and non-government organisations (Cooke and Morgan 1998; Perry 1999). Regarding Taiwan, which forms the basis of our study, the development of its regional systems of innovation is similar to that of Wales where the government planned Science-based Industrial Parks within which firms, research institutes, universities, intermediaries, and government-related organisations are located. For example the research institutes such as National Instrument Technology Research Center, National Center for High-performance Computing, National Nacho Device Laboratories, National Chip Implementation; universities such as National Chiao Tung University and National Tsing Hua University; and NSC's Science Park Administration locate in HSIP area to offer high-end experimental facilities, academic achievements and governmental supports for HSIP campus manufacturers (Fig 1). Asheim (2007) also highlighted Taiwan's Science-based Industrial Park as a regionalized national innovation system, in the form of an exogenous development model, an innovation system incorporating mainly the R&D functions of universities, research institutes and corporations.

There have been many attempts to study the effectiveness of regional innovation policies, and using diverse methods and conflicting measures of effectiveness. Several studies considered RIS as a group of firms, knowledge centers, research institutes, and technology transfer intermediaries clustered in a region promoted by government institutions through regional technology policies and where technological capability development and technology transfer and diffusion are conducted through technology alliances to build a specific specialised technology within the region (Asheim 2007; Cooke et al. 1997; Sternberg 1996; Walter 1997). This study termed it as the 'regional technology effect'. Still another group believed that for firms to strengthen or maintain their advantages, an emphasis on continuous improvement and innovation needs substantial and sustained investments which include venture capital and government subsidies to promote technology upgrade, share risks in industrial innovation, and nurture emerging technology-based industries; this is an important financial resource for industrial innovation (Asheim 2007; Maskell and Malmberg 1999; Porter 2000; Walter 1997). For this study, this resource is termed as 'finance injection for innovation.' Lastly, another group of scholars viewed those firms within the region which have a risk-taking and entrepreneurial spirit with a focus on potential opportunities and insistence on innovation, as building a mechanism for cooperation and sharing using the integration of resources; thus, firms can mutually and closely link these resources, bravely accept challenges and fully pursue financial opportunities (Asheim 2007; Baptista and Swann 1998; Cooke et al. 1997; Porter 2000). This is termed as 'innovation culture climate' for the purposes of this study. This has employed these three constructs, regional technology effect, finance injection for innovation, and innovation culture climate, to examine the operations of regional innovation systems.

2.4 Business performance

Performance is an indicator of business competitiveness as viewed by the firm. In businesses, performance measurement or performance evaluation is a measure or evaluative system using quantified standards or subjective evaluations usually employed in order for firms to understand the performance of their daily operational activities. Measuring business performance can help firms know whether strategies and organisational structures they adopted achieve target goals (Grady 1991). The management literature recognises numerous concepts and variables to measure performance. For example, March and Sutton (1997) mentioned profits, sales, market share, productivity, debt ratios, and stock prices. Ittner and Larcker (1997) differentiated between financial and non-financial measures of performance. Miranda (2004) argued that business performance management is one of the hottest topics in industry today.

Traditional performance assessment systems often stress on the 'outcome' and not on the 'process', easily overlooking conflicts caused by changes in the external environment. Key factors for business success are not grasped, firms thus failing to achieve the ultimate goal of performance assessment and losing its significance in management. Thus, the concept of balanced scorecard has been increasingly employed for performance assessment. The balanced scorecard (BSC) is both a performance framework and a management methodology. It was developed by Robert Kaplan and David Norton after an extensive research project in 1990 (Voelker et al. 2001). The BSC is essentially a customized performance measurement system that goes beyond conventional accounting and is based on organisational strategy. Kaplan and Norton (1996) performed a study on future performance assessment system in all kinds of industry by gathering the opinions from researchers and workers. Eventually, they came up with the framework of the balanced scorecard. This is a suite of new methodologies measuring firms' short- and long-term achievements and a tool that can be used for planning strategies and management decisions to measure performance in order to meet the demands of performance measurement and management and improve weaknesses caused by traditional performance assessment.

Traditional accounting-based performance measures evaluate business performance from a financial viewpoint. However, in addition to a financial perspective, the balanced scorecard also incorporates three other perspectives: customers, business processes, and growth and learning. Aside from measuring tangible and intangible assets, the balanced scorecard also evaluates whether strategies are effective and executes strategies against these dimensions and goals. The four perspectives are described in detail as follows:

i. Financial Perspective

The financial perspective typically considers analysis of certain lagging indicators, usually financial ratios and data that report on past performance. These include return on equity, return on assets, net income, revenue, and cash flow information. Consideration of this information has been a long-standing tradition in management of a firm (Bible et al. 2006). For firms, the financial perspective involves performance measure indicators discussed in finance such as reducing costs, improving efficiency, and enhancing productivity.

ii. Customer Perspective

Businesses must first distinguish between markets and customers and measure their performance in these areas. Indicators include market share ratio, customer satisfaction, continuation of customers, acquirement of customers, and profitability of customers. The balanced scorecard can assist firms in clearly identifying these indicators, seeking measuring standards, and exerting control over these. Kaplan and Norton (1996) believed that these five core measures are applicable to all types of organisations.

iii. Internal Business Process Perspective

Management needs to control essential internal processes to provide value and attract their customers in the target market. Kaplan and Norton (1996) considered that management from this perspective must establish the firm's important internal processes which - through improvements in internal procedures - assist them in creating customer value and reaching the financial returns expected by shareholders. Indicators include innovation process, operation process, and customer service process.

iv. Learning and Growth Perspective

Kaplan and Norton (1996) believed that the learning and growth perspective identifies infrastructure that must be built to create long-term growth and improvement of innovative companies. The balanced scorecard proposes that focus should not be only on investing in new products and new facilities; organisations must also invest in people, systems, and processes. Based on experience with the BSC, Kaplan and Norton (1996) categorised this perspective into three aspects: ability of employees, ability of information systems, and incentive, authority and fitness. Later in 2007, Kaplan and Norton (2007) validated that several well-known global companies using the balanced scorecard to measure performance which have surpassed the concepts put forth by the theory and derived more value. Thus, this study draws upon elements of the above perspectives to measure the performance of respondent firms.

3. Hypotheses - The relationship between knowledge innovation capability, regional innovation systems and industrial clusters on business performance

This study primarily examined the degree of knowledge innovation capability in campus firms and its impact on business performance in regional innovation systems and industrial clusters. First, on the matter of knowledge innovation capability and business performance, Garcia-Morales (2007) and team members pointed out that a technological organisation with greater organisational knowledge innovation capability achieves a better response from the environment, obtaining more easily the capabilities needed to increase organisational performance and consolidate a sustainable competitive advantage. Moreover, many systematic studies seem to reveal a positive relationship between innovation and performance in businesses (Garcia-Morales et al. 2007; Koellinger 2008; Zangwill 1993). From the above findings, the following hypothesis can be derived:

Hypothesis 1: Knowledge innovation capability has a positive effect on Business Performance.

On the aspect of industrial clusters and business performance, Morosini (2004) believed that if firms located in advanced country regions can be effective in promoting cooperation, this has a significant performance-enhancing effect on their performance. Moreover, he also viewed that the cluster's underlying social fabric has a potential for innovation and knowledge creation; and at the same time, elements such as competitive factors, geographic closeness, and degree of knowledge integration within industrial regions have a positive impact on the economic performance of industrial clusters. Lai and his colleagues (2005) argued that innovative activity comes from direct contact with a variety of sources (e.g. suppliers, customers, competitors, and providers of different kinds of services). Industrial clusters that accumulate high levels of innovative success have assembled information that facilitates the next round of innovation, since the ability to innovate successfully would be a function of the technological levels already achieved. Porter (2000) pointed out that the existence of a cluster has positive effects on the competitive advantage of firms in a number of ways, one of them being a positive impact on the innovation capabilities of the cluster firms. From the above findings, the following hypothesis can be derived:

Hypothesis 2: Industrial Clusters have a significant moderating effect between Innovation Capability and Business Performance.

On the aspect of regional innovation systems and business performance, many scholars believed that innovation nowadays is seen as a socially and territorially embedded process and the regional level is recognized as being the best context for the development of innovation-based learning economies (Asheim and Isaksen 1997; Cooke and Morgan 1998; Isaksen 2001). According to the Regional Innovation Systems theory, regions can play a central role in economic coordination, especially with respect to innovation, evolving into a "nexus of learning processes" (Cooke and Morgan 1998). In addition, Asheim (2007) considered that regional innovation systems have played and will continue to play a strategic role in promoting the innovativeness and competitiveness of regions. From the above findings, the following hypothesis can be derived:

Hypothesis 3: Regional Innovation Systems have a significant moderating effect between knowledge innovation capability and business performance.

Finally, on the difference impact of industrial clusters and regional innovation systems on business performance, Kyrgiafini and Sefertzi (2003) argued that theory of industrial clusters referring to enterprises connected directly with the production chain in a particular field focuses on the links developed within a group of firms and analyses modes of collaborating and networking between enterprises which constitute a spatial cluster. Kyrgiafini and Sefertzi (2003) also considered that the concept of regional innovation systems places emphasis on acquiring the necessary knowledge for the innovation venture through inter-firm collaborations and interactive behaviors, while generating of regional innovation policies to build a favorable environment for innovation. Several scholars have categorised industrial clusters using transaction behaviors among firms to examine how to reduce transaction costs and enhance external economies of scale in order to increase competitiveness of industrial clusters (Amin and Thrift 1995; Anderson 1994; Morosini 2004; Porter 1998; Rosenfeld 2002; Storper and Salais 1997).

On regional innovation systems, several scholars have classified these on the basis of the interaction between actors of the specific region where an innovation environment is created through learning mechanisms to conduct technological innovation or knowledge-value adding activities (Asheim 2007; Baptista and Swann 1998; Cooke et al. 1997; Freeman 1987; Lundvall 1992; Nelson 1993; Porter 2000; Walter 1997). It can be known that industrial clusters emphasize strengthening business competitiveness, while regional innovation systems focus on knowledge-value adding and innovation activities. From the above findings, the following hypothesis can be derived:

Hypothesis 4: Regional Innovation Systems and Industrial Clusters have different moderating effects on business performance.

4. Method

This study aims to examine the impact of knowledge innovation capability, regional innovation systems, and industrial clusters on business performance. It also observes whether the two moderating variables, regional innovation systems and industrial clusters, produce different effects on business performance. Thus, the conceptual framework developed for this study is presented in Figure 2.

4.1 Sample and data collection

Questionnaires were distributed to firms located in either Hsinchu Science-based Industrial Park (HSIP, locates in northern Taiwan) or TaiChung Science-based Industrial Park (CSIP, locates in central Taiwan), or the Tainan Science-based Industrial Park (TSIP, locates in southern Taiwan), while sampling was performed on the managers from these campus manufacturers. In the sampling design, this study sampled from IC, Optoelectronics,

Precision Machinery and Computer & Accessories campus firms. Companies were first contacted by phone in July 2011 to obtain their willingness to participate in the study. Upon confirmation, questionnaires were then distributed by post. A total of 131 questionnaires were collected until the end of 31, August, 2011, 126 of which were valid, giving a response rate of 77%.

4.2 Measurement scales

A seven-point Likert's scale was used to measure each of the constructs in the research model (1=strongly disagree, 7=strongly agree), except basic information about the respondents. This study constructed the questionnaire based on previous research on knowledge innovation capability, industrial clusters, regional innovation systems, and business performance and modified for adaptation to the context. SPSS17.0 was employed to conduct tests on the hypotheses. The questionnaire of this study was tested with a high reliability and validity, as shown in Table 5.

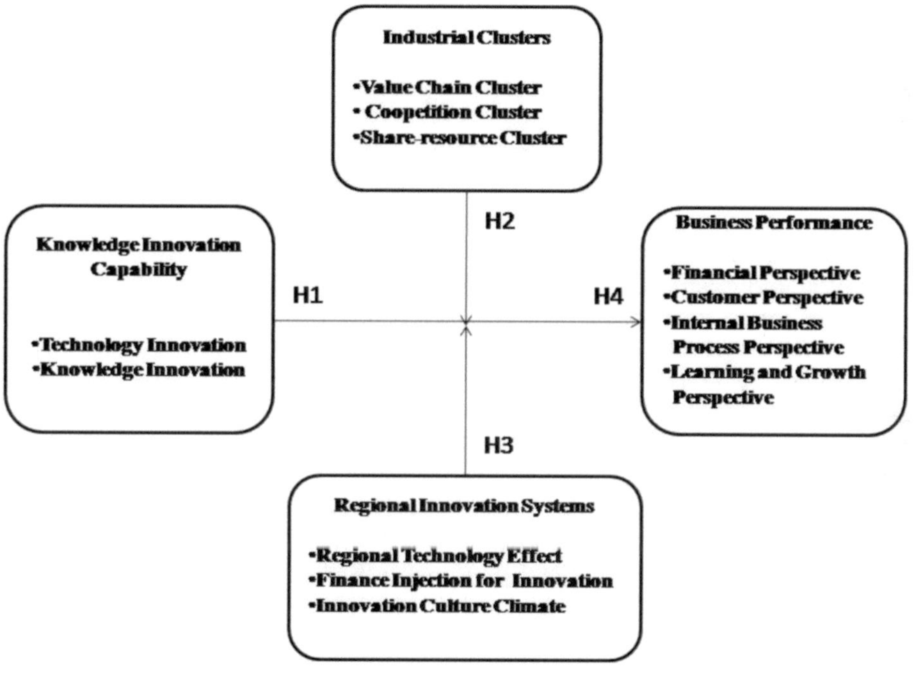

Fig. 2. Conceptual framework for this study

To ensure that the survey design has a high degree of reliability and validity, this study conducted reliability, validity and factor analysis tests. This study employed construct validity and criterion validity to evaluate the validity of the questionnaire. Zaltman and Burger (1975) and Kerlinger and Lee (2000) proposed a method of selecting factor dimensions using principal components analysis. Factors selected must conform to these conditions: (1) factor loadings must be greater than 0.5; (2) rotation sums of squared loadings must be more than 50%; and (3) the Kaiser-Meyer-Olkin measure of sampling adequacy must be greater than 0.7. When these conditions have been met, the test is considered stable. Table 5 shows that the validity value of this study exceeded that of the standard value. In measuring reliability, Nunnally (1978) proposed Cronbach's α coefficient as a measure of reliability; α coefficient greater than 0.7 is high reliability while less than 0.35 is low reliability. From Table 5, it can be seen that the composite reliability values are larger than 0.7, showing that this study has high reliability.

	Construct Validity		*Criterion validity*	*Reliability*
	KMO[a]	Rotation Sums of Squared Loadings	Factor Loading	
Knowledge innovation capability	0.931***	83.23%	0.707~0.901	0.948
Industrial Clusters	0.821***	74.97%	0.621~0.864	0.912
Regional Innovation Systems	0.878***	78.42%	0.643~0.875	0.929
Business Performance	0.924***	82.38%	0.684~0.892	0.937

Note:
a. Kaiser-Meyer-Olkin (KMO) is measure of sampling adequacy.
b. *** denote significance at the 0.1% level.

Table 5. Summary of validity and reliability analysis

4.3 Date Analysis and results

4.3.1 Knowledge innovation capability and business performance

Table 6 shows the results of multiple regression analyses. It can be seen here that the knowledge innovation capability of sample firms has a positive effect on business performance. Within this, technology knowledge innovation capability and management knowledge innovation capability have a positive impact on performance perspectives such as financial, customer, internal business process, and learning and growth. Thus, Hypothesis 1 is confirmed.

	Business Performance			
	Financial	Customer	Internal Business Process	Learning and Growth
Knowledge innovation capability				
Technology Innovation	0.417***	0.362***	0.252***	0.229***
Knowledge innovation	0.205**	0.298***	0.387***	0.322***
Adj. R^2	0.260	0.279	0.265	0.192
F	24.044***	26.317***	24.580***	16.573***

Note: 1. ** and *** denote respectively significance at the 0.5% and 0.1% level.
2. The regression coefficients in the table are standardised.

Table 6. Multiple regression results of Business Performance on Knowledge innovation capability

4.3.2 Moderating role of industrial clusters

To address changes in the impact of knowledge innovation capability, industrial clusters, and regional innovation systems on business performance due to firm age and size, this study employed a firm's history and number of employees as control variables proposed by several researchers (Bharadwaj and Menon 2001; Li and Atuahene-Gima 2001) to examine the moderating effect of industrial clusters and regional innovation systems.

Before conducting moderating effect analysis, this research considered the question of collinearity between these independent variables which possibly have significant correlations between them. Therefore, before hierarchical regression analysis is performed, this research separately subtracts each arithmetic mean from the factors of the knowledge innovation capability and the industrial clusters and contains the interaction items between them. The scholars, Neter and team members (1996), suggested the collinearity examination by Variance Inflation Factors and the path of the VIF. If the VIF value is greater than 10, collinearity exists in the model. Otherwise, non-collinearity exists. Table 7 shows the hierarchical regression results of Business Performance on Knowledge innovation capability and Industrial Clusters and the moderating role is Industrial Clusters. Several models are estimated in this set of analyses. Model 1 includes control variables only. Model 2 reports the direct effects of knowledge innovation capability on business performance. Model 3 tests the moderating effects of industrial clusters. Model 4 tests the moderating effects of both industrial clusters and interaction items. In addition, each VIF value of the Model 4 on Table 7 was discovered smaller than 10 and demonstrated non-collinearity on this level of hierarchical regression.

	Model 1	Model 2	Model 3	Model 4	Model 4 VIF
Control variables					
Company's History	0.079	0.054	0.028	-0.021	1.263
Number of Employees	0.191*	0.163	0.109	0.029	1.291
Independent variables					
Innovation Capability(IC)		0.294**	0.264**	0.228**	2.355
Moderating Variables					
Value Chain Clusters			0.267**	0.195*	2.039
Coopetition Clusters			0.011	0.103	1.836
Shared-Resource Clusters			0.109	0.042	1.754
IC×Value Chain Clusters				0.302**	1.913
IC×Coopetition Clusters				-0.068	1.972
IC×Shared-Resource Clusters				0.082	1.765
R^2	0.185	0.283	0.359	0.476	
F	19.277***	23.129***	17.864***	11.237***	
ΔR^2	0.185	0.098	0.076	0.117	
ΔF	19.277***	11.957***	8.147***	6.681**	

Note: 1. *, ** and *** denote respectively significance at the 0.1%, 0.5% and 0.01% levels, respectively.
2. The regression coefficients in the table are standardised.

Table 7. Hierarchical regression results of Business Performance on Innovation Capability and Industrial Clusters

From the Model 4 in Table 7, it can be seen that the interaction items of knowledge innovation capability and value chain clusters have a positive moderating effect (β=0.302, p<0.05) on business performance. In other words, if firms have a high degree of knowledge innovation capability and highly concentrated value chain clusters within the industry, then these can be effective on the firms' performance. Thus, Hypothesis 2 offers partial support.

4.3.3 Moderating role of regional innovation systems

Table 8 indicates the hierarchical regression results of Business Performance on Knowledge innovation capability and Regional Innovation Systems and the moderating role is Regional innovation Systems. Model 1 only contains control variables, and Model 2 indicates the direct effects of knowledge innovation capability on business performance. Model 3 tests the moderating effects of regional innovation systems while Model 4 tests the moderating effects of both regional innovation systems and interaction items. We found each VIF value of the Model 4 on Table 8 was smaller than 10 however the non-collinearity still exists in this level of hierarchy regression. This evidence is not consistent with Neter's (1996) suggestion on Variance Inflation Factors (VIF); and the reason behind, and algorithm relating to, this phenomenon will be explored in our future studies.

	Model 1	Model 2	Model 3	Model 4	Model 4 VIF
Control variables					
Company's History	0.069	0.074	0.023	-0.035	1.279
Number of Employees	0.191*	0.163	0.129	0.092	1.280
Independent variables					
Innovation Capability(IC)		0.294**	0.317**	0.253**	2.450
Moderating Variables					
Regional technology effect			0.234**	0.179*	1.524
Finance injection for innovation			0.152	0.051	1.984
Innovation culture climate			-0.087	0.103	1.980
IC×Regional technology effect				0.217**	2.450
IC×Finance injection for innovation				-0.074	1.897
IC×Innovation culture climate				0.186*	2.128
Adj. R^2	0.185	0.283	0.377	0.512	
F	19.277***	23.129***	18.520***	13.565***	
ΔR^2	0.185	0.098	0.094	0.125	
ΔF	19.277***	11.957***	9.089***	8.681***	

Note: 1. *, ** and *** denote respectively significance at the 0.1%, 0.5% and 0.01% levels, respectively.
2. The regression coefficients in the table are standardised.

Table 8. Hierarchical regression results of Business Performance on Innovation Capability and Regional Innovation Systems

In addition, Model 4 in Table 8 shows that the interaction items of knowledge innovation capability and regional technology effect have a positive moderating effect (β=0.217, p<0.05)

on business performance. In other words, if firms have a high degree of knowledge innovation capability and great regional technology effect within Science-based Industrial Parks, then these can be effective on the firms' performance. On another aspect, the interaction items of knowledge innovation capability and innovation culture climate have a positive moderating effect ($\beta=0.186$, $p<0.1$) on business performance. That is, if campus firms have a high degree of knowledge innovation capability and rich innovation culture climate in Science-based Industrial Parks, then these can be significant on the firms' performance. Thus, Hypothesis 3 offers partial support.

4.3.4 The comparison of moderating effect

Finally, from the comparison of the moderating effect on regional innovation systems and industrial clusters (Table 9), it can be observed that the moderating effect of RISs on knowledge innovation capability and business performance is greater than that of industrial clusters. Thus, Hypothesis 4 is confirmed. Hence, at present, the benefits provided by RISs concerning business performance are more evident than those by industrial clusters in Taiwanese HSIP, CSIP and TSIP.

Construct / Index Items	Industrial Clusters	Regional Innovation Systems
F	11.237	***13.565***
R^2	0.476	***0.512***
Number of significance on moderating variables	2	***3***
Mean/paired t-test	4.6685	***4.9701***
	5.411***	
Moderating effect	Low	***High***

Note: *** denote respectively significance at the 0.01% level, respectively.

Table 9. Comparison of moderating effect on Regional Innovation Systems and Industrial Clusters

5. Discussion

This study examined the moderating effect of regional innovation systems and industrial clusters on knowledge innovation capability and business performance from the perspective of innovation systems using Taiwan's HSIP, CSIP and TSIP parks as samples. Both concepts of industrial clusters and regional innovation systems emphasize that through the close social networked systems composed of actors from campus manufacturers, internal and external resources and information are easily obtained, diffused, and gathered to build innovation and other capabilities in campus manufacturers (Asheim 2007; Morosini 2004). Empirical results show a positive relationship existing between knowledge innovation capability and business performance, corresponding to arguments of a number of researchers (Garcia-Morales et al. 2007; Koellinger 2008; Zangwill 1993).

Further analysis from this study shows that when knowledge innovation capability is distinguished between technological and knowledge innovations; the technological and knowledge innovation capabilities of the sample firms have a significant positive relationship as Kaplan and Norton 's (1996) contributions such as financial, customer, internal business process, and learning and growth. This demonstrates that if campus firms can focus on each aspect of knowledge innovation capability, improvements in performance of firms are evident.

On the moderating effect of industrial clusters, this study observed that the interaction of knowledge innovation capability and value chain clusters has a positive moderating effect on business performance. This result consists with the finding of Morosini (2004) that individual firms having high knowledge innovation capability and, when clustered in a specific geographical region, create a social fabric where a high degree of cooperative effectiveness within vertical value chains leads to significant improvements in business performance. However, the interaction of knowledge innovation capability with coopetition clusters and shared-resource clusters did not demonstrate a significant level in our study. From these results, this study infers that the social fabric of campus manufacturers locate in the Science-based Industrial Parks have only achieved integration among vertical value chains. It has not yet evolved to that of horizontal coopetition fabric and of shared-resource clusters spanning a wide range of interactive dimensions.

On the moderating effect of regional innovation systems, this study observed that the interaction of knowledge innovation capability and regional technology effect has a positive moderating effect on business performance. This shows that high knowledge innovation capability along with high regional technology effect raises effectiveness in business performance. The interaction of knowledge innovation capability and the innovation culture climate has a positive moderating effect on business performance, illustrating that high knowledge innovation capability, coupled with a climate rich in innovation culture in Science-based Industrial Parks, enhances effectiveness in campus business performance. These findings confirm views from other researchers; that regional innovation systems can promote innovation while strengthening business competitiveness (Asheim and Isaksen 1997; Asheim 2007; Cooke 1998; Isaksen 2001).

In addition, the interaction of knowledge innovation capability and finance injection for innovation did not reach a significant level, implying that respondents consider that the lack of innovation incentives and subsidies in government policies do not significantly improve campus business performance. As a synthesis of the moderating effect of RIS, this study suggests that regional and local governments should provide a technological platform for the various research and development departments in industrial clusters, in order to strengthen technology flow and collaboration, and enhance the overall technology standards of the region. Furthermore, this study believes that knowledge innovation capability stems from attainments in culture; when technology has been developed to its peak, then promotion at the cultural level is needed. In other words, combining technology with humanities can improve overall living standards and create a high-value society. Thus, government policies should actively bring about an environment that supports an innovation culture.

Finally, after comparing the moderating effect of regional innovation systems and industrial clusters, it is observed that the moderating effect of RIS on knowledge innovation capability and performance is greater than that of industrial clusters to Taiwanese Science-based Industrial Parks. Thus, when looking at the assistance knowledge innovation capability brings to improving the performance of campus firms at present, the focus is on nurturing a favorable environment for regional innovation systems; this should be more beneficial than a good social fabric in industrial clusters. Under the concept of innovation systems, if campus manufacturers are able to make no distinction between themselves and focus on the sharing, transfer, and spread of technology, information, and knowledge among themselves, they can go so far as to create technological alliances in the park; this definitely has several positive contributions to make to business performance among firms. These findings offer evidence to support developing countries with the strategies and administration of regional Science-based industry by emphasizing coopetition effects to replace zero-sum effects among campus manufacturers, and at the same time, strengthen the effectiveness of resource-sharing among industries so that the whole industry and national economy becomes more robust.

6. Conclusion

Clarity on the relative advantages of industrial clusters and regional innovation systems (RISs) to enhance industrial innovations is critical for development policy that includes science-based industrial parks. This study concentrates on the Taiwanese IC, opto-electronics, precision machinery and computer & accessories campus industries to enumerate, compare and contrast the impact of knowledge innovation capability, regional innovation systems, and industrial clusters on business performance. Through empirical study of business performance of firms at three science parks, it is revealed that the knowledge innovation capability has a significant, positive effect on business performance. A comparison of the moderating effects of regional innovation systems and the fabric of industrial clusters shows that regional innovation systems have a greater moderating effect than the fabric of industrial clusters on knowledge innovation capability and business performance for campus manufacturers. Finally, from the perspective of assistance given by Taiwanese science-based industrial parks to promote business performance, a focus on the construction of regional innovation systems should be more beneficial than the promotion of industrial clusters.

7. Implications and limitation

A limitation of this study is the focus on campus industry IC, Opto-Electronics, Precision Machinery and Computer & Accessories in Taiwan only for its research sample. This sample is not enough for an overall representation. Therefore, it is suggested that future research widens its scope, such as to national innovation systems among countries or continents in the world. This study employed only industrial clusters and regional innovation systems as moderating variables for examining knowledge innovation capability and business performance. Future research can include more concepts such as knowledge-sharing mechanisms, organisational learning effectiveness, and innovation performance as intervening variables to allow for a more comprehensive study.

8. References

Adler, P.S. and Shenbar, A. (1990), 'Adapting your technological base: The organizational challenge', *Sloan Management Review,* Vol. 25, pp. 25-37.

Afuah, A. (1998), *Innovation Management: Strategies, Implementation, and Profits* (New York: Oxford University Press.).

Amin, A. and Thrift, N. (1995), 'Holding down the global', in A. Amin and N. Thrift (eds.), *Globalization, Institutions, and Regional Development in Europe* (Oxford: Oxford University Press), 257-260.

Anderson, G. (1994), 'Industry Clustering for Economic Development', *Economic Development Review,* Vol. 12, pp. 26-32.

Asheim (2001), 'Learning regions as development coalitions: Partnership as governance in European workfare states?, Concepts and Transformation. ' *International Journal of Action Research and Organizational Renewal,* Vol. 6, pp. 73-101.

--- (2007), 'Differentiated Knowledge Bases and Varieties of Regional Innovation Systems', *Innovation,* Vol. 20, pp. 223-241.

Asheim and Isaksen (1997), 'Location, Agglomeration and Innovation: Towards Regional Innovation Systems in Norway?' *European Planning Studies,* Vol. 5, pp. 299-330.

--- (2002), 'Regional innovation systems: the integration of local "sticky and global "ubiquitous knowledge', *Journal of Technology Transfer,* Vol. 27, pp. 77-86.

Asheim and Coenen, L. (2005), 'Knowledge bases and regional innovation systems: Comparing Nordic clusters', *Research Policy,* Vol. 34, pp. 1173-1190.

Baptista, B. and Swann, P. (1998), 'Do Firms in Clusters Innovate More?' *Research Policy,* Vol. 27, pp. 525-540.

Benn, L. and Danny, S. (2001), 'Developing innovation capability in organizations: A dynamic capabilities approach', *Industrial and Labor Relations Review,* Vol. 45, pp. 488-506.

Bharadwaj, S. and Menon, A. (2001), 'Making innovation happen in organizations: individual creativity mechanisms, organizational creativity mechanisms or both?' *The Journal of Product Innovation Management,* Vol. 17, pp. 424-434.

Bible, L., Kerr, S., and Zanini, M. (2006), 'The Balanced Scorecard: Here and Back ', *Management Accounting Quarterly,* Vol. 7, pp. 18-23.

Boschma, R. and Lambooy, J. (1999), 'Evolutionary economics and economic geography', *Journal of Evolutionary Economics,* Vol. 9, pp. 411-429.

Brenner, T. (2005), 'Innovation and Cooperation During the Emergence of Local Industrial Clusters: An Empirical Study in Germany', *European Planning Studies,* Vol. 13, pp. 921-938.

Cervantes, M. (1997), 'Diffusing Technology to Industry', *OECD Observer,* Vol. 207, pp. 20-23.

Cho, H. and Pucik, V. (2005), 'Relationship between Innovativeness, Quality, Growth, Profitability, and Market Value', *Strategic Management Journal,* Vol. 26, pp. 555-575.

Chuang, L.M. (2005), 'An Empirical Study of the Construction of Measuring Model for Organization Innovation in Taiwanese High-tech Enterprises', *Journal of American Academy of Business,* Vol. 6, pp. 299-304.

Cooke, P. (1992), 'Regional Innovation Systems: Competitive Regulation in the New Europe', *Geoforum,* Vol. 23, pp. 356-382.

--- (1998), 'Introduction: Origins of the Concept', in H. Braczyk, P. Cooke, and Heidenreich (eds.), *Regional Innovation Systems* (London: UCL Press), 2-25.

--- (2001), 'Regional Innovation Systems, Clusters, and the Knowledge Economy', *Industrial and Corporated Change,* Vol. 10, pp. 945-974.

Cooke, P. and Morgan, K. (1998), *The Associational Economy, Firms, Regions and Innovation* (New York: Oxford University Press).

Cooke, P., Uranga, G., and Etzebarria, G (1997), 'Regional innovation systems: Institutional and organisational dimensions', *Research Policy,* Vol. 26, pp. 475-491.

Damanpour, D. (1996), 'Organizational Complexity and Innovation: Developing and Testing Multiple Contingency Models', *Management Science,* Vol. 42, pp. 693-716.

Drucker, P. (1994), *Innovation and Entrepreneurship* (New York: Harper and Row).

Fernandez-Ribas, A. and Shapira, P. (2009), 'The role of national and regional innovation programmes in stimulating international cooperation in innovation', *International Journal of Technology Management,* Vol. 48, pp. 473-398.

Fester, E.J. and Bergman, E.M. [1999], 'Industrial and Regional Clusters: Concepts and Comparative Applications', (Regional Science).

--- (2000), 'National Industry Cluster Templates: A Framework for Applied Regional Cluster Analysis', *Regional Studies,* Vol. 34, pp. 1-19.

Freeman, C. (1987), *Technology Policy and Economic Performance: Lessons from Japan* (London: Pinter).

Fukugawa, N. (2008), 'Evaluating the strategy of local public technology centers in regional innovation systems: evidence from Japan', *Science and Public Policy,* Vol. 35, pp. 159-170.

Furman, J.L., Porter, M.E., and Strern, S. (2002), 'The determinants of national innovative capacity', *Research Policy,* Vol. 31, pp. 899-933.

Garcia-Morales, V.J., Ruiz-Moreno, A., and Llorens-Montes, F.J. (2007), 'Effects of Technology Absorptive Capacity and Technology Proactivity on Organizational Learning, Innovation and Performance: An Empirical Examination', *Technology Analysis and Strategic Management,* Vol. 19, pp. 527-558.

Geroski, P. A. (1994), *Market structure, corporate performance and innovative activity* (Oxford: Clarendon Press).

Gilbert, M. and Cordey-Hayes, M. (1996), 'Understanding the Process of Knowledge Transfer to Achieve Successful Technologic Innovation', *Technovation* Vol. 16, pp. 301-312.

Grady, M.W. (1991), 'Performance Measurement: Implementing Strategy', *Management Accounting Quarterly,* Vol., pp. 49-53.

Hu, A.G. (2007), 'Technology parks and regional economic growth in China', *Research Policy,* Vol. 36, pp. 76-87.

Isaksen, A. (2001), 'Building Regional Innovation Systems: is endogenous industrial development possible in a global economy', *Canadian Journal of Regional Science,* Vol. 24, pp. 101-120.

--- (ed.), (2005), *Regional clusters building on local and non-local relationships,* eds. A. Lagendijk and P. Oinas (Proximity, Distance and Diversity: Issues on Economic Interaction and Local Development, Aldershot: Ashgate) 129-152.

Ittner, C.D., Larcker, D.F., and Rajan, M.V. (1997), 'The choice of performance measures in annual bonus contracts', *Accounting Review,* Vol. 72, pp. 231-255.

James, S. (2002), 'Knowledge spillovers and reasons for concentration of innovation SMEs', *Urban Studies,* Vol. 39, pp. 885-902.

Jayanthi, S. and Sinha, K.K. (1998), 'Innovation Implementation in High Technology Manufacturing: A Chaos-theoretic Empirical Analysis', *Journal of Operations Management,* Vol. 16, pp. 471-494.

Kaplan, R.S. and Norton, D.P. (1996), *The balanced scorecard: Translating strategy intoaction* (New York: Harvard Business School Press).

--- (2007), 'Using the balanced scorecard as a strategic management system', *Harvard Business Review,* Vol. 85, pp. 150-195.

Kerlinger, F. and Lee, H. (2000), *Foundations of Behavioral Research* (Orlando: Harcourt College Publishers).

Kim, S. (2003), 'Industrial Clusters in Japan: The Regional System of Industrialization', *Korea Observer,* Vol. 32, pp. 369-392.

Koellinger, P. (2008), 'The relationship between technology, innovation, and firm performance—Empirical evidence from e-business in Europe', *Research Policy,* Vol. 37, pp. 1317-1328.

Kyrgiafini, L. and Sefertzi, E. (2003), 'Changing Regional Systems of Innovation in Greece: The Impact of Regional Innovation Strategy Initiatives in Peripheral Areas of Europe', *European Planning Studies,* Vol. 11, pp. 885-910.

Lai, H.C., Chiu, Y.C., and Leu, H.D. (2005), 'Innovation capacity comparison of China's information technology industrial clusters: The case of Shanghai, Kunshan, Shenzhen and Dongguan', *Technology Analysis and Strategic Management,* Vol. 17, pp. 293-315.

Li, H. and Atuahene-Gima, K. (2001), 'Product innovation strategy and the performance of new technology ventures in China', *Academy of Management Journal,* Vol. 44, pp. 1123-1134.

Lin, P.Y., Huang, J.Y., and Tung, Y.C. (2004), 'How Organizational Learning and Organizational Innovations Mediate Market Orientation and Organizational Performance: An Empirical Study of the Information Technology Industry in Scientific Industry', *Management Review,* Vol. 23, pp. 101-134.

Lundvall, B. (1992), *National Innovation Systems: Towards a Theory of Innovation and Interactive Learning* (London: Pinter).

March, J.G. and Sutton, R.I. (1997), 'Organizational performance as a dependent variable', *Organization Science,* Vol. 8, pp. 698-706.

Maskell, P. and Malmberg, A. (1999), 'Localized Learning and Industrial competitiveness', *Cambridge Journal of Economics* Vol. 23, pp. 167-185.

Miranda, S. (2004), 'Beyond BI: Benefiting from Corporate Performance Management Solutions', *Financial Executive,* Vol. 20, pp. 58-61.

Moore, G.A. (2004), 'Darwin and the Demon: Innovation within Established Enterprises', *Harvard Business Review,* Vol. 82, pp. 86-92.

Morosini, P. (2004), 'Industrial Clusters, Knowledge Integration and Performance', *World Development,* Vol. 32, pp. 305-326.

Nelson, R. (1993), *National Innovation Systems – A Comparative Analysis* (Oxford: Oxford University Press).

Neter, J., et al. (1996), *Applied Linear Statistical Model* (4 edn.; Chicago: Irwin).

Nunnally, J.C. (1978), *Psychometric Theory* (2 edn.; New York: McGraw-Hill).

Perry, M. (1999), *Small Firms and Network Economics* (London: Routledge).

Porter, M.E. (1998), 'Clusters and The New Economics of Competition', *Harvard Business Review,* Vol. 76, pp. 77-90.

--- (ed.), (2000), *Locations, clusters and company strategy,*, eds. G. Clark, M. Feldman, and M. Gertler (The Oxford Handbook of Economic Geography, Oxford: Oxford University Press) 253-274.

Rosenfeld, S. (1997), 'Bring business clusters into the mainstream of economic development', *European Planning Studies,* Vol. 5, pp. 3-23.

--- 'Creating Smart Systems: A guide to cluster strategies in less favoured regions', <www.rtsinc.org/publications/pdf/less_favoured.pdf>.

Schulz, M. (2001), 'The Uncertain Relevance of Newness: Organizational Learning and Knowledge Flows', *Academy of Management Journal,* Vol. 44, No. 4, pp. 661-681.

Shane, S.A. and Ulrich, K.T. (2004), 'Technological Innovation, Product Development, and Entrepreneurship in Management Science', *Management Science,* Vol. 50, pp. 133-144.

Shapira, P. (2008), 'Putting Innovation in Place: Policy Strategies for Industrial Services, Regional Clusters, and Manufacturing SMEs in Japan and the United States', *Prometheus,* Vol. 26, pp. 69-87.

Sternberg, R. (1996), 'Regional Growth Theories and High-Tech Regions', *International Journal of Urban and Regional Research,* Vol. 20, pp. 518-538.

Storper, M. and Salais, R. (1997), *Worlds of Production: the Action Frameworks of the Economy* (Cambridge: Harvard University Press).

Swann, G. and Prevezer, M. (1996), 'A Comparison of the Dynamics of Industrial Clustering in Computing and Biotechnology', *Research Policy,* Vol. 25, pp. 139-157.

Tidd, J., Bessant, J., and Pavitt, K. (1997), *Managing Innovation: Integrating Technological, Market and Organizational Change* (Chichester: Wiley).

Tsai , C.T., Huang, K.L., and Kao, C.F. (2001), 'The Relationships among Organizational Factors, Creativity of Organizational Members and Organizational Innovation', *Journal of Management,* Vol. 18, pp. 527-566.

Voelker, K.E., Rakich, J.S., and French, G.R. (2001), 'The Balanced Scorecard in Healthcare Organizations: A Performance Measurement and Strategic Planning Methodology', *Hospital Topics,* Vol. 79, pp. 13-24.

Walter, G.H. (1997), 'Emergence and Development of Regional Technology Policy in Germany-the Technologie Region Karlsruhe', *Innovation Conference: Technology Assessment Strategy Forecasting and Regional Policy,* pp. 73-87.

Zaltman, G. and Burger, P.C. (1975), *Marketing Research: Fundamentals and Dynamics* (Hinsdale: Dryden Press).

Zangwill, W.I. (1993), *Lightning Strategies for Innovation, How the World's Best Firms Create New Products* (New York: Free Press).

2

Applying Multiple Behavioral Pattern Analyses to Online Knowledge Management Environments for Teachers' Professional Development

Huei-Tse Hou
Graduate Institute of Applied Science and Technology
National Taiwan University of Science and Technology
Taiwan

1. Introduction

Given the trend toward digitalized knowledge management and the highly interactive Internet environments of Web 2.0, the digitalization of teaching resources and teachers' knowledge management have become important issues. In the field of digital learning, a growing number of studies are focusing on applying Web 2.0 technologies (e.g., blogs and social community software) to teaching (e.g., Fessakis et al., 2008; Kabilan et al., 2010; Mazman & Usluel, 2010). With diversified digital teaching contents, these technologies extend and integrate current teaching modes and help create many new online instructional strategies. In the future, teachers may need to use these growing and complex digital teaching materials, digital learning contents, and instructional strategies. To be utilizes by teachers, these resources must be efficiently and effectively integrated. From the perspective of knowledge management, teachers must also be able to share and integrate their teaching knowledge efficiently within their communities of professional development and, more importantly, effectively externalize and combine knowledge.

Many studies have investigated issues of teacher community and teacher knowledge management (Barab, et al., 2001; Carroll et al., 2003; Hou et al., 2009a, 2009b; Hsu, 2004; Snow-Gerono, 2005; Stigler & Hiebert, 1999), including the application of new technologies to teacher knowledge management (Carroll et al., 2003; Lee et al., 2010). Many studies have also pointed out the necessity of schools adopting knowledge management (Hargreaves, 1999; Kuo, 2003; McKenzie et al., 2001; Richard, 2001). Most teacher knowledge is tacit, and the goal of knowledge sharing is not definite (Carroll et al., 2003); thus, teachers require more assistance and guidance when sharing knowledge. There also exist differences in knowledge sharing behaviors in different types of organizations (Bock et al., 2005; Yang, 2007; Yang & Chen, 2007); therefore, knowledge management strategies should be customized based on teachers' organizations and teaching contexts so as to facilitate teaching knowledge sharing and management of teacher communities. Professional development knowledge sharing is increasingly important for teachers because the digitization of teaching contents has resulted in knowledge content becoming more diverse, including multimedia, learning objects, digital teaching materials edited by teachers, and teaching plans aided by digital technology. These materials are abundant and fast-emerging, adding complexity and difficulty to the process of internalizing teaching knowledge and leading to cognitive load for teachers as they search and combine various types of Internet information.

To meet the demands of knowledge management for teacher communities in the Web 2.0 environment, management strategy becomes a key topic of research because it controls the quality and effectiveness of teachers' professional development. Regarding current knowledge sharing limitations for teachers, Carroll et al. (2003) make several knowledge management suggestions: (1) establishing practice community, (2) building knowledge storage reservoirs, (3) establishing expert guiding mechanisms, (4) promoting peer-supporting mechanisms, and (5) practicing case sharing. Hansen et al. (1999) divides the knowledge sharing strategies of knowledge management systems into two dimensions, specifically, individual and file, and states that each should formulate its own strategies. Given the isolated nature of teaching and the tacit nature of teaching knowledge as well as the diverse and complex nature of knowledge files (digital content of teaching resources) and developing trends in new interactive technologies, the formulation of strategies should not refer solely to the current literature. This issue involves multi-aspect consideration and more precise analyses of knowledge sharing behaviors as aids and foundations to formulate knowledge management strategies effectively that are compatible with teaching practices, allowing for further development of proper knowledge management platforms for teacher communities. Though studies of teacher knowledge management (Carroll et al., 2003; Lee et al., 2010; Plass & Salisbury, 2002; Spector, 2002;) and analyses of teacher knowledge sharing behaviors (Hou et al., 2009a, 2009b) have been conducted, these studies are few in number, and a comprehensive discussion about integrating multiple analytical methods to analyze community behaviors is lacking.

Therefore, this research attempts to apply theories of knowledge transfer and creation to investigate possible phenomena of teaching knowledge transfer in the area of e-Learning. This study employs frequently used behavioral analysis techniques to propose an analytical and detecting framework for integrating different analysis techniques of teachers' professional development and knowledge transfer. By proposing this framework and model, this study expects to aid the development and management of teachers' professional development communities in the Web 2.0 environment.

2. Teaching knowledge transfer in the web 2.0 environment

Knowledge transfer and creation are key to knowledge growth in community organizations. According to widely discussed knowledge creation and transfer model (Nonaksa & Takeuchi, 1995), the transfer of knowledge can be divided into four processes: socialization, externalization, internalization, and combination. This study discusses the traits of these processes of teachers' organization of transferred knowledge below.

1. Socialization: Socialization refers to the process of transferring implicit knowledge to implicit knowledge. This process occurs when individuals transfer knowledge by conveying and sharing experiences in the organization mentally (as opposed to written texts). Knowledge senders and receivers learn knowledge sharing through observation, imitation, and practice. However, given the previously mentioned isolating nature of teachers' knowledge sharing, teachers may find it difficult to proactively share and

observe. In online communities that lack physical interaction, the process of building a socialization community environment requires further research and discussion. Some recent studies have used blogs to build environments for teachers to share knowledge and to observe (Hou et al., 2009b), but the limitation of diversity in social knowledge construction remains. Conducting real and timely empirical behavior analysis can help teacher educators understand the potential reasons for this limitation and formulate appropriate strategies for facilitating socialization. It is also worth applying empirical behavior analysis to analyze and understand the impacts of increasingly favored social network services (SNS) software (e.g., Facebook, Google +) on the socialization of teachers' communities.

2. Externalization: Externalization refers to the process of transferring implicit knowledge to explicit knowledge. This process occurs through mutual dialogues and documentation to initiate knowledge transfer. For example, individuals can communicate their ideas or opinions through language and writing. This process is crucial for teachers' professional development, particularly in building online teacher communities. The question of how to facilitate documentation and digitalization of teaching methods and materials for these busy teachers is an important issue. Several studies have emphasized employing reward mechanisms to increase sharing performance. However, it is important to consider if by applying a reward mechanism (e.g., monetary prize for competition or certification mechanism), the effects of sharing will be long-lasting. Also important to consider is if there is a mechanism to increase teachers' internal motivations to share and produce digital teaching materials and cases. Many studies have mentioned the limitations of online teachers' communities (Barab et al., 2001; Carroll et al., 2003) with the topic of motivation also being discussed. It is worth discussing the question of how to help the members of teacher communities understand precisely how they can benefit the community and themselves by externalizing their knowledge. When teachers find motivations to externalize their knowledge, their capabilities for conducting this externalization must also be evaluated. Many studies have mentioned that some teachers do not have sufficient knowledge of information technology (Leu et al., 1998). Thus, studies need to be conducted that examine how to ensure that teachers have sufficient capabilities for externalizing their knowledge as well as whether the externalized knowledge (e.g., multimedia teaching materials, teaching cases) is precise, of sufficient quality and is not repetitive. Behavioral analyses of the processes of teachers' externalization will allow us to better understand the continuity, depth of contents, and obstacles of externalization.
3. Internalization: Internalization refers to the process of transferring explicit knowledge to implicit knowledge. Internalization occurs through the integration of explicit files and photos such that individuals may absorb and internalize them as tacit knowledge. For example, individuals can learn a specific skill by reading Internet files. For teacher professional development, increasing professional knowledge depends on internalizing and absorbing explicit teaching knowledge. The process of internalization is similar to cognitive process of concept understanding in which knowledge is divided into declarative knowledge (e.g., disciplinary knowledge) and procedural knowledge (e.g., teaching process). To help teachers efficiently absorb sufficient teaching knowledge, the question of how to facilitate teachers' learning motivations in online communities becomes important. Increasing the depth of internalization by designing professional

development activities that assist meaningful learning and deepen cognitive levels may prove helpful. Many recent studies have investigated the knowledge construction phases of online learning communities (Hou et al., 2009a, 2009b), using various analysis methods (e.g., integrating lag sequential analysis, quantitative content analysis) to discuss cognitive characteristics and limitations. Applying different teaching strategies, such as role playing (Hou, 2011a) and problem solving (Hou et al., 2008, 2009a), also helps increase the cognitive diversity and depth of the internalization process. For teachers' professional development, applying these strategies may help teachers internalize professional knowledge, which may result in better professional development effects.

4. Combination: Combination refers to the process of transferring explicit knowledge to explicit knowledge. This process occurs through such modes as storage, addition, sequencing, categorizing, and reorganizing so as to systematize current explicit knowledge. For example, an organization can exchange information through files and the Internet or through databases that integrate and process different knowledge and incorporate it into the organization's knowledge. This process is key to teacher professional development community's production of new knowledge. After observing and internalizing teaching knowledge, teachers must optimize the combination of shared knowledge according to practical teaching contexts so that they may apply the learned knowledge. This process is logistically difficult because teachers should have the capability, time, and motivation to combine and share knowledge. The development of cross-disciplinary teaching knowledge, which has received increasing attention in particular, requires colleagues' cooperation on knowledge combination. As for difficulties in integrating and developing teaching materials, recent studies have found that material designers have difficulties in project control and have little interaction with cross-disciplinary colleagues when collaborating on the development of teaching materials (Albers, 1996; Plass & Salisbury, 2002). However, in the growing Web 2.0 environment, highly interactive Internet behaviors and the concept of collective intelligence are gaining attention (Musser et al, 2006). Cross-disciplinary knowledge integration and social knowledge construction may improve when teachers are more familiar with common social networking software and use it more frequently. Researchers conducted sequential analysis of the behavior of teacher communities using blogs to construct social knowledge (Hou et al., 2009b). The results show that the articles that teachers posted on blogs consisted primarily of sharing their feelings, experiences, or teaching information with limited social knowledge construction. Thus, the process of choosing and developing social software that meets teachers' communities' needs is a challenging topic for research, as is determining how to assist with proper strategies of facilitating teachers' observation (socialization and internalization), sharing (externalization), and combining innovative knowledge. In this way, teachers can achieve the goal of knowledge creation by accumulating knowledge through the cycle of socialization, externalization, internalization, and combination (Nonaksa & Takeuchi, 1995).

In conclusion, this study discusses the management of teacher professional knowledge and the limitations of current research by applying knowledge innovation and transferring model (Nonaksa & Takeuchi, 1995). As the results show, to facilitate professional knowledge transferring and innovation for teacher online community, besides the four essential tool categories in teaching knowledge management system (Spector, 2002) (i.e., communication, coordination, collaboration, and control), the design of assistance mechanism and functional module is also needed for the transferring process (i.e. socialization, externalization, internalization, and combination). We can embed the tools/modules that facilitate knowledge transfer into original digital teacher knowledge management systems. A related behavioral index (e.g., determining what kind of knowledge transferring is present when a teacher conducts a specific operation and browses a specific webpage) must then be set to implement a behavioral analysis of the transferred category's process. Thus, the point of restriction in teachers' interactions can be quickly diagnosed, allowing for direction in knowledge management strategy formulations and revision to platforms for teachers' professional development.

3. Frequently used behavioral analysis techniques for online communities

To implement behavioral analysis techniques in the teacher knowledge transferring process, we need a deeper understanding and discussion of current frequently used behavioral analysis techniques in online communities and of how to apply these techniques to knowledge management platforms for teachers' professional development.

Recent studies have used various techniques to analyze interaction in online communities. These techniques include the following:

1. Behavioral Frequency Analysis: This technique automatically records frequency/log of user operations in the system and performs an analysis. For example, analysis can be conducted on the percentages of all learners' operational behaviors and frequency in online game communities (Hou, 2011a).
2. Quantitative Content Analysis: With specific coding schemes, this technique encodes users' posted contents on knowledge management platforms and analyzes each code's frequency and percentage. For example, with knowledge construction coding schemes (Gunawardena et al., 1997) or with the cognitive processing dimension of the revised Bloom's taxonomy (Anderson & Krathwohl, 2001), analysis of discussions on discussion boards or blogs can be performed to understand the phenomena of discussions (Hou et al., 2009a, 2009b; Hou, 2011b).
3. Lag sequential analysis: This technique examines the sequential correlation of all behaviors during a specific period, either among the entire group or between users (Bakeman & Gottman, 1997, Hou, 2010). For example, this technique can investigate what behaviors users normally perform after a specific behavior to find if the sequence has reached statistical significance. To apply this analysis, behaviors must be encoded, arranged and analyzed according to time sequence, followed by the operations of sequential behavioral frequency transition matrixes. Calculations for these matrixes include calculating sequential transition frequency matrixes followed by the sequential transition conditional probability and expected values of the transition process between all codes, resulting in an adjusted residuals table and a visual behavioral frequency transition diagram. This technique is increasingly applied to behavioral analysis of online learning (e.g., Duran & Monereo, 2005; Hou et al., 2008, 2009a; Jeong, 2003). To investigate sequential transition changes in different time phases more deeply, Hou (2010) proposed progressive sequential analysis to reflect changes of behavioral sequences.
4. Time series analysis: This technique uses historical accumulated behavioral frequency during a specific period to establish proper time series models and to forecast

behavioral frequency for a future period. For example, Box and Jenkins's Autoregressive-Moving Average Models (ARMA) (Box et al., 1994) uses historical data to establish candidate time series models to forecast possible future behavioral trends. Indexes such as mean absolute deviation (MAD) and root mean square error (RMSE) are also used to calculate mean forecasting errors. This technique emphasizes forecasting future behavioral trends. Some researchers have applied this technique to student levels of discussion participation on blogs, finding that certain characteristics of student participation can be predicted (Hou & Ho, 2011).

5. Social network analysis: This technique finds various centrality coefficients centers by analyzing social interaction between members. This technique includes examples, such as degree centrality, betweenness centrality, and closeness centrality. Additionally, social network analysis can calculate the density and clusters of whole social network interaction. It helps significantly in understanding a community's interaction details, while also aiding community managers in better defining members with a high influence and members with low levels of interaction.
6. Cluster analysis: Cluster analysis helps investigate potential behavioral clusters of all behavioral categories for all members. For example, by using two-stage cluster analysis (Ward Method with K-mean method), researchers can investigate possible behavioral modes for members in a community as well as their behavioral characteristics (Hou, 2011a).

By reviewing the above-mentioned analysis techniques, we have found that all techniques have their own analytical dimensions, characteristics, and limitations. Increasing numbers of researchers are combining two or more techniques to increase the validity of their research. For example, by combining quantitative content analysis and lag sequential analysis (Hou et al., 2009a, 2009b), researchers can simultaneously investigate the interaction content and interaction behavior sequential patterns for community members.

4. Online Knowledge Transfer Analysis (OKTA) that integrates social network analysis and lag sequential analysis

Since the teachers' knowledge transfer is restricted by their organizational culture, based on the needs of teachers' online professional development communities, this study attempts to propose and integrate (1) lag sequential analysis to reflect the knowledge transfer behavioral patterns of the entire community and (2) social network analysis to reflect whole social interaction dynamics. The combination of these two techniques may help solve restrictions met when applying lag sequential analysis to detect the behavioral patterns of teachers' knowledge transfer. With social network analysis, it is possible to find influential teachers, formulate and revise strategies, and arrange interaction facilitators so as to effectively make progress in knowledge transfer.

This study proposes the Online Knowledge Transfer Analysis Framework (OKTA), which integrates social network analysis and lag sequential analysis as shown in the figure below.

Figure 1 shows the three analysis phases from top to bottom: (1) "constructing knowledge base of teacher professional development", (2) "lag sequential analysis of teaching knowledge transfer", and (3) "social interaction network analysis of knowledge transfer." The details of each phase are described below.

1. Constructing Knowledge Base of Teacher Professional Development

To analyze teachers' knowledge transfer, supporting function modules must be designed for each knowledge transfer phase (i.e., socialization, externalization, internalization, and combination). To aid analysis, a related behavioral index must be formulated (e.g., what type of knowledge transfer category is present when teachers conduct a specific operation or browse a specific webpage in the KM system?). When teachers conduct a specific operation in the KM system, the system can determine the category of knowledge transfer for that operation and record it in the knowledge base as shown in the top frame of Figure 1. The knowledge base will not only store the transferred contents (e.g., files, multimedia) but will also store the processes of the transfer (e.g., transfer category, operators, list of individuals who may be involved). These data are stored via proper and flexible relational databases. This study defines such databases as an *Interaction Tagged Knowledge Base* (ITKB); they are not only able to index the knowledge content and members but also serve as a dynamic behavioral analysis and index for knowledge transfer and social interaction.

2. Lag Sequential Analysis of Teaching Knowledge Transfer

After completing the construction of ITKB, the system can conduct lag sequential analysis on ITKB. Through serial calculation of behavioral transition matrixes (Bakeman & Gottman, 1997), the system can quickly monitor and analyze the retrieved knowledge transition data in chronological order. The result of this analysis is shown as the example in the middle frame of Figure 1. This allows us to quickly understand the percentage and frequency in a specific period between the four knowledge transition behaviors of the entire community or of a group of members and to understand the sequential relationship between these behaviors (e.g., in Figure 1, most members practice knowledge transfer of combination after knowledge externalization).

These behavioral patterns can be derived by automatic calculation and analysis and are helpful in discovering infrequent knowledge transfer behaviors and limitations of knowledge transfer behavioral patterns, thereby serving as references for formulators of knowledge management strategies.

For example, formulators of knowledge management strategies can understand if teachers are following the rational knowledge transfer process of socialization, externalization, internalization, and combination in a sequential order (Nonaksa & Takeuchi, 1995); they may also discover possible characteristics and limitations of knowledge transfer behaviors and thus design responsive interaction mechanisms and strategies to facilitate deeper teaching knowledge transfer.

3. Social Interaction Network Analysis of Knowledge Transition

Following lag sequential analysis, to better understand teachers' possible social interaction status in the four transfer-behavior process (e.g., what is the pattern of teachers' interaction in the process of knowledge externalization? Which teachers are more influential in this process?), this study conducts social network analysis (Scott, 2000) of the stored operators by ITKB in a specific knowledge transfer behavior and of individuals who may be involved. An example of the result is presented in the bottom frame of Figure 1. The social network map is produced along with all types of *centrality data* for each teacher (including *Degree centrality, Betweenness centrality, and Closeness centrality*). The sorting of the data helps operators of knowledge management strategies find the most influential members (e.g., t5 in Figure 1 may have higher *Degree centrality or Betweenness centrality*). When the crucial facilitators are located, proper knowledge management strategies can be formulated to improve teaching knowledge management.

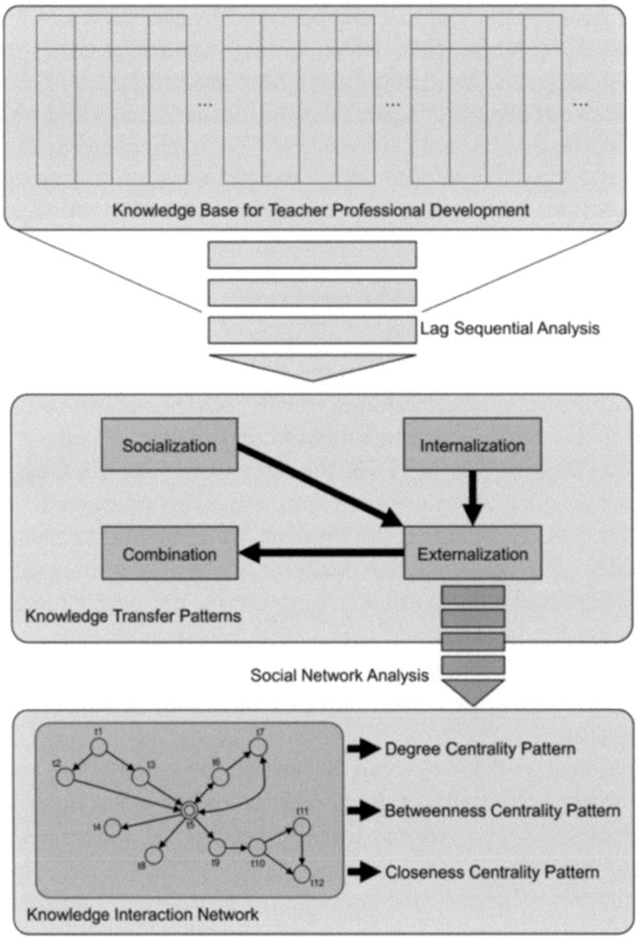

Fig. 1. Online Knowledge Transfer Analysis (OKTA) that Integrates Social Network Analysis and Lag Sequential Analysis

5. Conclusion

The importance of knowledge management in schools has been receiving increasing attention (Hargreaves, 1999; Kuo, 2003; Lee et al., 2010; McKenzie et al., 2001; Richard, 2001). This study attempts to apply knowledge creation and transfer theory (Nonaksa & Takeuchi, 1995) to investigate possible phenomena of teachers' teaching knowledge transfer in digital learning environments and proposes Online Knowledge Transfer Analysis (OKTA) that integrates social network analysis and lag sequential analysis. The behavior analysis framework proposed here will be helpful for investigating teaching knowledge transfer and multi-dimensional behavior patterns of social interaction in teacher communities in Web 2.0 environments. This study intends for this technique to allow for further researches into lack of knowledge sharing and teachers' online professional development. Additionally, through the automatic analysis mechanism of OKTA, this study hopes to visualize different types of behavioral patterns of knowledge transfer processes to allow for more efficient and crucial references for formulators of knowledge management strategies.

6. Acknowledgments

This research was supported by the projects from the National Science Council, Republic of China, under contract number NSC-100-2628-S-011-001-MY4, NSC-100-3113-S-011-001, NSC -99-2511-S-011-007-MY3, and NSC-97-2511-S-011-004-MY3.

7. References

Alber, A. F. (1996). *Multimedia: A management Perspective.* California, USA: Wadsworth Publishing Company.

Anderson, W., & Krathwohl, D. R. (Eds.). (2001). *A taxonomy for learning, teaching, and assessing: A revision of Bloom's educational objectives*, NY: Longman.

Bakeman, R., & Gottman, J. M. (1997). *Observing interaction: An introduction to sequential analysis.* (2nd ed.). UK: Cambridge University Press.

Barab, S. A., MaKinster, J. G., Moore, J. A., Cunningham, D. J., & The ILF Design Team (2001). Designing and building an on-line Community: The struggle to support sociability in the inquiry learning forum. *Educational Technology Research and Development, 49*(4), 71-96.

Bock, G. W., Zmud, R. W., Kim, Y., & Lee, J. (2005). Behavioral intention formation knowledge sharing: Examining roles of extrinsic motivators, social-psychological forces, and organizational climate. *MIS Quarterly, 29*(1), 87-111.

Box, G. E. P., Jenkins, G. M., & Reinsel, G. C. (1994). *Time series analysis: Forecasting and control.* Englewood Cliffs, NJ: Prentice Hall.

Carroll, J. M., Choo, C. W., Dunlap, D. R., Isenhour, P. L., Kerr, S. T., MacLean, A., & Rosson, M. B. (2003). Knowledge management support for teachers. *Educational Technology, Research & Development, 51*(4), 42-64.

Duran, D., & Monereo, C. (2005). Styles and sequences of cooperative interaction in fixed and reciprocal peer tutoring. *Learning and Instruction, 15*(3), 179-199.

Fessakis, G., Tatsis, K., & Dimitracopoulou, A. (2008). Supporting "learning by design" activities using group blogs. *Educational Technology & Society, 11*(4), 199-212.

Gunawardena, C., Lowe, C., & Anderson, T. (1997). Analysis of global online debate and the development of an interaction analysis model for examining social construction of knowledge in computer conferencing. *Journal of Educational Computing Research, 17*(4), 397–431.

Hansen, M. T., Nohria, N., & Tiemey, T. (1999). What's your strategy for managing knowledge? *Harvard Business Review, March-April*, 106-116.

Hargreaves, D. H. (1999). The knowledge-creating school, *British Journal of Educational Studies, 47*(2), 122-144.

Hsu, S. (2004). Using case discussion on the web to develop student teacher problem solving skills. *Teaching and Teacher Education, 20*(7), 681-692.

Hou, H. T., Chang, K. E., & Sung, Y. T. (2008). Analysis of Problem-Solving Based Online Asynchronous Discussion Pattern. *Educational Technology & Society*, 11, 1, 17-28.

Hou, H. T., Sung, Y. T., & Chang, K. E. (2009a). Exploring the behavioral patterns of an online knowledge sharing discussion activity among teachers with problem-solving strategy. *Teaching and Teacher Education*, 25, 1, 101-108.

Hou, H. T., Chang, K. E., & Sung, Y. T. (2009b). Using Blogs as a Professional Development Tool for Teachers: Analysis of Interaction Behavioral Patterns, *Interactive Learning Environments*, 17, 4, 325-340.

Hou, H. T. (2011a). Learning English with online game: a preliminary analysis of the status of learners' learning, playing and interaction, paper presented at the Sixth

International Conference on E-Learning and Games (Edutainment 2011), September 7-9, 2011, Taipei, Taiwan.

Hou, H. T. (2010) Exploring the Behavioural Patterns in Project-Based Learning with Online Discussion: Quantitative Content Analysis and Progressive Sequential Analysis, *Turkish Online Journal of Educational Technology*, 9, 3, 52-60.

Hou, H. T. (2011b). A case study of online instructional collaborative discussion activities for problem solving using situated scenarios: an examination of content and behavior cluster analysis, *Computers and Education, 56*, 3, 712-719.

Hou, H. T., & Ho, C. C. (2011). Applying time series analysis to forecast learners' participation patterns in blog instructional activities: A preliminary study. *British Journal of Educational Technology*, 42, 5, e91-93.

Jeong, A. C. (2003). The sequential analysis of group interaction and critical thinking in online threaded discussions. *American Journal of Distance Education, 17*(1), 25–43.

Kabilan, M. K., Ahmad, N., & Abidin, M. J. Z. (2010). Facebook: An online environment for learning of English in institutions of higher education? *Internet and Higher Education, 13*(4), 179-187.

Kuo, Y. F. (2003). A study on service quality of virtual community, *Total Quality Management & Business Excellence, 14*(4), 461-473.

Lee. C. L., Lu, H. P., Yang, C., & Hou, H. T. (2010). A Process-based knowledge management system for schools: a case study in Taiwan, *Turkish Online Journal of Educational Technology*, 9, 4, 10-21.

Leu, D. J., Hillinger, M., Loseby, P., Balcom, M., Dinkin, J., Eckels, M., Johnson, J., Mathews, K., & Raegler, R. (1998). Grounding the design of new technologies for literacy and learning in teachers' instructional needs. In D. Reinking, M. McKenna, L. D. Labbo, & R. Kieffer (Eds.), *Handbook of literacy and technology: Transformations in a post-typographic world* (pp. 203-220). Mahwah, NJ: Erlbaum.

Mazman, S. G., & Usluel, Y. K. (2010). Modeling educational usage of Facebook. *Computers & Education, 55*(2), 444-453.

McKenzie, J., Truc, A., & Winkelen, C. (2001). Winning commitment for knowledge management initiatives. *Journal of Change Management, 2*(2), 115-127.

Musser, J., O'Reilly, T., & the O'Reilly Radar Team (2006). *Web 2.0: Principles and best practices*. CA: O'Reilly Media, Inc.

Nonaksa, I., & Takeuchi, H. (1995). *The knowledge creating company*. NY: Oxford University Press.

Plass, J. L., & Salisbury, M. W. (2002). A living-systems design model for Web-based knowledge management systems. *Educational Technology, Research and Development, 50*(1), 35-56.

Richard, D. R. (2001). Technology: Where students learn. *American School & University, 47*(3), 360-363.

Scott, J. (2000). *Social network analysis: A handbook*. London: SAGE Publications.

Snow-Gerono, J. L. (2005). Professional development in a culture of inquiry: PDS teachers identify of benefits of *professional learning communities. Teaching and Teacher Education, 21*(3), 241-256.

Spector, J . M. (2002). Knowledge management tools for instructional design. *Educational Technology, Research and Development, 50*(4), 37-47.

Stigler, J. W., & Hiebert, J. (1999). *The teaching gap*. New York: Free Press.

Yang, J. T. (2007). Knowledge sharing: Investigating appropriate leadership roles and collaborative culture. *Tourism Management, 28*(2), 530-543.

Yang, C., & Chen, L. C. (2007). Can organizational knowledge capabilities affect knowledge sharing behavior? *Journal of Informational Science, 33*(1), 95-109.

3

Knowledge Management Practice Assessment and the Relationship Between Knowledge Management Practices and Organizational Strategy Development: Empirical Evidence From Turkey

Rifat Kamasak
Yeditepe University, Istanbul
Turkey

1. Introduction

Knowledge became one of the most important intangible assets that enable organizations to create core competencies and achieve sustainable competitive advantage. In the business era where knowledge intensive organizations compete to survive, a practical understanding and application of Knowledge Management (KM) is essential for a fast and efficient exchange of information. Several authors (*i.e.*, Handzic *et al.*, 2008; Frappaolo, 2008; Sveiby, 2001; Zack, 1999) suggest that organizations which successfully manage their tacit, implicit and explicit knowledge have a greater ability in adapting the dynamic and complex new business environment.

Although KM is a substantially investigated issue, there is still no widespread agreement on what KM actually is, because of its very broad spectrum integrating business strategy and process, organizational community and culture, collaboration, learning, expertise, and technology (Skadiang, 2009; Haggie & Kingston, 2003; Silver, 2000). While knowledge literature offers many studies related to the different dimensions of KM, the research regarding the assessment of organizational knowledge management is very limited. Moreover, a multidimensional standard scale that can be used for greater universality and coherence in several areas is lacking.

Since people can understand different things from knowledge issues and knowledge management (KM), assessment of knowledge management practices has been a controversial issue in management literature. However, different dimensions of KM have to be clarified thoroughly for an effective knowledge management. Choi (2003) claimed that there was a scarcity of studies on a survey scale that might assess the critical attributes of organizational knowledge management and evaluate KM success factors. The study attempts to bridge this literature gap by employing a standardized KM scale that would assess the multidimensional nature and practice of organizational knowledge management among Turkish firms.

The aim of this research is to investigate the reliability and validity of the Knowledge Management Scale developed by The University of Southern Queensland (USQ) as a measurement tool for assessing the extent of organizational knowledge management (OKM) practices in Turkish firms. In other words, the question of "how KM practices are perceived by Turkish managers in organizations" is tried to be answered. In order to achieve this, a self-administered e-mail survey is selected as the appropriate method for the research and a 16-item KM scale developed by USQ researchers (known as the USQ KMS-16) is used as the measurement instrument. The research also purposes to identify any perceived links and influence between knowledge management practices and the development and execution of organizational strategies.

2. Literature review

"If you can't define something, you can't measure it.
If you can't measure something, then you can't manage it".
Peter Drucker

Since the 1960's, just after Drucker used the terms "knowledge work" and "knowledge worker", there has been a growing interest in knowledge and its management which have been gaining momentum (Wiig, 1997). Although the interest was initially focused on information technology, more recently the nature of the issue has shifted to knowledge management which includes some other aspects of social sciences such as the human, sociology, communications, learning, business and strategy (Stephens, 2001). According to Clarke (2001), whilst knowledge became one of the most strategically important resources, learning was promoted to the most strategically important capability for business organizations with the boost of global competition.

Smith *et al.* (2005) defined organizational knowledge as the validated understanding and beliefs in a firm about the relationship between the firm and its environment. Keskin (2005) defines knowledge as an organized combination of data, integrated with a set of rules, procedures, and operations that have developed through experience and practice. Walczak (2005) provided a similar concept to this definition, but considers an additional issue; high quality decision making.

Knowledge is a key resource in a rapidly changing global market where the development of innovative services, products and solutions is required to attract and retain customers and get ahead of the competition (Spender, 1996). Several researchers (*e.g.*, Schulze *et al.*, 2008; Nilakanta *et al.*, 2006; Nonaka *et al.*, 2006; Nonaka, 1991) who explain the strategic nature of knowledge also emphasize its importance of usage in organizational strategy development processes. Moreover, some others (*e.g.*, Hamel, 2002; Pemberton *et al.*, 2001; Davenport & Prusak, 2000; Leonard-Barton, 1998; Nonaka, 1991) claim that "knowledge is the cornerstone of competitive advantage".

McDermott and O'Dell (2001) suggest that it is very unlikely to succeed unless KM initiatives are integrated with business strategy and "related to the development of organizational core capabilities". Dilnutt (2000: 64) states that, "knowledge management brings together the concepts of knowledge work and strategic management, in order to manage the required resources and capabilities through the facilitation of knowledge development, creation, representation, access and transfer". For these reasons, KM as an emerging discipline became crucial for the organizations that seek to improve their efficiency and competitive abilities. It is clear that effective implementation of a sound organizational knowledge management (OKM) strategy is considered mandatory for the organizations in the knowledge economy (Binney, 2001).

For knowledge to be managed more effectively and efficiently, assessment of the critical attributes of OKM and evaluation of KM success factors have to be clarified thoroughly.

However, because of the dominant effects of culture, the predilection towards the acceptance and use of knowledge management varies from country to country. Some researchers (*e.g.*, Cohen, 1998; De Long & Fahey, 2000; Andriessen, 2006; Andriessen & van den Boom, 2007; Jelavic & Ogilvie, 2010) conducted studies on the knowledge perceptions of different countries. Cohen's (1998) study identified the differences in the perception of knowledge management in American versus Japanese organizations. The study revealed that "while the west emphasized the re-use of explicit knowledge and the management of projects and markets, the east focused on the creation of tacit knowledge and the management of cultures and communities" (Jelavic & Ogilvie, 2010: 54). Figure 1 exemplifies the traditional US-Japanese differences on knowledge view.

American	**Japanese**
Focus on explicit knowledge	Focus on tacit knowledge
Re-use	Creation
Knowledge projects	Knowledge cultures
Knowledge markets	Knowledge communities
Management and measurement	Nurturing and love
Near-term gains	Long-term advantage

Fig. 1. US-Japanese contrast on knowledge view (Jelavic & Ogilvie, 2010, p. 56)

According to De Long and Fahey (2000: 116), "cultures that are more inclined to rewarding creativity develop differing patterns of interaction around knowledge than cultures that uncover and leverage existing knowledge". Similarly, Andriessen and van den Boom (2007: 647) suggest that "the western knowledge management literature has a tendency to conceptualize knowledge as a physical manifestation or a, substance whereas the eastern literature views it as part of a process". Figure 2 summarizes Andriessen and van den Boom's comparison of metaphors for knowledge in the east and the west.

Origin	**Western literature**	**Asian Philosophy**
Dominant metaphors	-Knowledge as a thing that can be controlled and manipulated. -Knowledge as information that can be codified, stored, accessed and used. -Knowledge as resource that can be created, stored, shared, located, or moved, as that is part of the input-throughput-output system of the organization. -Knowledge as capital that can be valued, capitalized and measured; that is part of the financial flow and requires a return on investment. -Knowledge as thoughts or feelings that is tacit but can be made explicit; that can be communicated and shared.	-Knowledge as spirit and wisdom. -Knowledge as unfolding of truth. -Unity of universe and human self. -Unity of knowledge and action. -Knowledge as illumination or enlightenment of an underlying, deeper reality. -Knowledge as essence-less and nothingness (Japan). -Knowledge creation as a continuous, self-transcending process.

Fig. 2. Metaphors for knowledge in East and West (Jelavic & Ogilvie, 2010, p. 56)

In management literature, KM assessment is still a controversial issue. Although a few researchers (*e.g.*, Choi, 2003; Darroch, 2003; Wickramasinghe, 2003; Maier, 2002; Bennett & Gabriel, 1999) put some efforts in order to assess the critical attributes of OKM, it is observed that there is still a lack of empirical research on *KM assessment* (how to gauge the extent of KM practice) using a standard, multidimensional scale that reflects the breadth and depth of OKM in organizations across industries.

Maier's (2002) study which was conducted on 445 German-speaking companies resulted that KM was mostly an information technology (IT) and information systems (IS) issue. Accordingly, Maier (2002) focused on the pure technological side of KM and suggested that especially all large organizations should have highly complex IT and communication technology systems such as interactive tools, social software and networks. However, Wickramsinghe's (2003) research found that only technological side of KM was not enough for a successful OKM and KM systems were found to be unable to support subjective knowledge.

These results revealed the importance of the organic side of knowledge management rather than the mechanistic side. Another study was conducted by Choi (2003) in which 1,000 questionnaires on 39 attributes were distributed to 1,000 selected firms in the USA. Results of the study showed the importance of a KM-supportive culture, capability of information systems technology, commitment of the top management to KM implementations and KM education and learning (Skadiang, 2009).

Moreover, especially information systems capability was positively associated with KM success although "numerous studies have shown that organizational culture had been singled out as the most critical factor for KM implementation" (Skadiang, 2009: 41). So, Choi's (2003) study has emphasized the importance of both technology and organizational culture for a successful KM management. The last noteworthy study came from Darroch in 2003. Darroch (2003) developed a scale to measure KM behavior and practices in organizations with at least 50 employees in New Zealand. Results of the study confirmed that KM was significantly correlated with strategy, culture and technology.

The review on KM literature reveals that the interest was initially focused on information technology. However, the nature of the issue has shifted to some other aspects of social sciences such as the human, sociology, communications, learning, business and strategy. According to Bollinger and Smith (2001), "a strong, positive organizational culture is vital to learning, development and the sharing of skills, resources and knowledge". Consequently, previous KM research leads us to three dimensions for OKM; OKM strategy, OKM culture and OKM process and technology. In this literature review, it was aimed to synthesize previous research on organizational knowledge management (OKM) as well as to identify and to analyze gaps and key research issues. The following section continues with the empirical part of the study.

3. Methodology

The literature review revealed that there has been limited research about how knowledge management practices are assessed and what their relationship with the organizational strategy development is. This is particularly true in the Turkish business context where there has been little research into Knowledge Management itself. Hence, the nature of the research is exploratory and theory-building.

3.1 Sample and demographics

The study focused on a broad set of Turkish firms in both the manufacturing and the services industries. A total of 1000 firms, namely, the first 500 and the second 500 largest firms announced by Istanbul Chamber of Industry (ISO) annually have composed the sample frame of this research. Since organizational strategy is developed and executed by the firms' owners and senior managers, a database that includes the names and the e-mail addresses of the firms' top executives was obtained.

Because unit of analysis is at the firm level, a single informant is used in the study and the questionnaire was mailed to only one executive from each firm. The questionnaire developed by Erwee *et al.* (2007) was sent to the e-mail addresses of the top managers as a web-link with a covering letter. Three weeks after the initial mailing, a reminder follow-up e-mail was also sent to be able to increase the response rate of the study. The survey was conducted on-line and a total of 171 responses were obtained from the managers of the largest 1000 firms, resulting in a response rate of 17.1 percent. Demographic statistics revealed that the mean firm size was 312 employees while the mean firm age was 22.7 years (Table 1).

Variables	
Firm size (employees)	312
Firm age (years)	22.7

Table 1. Composition of the firms based on size and age

The mean age of the respondents was 35.3. A predominant 69 percent of the respondents were top level managers and the remaining 31 percent was mid-level managers (Table 2).

Position	Composition	Number	Percentage
Top level		118	% 69
Mid-level		53	% 31

Table 2. Composition of the respondents based on the managerial positions

While male respondents were at the majority with 73%, females comprised only 27% of the sample. 21% of the respondents were between 30-40 years of age, whereas, 62% were between 41-50 and 17% were above 51 years of age (Table 3).

Gender/Age	Composition	Number	Percentage
Male		125	% 73
Female		46	% 27
30-40		36	% 21
41-50		106	% 62
51+		29	% 17

Table 3. Composition of the respondents based on gender and age

The sectors in which the majority of the respondents work are, finance and banking, food, drugs, automotive and automotive parts, textile, electronics, and construction as shown in Table 4.

Industry	**Composition**	**Number**	**Percentage**
Finance and Banking		36	% 21
Food		26	% 15
Drugs		24	% 14
Automotive		21	% 12
Textile		19	% 11
Electronics		16	% 9
Construction		12	% 7
Others		17	% 11

Table 4. Composition of the firms based on the industry

3.2 Measurement instruments

Self-administered e-mail survey was selected as the appropriate method for this research. In order to assess the dimensions of KM practices of the organizations, a multi-dimensional standard scale that was consisted of 16 questions (known as the USQ KMS-16 by Erwee *et al.*, 2007) was used as the measurement instrument. Another 6 questions were developed by the researcher and added to the questionnaire in order to investigate the relationship between the knowledge management practices and the development and execution of organizational strategies.

So, the questionnaire is consisted of a total number of 22 questions excluding demographics; 4 questions for OKM strategy, 6 questions for OKM culture, and 6 questions for OKM process/technology. The last 6 questions are employed in order to explore the knowledge management practices' influence on the development of an organization's strategy.

To test for non-response bias, the means of all variables obtained from early and late respondents were examined. According to Spanos and Lioukas (2001: 915), "the rationale behind such an analysis is that late respondents (*i.e.*, sample firms in the second wave) are more similar to the general population than the early respondents". No statistically significant differences were found in all variables.

In order to test representation capability of the respondents for the broader population, the means of early and late respondents on two key demographic variables were compared (Galbreath & Galvin, 2008). The comparison of early and late respondents did not reveal a significant difference on firm size (t=−.319, p=.298) and age (t=−.542, p=.203). Hence, non-response bias was not considered as a serious issue in the study. Responses were recorded on a five-point Likert-type scale, with anchors of "strongly disagree" and "strongly agree".

4. Analysis and results

Data obtained from 171 managers were analyzed by SPSS 18.0 version. Principal Component Analysis with Varimax rotation which indicated .82 Cronbach's-alpha reliability yielded three factors as in the original instrument; namely OKM culture, OKM strategy and OKM process/technology. Consequently, all dimensions showed consistency with the original scale and these findings revealed the validation of the scale for the Turkish sample.

This implication has also supported the efforts of testing a new organizational knowledge management scale for extensive variety of populations. The variables were observed to be moderately correlated which indicates that each variable is distinct and it makes a unique contribution to the overall model. Variance inflation factors (VIF) were also below the score recommended as problematic, which is 10. So, multi-collinearity was not likely to be a problem in this data set. Correlations for all the variables with descriptive statistics and the factor pattern of the measurement instrument are presented in Table 5 and Table 6, respectively.

Variables	N	Mean	SD	1	2	3	4	5	6
1. Firm size	171	312.07	737.61	–					
2. Firm age	171	22.71	33.45	.11	–				
3. Respondent age	171	35.34	.73	.19**	.08	–			
4. OKM strategy	171	3.98	.49	.20**	.24**	.05	–		
5. OKM culture	171	3.49	.53	.16**	.07	.18**	.29**	–	
6. OKM technology	171	3.27	.61	.35**	.23**	-.19*	.08*	.21**	–

*P <0.05 **P <0.01

Table 5. Correlations among variables

The influence of knowledge management practices in developing organizational strategies was also investigated by regression analysis. Regression analysis found significant relationships between all knowledge management dimensions, and organizational strategy development. The results can be seen in Table 7.

5. Conclusion and discussion

The aim of this study was to investigate the reliability and validity of the Knowledge Management Scale developed by University of Southern Queensland (USQ) as a measurement tool for assessing the extent of organizational knowledge management (OKM) practices in Turkish firms along with the exploration of OKM practices' influence in developing organizational strategy. Exploratory factor analysis yielded three factors as in the original instrument; namely OKM culture, OKM strategy and OKM process/technology. So, the most important finding of the study can be considered as all dimensions showed consistency with the original scale and these findings revealed the validation of the scale for the Turkish sample. In organization literature, information systems and technology were the main issues associated with knowledge management. And the other dimensions that could influence an effective management of knowledge were generally omitted. However, knowledge is a unique, valuable and inimitable resource that affects profitability and performance of the organizations and it should be analyzed from a larger perspective (Taylor & Lowe, 1997). The proponents of Knowledge Based View (KBV) perceive organizations as a body of knowledge (Spender, 1996). Theorists (*e.g.*, Dehning & Stratopoulos, 2003; Barney & Wright, 1998; Foss, 1996) consider the firm as a heterogeneous knowledge production entity and stress that knowledge, especially tacit knowledge, is the very source of sustainable competitive advantage. The findings of the study concur with the extant literature that posits knowledge as a strategic resource rather than a simple IT or an IS issue. According to the results, managers acknowledge KM to be a core part of their organizational strategy and

Table 6. Factor pattern of USQ Knowledge Management Scale

		Factor Loadings		
		1	2	3
Factor 1: OKM Culture				
Employees are actively encouraged to make contributions to the organization's knowledge.		.798		
Employees are actively encouraged to use the organization's knowledge.		.761		
The organization has a strong culture of performing work to a high standard.		.735		
Employees are actively encouraged to look for new ideas internally.		.693		
Employees actively use new ideas to improve organizational performance.		.634		
The organization actively supports the formation of close working relationships among employees.		.582		
Factor 2: OKM Strategy				
Managing knowledge is a core part of the organization's strategy.			.902	
The organization has strategies to implement its KM capabilities externally.			.817	
Priorities are established for addressing goals that improve organizational performance.			.764	
In managing knowledge, goals that improve organizational performance are purposely identified.			.729	
Factor 3: OKM Process/Technology				
Acknowledged subject matter experts' among employees are rewarded by the organization for their expertise.				.756
The organization invests resources to ensure its information can be trusted.				.694
Periodically reviewing the quality of its knowledge resources is a formalized process in the organization.				.651
The organization deliberately identifies optimal external practices.				.607
The organization measures employees' contributions to its knowledge resources.				.593
Transferring optimal practices among employees is a formalized process in the organization.				.556
Percentage of explained variance		29.8	20.6	19.3
Total variance	69.7			
Factor's Cronbach alpha reliability coefficient		.86	.79	.77
Kaiser-Meyer-Olkin sampling adequacy	.735			
Barttlet's test of approx. Chi-Square Sphercity	1996.72**			

$^{**}P < 0.01$

Dependent Variables	Adjusted R^2	F	β	P values
OKM Culture	0.69	874.49	0.83	0.001*
OKM Strategy	0.62	537.62	0.79	0.001*
OKM Process/Technology	0.46	486.78	0.68	0.014*

*p<0.05 Predictors: (Constant), Organizational strategy development

Table 7. Regression analysis results

they affirm that knowledge needs to be effectively shared in the organization and integrated with business strategy. Obviously, these findings confirm the strategic nature of knowledge and its management.

Another noteworthy result is OKM culture factor's high explanatory power (29.8 percent) in the total variance. Literature also suggests that organizational culture which promotes learning, development and the sharing of skills, resources and knowledge is a key component of OKM. The survey findings affirm the dynamics of other OKM elements such as the "process of socialization, the sharing of knowledge as a natural, on-going part of work and the synergy and collaborative efforts of employees" (Skadiang, 2009: 107).

The research also revealed that knowledge was a strategic variable to organizations since a clear and significant relationship between each of the organizational knowledge dimension and organizational strategy development was found. The data indicated that OKM culture have the strongest influence on strategy development which means organizations may especially use their internal knowledge creating resources such as employees, managers, organizational culture and climate to execute their strategies, and to formulate and evaluate them. Strategic side of knowledge should not be ignored by organizations. Undoubtedly, high explanatory power of OKM culture reflects the crucial role of the OKM culture components such as organizational culture (Stewart, 1991; Biren *et al.*, 2000; Sindell, 2001), group characteristics (Moorhead & Griffin, 1995), process of socialization (Nonaka & Takeuchi, 1995), compensation structure and rewards for new ideas (Quinn *et al.*, 1996; McDermott & O'Dell, 2001; Tiwana, 2002), supportive social atmosphere (Davenport *et al.*, 1998; Figallo & Rhine, 2002), trust, honesty and collaboration (Bollinger & Smith, 2001; Behrend & Erwee, 2007), expertise and creativity (Amabile, 1999), and open communication and knowledge exchange (Badaracco, 1991; Perez & de Pablos, 2003; Collison & Parcell, 2006) in developing organizational strategy. Davenport *et al.* (1998) delineate knowledge as a fuzzy and invisible asset that is closely linked to the human brain. This valuable asset can only be revealed through sharing with others.

Taking a knowledge (centric) view of an organization can also help in understanding: what the organization does; what its core competences are; and where value adding occurs. It should not be forgotten that many companies (*e.g.*, Google, Apple, Virgin) have created knowledge by their human related skills, distributed knowledge with their IT technologies in order to increase their creativity, and produced know-how as a source of core competency. It is obvious that the balance between knowledge and resources will continue to shift towards the knowledge and perhaps knowledge will not only be the most important factor in creating competitive advantage for the organizations but also will be the unique asset in determining the standard of living for nations. Based on the results on the study, it should be noted that, in order to make the organizations achieve sustainable competitive advantage and superior firm performance, the firms need to focus on the elements of OKM culture and provide a balance between the technological and human-related resources rather than make all their investment to the IT and IS issues. This suggestion can be deemed as the most important managerial implication of the study.

Lastly, the measurement tool used in this study is found to be a reliable measure for KM assessments within the context of Turkish companies. It is also believed that USQ KMS-16 as a multidimensional standard knowledge management scale can be used for greater universality and coherence in organization literature. However, applying the instrument on more extensive variety of populations would not only increase the validity of the scale but it would also help the future researchers to add supplementary questions to address the items that were not specifically highlighted in the USQ KMS-16 questionnaire. With some felicitous modifications, the USQ KM scale could be used, on a macro level, as a benchmark by researchers, industry associations, professional bodies or government agencies to analyze OKM practice across selected industries.

6. References

Amabile, T. (1999). *Harvard Business Review on Breakthrough Thinking,* Harvard Business School Press, Boston, USA.

Andriessen, D. (2006). On the metaphorical nature of intellectual capital: a textual analysis. *Journal of Intellectual Capital,* Vol. 7, No. 1, pp. 93-110.

Andriessen, D., & van de Boom, M. (2007). East is East, and West is West, and (n)ever its intellectual capital shall meet. *Journal of Intellectual Capital,* Vol. 8, No. 4, pp. 641-652.

Badaracco, J.L., Jr. (1991). *The Knowledge Link: How Firms compete through Strategic Alliances,* Harvard Business School Press, Boston, USA.

Barney, J.B., & Wright, P.M. (1998). On becoming a strategic partner: the role of human resources in gaining competitive advantage. *Human Resource Management,* Vol. 37, No. 1, pp. 31-46.

Behrend, F., & Erwee, R. (2007). Using social network analysis to map information and knowledge flows in virtual project teams, 15 May 2010, Available from: http://eprints.usq.edu.au/view/people_yr_title/Behrend,_Frank.html

Bennett, R., & Gabriel, H. (1999). Organisational factors and knowledge management within large marketing departments: an empirical study. *Journal of Knowledge Management,* Vol. 3, No. 3, pp. 212-225.

Binney, D. (2001). The knowledge management spectrum - understanding the KM landscape. *Journal of Knowledge Management,* Vol. 5, No. 1, pp. 33-42.

Biren, B., Dutta, S. & van Wassenhove, L.N. (2000). Xerox: building a corporate focus on knowledge, 20 July 2011, Available from: http://knowledge.insead.edu/docs/Xerox.pdf

Bollinger, A.S. & Smith, R.D. (2001). Managing organizational knowledge as a strategic asset. *Journal of Knowledge Management,* Vol. 5, No. 1, pp. 8-18.

Choi, Y.S. (2003). Reality of knowledge management success, In: *Journal of the Academy of Business and Economics,* March [Online], 7 June 2011, Available from: http://www.findarticles.com/p/articles/mi_m0OGT/is_1_2/ai_113563644

Clarke, T. (2001). The knowledge economy. *Education + Training,* Vol. 43, No. 4, pp. 189-196.

Cohen, D. (1998). Toward a knowledge context: report on the first annual U.C. Berkeley forum on knowledge and the firm. *California Management Review,* Vol. 30, No. 3, pp. 22-39.

Collison, C., & Parcell, G. (2006). *Learning to Fly: Practical Knowledge Management from Leading and Learning Organizations,* Capstone Publishing Limited, West Sussex, UK.

Darroch, J. (2003). Developing a measure of knowledge management behaviors and practices. *Journal of Knowledge Management,* Vol. 7, No. 5, pp. 41-54.

Davenport, T.H., & Prusak, L. (2000). *Working Knowledge: How Organizations Manage What They Know,* Harvard Business School Press, Boston, USA.

Davenport, T.H., DeLong, D.W., & Beers, M.C. (1998). Successful knowledge management projects. *Sloan Management Review*, Vol. 39, No. 2, pp. 43-57.

De Long, D.W., & Fahey, L. (2000). Diagnosing cultural barriers to knowledge management. *Academy of Management Executive*, Vol. 14, No. 4, pp. 113-128.

Dehning, B., & Stratopoulos, T. (2003). Determinants of a sustainable competitive advantage due to an IT-enabled strategy. *Journal of Strategic Information Systems*, Vol. 12, No. 1, pp. 7–28.

Dilnutt, R.P. (2000). *Knowledge management as practiced in Australian organisations: A case study approach*, DBA thesis, Southern Cross University.

Drucker, P.F. (1993). *Post Capitalist Society*, Harper Business, New York, USA.

Erwee, R., Skadiang, B., & Reynolds, M. (2007). *Dimensions of organizational knowledge management*, Unpublished working paper, University of Southern Queensland, pp. 1–13.

Figallo, C., & Rhine, N. (2002). *Building the Knowledge Management Network*, John Wiley & Sons, New York, USA.

Foss, N.J. (1996). Knowledge based approaches to the theory of the firm: some critical comments. *Organization Science*, Vol. 7, No. 5, pp. 470–476.

Frappaolo, C. (2008). Implicit knowledge. *Knowledge Management Research & Practice*, Vol. 6, No. 1, pp. 23–25.

Galbreath, J., & Galvin, P. (2008). Firm factors, industry structure and performance variation: new empirical evidence to a classic debate. *Journal of Business Research*, Vol. 61, No. 2, pp. 109–117.

Haggie, K., & Kingston, J. (2003). Choosing your knowledge management strategy. *Journal of Knowledge Management Practice*, Vol. 13, No. 1, pp. 1–24.

Hamel, G. (2002). *Leading the Revolution*, Plume, New York, USA.

Handzic, M., Lagumdzija, A., & Celjo, A. (2008). Auditing knowledge management practices: model and application. *Knowledge Management Research & Practice*, Vol. 6, No. 1, pp. 90–99.

Jelavic, M., & Ogilvie, K. (2010). Knowledge Management views in Eastern and Western cultures: an integrative analysis. *Journal of Knowledge Globalization*, Vol. 3, No. 2, pp. 51-69.

Keskin, H. (2005). Relationships between explicit and tacit oriented KM strategy, and firm performance. *Journal of American Academy of Business*, Vol. 7, No. 1, pp. 169–175.

Leonard-Barton, D. (1998). *Wellsprings of Knowledge: Building and Sustaining the Sources of Innovation*, Harvard Business School Press, Boston, USA.

Maier, R. (2002). *Knowledge Management Systems: Information and Communication Technologies for Knowledge Management*, Springer, Berlin, Germany.

McDermott, R., & O'Dell, C. (2001). Overcoming cultural barriers to sharing knowledge. *Journal of Knowledge Management*, Vol. 5, No. 1, pp. 76–85.

Moorhead, G., & Griffin, R.W. (1995). *Organizational Behavior: Managing People and Organizations*, 4th edn, Houghton Mifflin Company, Boston, USA.

Nilakanta, S., Miller, L.L., & Zhu, D. (2006). Organizational memory management: technological and research issues. *Journal of Database Management*, Vol. 17, No. 1, pp. 85–95.

Nonaka, I. (1991). The knowledge creating company. *Harvard Business Review*, Vol. 69, No. 6, pp. 96–104.

Nonaka, I., & Takeuchi, H. (1995). *The Knowledge-Creating Company*, Oxford University Press Inc., New York, USA.

Nonaka, I., Toyama, R., & Konno, N. (2000). SECI, ba, and leadership: a unified model of dynamic knowledge creation. *Long Range Planning*, Vol. 33, No. 1, pp. 5–34.

Nonaka, I., von Krogh, G., & Voelpel, S. (2006). Organizational knowledge creation theory: evolutionary paths and future advances. *Organization Studies*, Vol. 27, No. 8, pp. 1179–1208.

Pemberton, J.D., Stonehouse, G.H., & Yarrow, D.J. (2001). Benchmarking and the role of organizational learning in developing competitive advantage. *Knowledge and Process Management*, Vol. 8, No. 2, pp. 123–135.

Perez, J.R., & de Pablos, P.O. (2003). Knowledge management and organizational competitiveness: a framework for human capital analysis. *Journal of Knowledge Management*, Vol. 7, No. 3, pp. 82-91.

Quinn, J.B., Anderson, P., & Finkelstein, S. (1996). Managing professional intellect: making the most of the best. *Harvard Business Review*, Vol. 74, No. 2, pp. 71-80.

Schulze, P., Heinemann, F., & Abedin, A. (2008). Balancing exploitation and exploration organizational antecedents and performance effects of ambidexterity", *Best Paper Proceedings – Academy of Management (AOM) Annual Meeting*, Anaheim, CA, pp. 1–6.

Silver, C. A. (2000). Where technology and knowledge meet. *The Journal of Business Strategy*, Vol. 21, No. 6, pp. 28–33.

Sindell, M.T. (2001). Knowledge management conversation: co-workers chat, guidance unfolds. *Training & Development*, November issue, American Society for Training & Development Inc., USA.

Skadiang, B. (2009). *Dimensions of organisational knowledge management (OKM): A study on Malaysian managers using the multidimensional USQ KM scale*, Doctoral Dissertation, University of Southern Queensland, Australia.

Smith, K.G., C.J. Collins, & Clark, K.D. (2005). Existing knowledge, knowledge creation, capability, and the rate of new product introduction in high-technology firms. *Academy of Management Journal*, Vol. 48, No. 2, pp. 346–357.

Spanos. Y.E., & Lioukas, S. (2001). An examination of the causal logic of rent generation: contrasting Porter's competitive strategy framework and the resource-based perspective. *Strategic Management Journal*, Vol. 22, No. 10, pp. 907–934.

Spender, J.C. (1996). Making knowledge the basis of a dynamic theory of the firm. *Strategic Management Journal*, Vol. 17, Winter Special Issue, pp. 45–62.

Stephens, D. (2001). Knowledge management in the APS: a stock-take and a prospectus, *Canberra Evaluation Forum*, 15 March 2001, Canberra, p. 23.

Stewart, T.A. (1991). Brainpower. *Fortune*, Vol. 123, No. 11, pp. 44-50.

Sveiby, K.E. (2001). A knowledge-based theory of the firm to guide strategy formulation, 12 May 2011, Available from:
http://www.sveiby.com/Portals/0/articles/Knowledgetheoryoffirm.htm

Taylor, P., & Lowe, J. (1997). Are functional assets or knowledge assets the basis of new product development performance?. *Technology Analysis & Strategic Management*, Vol. 9, No. 4, pp. 473–488.

Tiwana, A. (2002). *The Knowledge Management Toolkit*, 2nd edn, Pearson Education Inc., New Jersey, USA.

Walczak, S. (2005). Organizational knowledge management structure. *The Learning Organization*, Vol. 12, No. 4, pp. 330–339.

Wickramasinghe, N. (2003). Do we practice what we preach: are knowledge management systems in practice truly reflective of knowledge management systems in theory?. *Business Process Management Journal*, Vol. 9, No. 3, pp. 295–316.

Wiig, K.M. (1997). Knowledge management: an introduction and perspective. *The Journal of Knowledge Management*, Vol. 1, No. 1, pp. 6–14.

Zack, M.H. (1999). Managing codified knowledge. *Sloan Management Review*, Vol. 40, No. 4, pp. 45–58.

4

Facts, Processes and Common Understandings: The Management of Knowledge in Project Based Organisations

Karina Skovvang Christensen and Per Nikolaj Bukh
Aarhus University and Aalborg University
Denmark

1. Introduction

During the last couple of decades, project based organisations (PBOs) have been on a strong increase (e.g. Prencipe and Tell, 2001; Whitley, 2006) as the fast changing environment and conditions for conducting business call for more flexible, innovative organisational designs. Project teams are one way to organise for these changes. PBOs are especially suited to react to changes and initiate team learning, and they are also said to be the key learning unit in organisations (Senge, 1990). In this way PBOs can be seen as small knowledge intensive factories where knowledge is created, adapted, and re-framed.

However, PBOs face a number of challenges. One of these is not to "reinvent the wheel" as organisational knowledge can be fragmented and very team specific. In such organisations it may be difficult to know what knowledge is available in the organisation if there are no formal mechanisms or established department responsible for capturing, storing and sharing knowledge in and between project teams. More specifically one has to assess whether the organisation is able to capitalise on knowledge gained in one project and transfer it to other projects. Will team members with diverse skills - who work together for at limited period of time, who might not know each other, and who may not expect to collaborate again - be able and willing to share knowledge? Do team members even have to handle multi-teaming? All these issues, and more, aim at an effective understanding of knowledge management.

Paying attention to the role of knowledge management as well as the role of social processes, practises and patterns is relatively new in relation to knowledge management in projects and PBOs as Bresnen et al. (2003) have pointed out. According to Ajmal and Koskinen (2008) the benefits of knowledge transfer have long been recognized in PBOs, but the effectiveness of the knowledge transfer varies considerably.

Effective knowledge management is complex, but essential. Therefore, this paper focuses on how the alignment between an organisation's strategy, products, and knowledge management strategy can help clarify which knowledge management initiatives will be most effective.

The aim is to discuss how different types of knowledge enable various ways of managing knowledge, i.e., how they create, share and transfer knowledge in and between projects. Therefore, we study how more views on knowledge management and related initiatives in relation to developing and sharing knowledge in projects can extend the managerial palette of options and how it might help project managers choose the most effective knowledge management tools to facilitate knowledge management activities in general. Further, we examine how a particular project management model used in two specific organisations differs when the package of knowledge management tools differs.

The significant role of knowledge and effective knowledge management in PBOs is for instance essential for improving the utilisation of core capabilities and technological platforms and reduce development time in projects (Oshri et al., 2005). Aamodt and Plaza (1994) argue that 4R, i.e., Retaining, Retrieving, Reusing and Revising previously developed knowledge from other projects, is an essential goal of knowledge management in PBOs as this previously generated knowledge is to support future project work. This approach supports the view that knowledge can be retained, retrieved, revised and reused, which corresponds to what is called the artefact oriented perspective (e.g. Christensen & Bang, 2003; Christensen & Bukh, 2005) in this article. This perspective is rooted in the decision support literature which means that the 4Rs constitute the backbone of knowledge management in the sense that they support new problem solving by using previous knowledge. The artefact oriented perspective focuses on the explicit dimension of knowledge where information can be captured, stored, retrieved and re-used using knowledge management systems.

An alternative way to view knowledge management is the process oriented perspective (e.g. Christensen & Bang, 2003; Christensen & Bukh, 2005) which primarily focuses on the interplay between the tacit and explicit dimensions of knowledge. From this perspective the context for understanding the information is more important, and it is emphasised that the essential issue of knowledge management is the process of creation and sharing of knowledge. This perspective is in agreement with the organisational culture perspective presented by Ajmal and Koskinen (2008, p. 8) which "encourages informal interactions between individuals to ensure that knowledge is created and transferred".

By using these two perspectives to analyse knowledge management in two Danish PBOs: The development division at Bang & Olufsen and FKI Logistex Crisplant, this article shows how project management, which on the surface looks alike - as it is based on the same basic project management model, i.e., Cooper's (2001) stage-gate-model - might be very different in practice as important differences are found.

The article shows how project management in the two companies differs and how it, together with the differences in the production processes, influences how the involved knowledge resources are managed. In the conclusion it is suggested that if a company offers standardized products, a codification strategy departing in the artefact oriented perspective will be most effective, whereas the personification strategy departing in the process oriented perspective will be most effective if a company offers customized solutions. Further, the analysis from the two perspectives may contribute to understanding the implications of the lack of agreement on what knowledge management is (cf. Firestone, 2008).

The remainder of the article is structured in the following way: Section 2 introduces knowledge management in projects and the two perspectives on knowledge management. Further, two different strategies for knowledge management are discussed. In Section 3 the methodology is presented and a short description of the two companies is given. In section 4 the companies' different initiatives in relation to knowledge management are presented and it is illustrated how knowledge management is an integrated part of project management. In section 5 knowledge management is analyzed from the two different perspectives, and finally, section 6 discusses how the perspectives may help to show a more balanced picture of knowledge management by focusing on different aspects of knowledge management.

2. Knowledge management in projects

In management literature there has been an overwhelming interest in the concept of knowledge and knowledge based resources. This is not only reflected in the importance of knowledge-intensive companies but also in an interest in how knowledge based resources interact in the creation of value in companies and how knowledge can be managed. Paying similar attention to the importance of knowledge, knowledge based resources and processes as well as the role played by social processes, practises and patterns in relation to the management of knowledge in projects and project organisations (e.g. Huang & Newell, 2003; Cummings, 2004; Brookes et al., 2006) is, however, a more recent phenomenon as was emphasised already by Bresnen et al. (2003).

This is somewhat surprising as PBOs are becoming an increasingly important mode of organising and as product development and innovative activities, which are often based on project organisations, are the prototype of knowledge intensiveness (Brookes et al., 2006). The importance of knowledge management in PBOs arises from several aspects of the role of knowledge as well as the characteristics of PBOs (e.g. Koskinen, 2004). Employees are the primary carrier of knowledge in PBOs opposite more functionally based organisations with established departments responsible for knowledge storage and sharing (Ajmal and Koskinen, 2008).

This demands special attention. Projects are often based on a specific task with a budget, assigned project members and a schedule to be kept (e.g. Reich et al., 2008), and they are evaluated based on their performance in relation to specific task related milestones. However, projects are also expected to function as a place where knowledge is shared and developed. Individuals, teams and organizations are expected to optimize performance and learning, but learning and performance often work at cross-purposes - especially in teams (Bunderson & Sutcliffe, 2003; Singer & Edmondson, 2008; cf. O'Leary et al., 2011). Regularly, changes in projects often disrupt the time schedule which can be very costly. Therefore, Senaratne and Sexton (2009) argue that understanding the role of knowledge and what type of knowledge is shared and developed in the project during the change event is crucial.

Additionally, the amount of R&D activities carried out in projects has increased dramatically (von Zedtwitz et al., 2004), and knowledge management has been argued to facilitate integration between R&D and marketing (Sherman et al., 2005). Further, the increasing geographical distribution of projects and project members affects how project management can be carried out, and knowledge management becomes a difficult task because of distance and cultural barriers (Evaristo et al., 2004; Ajmal & Koskinen, 2008).

Finally, knowledge is in general a vital resource in project based industries as Love et al. (2003) remark, and effective knowledge management, in project organisations for instance, is essential for establishing a learning project organisation (e.g. Kasvi et al., 2003) and for improving the utilisation of core capabilities and technological platforms and to reduce development time in projects (Oshri et al., 2005). Thus, knowledge management in projects and PBOs is expected to be of importance, and it strives for an effective understanding of knowledge management.

2.1 The two perspectives on knowledge management

The discussion of the concept of knowledge is still an ongoing process. Several categorisations and frameworks have been suggested (e.g. Blackler, 1995; Li & Gao, 2003; Meyer & Sugiyama, 2007), however, Polanyi's (1966) dichotomy of tacit and explicit knowledge is still a point of departure for understanding the nature of knowledge as it was found by Alavi & Leidner (2001) as well as Jennex & Croasdell (2005), cf. Jennex & Olfman (2006).

The notion of implicit knowledge has often been used to span the two poles (e.g. Frappaolo, 2008; Li & Gao, 2003; Meyer & Sugiyama, 2007), and the continuum perspective, in which knowledge has both an implicit and explicit dimension in a specific context, is developing (Jasimuddin et al., 2005; Klein, 2008; Kogut & Zander, 1992; Mohamed et al., 2006). When managers as well as scholars discuss knowledge, different perspectives are often taken. The difference often consists of the way in which knowledge is perceived. In other words, the basic epistemologies differ. Although for example Nonaka & Takeuchi (1995) use the term 'tacit' knowledge, we will follow Klein's (2008, p. 42) suggestion and mainly distinguish between explicit and implicit knowledge. The latter is a subset of tacit knowledge since Polanyi's (1966) notion of tacit knowledge implies a kind of knowledge that fundamentally cannot be shared. Further, the distinction between the artefact oriented and the project oriented perspectives will be outlined in more details below.

The first perspective on knowledge and knowledge management will be termed the *artefact oriented* perspective. Focus is often on information technology and the ways in which technology may be applied for the codification of knowledge. It is more or less explicitly assumed that everything can be described, and the more data a company collects, the more knowledge it possesses. Knowledge management is therefore mostly based on collecting, storing and distributing knowledge, for example, in the form of documents and specific information (e.g. Huber, 1991; Lyles & Schwenk, 1992).

From the artefact-oriented perspective, knowledge management focuses mostly on project memory (cf. Jennex & Olfman, 2006; Kärreman et al., 2004) and manuals for organisational processes (Malone et al., 1993). This is in agreement with the R4s - retrieve, reuse, revise and retain - emphasised by Aamodt and Plaza (2004). According to Karni & Kaner (2008) R4 constitutes the backbone of case-based reasoning which was developed to support new problem solving by using previous knowledge. See also a similar perspective termed "knowledge as a solution" suggested by Snider and Nissen (2003); cf. Ajmal and Koskinen (2008, p. 8).

Many authors (e.g. Blackler, 1995; Tsoukas, 1996) have indicated that the artefact oriented perspective has become insufficient when handling management challenges in relation to the complexity of the knowledge society and hence has criticised the reductionist view of knowledge expressed by the artefact oriented perspective emphasising instead that knowledge is situated in social and organisational practises as well as relationships (Tsoukas & Vladimirou, 2001). The problem is not lack of documents, data, or access to information. The limitation is rather to be found in the quality, content, and organisation of the material. This has given rise to the second perspective, which we term the *process oriented perspective*. Here, knowledge is related to experience and is more dependent on the context as it is socially created, to use Snider and Nissens (2003) expression.

The process oriented perspective is most clearly exemplified by Ikujiro Nonaka's research in which knowledge is perceived as a "dynamic human process of justifying personal beliefs as a part of an aspiration for the 'truth'" (Nonaka 1994, p. 15). An essential point is that focus is on the process in which knowledge is created and not on the documents or the rules based on the process. This implies that continuous and dynamic adaptation to 'real life' takes place.

From the process-oriented perspective knowledge creation and sharing is considered to be a continuous process where knowledge is transformed between tacit and explicit knowledge and between people and technology. Here the point of departure is the so-called SECI-model (Nonaka & Takeuchi 1995) which consists of four types of processes, identified by Nonaka & Takeuchi (1995) as central in relation to knowledge management: Socialisation, Externalisation, Combination and Internalisation. According to Nonaka & Takeuchi (1995, pp. 70-71) the development of organisational knowledge is a continuous and dynamic interaction between tacit and explicit knowledge.

More effective knowledge management may also result from adapting management tools that fit the prevailing perception of knowledge. For instance Marr et al. (2003) state that knowledge management practises will be perceived as more effective if they match the personal epistemology of the employees. In relation to an in-depth study of knowledge management in a project case study in an Australian industrial engineering organisation, Sense (2007, p. 17-18) documents similarly that the project members favour knowledge sharing techniques that align with their cognitive style type and further that they acknowledge the personal bias towards specific modes of sharing knowledge.

2.2 Strategies for knowledge management

Hansen et al. (1999) argued that two strategies dominate practice in general: the *codification strategy*, which is associated with the understanding of knowledge management in the artefact oriented perspective and the *personification strategy*, which can be related to the process oriented perspective. Even though the two strategies may be presented as alternatives, they are often seen as supplementing each other instead of being mutually exclusive. While the codification strategy is a cornerstone in the bureaucratic organisation, the personification strategy is seen to have its strength in knowledge intensive organisations. As knowledge complexity grows, capturing the context and culture information needed to ensure that knowledge is reusable becomes more difficult (Jennex & Olfman, 2006) and the personification strategy gains more importance. While Hansen et al. (1999) originally claimed that one of the strategies often will have a more prevailing position in the organisation's consciousness, other authors (e.g. Jennex & Olfman, 2006, p. 58) argue that the two strategies may be of equal importance.

Although recent knowledge management researchers favour a combination approach as mentioned above, many find that practice is often grounded in one of the two perspectives (e.g. Christensen & Bukh, 2005; Hoegl & Schulze, 2005; Liebowitz & Megbolughe, 2003; Pretorius & Steyn, 2005). In a case study of knowledge management in a South African Bank, Pretorius & Steyn (2005) find that management of explicit knowledge has the most focus in relation to projects. So while explicit knowledge could be captured in project documentation such as schedules and technical reports when a codification strategy is followed, implicit knowledge is most easily transferred between people.

One reason that a codification strategy seems to be widespread in PBOs could be that project team members are often dispersed organisationally and geographically (Kasvi et al., 2003) thus reducing the possibility of face-to-face communication which otherwise has a positive effect on implicit knowledge transferring as was concluded by Koskinen et al. (2003). Further, as a project has a limited duration there will be a tendency for people not to get familiar enough with each other to develop the trust necessary for a personification strategy to work (Bresnen et al., 2003; see also Pretorius & Steyn, 2005).

3. The methodology

The practises studied in the companies include activities that are not perceived beforehand as knowledge management initiatives in the two companies. Therefore a case study approach seems appropriate. Such an approach offers the possibility of dealing with a variety of evidence, documents, questionnaires, interviews and observations in a flexible manner (Yin 2003). In the present context this means the opportunity to observe and describe a complicated research phenomenon in a way that allows analytical (Eisenhardt, 1989; Tsoukas, 1989) or analogical (Smaling, 2003) generalisations of the observations.

3.1 Focus on the perception of knowledge

The view of knowledge pervading much research especially from the artefact oriented perspective - but not limited to that - is positivist, i.e., it follows the Platonic view that knowledge is 'justified true belief'. However, recent knowledge management researchers (e.g. Nonaka & Takeuchi, 1995; Christensen and Bang, 2003; Ajmal and Koskinen, 2008) have initiated a move away from seeing the subject in a static, cognitive relationship to propositions stating facts about the empirical world (se also Jackson & Klobas, 2008).
Following this recent tradition we adopt an approach where knowledge, neither as an object to be managed nor as a research object, is strictly defined beforehand. As the basic idea of simultaneously working with different perspectives on knowledge as presented in the previous section, we let the nature of knowledge be based on the individual's set of beliefs or mental models used to interpret actions and events in the world. This opens up for different perceptions of knowledge and knowledge management. In an organisation such as Roos & von Krogh's (1995, p. 1) this is reflected in their statement that "[w]hat you see depends on who you are", which implies that knowledge should be regarded as a subjective term.

3.2 The data collection

The empirical material includes ten semi-structured interviews, five in each of the two companies. The five respondents in each company held similar positions across the companies. We interviewed the senior executive responsible for the development projects, a project manager, a manager responsible for project methods and two engineers (one who had been with the company for many years and one who had been with the company less than 2 years) actually working on the projects.
The interviews were structured according to the interview guide shown in Figure 1. The overall themes were followed in each interview but the questions listed under each theme were only a tentative list of areas to be covered in the interviews. First, the interviewees were asked to tell about the company's history. Next, according to the interview guide, they were asked to enter conversation about how knowledge management affects their daily work, how knowledge is created and shared, as well as how they work with different tools (e.g. project models and IT-systems). The interviews lasted approximately 1½ hours on average, and they were taped and transcribed.

A: What is the overall purpose of knowledge management?
Why do you work with knowledge management? What are the expected gains, short and long term?
B: How does the company work with knowledge management?
How are the activities organized? How are project teams formed and how are they organized? How is co-operation in the teams facilitated? What knowledge does the firm acquire, how is knowledge shared, stored and used in daily work? Are any models or frameworks used in the work with knowledge management?
C: How is knowledge created, stored, retrieved, and shared?
What about knowledge in projects and teams? How do you avoid losing knowledge, e.g., when employees leave? How are tasks coordinated? How is the relevant competences brought into projects? How do personal networks affect the work? How are information technologies and systems used? How are experiences from projects collected, stored and reused?
D: How does the project management model function?
How do you actively work with the phases in the model? How does it affect daily practice that you work with gates? Does it make a difference that you use gates and not milestones? What does it mean for the collection, storing and sharing of knowledge? How do you collect knowledge in the evaluation of projects and learn from experience?
E: How are systems and technologies used?
What kinds of systems support your project work? How are these systems used? What kinds of knowledge are stored and retrieved from these systems? How is knowledge organized in order that it can to be retrieved and reused? How do you feel about the technological support for sharing of knowledge? What kinds of communication take place in projects? What form of communication is the most important?

Fig. 1. Interview guide

The interviews at B&O were collected through the period 28-29 August 2003, whereas the interviews at Crisplant were collected almost two years earlier, i.e., they took place in the period 29 October to 12 December 2001. Moreover, documents, reports, and observations were collected. General attitudes will be expressed by the company name, whereas the respondent's function is emphasized where this is of importance in connection with a statement.

3.3 The two companies

Bang & Olufsen (B&O), which is known for its distinguished design and quality, manufactures and sells products to the audio, video and multimedia market. In recent years the company has also increased its revenues from audio systems developed exclusively for automotive manufacturers such as Aston Martin, AMG and Audi. Development of new products is a decisive competitive parameter and Research & Development costs represent more than 9 per cent of the company's revenue. At the time of interviewing, the export share was 83 per cent of the revenue of DKK 3,613 millions (Euro 480 millions), and the B&O group employed approx. 2,700 people. This article only addresses knowledge management in the product development division of B&O.

FKI Logistex Crisplant A/S (Crisplant) develops, produces, and installs solutions within the so-called automatic high-speed transport and sorting systems (ATS) area which forms a substantial part of operations at airports, postal centres, libraries, mail order businesses, distribution centres etc. all over the world. Their systems are developed and implemented in close cooperation, not only with the customer, but also with a number of other companies. These supply various parts of the installation of which the sorting system must be an integrated part. At the time of interviewing, Crisplant had approximately 700 employees and a revenue of DKK 840 millions (Euro 113 millions).

4. Knowledge management in the two companies

The two organisations were chosen because they represent two different types of PBOs both focussing on product development. B&O has organised product development in a department separated from production with products being manufactured at assembly plants and sold as a mass product to customers all over the world. Crisplant develops customer specific solutions in projects more like a construction company with development and installation at the customer site being separate phases of the same project.

Product development as it is undertaken in both companies has traditionally been described a knowledge intensive activity (Meyer & Utterback 1993). Managers, engineers and technicians apply the knowledge they have developed through formal training and from experience. At the same time they enhance their skills and capabilities through the project. Such knowledge-intensive companies are dependent on their employee based knowledge resources. However, neither B&O nor Crisplant have a separate strategy for knowledge management. Instead, the analysis stresses the importance of knowledge management being an integrated part of the companies' processes and management activities embedded within an organizational culture which encourages development, sharing, and anchoring of knowledge.

4.1 Knowledge management in Bang & Olufsen

In the first phases of a development project in B&O, knowledge management is based on personal interactions where employees meet across departments and enter into a dialogue where creative ideas are being conceived and new knowledge generated. Thus, the dissemination of existing knowledge is important in B&O. Further, the company is dependent on tacit knowledge or unique competencies such as employees who have "a pair of good ears", as it was expressed by a project manager, which are able to hear precisely when a loudspeaker or an amplifier sounds correct. Such knowledge is very difficult to transfer and therefore B&O is committed to the fact that this kind of knowledge transfer takes place through close cooperation where competences are disseminated in the organisation.

The development processes are built around the unique knowledge resources of key people in a way that makes it difficult for competitors to imitate B&O's products. To disseminate the specialist knowledge in the interviews, the importance of the availability of these "knowledge keepers" is stressed to the organisation. It must be known who possess specific types of knowledge so that, instead of being a hidden resource, the individual key person becomes an available resource to be relied on all over the organisation. A manager at B&O explains:

We have a culture in the development division where everybody walks around and talks to everybody about the problems they encounter ... when an employee is designing something, the person knows that he needs to go and talk to a specific colleague because the colleague knows something special about this. And then he does so and they have a chat about it. So in most cases there is free and open access to all the knowledge available, you could say, via personal contact.

Consequently, making the implicit explicit will improve the knowledge management of an organisation (Matzkin & Cupcham, 2011). This may be part of the culture (Ajmal and Koskinen, 2008) or enabled by the autonomy that employees are granted by management similarly to what Oshri et al. (2005, p. 16) found in a case study of knowledge transfer in a multiple-project environment. Further, key employees' expert knowledge is made available to the organisation by holding a large number of internal courses at B&O where the employees teach each other.

However, explicit and codifiable knowledge is also applied to a great extent in all development projects. It may both be knowledge which is unique to B&O, and at the same time it may be knowledge which in principle is available on the world market. To capture knowledge, B&O uses the so-called TOP-model, an adopted version of Cooper's (2001) stage gate model, in all development projects. In practice this means that when the first phases of a development project (physical proximity and face-to-face contact) are completed, only a few people from the quality department are responsible for making sure that knowledge is shared both in the individual project and across projects.

In addition to this, B&O has strict documentation requirements during the development projects. This is partly due to the company's ISO-certification and partly due to the internal strategies for knowledge sharing where the possibility to reuse earlier developed elements in future products is seen as important. In this way explicit knowledge becomes a focal point similar to what Tsai (2001) demonstrated in a study where transferring knowledge from one base project to other projects enhanced organisational innovation and performance. B&O thus is very conscious about the importance of documentation. It attempts to extend the documentation activities further so that the company may reuse more knowledge and thus reuse more solutions by building up modular products.

4.2 Knowledge management in crisplant

From development over production to implementation, all project activities in Crisplant are project-organised and run according to Crisplant's Project Management Model (CPMM), which is also an adapted version of a state gate model (cf. Cooper, 2001). Due to the nature of the customer specific solutions, the context is somewhat similar to that of the construction industry where for example Bresnan et al. (2003) emphasise that organisations face substantial obstacles to be overcome in "capturing knowledge and in re-cycling of project based learning that stem from the relatively self-contained, idiosyncratic and finite nature of project tasks" (ibid, p. 158).

Crisplant develops solutions with a high degree of customisation, the individual projects are very different from each other, and the composition of project teams takes place more on the basis of employees' competencies than on the basis of specific technical components which must be included in the project. Thus, knowledge management has to focus specifically on employees, and as a consequence the development, sharing, and anchoring of the accumulated knowledge is an integrated part of the company's way of working. In an interview it was for instance said that: "It is natural for us to live by having knowledge and trying to give our customers value through a continuous development and creative use of our knowledge".

Thereby, knowledge management becomes an integrated part of the management activities that influence organisational culture and support the overall main strategic goals. Furthermore a manager at Crisplant says: "Knowledge management is about presenting favourable conditions for the creative process of the individual in cooperation with others and hence set the knowledge resources of the company at play".

But Crisplant also uses a range of IT-tools for supporting the creation and transfer of knowledge as standardised and codified knowledge collected by the project leaders in progress reports each month.

This is of importance in relation to documenting the experience from the separate development phases. Crisplant is, however, of the opinion that the employees' implicit knowledge is essential for the company's progress and growth.

The company is convinced that the informal knowledge sharing taking place daily as "face-to-face" contact is by far of greatest strategic importance. Crisplant's management thus attempts to make the frames for knowledge sharing and knowledge creation available by focusing on teamwork in the project organisation and by integrating a dialogue-based company culture which cultivates trust norms and shared values by which projects take the character of communities of practice (Brown & Duguid, 1991, 2001).

The manager responsible for organisational development explains that "the day-to-day knowledge sharing and knowledge creation to a wide extent is expressed through the work with CPMM as well as a continuous focus on creativity in all processes". To improve creativity, Crisplant works intensely with a model internally named the 'Creative Working Model' (CWM). This model facilitates the process at all levels, from structuring a project, over the way a certain meeting is structured, to how the individual employees structure their working day.

The CWM consists of five phases. A *seeing phase* which focuses on dialogue about expectations with regard to the final goal and thus which objectives must be obtained to reach the overall goals for the task or project. Following this comes the *idea phase* in which it is established how the objectives and goal should be obtained. The third phase is the *planning phase* which is carried through in interaction with Crisplant's Project Management Model. When the planning is done, the project participants begin *executing* the plan as the fourth phase, and subsequently, the project group goes into a *seeing again phase* where the course of events is evaluated and the project team learns from its experiences. Additionally, the CWM is accomplished in each of the phases in the CPMM.

4.3 Knowledge management as project management

B&O's product development division as well as Crisplant are organized as PBOs. Competent, efficient and reliable project implementation is decisive for business success in B&O as well as Crisplant. For several years, both companies have applied a project management model inspired by Cooper's 'stage gate model' (Cooper, 2001).

At Crisplant, the purpose of working with the Stage-Gate model is to establish "a common set of rules for project control, management and execution internally as well as in cooperation with customers, suppliers and other partners" (Crisplant, 1999, p. 4). In the product development division at B&O, the Stage-Gate model has a more direct role as knowledge management tool. Also, the method department continuously adjusts it according to the experiences from different product development projects. At B&O, the

Stage-Gate model thus functions as a dynamic model according to which knowledge is accumulated and later disseminated through the application in the individual projects.

Each phase of the Stage-Gate models ends with a *gate*. In this connection, the project managers of both companies prepare a gate report on the status of the project, both with regard to progress and budget. At the same time, major replacement among employees often takes place in between the individual phases. Therefore a gate also represents a critical point in relation to knowledge management, as knowledge needs to be transferred from one team to another.

With respect to knowledge, B&O has high documentation requirements in all projects, but at the same time, the company is aware of the value of face-to-face knowledge transfer along the way. The Method Manager in B&O expresses it in the following way:

> it is not such an explicit transfer taking place at each individual gate. It is not the documentation that ensures knowledge transfer in the projects ... it is only because people talk together and we agree on how things should be that it works ... it is not due to our documentation.

Like B&O, Crisplant is aware that not all types of knowledge can be passed on in written-down documentation, and therefore it works with the CWM-model.

Both companies apply pre-determined checklists which the project manager goes through. On this basis he prepares a phase report after each individual phase of the Stage-Gate model. These phase reports are saved and used for example when the project management tool is being updated at B&O. At the end of a project, a project evaluation meeting is held at both Crisplant and B&O. Here the project's experiences, good as well as bad, are collected in a final report.

5. Knowledge management in perspective(s)

In the following two subsections the project management of the two companies is analysed according to the two epistemological perspectives on knowledge management: the artefact oriented and the process oriented. Hereby, it is illustrated how the presentation and the perception of knowledge management depend on the epistemological starting point.

5.1 Artefact-oriented perspective

As a part of B&O's codification strategy, artefacts in the form of process documentation, product specifications, development documentation etc. are pointed out as essential elements of the knowledge management activities. At Crisplant, such documents also form an important part of the knowledge collecting process which the Managing Director at the time expressed in this way:

"...As we work out a concept proposal and a solution to our customer, we document the thoughts and ideas we have concerning the solution to a specific project. Thus, the knowledge stays in the company so to say - because it has been put down in writing."

From this perspective, knowledge in both companies is about writing and documenting in order to make the company capable of leaning from previous project descriptions etc. when new quotations are given and on the whole when working on the projects. Thus, the project management systems function as a repository for routine solutions where explicit knowledge can be reused (cf. Markus 2001, p. 59). Within the artefact-oriented perspective, knowledge management thus focuses on the types of knowledge which may be explicated, formalized, and ultimately codified. Project management in the two companies appears to consist of more or less the same components. Although, the continuous update of the state-gate-model is more important in B&O than in Crisplant, whereas the process based on the basic principles in the model is more important in Crisplant than in B&O.

From a pure artefact oriented perspective having knowledge management such as management control systems, databases, administrative systems etc. ensures knowledge management. At both B&O and Crisplant artefact oriented knowledge management focuses on consistent documentation of development activities via Stage-Gate models, quality management, and data collection. In the artefact oriented perspective less focus is on the context in which knowledge was created because the underlying assumption is that this knowledge can be re-used even though the context in which it was created is less explicit. From this perspective knowledge management looks similar in the two organisations.

5.2 Process oriented perspective

Contrary, from a process-oriented perspective (with emphasis on the SECI model), knowledge management is also apparent in both B&O and Crisplant. This may be illustrated by the fact that the companies, besides anchoring knowledge through progress reports, Stage-Gate models and quality control systems, focus on personal relations. Crisplant has systematized the transfer of knowledge between project phases in the Stage-Gate model. This has been achieved through support from the CWM, and B&O works with mentor arrangements and which creating a dialogue-based culture. By sharing knowledge across the organizations, the companies attempt to internalize employee knowledge.

At Crisplant the process-oriented perspective is predominant in the work with the CWM which structures the processes, ensures the process and becomes instrumental in creating, sharing, and internalizing knowledge. At both B&O and Crisplant, the socialization phase is stressed by attaching importance to physical meetings between project teams. These are utilized to share opinions, values, and knowledge and to obtain a common framework of understanding.

The externalization phase should be understood as the phase where the employees express their ideas. Nonaka et al. (2000) stress that the use of images, metaphors, analogies etc. in this phase may help employees express a point without really being able to explain it. This is exactly what happens in the idea phase of the CWM at Crisplant. When all thoughts and ideas have been aired and placed on the boards, these are combined and reduced in order to make a realistic plan for the development of the project. At B&O the idea phase is not formalized in the same way. The ideas from Crisplant's idea phase and B&O's development department are both incorporated in the companies' Stage-Gate models which structure the development of the projects. This is the equivalent of what takes place in Nonaka's combination phase in the SECI-model.

The internalization phase is the last phase of the SECI-model. In this phase the objective is to embody common guidelines, goals and objectives. In Crisplant this is accomplished in the executing phase of the CWM and the phases in the companies' Stage-Gate model where the products are actually developed and installed at the customers site. Although, our study is based on the development division at B&O, and B&O does not install their products at the customer's site and thereby share knowledge and get feedback from the customers. This may, however, be done by their retailers. Either way, the experiences gained during the projects are incorporated as far as possible in the stage gate model in order to be available for later project.

5.3 Knowledge management strategies in the two companies

Crisplant's highly customized products are assembled and implemented at the customer's site often in collaboration with the customer and suppliers of subparts causing changing settings from customer to customer and from project to project. This is in agreement with the predominant personification strategy based on CMW, which according to Hansen *et al.* (1999) is the optimal knowledge management strategy for highly customized products.

B&O's knowledge management strategy is not as clear as it involves more elements from both the codification strategy and the personification strategy. In the same way as Crisplant, B&O acknowledges the importance of face-to-face communication, but in B&O it is more a question of making the structures and frameworks available to the organisation, thus leaving it to the initiatives of the employees to communicate when needed. Thus the experiences from B&O is in line with Keegan & Turner (2001) who in a study of learning across projects found that the informal networks within companies are the most important conduit for transferring knowledge between projects (cf. Sense, 2007).

The ideal context of knowledge creation and sharing depends on the type of knowledge. For instance, both B&O and Crisplant find it important that the members of a project team meet physically in the initial phases where the objective is to express thoughts and ideas concerning the project. At B&O, product development begins in a separate organisational unit known as *Idea Land* where a group of designers are seated closely together. Later, in the construction phases physical proximity is not imperative to the same degree.

Following the process oriented perspective both implicit and explicit knowledge and not least the interplay between the two knowledge types are in focus. From a process oriented perspective the second and third phases of the SECI model (Externalization and Combination) differ the most between the two companies, whereas the first and last phases (Socialization and Internationalization) are more similar. In the Externalization phase the employees at Crisplant meet physically and discuss their ideas: At B&O the freedom of the projects are restricted by directions from the designers from Idea Land, and the rest of the project members must make their ideas and components fit. In the Combination phase, knowledge management is primarily centred on working with the Stage-Gate models and the use is very different. In B&O the state gate is continuously adapted and used as a knowledge management tool within and between projects, whereas it is primarily used for notification in Crisplant. In the Internalization phase the specific development work is conducted, and contrary to B&O, Crisplant still give priority to physical proximity in the last phase, as Crisplant focuses on a common internalization phase for the group in preference to the individual.

6. Concluding remarks

The analysis illustrates how the understanding of specific project related activities differs depending on the perspective taken in the analysis. In practice, an understanding of different perspectives will give a company a more nuanced picture of the organization, knowledge, and management, thereby expanding the optics which is used for identification of potentials or problems in relation to the management of knowledge.

In the analysis of the knowledge management activities in Crisplant, the process oriented approach was most prevalent. All activities, from meetings to large projects, were structured according to the CWM model used by the firm. Further, the sharing of knowledge is encouraged by initiatives where the employees are physically located in relation to the projects so as to enable a 'space' for communication.

However, when an organisation is project based, project leaders need to be very attentive and create an atmosphere of trust and care to encourage the project members to share knowledge with each other. Otherwise it may be difficult to perform as a team and achieve the overall goal, keep the budget, the schedule etc. This directs attention to the personification strategy, which is in accordance with Hansen et al. (1999) who emphasize the importance of implicit and human interaction in the development of new products.

Knowledge management in the development division at B&O is not equally clear. This may reflect the fact that the development division acts as an intermediary between the department termed Idea Land, where knowledge management is based on the process oriented perspective, and the rest of the organisation, where knowledge management is more oriented towards the artefact oriented perspective. For instance, this is expressed by the higher priority continuous documentation and updating of the state gate model is given in B&O compared to Crisplant.

As B&O's end products are mass products, they supports Hansen et al.'s (1999) finding that knowledge management in relation to mass produced products is most effectively managed following the codification strategy. However, in the development division and in particular in Idea Land, the knowledge management activities are primarily based on the process-oriented perspective. In practice both tacit or implicit knowledge as well as explicit knowledge seem to be of equal significance in B&O, which means that the company combines the personification and the codification strategy. And the dominating strategy depends on which part of the company is in focus. Generally seen, it also fits the line of thought that B&O's design structure includes a special department, the methods department, to continuously adjust and update the Stage-Gate model enabling all employees to use the experiences gained by colleagues.

The evidence from the two companies does not allow for a statistical generalisation. However, based on analogical generalisation (Smaling, 2003), we suggest that the more standardized solutions a company offers, the more a codification strategy will be effective. This results in a knowledge management strategy which departs directly from the artifact oriented perspective. Further, when a company provides more customized solutions, complexity increases, the process-oriented perspective comes in focus, and the personification strategy is most effective. In both cases the primary strategy should be supported by the secondary strategy.

The two strategies call for different factors to enable successful knowledge management. Several studies (e.g. Ajmal et al., 2010; Bresnen et al., 2003; Lindner & Wald, 2010) have identified various factors which specifically enable or prevent effective knowledge management in projects as they also need to compensate for the lack of organisational routines and organisational memory. Most studies (e.g. Ajmal et al., 2010; Bresnen et al., 2003) are based on a single or a few case studies limiting the generalisability of the results. However, most scholars (Ajmal et al., 2010; Ajmal & Koskinen, 2008; Lindner & Wald, 2010) agree on the factors, only the ranking varies.

Lindner & Wald (2010), for instance, did a cross-industry study based on 414 organisations. They argue that cultural factors are the most important for successful knowledge management as they bridge the various organisational design gaps. This is in line with the process oriented perspective. Further, Lindner & Wald (2010) highlight not only availability to systems - but that the quality and usefulness of the supporting communications systems (ICT) for sharing, storing and retrieving knowledge are essential, and if multi-teaming, the design element is also important. Systems and design support the artefact oriented perspective. However, successful knowledge management depends on balancing the interplay of the two perspectives and thereby also their respective enabling factors.

If differences in epistemological assumptions have to be taken into consideration in managerial practice, this is likely to place heavier demands on the manager. It is no longer sufficient 'only' to act and make decisions. Conscious reflection in relation to own behaviour and acts and the opportunity to take another point of departure involving another decision become part of the decision process. The reflective manager must be familiar with different epistemologies, which is also emphasized by Venzin et al. (1998, p. 36), as this provides a much larger managing scope and ensures a better understanding of the limitations to the various sets of actions. More effective knowledge management may result from adapting management tools that fit the prevailing perception of knowledge. The more the organization focuses on knowledge, the more important it becomes to understand the epistemological implications.

The two perspectives on knowledge management bring different activities and priorities into focus. As was especially evident in the case of B&O, the perceptions of knowledge management and thus also the priorities may differ between different parts of the organisation. In general this has implications for the cross-functional co-operation and multi-teaming in an organisation. In PBOs this may be especially important as employees from different parts of the organisation are brought into the projects (for limited time).

As projects pass through different phases, cf. the stage-gate model, different people may be involved in the projects and the importance attached to different initiatives may differ. We did not follow the life of specific Projects. Consequently we were not able to assess the consequences of the changes in emphasis during projects. Yet, based on the study we expect that managerial awareness of the epistemological differences may improve knowledge management in projects.

7. Acknowledgement

*The authors are grateful to Allan Krogh Erlandsen, B&O, and Hanne Buje Jensen, former employee at FKI Logistex Crisplant, for access to the companies.

8. References

Aamodt, A. & Plaza E. (1994). Case-based reasoning: foundational issues, methodological variations, and system approaches. *AI Communications*. Vol. 7, No. 1, pp. 39-59.

Ajmal, M. M. & Koskinen K. U. (2008). Knowledge Transfer in Project-Based Organizations: An Organizational Culture Perspective. *Project Management Journal*, Vol.39, No.1, pp. 7-15.

Ajmal, M.; Helo P. & Kekäle, T. (2010). Critical factors for knowledge management in project business. *Journal of Knowledge Management*, Vol. 14, No. 1, pp. 156-168.

Alavi, M. & Leidner, D. E. (2001) Knowledge management and knowledge management systems: Conceptual foundations and research issues. *MIS Quarterly* Vol. 25, No. 1, pp. 107-136.

Blackler, F. (1995). Knowledge, knowledge work and organizations: An overview and interpretation. *Organisation Studies*, Vol. 16, No. 6, pp. 1021-1041.

Bresnen, M.; Edelman, L.; Newell, S.; Scarbrough, H. & Swan, J. (2003). Social practices and the management of knowledge in project environments. *International Journal of Project Management*, Vol. 21, No. 3, pp. 157-166.

Brookes, N. J.; Morton, S. C.; Dainty, A. R. J. & Burns, N. D. (2006). Social processes, patterns and practice and project knowledge management: A theoretical framework and an empirical investigation. *International Journal of Project Management*, Vol. 24, pp. 474-482.

Brown, J. S. & Duguid, P. (1991). Organizational learning and communities-of-practice: Towards a unified view of working, learning, and innovation. *Organization Science*, Vol. 2, No. 1, pp. 40-55.

Brown, J. S. & Duguid, P. (2001). Knowledge and organisation: a social practice perspective. *Organization Science*, Vol. 12, pp. 198-213.

Bunderson, J. S. & Sutcliffe, K. M. (2003). Management team learning orientation and business unit performance. *Journal of Applied Psychology*, Vol. 88, pp. 552-560.

Christensen, K. S. & Bang, H. K. (2003). Knowledge Management in a Project Oriented Organization: Three Perspectives. *Journal of Knowledge Management*. Vol. 7, No. 4, pp. 116-128.

Christensen, K. S. & Bukh, P. N. (2005). Knowledge Management: Two Perspectives. In P N Bukh, K S Christensen & J Mouritsen (Eds.) *Knowledge Management and Intellectual Capital: Establishing a Field of Practice*. Houndmills: Palgrave MacMillan, pp. 15-34.

Cooper, R. G. (2001). *Winning at new products*. Perseus, Cambridge, MA.

Crisplant (1999). Crisplant Project Management Model (In Danish: Faseplan for projektgennemførelse på Crisplant).

Cummings, N. (2004). Work groups, structural diversity and knowledge sharing in global organisations. *Management Science*, Vol. 50, No. 3, pp. 352-365.

Eisenhardt, K. (1989). Building theories from case study research. *Academy of Management Review*, Vol. 14, No. 4, pp. 532-550.

Evaristo, J. R.; Scudder, R; Desouza, K. C. & Sato, O. (2004). A dimensional analysis of geographically distributed project teams: a case study. *Journal of Engineering and Technology Management*, Vol. 21, pp. 175-189.

Firestone, J. M. (2008). On doing knowledge management. *Knowledge Management Research & Practice*, Vol. 6, No. 1, pp. 13-22.

Frappaolo, C. (2008). Implicit knowledge. *Knowledge Management Research & Practice*, Vol. 6, No. 1, pp. 23-25.

Hansen, M. T.; Nohria, N. & Tierney, T. (1999). What's your strategy for managing knowledge?. *Harvard Business Review*, Vol. 77, No. 2, pp. 106-116.

Hoegl, M. & Schulze, A. (2005). How to Support Knowledge Creation in New Product Development: An Investigation of Knowledge Management Methods. *European Management Journal*, Vol. 23, No. 3, pp. 263-273.

Huang, J. & Newell, S. (2003). Knowledge integration processes and dynamics within the context of cross-functional projects. *International Journal of Project Management*, Vol. 23, No. 1-2, pp. 157-166.

Huber, G. (1991). Organizational learning: the contributing process and the literature. *Organization Science*, Vol. 2, No. 1, pp. 88-116.

Jackson, P. & Klobas, J. (2008). Building knowledge in projects: A practical application of social constructivism to information systems development. *International Journal of Project Management*, Vol. 26, No. 4, pp. 329-337.

Jasimuddin, S. M.; Klein, J. H. & Connell, C. (2005). The paradox of using tacit and explicit knowledge: Strategies to face dilemmas. *Management Decision*, Vol. 43, No. 1, pp. 102-112.

Jennex, M. E. & Croaswell, D. (2005). Knowledge management: Are we a discipline?. *International Journal of Knowledge Management*, Vol. 1, No. 1, pp. i-v.

Jennex, M. E. & Olfman, L. (2006). A model of knowledge management success. *International Journal of Knowledge Management*, Vol. 2, No. 3, pp. 51-68.

Karni, R. & Kaner, M. (2008). Knowledge Management of Interconnected Decisions with Application to Project Management. *Knowledge and Process Management*, Vol. 15, No. 4, pp. 211-223.

Kärreman, D., Alvesson, M. & Blom, M. (2004). Knowledge Management and »Organisational Memory« - Remembrance and Recollection In a Management Consultancy Company. In: Bukh P N, Christensen K S, Mouritsen J (Eds.) *Knowledge management: establishing a field of practice*. Palgrave Macmillan, Houndsmill, pp. 124-148.

Kasvi, J. J., Vartianen, M. & Hailikari, M. (2003). Managing Knowledge and knowledge competencies in projects and project organisations. *International Journal of Project Management*, Vol. 21, No. 8, pp. 571-582.

Keegan, A. & Turner, J. R. (2001). Quantity versus quality in project based learning practises. *Management Learning*, Vol. 32, No. 1, pp. 77-98.

Klein, J. H. (2008). Some directions for research in knowledge sharing. *Knowledge Management Research & Practice*, Vol. 6, No. 1, pp. 41-46.

Kogut, B. & Zander, U. (1992). Knowledge of the firm, combinative capabilities, and the replication of technology. *Organization Science*, Vol. 3, pp. 383-396.

Koskinen, K. U.; Pihlanto, P. & Vanharanta, H. (2003). Tacit knowledge acquisition and sharing in a project work context. *International Journal of Project Management*, Vol. 21, pp. 281-290.

Koskinen, K. U. (2004). Knowledge Manamgenet to Improve Project Communication and Implementation. *Project Managment Journal*, Vol. 35, No. 1, pp.13-19

Li, M. & Gao, F. (2003). Why Nonaka highlights tacit knowledge: a critical review. *Journal of Knowledge Management*, Vol. 7, No. 4, pp. 6-14.

Liebowitz, J. & Megbolugbe, I. (2003). A set of frameworks to aid the project manager in conceptualizing and implementing knowledge management initiatives. *International Journal of Project Management*, Vol. 21, pp. 189-198.

Lindner, F. & Wald, A. (2010). Success factors of knowledge management in temporary organizations. *International Journal of Project Management*, Vol. 29. No. 7, pp. 877-888.

Love, P. E. D.; Edum-Fotwe, F. & Irani, Z. (2003). Editorial, Management of Knowledge in project environments. *International Journal of Project Management*, Vol. 21, No. 3, pp. 155-156.

Lyles, M. & Schwenk, C. (1992). Top management, strategy and organizational knowledge structures. *Journal of Management Studies*, Vol. 29, No. 2, pp. 155-74.

Malone, T. W., Crowston, K., Lee, J. & Pentland, B. (1993). Tools for inventing organizations: toward a handbook of organizational processes. In *Proceedings of the 2nd IEEE Workshop on Enabling Technologies Infrastructure for Collaborative Enterprises*, Morgantown, WV.

Markus, L. M. (2001). Towards a theory of knowledge reuse: Types of knowledge reuse and factors n reuse success. *Journal of Management Information Systems*, Vol. 18, No. 1, pp. 57-93.

Marr, B.; Gupta, O.; Pike, S. & Ross, G. (2003). Intellectual capital and Knowledge management effectiveness. *Management Decision*, Vol. 41, No. 8, pp. 711-781.

Matzkin, D. & Cupcham, T. (2011). A comparative analysis between some South American and European organizations in their implicit and explicit knowledge management practices. In Huei-Tse Hou (Ed.). *Knowledge Management / Book 2*. Intech.

Meyer, B. & Sugiyama, K. (2007). The concept of knowledge in KM: a dimensional model. *Journal of Knowledge Management*, Vol. 11, No. 1, pp. 17-35.

Meyer, M. H. & Utterback, J. M. (1993). The product family and the dynamic of core capabilities. *Sloan Management Review*, Vol. 34, No. 3, pp. 29-38.

Mohamed, M.; Stankosky, M. & Murrey, A. (2006). Knowledge Management and information technology: can they work in perfect harmony?. *Journal of Knowledge Management*, Vol. 10, No. 3, pp. 103-116.

Nonaka, I. (1994). A Dynamic Theory of Organizational Knowledge Creation. *Organization Science*, Vol. 5, No. 1, pp. 14-37.

Nonaka, I. & Takeuchi, H. (1995). *The Knowledge-creating Company*. Oxford University Press, Oxford.

O'Leary, M. B.; Mortensen, M. & Woolley, A. W. (2011). Multiple Team Membership: A Theoretical Model of Its Effects on Productivity and Learning for Individuals and Teams. *Academy of Management Review*, Vol. 36, No. 3, pp. 461-478.

Oshri, I.; Pan, S. L. & Newell, S. (2005). Trade-offs between knowledge exploitation and exploration activities. *Knowledge Management Research & Practice*, Vol. 3, pp. 10-23.

Polanyi, M. (1966). *The Tacit Dimension*. Peter Smith, Gloucester, MA.

Prahalad, C. K. & Hamel, G. (1990). The Core Competence of the Corporation. *Harvard Business Review*, Vol. 68, No. 3, pp. 79-88.

Prencipe, A. & Tell, F. (2001). Inter-project learning: processes and outcomes of knowledge codification in project-based firms. *Research Policy*. Vol. 30, No. 9, pp. 1373-1394.

Pretorius, C. J. & Seyn, H. (2005). Knowledge management in project environment. *South African Journal of Business Management*, Vol. 36, Vol. 3, pp. 41-50.

Roos, J. & von Krogh, G. (1995). What you see depends on who you are: Think about epistemology. *IMD Perspectives for Managers*, Vol. 7, pp. 1-4.

Senaratne, S. & Sexton, M. G. (2009). Role of knowledge in managing construction project change. *Engineering, Construction and Architectural Management*, Vol. 16, No. 2, pp. 186-200.

Senge, P. M. (1990). *The fifth discipline*. Doubleday.

Sense, A. J. (2007). Stimulating situated learning within projects: personalizing the flow of knowledge. *Knowledge Management Research & Practice*, Vol. 5, pp. 13-21.

Sherman, J. D.; Berkowitz, D. & Souder, W. E. (2005). New Product Development Performance and the Interaction of Cross-Functional Integration and Knowledge Management. *Journal of Product Innovation Management*, Vol. 22, pp.399-411.

Singer, S. J. & Edondson, D. C. (2008). When learning and performance are at odds: Confronting the tension. In P. Kumar & P. Ramsey (Eds.) *Performance and learning matters*. Singapore: World Scientific, pp. 33-60

Smaling, A. (2003). Inductive, analogical and communicative generalization. *International Journal of Qualitative Methods*, Vol. 2, No. 1.

Snider, K. F. & Nissen, E. (2003). Beyond the body of knowledge: A knowledge-flow approach to project management theory and practice. *Project Management Journal*, Vol. 34, No. 2, pp. 4-12.

Tsai, W. (2001). Knowledge transfer in intraorganizational networks: Effects of network position and absorptive capacity on business unit innovation and performance. *Academy of Management Journal*, Vol. 44, No. 5, pp. 996-1004.

Tsoukas, H. (1989). The validity of idiographic research explanations. *Academy of Management Review*, Vol. 14, No. 4, pp. 551-61.

Tsoukas, H. (1996). The firm as a distributed knowledge system: A constructionist approach. *Strategic Management Journal*, Vol. 17, pp. 11-25.

Tsoukas, H. & Vladimirou, E. (2001). What is organizational knowledge?. *Journal of Management Studies*, Vol. 38, pp. 973-993.

Venzin, M.; von Krogh, G. & Roos, J. (1998). Future research into knowledge management. In: von Krogh, G.; Roos, J. & Klein, D. (Eds). *Knowing in Firms: Understanding, managing and measuring knowledge*. Sage, London.

Von Zedtwitz, M.; Gassmann, O. & Boutellier, R. (2004). Organizing global R&D: challenges and dilemmas. *Journal of International Management*, Vol. 10, pp. 21-49.

Whitley, R. (2006). Project-based firms: new organizational form or variations on a theme? *Industrial and Corporate Change*, Vol. 15, No. 1, pp. 77-99.

Yin, R. K. (2003). *Case Study Research: Design and Methods*, 3rd edition. Sage, London.

5

From Intention to Sharing: A Qualitative Study of Barriers to Knowledge Sharing Practices

Mei-Lien Young and Feng-Yang Kuo[1]
Nanhua University
Sun Yat-sen University
Taiwan

1. Introduction

Previously, we have published a quantitative study (Kuo & Young, 2008) that reported an intention-action inconsistency in knowledge sharing practices on Internet-based knowledge management system (KMS), called SCTNet. The SCTNet has been put in place to facilitate teachers' knowledge sharing tasks in Taiwan since 1999. With the aid of the government, over 100,000 registered members, most of whom are teachers, joined SCTNet over a period of ten years. Still, even though most members have indicated their desire to create, store, distribute, and discuss their teaching knowledge, the observed actual activities on SCTNet have been lacking. The teachers undoubtedly possess knowledge potentially useful to others, and they do desire to learn from others in order to fulfill their ever-demanding daily teaching assignments, but they simply fail to enact their desires to conduct knowledge sharing tasks.

Our quantitative study, couched in the Theory of Planned Behavior (Ajzen & Fishbein, 1980; Ajzen, 1988, 1991, 2002), has investigated four types of volitional control (intention toward behavior, perceived self-efficacy, perceived controllability, action control) mechanisms that may impact people's knowledge sharing practices. Our results show that the perceived controllability of using a knowledge management platform is not critical, confirming many previous findings that perceived ease or difficulty related to IT usage does not play a central role in successful knowledge management implementations. However, perceived self-efficacy, i.e. one's conviction of his or her ability to conduct knowledge management tasks, is an important factor directly influencing knowledge sharing practice. In addition, one's action/state orientation moderates his or her enactment of subjective norms and self-efficacy beliefs into intentions, and his/her enactment of controllability into behaviors. Overall, the result indicates that people of high self-efficacy and action orientation are more likely to overcome the impediment in knowledge sharing. But, more important, the low R square value of 0.04 indicates that the overall explanatory power of the quantitative study is rather low. This weak R square value may be caused by the limitation of the quantitative approach to study a fundamentally social act such as knowledge sharing.

In this paper, we report the results of our follow-up qualitative study, in which more than 40 SCTNet members have been interviewed to further comprehend the intention-action

---

[1] Feng-Yang Kuo is the corresponding author. Both authors contributed equally to this article.

inconsistency in knowledge sharing practices and explore the possible categories of barriers that impede SCTNet members' volitional control from knowledge sharing behaviors. In this paper, we first briefly report the case of SCTNet and the intention-action gap of knowledge sharing. Next, we elaborate on the phenomenological-based qualitative study and identify the barriers to knowledge sharing. Discussions and reflections from this investigation are also discussed.

2. The SCTNet and the intention-action gap

During the early 1990s in Taiwan, educational polices were dramatically changed, and teachers found themselves in a continuous struggle to grow in professional knowledge, to design teaching materials, and to develop flexible course measurements to evaluate students' learning. An Internet-based Knowledge Management System, named SCTNet was developed as a response to this need in 1999 along with government funding, university professors' leadership in systems development, and K-12 teachers' endorsement.

Smart Creative Teacher Network (SCTNet, http://SCTNet.edu.tw) is a KMS with features such as Discussion Board, Professional Workshop, Resource Sharing, and Coffee Shop for facilitating knowledge sharing among members. The Discussion Board enables teachers to raise and discuss educational issues. Typical issues revealed on the Discussion Board include educational policies and welfare matters. The Professional Workshop is a place for teachers who have similar interests to share their teaching experiences. Resource Sharing is intended for teachers to share their class designs; while Coffee Shops are for teachers to share news about placement service and career planning.

Teachers have to be registered to become SCTNet members in order to post work-related issues, participate in discussions, critique postings from other professionals, and to upload and download instruction materials. These shared knowledge units are verified and administered as "right" knowledge into SCTNet knowledgebase by knowledge managers who are selected from SCTNet members that possess in-depth knowledge in a certain teaching domain.

From the time of its implementation, various stakeholders, such as central and local governments, university professors, and the tactical team formed by primary/junior school teachers, have expended considerable effort in promoting SCTNet. These efforts include government-backed countrywide workshops, top-down formal policy reinforcements from education administrations, anniversary celebration meetings, and bottom-up informal verbal recommendations among teachers. By 2010 SCTNet had over 100,000 registered members and over 20,000 verified knowledge units were stored. However, despite this apparent success, the actual knowledge sharing activities on SCTNet are rather meagre. For example, according to the official log maintained by the system, only 2% of the total registered members access SCTNet each day, and 80% of the overall knowledge posted is contributed by less than 5% of those who access SCTNet.

3. Research methodology

The phenomenological research method provides a systematic exploration and description of the essence and meaning of lived-experience. Such a method is used in researching the "lived" world (Husserl, 1999; Schutz and Luckmann, 1973; Bergum, 1991) and addresses the question, "Why is a phenomenon like this?" (Van Manen, 1990, p. 9). In this approach, it is asserted that "being is never isolated from the world but is always experienced as in-the-world" (Pollio et al. 1997, p. 15). For this reason, the social, cultural and historical traditions can help in capturing the whole sense of knowledge sharing for the teacher (Van Manen, 1990, p. 12).

In light of this, the goal of our interview was to discover the shared meanings of knowledge and knowledge sharing held by the teachers as they practiced knowledge sharing within the complex social setting of schools and Internet-based SCTNet. We took the position that people, things and objects that we experienced in our life could not be separated from the culture in which we lived and the language we spoke. Hence, our actions, language, and concepts could embed shared meanings within a social and linguistic frame of reference. Furthermore, as Geertz (1983) noted, detailed descriptions of microcosmic phenomena within a domain could reveal general forms of life by examining the vehicles of life in which those forms were meaningfully embedded. In this study, the microcosmic area of schools and the Internet-based SCTNet where teachers practiced their knowledge sharing was treated in detail and related back to the larger context of Taiwan's culture and school system.

3.1 Sampling and procedures

Theoretically, in phenomenological research, the sample size is approximately 6 participants (Morse 1991). However, in practice, the number of participants varies from 10 to 15 or more, depending on whether the data are considered to reach saturation. According to Glaser and Strauss (1967), data saturation means that

> *...no additional data are being found whereby the [researcher] can develop properties of the category. As he sees similar instances over and over again, the researcher becomes empirically confident that a category is saturated...when one category is saturated, nothing remains but to go on to new groups for data on other categories, and attempt to saturate these categories also. (Glaser & Strauss 1967, p. 65)*

In this study, data collections during a 6-month period of fieldwork were obtained through "snowball" effect as well as purposeful sampling. A total of 49 participants, consisting of 21 males and 28 females were interviewed in our study. The age of the informants ranged from 25 to 55 years old, with a mean of 35. Among these informants, 5 were school principals, 18 were school deans, and 26 were teachers. The length of time that informants had been using SCTNet for knowledge sharing ranged from 1 to 5 years, with a mean length of 3 years. The profile of participants is shown in Table 1.

All participants were given the research purpose and procedure of the interview prior to the start, and each signed the participation agreement describing both the duties of the researcher with regard to the research ethic and the informant's rights in the context of participation in the research. To permit participants to structure and sequence their accounts of events with minimal instruction from the interviewer (White, 1980), Van Manen (1990) has suggested that interviews be designed to elicit narratives about the life histories and daily lives of the participants. Hence, each interview began with the question, "What is the knowledge-sharing experience like in school life and on SCTNet?" The length of the interview varied from two to three hours for each participant. Four participants required a second interview to clarify their narratives. Most of the interviews were conducted in the school setting, whereby the interview location was chosen by the informant. These locations included the classroom, conference room, library, or computer lab. A few interviews were held in cafes on the weekend. The interviews were recorded by a multifunction digital recorder and were transcribed verbatim to maintain data integrity and to reduce perceptual bias. After the interview, the transcripts were shared with the participants for their approval.

County/City		Gender		Age (Seniority)			Title			Total Participants	
		Male	Female	<=30	31–40	>41	Director	Dean	Teacher	Count	Total
City	Kaohsiung	10	9	7	5	7	1	5	13	19	29
	Pingtung	1	1	1	0	1	0	2	0	2	
	Tainan	1	0	0	1	0	1	0	0	1	
	Taichung	3	3	1	5	0	0	4	2	6	
	Taipei	1	0	0	1	0	0	1	0	1	
	Count	**16**	**13**	**9**	**12**	**8**	**2**	**12**	**15**	**29**	
County	Kaohsiung	0	4	3	1	0	0	3	1	4	20
	Pingtung	2	3	4	1	0	0	3	2	5	
	Tainan	0	1	0	1	0	0	0	1	1	
	Yunlin	0	1	1	0	0	0	0	1	1	
	Miaoli	0	3	2	1	0	0	0	3	3	
	Taoyuan	0	1	1	0	0	0	0	1	1	
	Ilian	2	0	1	1	0	0	0	2	2	
	Taitung	0	1	0	1	0	1	0	0	1	
	Penghu	1	1	0	0	2	2	0	0	2	
	Count	**5**	**15**	**12**	**6**	**2**	**3**	**6**	**11**	**20**	
Total		**21**	**28**	**21**	**18**	**10**	**5**	**18**	**26**	**49**	**49**

Table 1. The Demographics Distribution and Profile of Interview Participants

3.2 Data analysis

The purpose of data analysis in phenomenological research is to organize the interviews to present a narrative that explains what happened or to provide a description of the norms and values that underlie cultural behavior (Rubin & Rubin, 1995). For this study, more than one million words of interview transcripts and field notes were collected for data analysis. To reduce possible bias introduced by the investigator (Mitchell 1986), three teachers who had elementary and junior high school teaching experience as well as one SCTNet administrator were asked to participate in the analysis process.

The analysis procedure began with the immersion phase, in which we read transcripts several times and immersed ourselves in these data. The aim of this immersion was to establish an orienting gestalt, which provided an initial interpretation of the data that would drive later coding of the data in subsequent phases of analysis. In this phase, we identified the essential characteristics in the data from each interview. Next, we eliminated digressions that were clearly off topic, abrupt changes in topics, and verbal ticks. After this phase, the data were ready for line-by-line coding. During the coding process, as an understanding of the overall text was obtained, phrases in the text were underlined and tentative concept names were written in the margins of the text. Transcripts were examined line by line, and all important phrases were labeled with these tentative concept names. We then extracted passages that had similar concepts that could be grouped together into themes. A sample of the data analysis process is shown in Figure 1.

As the coding was completed, the researchers compared what different people had said, what themes were discussed, and how concepts could be understood from Taiwan's cultural arena. Finally, we constructed a textual-structural description of the meanings and essences of informant's experience (Kahn, 1993; Sandelowski, 1993, 1994; Moustakas, 1994). More than 200 concepts were identified from the text and constructed into 15 themes that related to the barriers of knowledge sharing.

4. Research results

The Taiwanese school system was administered by the Ministry of Education (MOE), which in turn supervised the Department of Education in each city/county where schools were located. Many decisions were centrally made by the MOE, and the school directors' main responsibility was to ensure comprehensive execution of these decisions.

Theme	Concept/Label	Case	Meaning Unit (Data)
Mistake free culture Face concern	Afraid of making mistake Not good enough Self-presentation	1	I am afraid ... afraid to say something wrong, to be laughed at, have not enough insight, or without being saturated with knowledge.
Mistake free culture Face concern	Being a teacher Self-presentation	1	I am a teacher now, I should think carefully before I post my thought or make response to the inquiry on SCTNet. "Does my posting inspire any one? Or does it helpful? And am I professional enough?" are always in my mind while I perform sharing on SCTNet......because I am a teacher now...
Face concern	Self-presentation Private setting	2	I will ask my friends about how to deal the problem with children and their parents only in private setting...

* Concepts are given for each meaning unit. The concepts essentially are labels placed on utterances or events. These identified concepts are then further grouped into the higher abstract level called themes.

Fig. 1. Sample of the data analysis process *

Meanwhile, the teachers also formed a large family that was rooted in the few colleges that specialized in teacher education. Students in these colleges not only knew each other within their schools but also learned about early graduates through the teacher family system. Furthermore, as they finished college, students were sent to different schools for their practical training, during which time they learned as apprentices from their mentors. These apprenticeships reinforced the teacher family system's rigidity and tightness.

It is in this background that SCTNet was introduced as a means to facilitate teachers to share their knowledge. Our qualitative analysis, presented in Figure 2, further shows that the barriers to SCTNet knowledge sharing practices can be classified into three main categories: the school system, the teacher community, and the SCTNet technology. In the following sections, the three main categories and their respective sub-categories are discussed in detail.

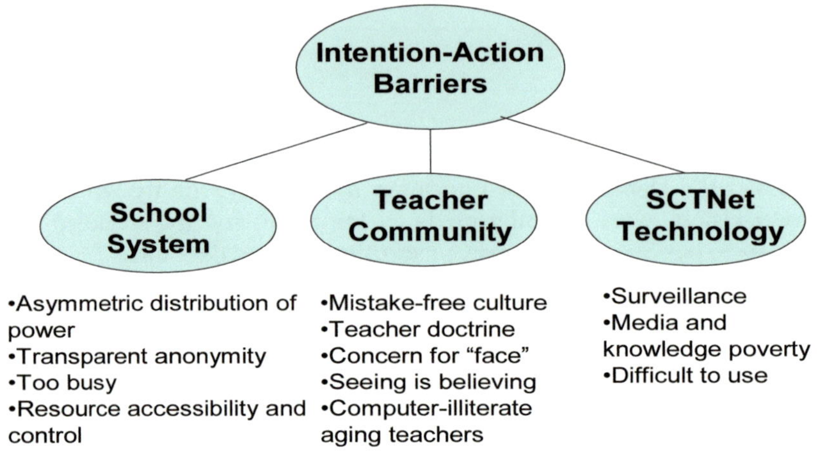

Fig. 2. The category-hierarchy regarding the barriers of Intention-Action Gap in knowledge sharing Practice on SCTNet

4.1 The school system

Asymmetric distribution of power. Situated in the hierarchically organized school system in which power asymmetry is the norm, teachers choose to be quiet both in the school setting and on the SCTNet. This is not surprising because teachers are those who possess the least power in the school system and are highly dominated and coerced. A typical statement depicting the scene of the school in terms of asymmetric power distribution and decision-making is:

> *"In fact, the school system is a top-down hierarchical structure. What the school principal says determines the way teachers do. Although school principals like to ask 'Is there any question?' yet teachers are always keeping quiet. They know their words are of no use.*

In realizing that their words were useless, teachers choose to be quiet to prevent arousing the anger of the director. This appeared in the sharing practice both within the school and in the SCTNet. One teacher provided details on this:

> *"In the school setting, the hierarchical system and the asymmetric distribution of power form a tone of conflict between director and teachers. This makes teachers afraid of speaking out what they think. Even in the forum of SCTNet, teachers still choose being quiet in response to the director of the school or the Ministry of Education's demands in avoiding the argument.*

In fact, the exercise of power was both public and profound so that the teachers felt that they had no way of breaking out from the pressure from the central administration. Two typical statements depicted by informants were:

> *"Sometimes, the Education Administrator calls the roll of the schools' deans on the SCTNet. If any dean doesn't sign in on time on SCTNet, the Education Administrator would demand him to sign in again. Basically, we do not agree upon the administration power that penetrates into the sharing practice on SCTNet."*
>
> *"They forced all deans in schools to use SCTNet. I have had the experience of being deprived of my access right by the city's Education Bureau because I did not follow its order to sign in on time ..."*

Transparent anonymity. Transparent anonymity refers to the fact that teachers' identities on SCTNet could be recognized despite the anonymity provided by the SCTNet. Informants depicted their concerns that the rigid and tight network could expose who they were. Two typical statements were the following:

> *"I have some concerns that if I put my viewpoints in detail, unknown others can easily recognize who I am via the traceable content and context that I depict. The teacher community is rigid and tight… Even though on SCTNet with the anonymity protection via information technology, it still is easy to recognize."*

> *"Through detailed description of the context, people can tell who I am and my identity would expose...then, the anonymous character of the IT is lost. The community of teachers is very tight. Any clue can be traced to find out who I am."*

Consequently, although in theory SCTNet provided anonymity protection for teachers so that they could express themselves and discuss topics freely, teachers became ambivalent in their sharing. A typical statement was:

> *"To talk on SCTNet has to be very cautious in the school setting since the teacher community is so rigid and tight that my depiction might arouse someone. Thus, in terms of sharing, I need to take this into my concern while I express my idea on SCTNet.*

Too busy. Repeatedly, our teacher informants stated that they were too busy to conduct knowledge sharing on SCTNet. They were busy because they were asked to play a large number of roles. For example, inside a typical classroom of a Taiwanese school, a teacher's roles included knowledge transmitter, agent of ideological apparatus of the Confucian tradition, and care provider. Outside the classroom but inside the school, a teacher could be an administrative clerk and a cultural worker.

> *"Normally, a 24 hours course instruction for students per week is the major work in our agenda. Also, we have to grade homework, join the routine meeting, consult student problems, and perform administration service …"*

> *"I teach first grade students. The kids always follow me while I go somewhere. They depend on me so much that they always come to me for help. Thus, I can't concern on doing other things but taking care of them."*

> *"In school, there are many scheduled administrative works that need teachers' help in implementation. For example, arranging kids' teeth check and vision test, and following up the results of treatment. In addition, teachers are responsible for policy announcement and broadcasting to ensure kids and their parents are well informed."*

If the school were located in a rural area that lacks resources, the teacher would then be responsible also for operational duties, such as repairing the fans and typing in purchasing orders.

> *"After each class, I need to open the school snack shop and serve as a clerk in selling the soft drinks, bread, and so on. In addition, I am also responsible to handle the purchase orders and dealing with the stock suppliers of school grocery store."*

> *"I am so busy that I always get home late. Too many jobs which are not related to teaching. Later on, I need to fix fans, lamps, and so on. I always lose control over my time. "*

Each of these roles demands responsibility and resources and teachers are expected to perform well in all of these roles between 8:00 am and 5:00 pm, from Monday to Friday. But there is more. When returning home, the teacher would still be responsible for affairs of his or her own children and, possibly, dealing with inquiries from the student's parents. Normally, it is late at night by the time the teachers' time is freed up to use SCTNet. Two typical statements show teachers' helpless. They said:

> *"As a teacher, we have to respond to parents' phone calls during the school or handle the inquiry while parents come to school. Sometimes, as teachers return to home, they are hardly able to refuse to answer the kids' parents' inquiries."*

"I need to wait until my kids fall asleep, then I can access to SCTNet. However, most of the cases I am burned-out and I can't use SCTNet."

Yet, knowledge sharing is another task that demands a great amount of time for understanding, reflecting, and organizing. Many teachers simply feel the loss of control over their time, hardly enough for knowledge sharing behavior on SCTNet. Three typical informants elaborated on this:

"Although I want to share what I know, yet it really bothers me in time management! I have to serve as an administrative clerk, teaching, care providing, and get on the homepage of the Ministry of Education to check some announcements. These tasks divide my time into pieces and cause me not to spend more time on SCTNet."

"Sometimes, I try to answer proposed questions on SCTNet and sometimes I ignore them. It all depends on whether I am free or not. My job takes up most of my time and I can hardly share what I know on SCTNet. Sharing knowledge on SCTNet demands a great amount of time, thus how long I will stay on SCTNet and how much I will share with others depend on the time I have."

"I can't even handle teaching well since it takes a lot of time to conduct the course design. Now I get on SCTNet only upon the administration demands."

Resource accessibility and control. In most schools, teachers are required to share computers that are centrally placed in a public area. This is especially common for teachers in rural schools. In the meantime, school administrators may not value the teachers' use of these computers to surf SCTNet, viewing these activities as non-productive or "playing," and subsequently expressing negative attitudes towards the teachers. As a result, teachers may feel that computers are inaccessible to them in the school unless they are doing administrative work. For instance, two teachers stated:

"Not every classroom has a PC. For shared PC, administration tasks always go first, personal stuff goes next..."

"In the school, when I use the computer to search on SCTNet, I always have pressure. I am afraid that my peers will interpret that I am not working hard since I have time to use computer to search and read the data. ...The principal and teachers are all in this office and share a few computers. If you use the computer, then others cannot perform their administrative work."

4.2 The teacher community

Mistake-free culture. The teacher community has a mistake-free culture. This can be understood from Taiwan's cultural tradition. In Taiwan, September 28 is National Teachers' Day, which was Confucius's birthday and is now the day for thanking teachers. As the teaching profession carries a high degree of respect within the society, teachers are expected to embody wisdom, excellence, knowledge, and perfection. Accordingly, "being free of error" becomes the belief of both the teacher community and the society. Being aware of this teacher's sacred role, teachers act cautiously on SCTNet, as shown by the following statements:

"I am afraid...afraid to say something wrong, to be laughed at, have not enough insight, or to be perceived as having inadequate knowledge."

"Before logging in SCTNet, I will consider all possible situations that can happen and prepare well to deal with them. ... Actually, I am afraid to fail...fail as a professional teacher. Thus, while I share my opinion on SCTNet, I go to great lengths to prevent any problems occurring in advance."

Teachers are also keenly aware that the intent of SCTNet is to provide a virtual forum for talented teachers from all over the country. They know that the first two letters of

SCTNet, SC, represented Smart and Creative, respectively. Consequently, they are constantly questioning if the quality of their input on SCTNet is "smart enough" or "creative enough" when viewed by the many "virtual grand masters" of the SCTNet teacher community. This was evidenced in many statements made in the interviews, such as "SCTNet is a professional forum" and "There are plenty of grand masters on SCTNet." Thus, to share knowledge on SCTNet and to be free of error became a commonly expressed concern about professionalism when teachers attempted to use SCTNet. Two typical informants expanded on this:

"'Is my posting helpful to others or can I impart rudimentary knowledge to beginners?' I have to think more before responding to the question. I am a teacher now!"

"There are so many grand masters on SCTNet! It always makes me sad that I don't understand what they talking about… Keeping quiet seems the best choice for me while I am on SCTNet. I think I need more training to make myself be professional so that I can discuss with them. Yet, it takes long time to achieve that!"

The teacher doctrine. In Taiwan's professional teacher community, there exists a set of rigorous doctrines: be kind, be honest, be reverential, be provident, and be modest. In practice, this means that teachers are expected to "respect seniority," "love colleagues," "not argue or fight against peers," and "not show off." As informants revealed, these doctrines regulated their behaviors both in school and on SCTNet. Anyone who violated these rules would receive a warning. Thus, although these doctrines helped to create a harmonious community, they unfortunately inhibited knowledge sharing. For example, two teachers depicted their experiences of sharing in school but were interpreted as "showing off":

"I am enthusiastic about helping others via providing my opinion, yet it always being rejected. Other teachers tell me that as a junior teacher, I should not rush to present myself."

"For professional teaching knowledge, I am afraid to share except with my best friend! I don't want be criticized: 'Who do you think you are? How do you dare to show me this?' Thus, I would rather not share the professional knowledge with others."

Another teacher depicted her experience of violating the doctrines as she questioned another teacher. Her behavior was viewed as bad manners:

"In a workshop, I found that the instructor didn't prepare well and simply gave the same content from a previous workshop. Thus, I made some comments on his lack of preparation. This event was passed back to my school next day. Yet, the interpretation was that I was rude."

As a result of these deeply rooted doctrines, teachers' knowledge sharing behaviors on the anonymous SCTNet differed little from their real world life. The following two statements were typical examples of avoiding showing off on SCTNet:

"I always answer the questions passively on SCTNet. I am afraid that if I respond to the inquiry actively, people may think I am boasting about my knowledge."

"While I post my idea on SCTNet, I will give my words carefully. Because I don't want to offend anybody on SCTNet."

Teachers might also play the role of a good listener on SCTNet to avoid fighting. One informant elaborated on this:

"'May my statement arouse the anger of others?' Instead of worrying about it, I would choose being a listener on SCTNet."

Some teachers were actually cognizant of the fact that few teachers choose to act against the teacher doctrines while they conducted knowledge sharing on SCTNet. One informant said,

"We teach and encourage our kids to express what they think in public, yet, we, as an adult and teacher, are hesitating in public presenting [on SCTNet]! Can we discuss in the public forum? Can we fight for our thinking? Unfortunately, I saw little debate happened on SCTNet."

The concern for "face." Our teacher informants expressed concern for failing to demonstrate that they are smart and creative, they might "lose their faces". Here, "face" is what others have recognized and extended to individuals (Ho, 1976). It is "something that is not lodged in or on individuals' body, but rather something that is diffusely located in the flow of events in the encounter and becomes manifest only when these events are read and interpreted for the appraisals expressed in them" (Goffman 1995, p. 214).

The "face" concern made teachers ambivalent in their presentations especially when they were situated in the mistake-free culture of the teacher community. Meanwhile, the desire to gain "face" from others also drives teachers to grasp any opportunity from which they can improve their image. It could be said that in a way teachers were trapped in a possible no-win situation: on any occasion when teachers did any kind of presentation, they had to tread the discourse carefully to ensure that they were neither under any risk of losing "face" nor that the presentation was not noticed. Consequently, sharing in private settings with good friends became the most comfortable place for teachers to conduct knowledge sharing. Typical statements are:

> *"I will ask my friends about how to deal the problem with children and their parents only in private setting..."*
>
> *"I prefer to share my thinking and my experience with well-known friends privately. Because sharing actively with unfamiliar others may be perceived as abrupt behavior."*

The concern for "face" was especially critical for teachers in unfamiliar, public settings such as SCTNet, where one's social position was well known and where there was an overriding public expectation of how one should behave. Two teachers expressed their concerns:

> *"I am afraid ...afraid to say something wrong, to be laughed at, have not enough insight, or to be perceived as having inadequate knowledge while I depict my idea on SCTNet."*
>
> *"Some of my teaching experiences are successful, yet some of them are failed. Especially for those failed experiences, I would rather share them with my closest friend in the teaching domain rather than those strangers on SCTNet."*

Impression management became a challenge to teachers due to the need to deal with possible negative repercussions from their SCTNet discussions. One teacher said:

> *"Writing my feelings or teaching experience in the virtual environment is just like making me naked in a public area. You know people pass by, yet you don't know how they look at you!"*

Seeing is believing. For teachers in Taiwan, whether one has actually seen another is important in sharing behaviors. Teachers in Taiwan learned domain knowledge from their teachers through face-to-face, direct verbal instruction while they were in college and from their mentors during their practical training:

> *"When we were students, our teachers always transfer their knowledge via face-to-face, verbal class instruction."*
>
> *"As an apprentice, I always sit at the end of the classroom watching the course instruction given by my mentor. Occasionally, I will sit by her and study the course material design."*

Furthermore, when the participants graduated to become school teachers themselves, most of their own interactions have been face-to-face. SCTNet, although powerful, provides only a text-based setting that is inconsistent with the collective habit of face-to-face meetings. Our informants illustrated this point in the following remarks:

> *"While I have wonderful experience in my class, I would share with my friend directly through face-to-face, vocal interaction. Particularly, when I am excited, I won't sit in the front of computer to write my feeling..."*

"In general, I prefer to interact via verbal and face-to-face contact that I get used to. It is more effectively in comparing with communication via writing on SCTNet as well."

It also appears that teachers rely on direct social contact to make judgments concerning competence, trustworthiness, and safety related to another teacher. This is not surprising in Taiwan, which has a very strong culture of direct human contact. "Saw or met you before" thus becomes a vehicle for either accepting or rejecting knowledge sharing. Our informants said:

"If we saw each other before provides the basis of judgment of how and what I shall share."

"It's our culture — I prefer to see you and you prefer to see me before. We can hardly accept the way to interact on the Internet. It is so strange to rely only on the interaction via screen…I can't go through that feeling without knowing who I interact with."

Another depiction of the uncomfortable feeling in interacting with unfamiliar others on SCTNet was,

"As I express my thinking in front of unfamiliar people, I feel I am gazed by these people. This kind of feeling is very like a monkey in the zoo gazed by the tourists outside the cage. It makes me so uncomfortable!"

One informant spoke about his decisions to keep quiet while he interacted with a group of unfamiliar others on SCTNet:

"I would rather choose to remain quiet in front of unknown others on SCTNet...I have experience of expressing my opinion in front of unfamiliar others [in SCTNet] and have borne their criticism. I felt so stupid that I should keep quiet in front of them."

Computer-illiterate aging teachers. In the past, there has been a lack of emphasis on computer and Internet literacy in Taiwan's teacher education program. As a result, the level of computer and Internet self-efficacy for Taiwanese teachers dwindles, especially for older teachers. As two teachers said:

"As I know that many of the elder teachers do not have enough computer literacy, they feel that using computer is troublesome. … They would rather choose not to use SCTNet".

"About one third of the teachers who are elder can't even use e-mail. They resist using computer since they are afraid of it. Thus, most of the time, when they encounter computer problems, they always come over to me for help."

A similar phenomenon was also observed for female teachers. For example, one teacher said the following:

"In our school, female teachers are more than male teachers. They are not good at computer operation. Thus, whenever they run into the computer problem, they would come over to me."

Some young teachers were also insufficient in their computer skills, as one young informant indicated:

"In fact, many young teachers in our school possess little computer literacy as elder teachers do. They are about the same age as me, yet, they lack basic knowledge of using the computer."

4.3 Information technology: Smart, Creative, Teacher Network (SCTNet)

Surveillance. Today's information technology could be a powerful surveillance facility for social control (Lyon, 1994). SCTNet, as a technological knowledge management platform, is no exception. It is not only a place for teacher professionals to share knowledge but also a setting for institutional surveillance. For examples, two active SCTNet informants said:

"Some of the topics are not touchable! Here [SCTNet], everyone knows my ID… using ID is the same as using my name! In fact, I critiqued about the education policy of Education Administrator once, after that I was told to shut up …via someone indirectly…"

> *"I use several IDs [on SCTNet] to secure the anonymity because I have the experience that my ID was identified and my opinions which I posted on SCTNet were distributed back to my school. This bothers me seriously…"*

Another informant remarked that he viewed KMS as a "gazed place" and behaved cautiously:

> *"When I joined a discussion on SCTNet, I posted my opinion, yet, after I did that everyone stop discussing…I sensed a symbol of warning – 'Where is everybody?'…I got a big shock and realized that I was in a trouble…"*

In fact, the anonymity of the IT function in KMS was rendered almost useless because of the tight teacher community, as discussed earlier. Several teachers discussed this phenomenon of transparent anonymity:

> *"It is easy to tell who proposed the message as I read the tone of speaking, the pattern of writing, and the content of the event description. It doesn't even need to write the name… Actually, the community is too tight that it is hard to retain the anonymity …"*
>
> *"Actually, from the text, it is easy to know who the author is…if you stay there [SCTNet] long enough. The community is tight…That's why I need to put an extra note after I depict my opinion to state 'this is only my personal perspective, it doesn't regard to my school's policy'…"*

Thus, it seemed that the more powerful technology that the technical experts inject into the SCTNet, which ironically was necessary for knowledge management but easily became a tool of surveillance, the more insecure some teachers felt toward sharing their experiences on SCTNet. In this rigid and tight community, the perception of being "gazed" created a mental barrier to knowledge sharing among teachers, who were asked to be kind, honest, reverential, provident, and modest.

Media and knowledge poverty. Because SCTNet stripped away the social cues, teachers were unable to detect the shared social meaning from face-to-face-impeded knowledge sharing. Typical statements expand on this concern,

> *"In a face-to-face setting, even you say nothing; I still can tell if you agree upon my opinion or not from the cues of face. Yet, on SCTNet, I can't see your face and have no way to know your response."*
>
> *"I can't see the partner's face since the interaction on SCTNet strips away many of the cues and signs that are part of face-to-face interaction. Thus, it is hard to tell what peers think about my sharing."*

In addition, the textual expressions of SCTNet are structured sequentially according to the temporal order of verbal conversations. Thus, any participants who are unfamiliar with the history of the interactions have to go through a sea of background information of the community to become familiar with it before they can start sharing. Meanwhile, learning this history is no trivial task for any teacher. Many participants have to stay in this platform long enough to know the discourse so they can trace the text depictions, which are dispersed across various conversation sections. Two typical comments on this situation were:

> *"The content of our conversation is dispersed across many dialogue sections. It is difficult for SCTNet new members to obtain the whole picture. They have to trace back all of our conversation to know the detail. As a result, they always show their anxiety in participating the sharing without having the background knowledge of our conversation.*
>
> *"It's hard for me to understand what they talk about … I need to stay there [SCTNet] long enough to understand the context of the dialogue ..."*

Furthermore, in-depth semantic knowledge is often required for one to find the proper content. For example, a certain community might invent its own specific buzzwords that outsiders would not know. Without a comprehensive understanding of this local invention, teachers feel detached from the group on the SCTNet and rarely access SCTNet. Two relevant statements were:

> *"Usually, I am silent while I am on SCTNet. I need to know the context of their sharing; yet, it is difficult for me since most of the depictions are short. If I don't know more about the background of the depiction, I can hardly catch the point of the discussion."*
>
> *"They have their own writing patterns and symbols on SCTNet. I can hardly use their language since I don't understand their shared meaning. Therefore, I do not get on SCTNet gradually."*

Difficult to use. The difficulty in using SCTNet is a key factor that impedes teachers' access to SCTNet. For instance, many teachers expressed their loss of control over the SCTNet operation functions. Two informants said:

> *"The enrollment and search procedure are so complex that many of the teachers hesitate to use it. They fully lost their control in operating and using SCTNet."*
>
> *"For example, while I try to upload my posting, I need to go through several processes to identify which category and what type my posting is; yet, at the end I still receive the result of failed uploading! While I try several times, I give up finally!"*

In fact, the more that advanced technological features were added to SCTNet, the more loss some teachers felt. As the old saying "beauty is in the eyes of the beholder" has indicated, what is perceived by the IT experts as superb achievements often become the barriers hindering teachers from using SCTNet. Teachers expressed:

> *"I know there are many functions on SCTNet, but it is too complex for me that I am afraid of losing control in using SCTNet. Therefore, I choose not to touch it."*
>
> *"The SCTNet is a good forum for sharing our teaching experience, but too complex in its functions. Some of my friends give up after several tries."*

Especially, for older teachers, the difficulty in use is usually the most important factor preventing them from using SCTNet. A typical statement made by an older teacher was:

> *"I am not familiar with SCTNet. I try several times then I realize that registering is one step and getting into the forum is another step. After I get into the forum, I still don't know how to search the material that I want. Usually, I give up after several trials. I know many of my colleagues can't even get into the first door of the SCTNet. Finally, they stop trying to get into SCTNet."*

For younger teachers, the need to continuously help older teachers resolve the technical problems also becomes burdensome. One stated that:

> *"The function of SCTNet is so complex that many of my friends can't get access to it. They always ask me to register for them ..."*

5. Discussion and conclusions

5.1 Teachers, not teaching robots

Many theorists have seen the implementation of knowledge management systems as a matter of extracting the right knowledge from people's memory and storing it in networked computers for later distribution (Tiwana, 2001). This is also the focus of SCTNet, which is intended to become the platform that stores and distributes teaching materials and experiences. "Build a KMS, and the knowledge will be delivered" has become the belief of the IT architects of SCTNet. Yet, teachers are humans, situated in an environment that is rich in Confucian culture. In this tradition, teachers can easily know each other via their social networks, which in turn shape teachers' knowledge sharing in public; for example, they would not like to be seen as behaving inappropriately. Therefore, knowledge sharing has many different facets, such as seniority and face, which are far more subtle and difficult to manage than the exchange of one another's materials and experience in a mechanical fashion. The IT experts have failed to appreciate this rich tradition and have placed too much emphasis on technology. Sadly, for them, teachers have become SCTNet robots who would simply retrieve and deposit their knowledge. Thus, despite the fact that teachers are aware of the importance of advancing their knowledge through SCTNet, they do not enact their intention by using SCTNet.

5.2 Old habits die hard, even with information technology

In Taiwan, teachers are taught and trained to respect their own teachers and love their school classmates like brothers and sisters. Be kind, be honest, be reverential, be provident, and be modest engender the five values that every teacher must learn. These future prospective teachers always listen and take notes quietly in classrooms. Vicarious observation is praised, and open discussion or confrontation is discouraged. After graduation, these teachers step into schools and find that the same values are still instituted in their everyday lives. The school principal may be the classmate of a former teacher whom they must respect and accommodate. The colleagues are friends of classmates with whom they should be gentle. Teaching, as a social system, is composed of various habitual routines. Teachers must change those routines if they wish to adopt technology effectively. Yet, the force of the old habits is so enormous that teachers follow the same habitual patterns on SCTNet, where they feel that they must maintain the image of a gentle, kind, respectful, prudent, and compliant teacher. They do not risk being seen as rude or showing anything that violates the norms of their community. The architects of the SCTNet have failed to understand the significance of those habits and have designed a one-size-fits-all public knowledge management platform. But even advanced information technology is no match for old habits.

5.3 More technology… May be harmful for knowledge sharing

Throughout the design of SCTNet, new search engines, new security features, and new reports have been continuously added. The architects of SCTNet have seen the addition of new features as an enhancement of SCTNet to help teachers. Yet, for teachers to share knowledge on SCTNet, nothing comes easy. As stated previously, teachers on average are assigned 24 hours of course instruction per week. Also, they have to grade homework, perform administrative service, and counsel students who have problems. Many teachers are parents of their own school-age children and have their hands full with their own family routines. In addition, teachers are expected to internalize, socialize, combine, and externalize their knowledge (Nonaka 1994; Nonaka & Takeuchi 1995) on SCTNet, which requires great skill and time. They are, in essence, expected to become supermen or superwomen above their capacity. The architects of SCTNet have somehow forgotten the golden rule of information management: "Keep it Simple, Stupid" (KISS), and have overwhelmed the teachers with the best and most advanced technology.

5.4 For knowledge management, success is a journey, not a set of numbers

The government holds a strong belief that as long as the knowledge stored in SCTNet grows, the knowledge of teachers who access the SCTNet would also grow. The central government, therefore, employs several indices, such as the number of teachers logging onto SCTNet, the volume of stored knowledge in SCTNet, and so forth, as measures of success to evaluate the performance of school districts. Some districts, in turn, set up incentive programs to ensure good numbers, whereas others rely on administrative pressures. However, the result is not an overall increase in SCTNet usage by most teachers; rather, a small number of teachers carry the burden of meeting administrative expectations.

In addition, many districts often use SCTNet as an administrative tool for such purposes as policy announcements and data collection. Although the intent to facilitate the administration is good, the result is an SCTNet that is a one-way communication that eliminates the possibility of feedback from the teachers. Consequently, teachers feel increasingly detached from SCTNet. Knowledge and politics, after all, are not easily mixed.

The overemphasis on the set of numbers required by the government makes the artifact, SCTNet, become an invisible barrier that is counter to its initial purpose as a facilitator in knowledge sharing practices. Teachers thus perceive using SCTNet as an index of the policy coordinator or betrayer. Yet, being a policy betrayer is a serious mistake in conflict with the belief that being a teacher is to be gentle, be kind, be respectful, be prudent, and be compliant. As a result, choosing to be a policy coordinator to use SCTNet becomes a form of "show" but not knowledge growth.

6. Conclusions

In this paper, we reveal insights into how teachers' enactment of their knowledge sharing practices may be impeded by the structure of the school system, the culture of the teacher community, and the information technology design.

We should caution that the result of our study should not be interpreted as saying that information technology is useless to facilitate knowledge management, but rather that the architects of knowledge management platforms should focus on the human agencies and the social and cultural forces that influence their sharing behaviors. Knowledge is not meant to be managed mechanically; rather, it should be viewed as inseparable from the people who possess it. The designers of the knowledge management system should therefore be aware that their role is not simply to put the technology to use but to bind together the network of people who identify with the community of practice in achieving learning and knowing.

Introducing information technology into a community to perform an activity can change the nature of that activity. SCTNet reifies a view of the activity of knowledge sharing, but it also changes how one goes about sharing. It can enable new social groups to form, develop, and maintain a sense of shared meaning and identity. The newly formed identity and language will elicit different actions in participation of the community. Thus, viewing information technology as a mere competing tool, without being bound in people's minds, context, and culture, overlooks its social role and can lead to "an expensive and useless information junkyard" (McDermott 1999).

7. Reflection: Phenomenology, a new way for knowledge management research

Many advocates and theorists see KMS as a mechanism of extracting, storing, and distributing "codified knowledge" in which human beings are reduced to "nothing but" automatic behavior (Tiwana, 2001). Yet, knowledge sharing is a human act and is inextricably bound up with human cognition (Thomas et al., 2001). The study of knowledge sharing is therefore difficult because the hypothesis-based, cognitive psychological approach is inadequate in exploring and elucidating the insights of the intention-action gap. To discover the insights of the knowledge sharing intention-action gap, we are therefore required to let the voices of individuals' experiences emerged. The phenomenological method allows us to treat knowledge as the accumulation of individuals' lived-experiences over time, and this lived-experience is "residing in the content of sense-giving act(s)" (Husserl 2001, p. 23) in the second phase of our study. With this, we are able to develop insights into how human subjects of knowledge sharing enact their sharing practices. Our study demonstrates the importance of phenomenology for knowledge management research and provides a new way of viewing knowledge sharing problems in terms of human consciousness.

8. References

Ajzen, I. (1988). *Attitudes, Personality and Behavior*. The Dorsey Press, ISBN, 0335217036, Chicago.

Ajzen, I. (1991). The theory of planned behavior. *Organizational Behavior and Human Decision Processes*, Vol. 50, pp. 179-211, ISSN 0749-5978

Ajzen, I. (2002). Perceived behavioral control, self efficacy, locus of control, and the theory of planned behavior. *Journal of Applied Social Psychology*, Vol. 32, No. 4, pp. 665-683, ISSN 0021-9029

Ajzen, I. & Fishbein, M. (1980) *Understanding Attitudes and Predicting Social Behavior*, Prentice-Hall, Englewood Cliffs, ISBN, 0139364358, New Jersey.

Bergum, V. (1991). Being a phenomenological researcher. In: *Qualitative Nursing Research: A Contemporary Dialogue*, J. M. Morse (Ed.), pp. 55-71, Sage, Newbury Park, ISBN 0834200112, California.

Constant, D., Kiesler, S., & Sproull, L. (1994). What's mine is ours, or is it? A study of attitudes about information sharing. *Information Systems Research*, Vol. 5, No. 4, pp. 400-421, ISSN 1047-7047

Geertz, C. (1983). *Local Knowledge: Further Essays in Interpretive Anthropology*, Basic Books, ISBN 0465041620, New York.

Glaser, B. G. & Strauss, A.L. (1976). *The Discovery of Grounded Theory Strategies for Qualitative Research*. Aldine Publishing Company, ISBN 0202302601, New York.

Goffman, E. (1955). On face-work: An analysis of ritual elements in social interaction. *Psychiatry*, Vol. 18, pp. 213-231, ISSN 0022-3050

Ho, D. (1976). On the concept of face, *The American Journal of Sociology*, Vol. 81, No. 4, pp. 867-884, ISSN 0002-9602

Husserl, E. (1999). *The Idea of Phenomenology*. Kluwer Academic Publication, ISBN 0792356918, Boston.

Husserl, E. (2001). *Analyses Concerning Passive and Active Synthesis: Lectures on Transcendental Logic*. Translated by Steinbock AJ, Kluwer Academic Publishers, ISBN 079237066X, Boston.

William, J. (1980). *The Principles of Psychology*, Vol I and II. Henry Holt and Co., ISBN, 0486203816, New York.

Kahn D. L. (1993). The technical notes: Ways of discussing validity in qualitative nursing research. *Western Journal of Nursing Research*, Vol. 15, pp. 122-126, ISSN 0193-9459

Kuo, F.-Y. & Young, M.-L. (2008). A study of the cognition-action gap in knowledge management, *Journal of the American Society for Information Science and Technology*, Vol. 59, pp. 1224-37, ISSN 1532-2882

Kendzierski, D. (1990). Decision making versus decision implementation: An action control approach to exercise adoption and adherence. *Journal of Applied Social Psychology*, Vol. 20, No. 1, pp. 27-45, ISSN 0021-9029

Lyon, D. (1994). From big brother to electronic panopticon. In *The Electronic Eye: The Rise of Surveillance Society*, D. Lyon (Ed.), pp. 57-80, University of Minnesota Press, ISBN 0816625158, Minneapolis.

McDermott, R. (1999). Why information technology inspired but cannot deliver knowledge management. *California Management Review*, Vol. 41, No. 4, pp. 103-117, ISSN 0008-1256

Mitchell, E. S. (1986). Multiple triangulation: A methodology for nursing science. *Advances in Nursing Science*, Vol. 8, No. 3, pp. 10-26, ISSN 1550-5014

Morse, J. M. (1991). *Qualitative Nursing Research: A Contemporary Dialogue*. Sage, ISBN 0803940793, Newbury Park, California.

Moustakas, C. (1994). *Phenomenological Research Methods*. Sage Publications, ISBN 0803957998, California.

Nonaka, I. (1994). A dynamic theory of organizational knowledge creation. *Organization Science*, Vol. 5, No. 1, pp. 14-37, ISSN 1047-7039

Nonaka, I. & Takeuchi, H. (1995). *The Knowledge Creating Company*. Oxford University Press, ISBN 0195092694, New York.

Pollio, H. R., Henley, T. B., & Thompson, C. J. (1997). *The Phenomenology of Everyday Life*. Cambridge University Press, ISBN 9780521031400, Cambridge, United Kingdom.

Rubin, H. and Rubin, I. (1995). What did you hear? In *Qualitative Interviewing: The Art of Hearing Data*, H. Robin & I. Robin I (Eds.), pp 226-255, Sage, ISBN 9780761920748, Thousand Oaks, California.

Sandelowski, M. (1993). Rigor or rigor mortis: The problem of rigor in qualitative research revisited. *Advances in Nursing Science*, Vol. 16, No. 2, pp. 1-8, ISSN 1550-5014

Sandelowski, M. (1994). The proof is in the pottery: Toward a poetic for qualitative inquiry, In *Critical Issues in Qualitative Research Methods*, J. M. Morae (Ed.), pp 46-63, Sage, ISBN 9780803950429, Thousand Oaks, California.

Schutz, A & Luckmann, T. (1973) *The Structures of the Life-world*, Northwestern University Press, ISBN 0810103958, Evanston, Illinois.

Thomas, J. C., Kellogg, W. A., & Erickson, T. (2001). The knowledge management puzzle: Human and social factors in knowledge management. *IBM Systems Journal*, Vol. 40, No. 4, pp. 863-884, ISSN 0018-8670

Tiwana, A. A. (2001). Design knowledge management system to support collaborative information product evolution. *Decision Support Systems*, Vol. 31, No. 2, pp. 241-262, ISSN 0167-9236

Toumi, I. (1999-2000). Data is more than knowledge: Implications of the reversed knowledge hierarchy for knowledge management and organizational memory. *Journal of Management Information Systems*, Vol. 16, No.3, pp. 103-117, ISSN 0742-1222

Van Manen, M. (1990). *Researching Lived Experience: Human Science for an Action Sensitive Pedagogy*, University of Western Ontario Press, ISBN 0791404269, New York.

White, H. (1980). The value of narrativity in the representation of reality. *Critical Inquiry*, Vol. 7, pp. 5-27. ISSN 00931896

6

An Empirical and Modeling Approach to Knowledge Management Practices in South American Organizations

Daniel Matzkin-Jakubowicz[1] and Mildred Berrelleza-Rendón[2]
[1]*Universidad Virtual del Instituto Tecnológico y de Estudios Superiores de Monterrey*
[2]*Instituto Tecnológico y de Estudios Superiores de Monterrey*
Mexico

1. Introduction

The following chapter explores Knowledge Management (KM) practices in some South American organizations operating in Spanish speaking countries: Argentina, Bolivia, Chile, Colombia, Ecuador, and Peru. More specifically, empirical results are confronted to a functional KM guideline based on balanced scorecard architecture and used as a diagnosis tool. Some fundamental KM issues are previously discussed.

A dominant trend within researchers and practitioners is to relate Knowledge Management (KM) with innovative organizations, their sustainable economic growth, and the development of information management systems (e.g., Maier and Hadrich, 2006, Salojärvi et al., 2005, Tedmori et al., 2006). Technological innovation has for example been cited as a major reason for the current interest in knowledge management (Bouthillier and Shearer, 2002). According to this dominant perspective, in the "knowledge era" in which we are, the ways intangible assets are managed and converted into actionable knowledge contribute to organizational learning, competitive advantage, and organization's overall success (e.g., Dorey and Gobat, 1996, Roos et al., 1997, Senge, 2006).

Based on well established cognitive psychology findings on learning and memory Nonaka and Takeuchi (1995) described the two fundamental categories of knowledge found in organizations: on the one hand tacit knowledge that is distributed among the personnel and which is hard to articulate. On the other hand, explicit knowledge which can be codified and that will eventually contribute to feed technological systems such as data bases, and expert systems. Converting tacit into explicit actionable knowledge is one important challenge faced by any KM program (see Toledano O'Farrill, 2011); this being particularly true in the South American context.

However, there are still many gaps for a global theoretical scheme on KM dynamics. This is currently reflected in the existence of a variety of concepts and methods surrounding KM research. For instance Andriessen (2008) showed that metaphors are largely used to conceptualize knowledge in a KM context (Andriessen, 2008). For example Andriessen (2006 cited by Andriessen, 2008) found a list of 22 metaphors used by researchers and practitioners to describe what knowledge is (for example "knowledge as capital" or "Knowledge inventory"). As Andriessen explains, the use of metaphors to describe knowledge isn't a bad thing though it can easily bring up misunderstandings and lack of conceptual consistency. Our view is that this "KM black box" shouldn't be considered as a limitation but rather as a stimulating opportunity to enlarge a multidisciplinary field - encompassing computer science, to human, social, and administration sciences, as reflected in the variety of topics covered by this book.

The work presented hereafter is less focused on theoretical implications regarding KM but is more oriented to day to day KM practices inside South American organizations. Specifically, the following section explores the structural and management factors that constrain - or favor, KM practices.

2. Structural and management requirements for KM deployment

Less widespread is the study and understanding of the constraints underlying knowledge creation and sharing inside organizations. This is particularly true in South American organizations. These organizational requirements are among others based on organizational values and culture, management and leadership practices, motivational incentives, size, and technology availability (Ko et al, 2005). It seems important to emphasize that most research in KM consider these requirements as granted or given a priori. Therefore one of the direct questions addressed in this chapter is: how do these organizational constraints affect KM practices and deployment inside South American organizations?

Firstly, regarding the organizational values only an effective organizational culture can promote the deployment of systematic KM practices as employees' skills and only motivation isn't self sufficient. For that reason explicit efforts to cultivate a knowledge sharing culture are essential (De Long and Fahey, 2000). Past research has focused on organizational, social, motivational, and technical factors that favor or inhibit knowledge sharing. The complexity to act over these factors explain some of the difficulties encountered by managers in creating knowledge mindsets and effective and sustainable KM programs in their organizations (see Smith et al., 2010, De Long and Fahey, 2000). Mindsets can be associated to mental models acting as cognitive filters that influence decision making processes (Smith et al., 2010).

Secondly, promoting knowledge mindsets, cultures and knowledge sharing values isn't sufficient if other important organizations structural factors are ignored. One of them that to our knowledge hasn't yet been considered in the KM literature is organizational justice. The organizational justice concept refers to the personnel's fairness perception regarding the equity in distributions (e.g., rewards allocation), the fairness of organizational procedures (e.g., assessment evaluation, types of labor contracts that are offered) and the fairness in interactions (e.g. treatment made by a manager or the shared information; Adams, 1963; Leventhal, 1976; Bies and Moag, 1986) If one of these three dimensions is perceived as unfair it will act on employee's motivation and loyalty and thus affect the knowledge sharing and transfer process independently of the existence of explicit KM values in the organization. A secondary variable to consider is the size of the organization that has an effect in the existence of KM practices: the bigger the organization, more likely it is to exhibit KM practices whether these are implicit or explicit (Matzkin, 2008).

Hence, the above dynamics (i.e.: bottom-up and top-down information and knowledge flows, knowledge sharing mindsets, values, and a number of structural variables) are essential to generate the necessary capacity for openness in order to transform tacit into actionable explicit knowledge. It must be added that though the role of culture and values is difficult to measure its impact in the organization is clearly perceived by top managers in their day to day work (De Long and Fahey, 2000).

When the antecedent conditions exist in the organization it affects positively the management style of a business unit or team management by creating the conditions to generate knowledge mindsets at different levels of the organization (Smith et al., 2010; Zhu and Sun, 2010). As a matter of fact, in what sense does management style interact with KM practices? Management sends strong signals for example by supporting mechanisms of socialization, empowerment, mentorships, talent retention programs, training, face-to-face communication, and networking practices. Nonaka and Takeuchi (1995) illustrate many business cases showing the impact of management practices in team building and business processes and performance. These core management mechanisms have also been positively correlated with job satisfaction, performance, and motivation (Gelade, 2003; Ryan et al., 1996, Spreitzer et al., 1997, Abdul Hamid and Sulaiman 2011), settling the basis for an appropriate learning environment (Eriksen, 2010). Consequently, at a more operative level, many empirical data show how successful KM practices in organizations relate to the existence of core management styles and cultures (Zhu and Sun, 2010).

Finally when considering technology, although it is widely admitted that technical issues of electronic collaboration aren't a sufficient condition in order to manage knowledge and generate actionable processes, day to day evidence experienced by managers and employees show the strong impact they have in knowledge sharing (Newell et al., 2006; Nonaka and Takeuchi, 1995). This is understandable considering that the bigger is the organization, information and knowledge are widely dispersed and wherever it is needed it is not always accessible or is time costly to get it. Therefore the presence of intranets, ERPs, and collaboration devices inside the organization is another evidence of the existence of knowledge sharing mindsets.

At this point of the discussion only internal factors such as values, organization's characteristics, management style, and technology, have been considered as facilitating or constraining factors in KM practices. Byounggu and Heeseok (2003) correctly assume that external factors, such as industry types are also likely to constrain KM practices in organizations. Certainly, industry types (e.g.; manufacturing, financing, and service) require different KM styles and needs. This being said, we now turn to analyze the current situation of KM practices in South American organizations

3. Knowledge management in South America

In a snapshot, Bolivia, Ecuador, Peru and Colombia are considered geographically and culturally as Andean countries sharing many cultural traits as a common pre Hispanic past. Chile and Argentina are two distinct countries that have higher economic weight, income, and share similar human development index according to UNPD (2010) statistics. These 6 countries represent a population of about 161.4 million inhabitants.

Unlike an European perspective on KM where knowledge is considered a prominent factor of production and source of competitive advantage (see Tome 2011), the South American context presents significant differences with the European one. Literature on KM practices in South America exist though it is largely widespread with a strong emphasis in rural, social, educational, and cultural aspects that are mostly concerned with the nonprofit sector (e.g. Michel et al., 2010, Matzkin 2008, Ferreira and Neto, 2005). In Spanish speaking countries only a small number of published empirical researches on KM are available in

English and are limited to a few countries. For this reason the current work aims to present a global picture of KM management practices in some South American organizations starting from little or no data.

South American organizations are an interesting field of research for a better understanding of the diversity and scopes of existing KM practices in organizations outside North America and Europe. Firstly, we believe that South America represents many organizational contexts specific to developing countries characterized by deficient levels of innovation (this is measured by the number of patents fillings per country, see for example WIPO 2007 and EPO 2010), of human capital, and in many cases limited financial resources. Therefore in a South American context, efficient KM practices could profitably help organizations to fulfill their objectives despite their structural deficiencies. Secondly, according to World Bank statistics the past ten years have been quite profitable in terms of economic growth (this is measured in GDP, World Bank 2010) for the majority of South American countries. As a result, it inserted the region into the globalized economy generating high levels of investments from international firms that export their knowhow, and that has probably affected the way organizations are managed in the region. Thirdly, as Europe, South America is irregular in terms of local cultures (i.e.; traditions, population's origin, and beliefs), levels of economic development, and regarding political lines followed by governments (i.e., free trade economic models versus State controlled economy ones).

In the case of Colombia, 46 percent of the 50 organizations that have been surveyed by Baquero and Schulte (2007), consisting of a mix of educational, public, and private organizations, were planning to develop KM practices in a span of time of 2 years. The authors report that very few of these organizations had values systems and cultures that facilitated knowledge sharing practices. Additionally, most of the organizations had not heard about programs that were specifically intended to promote employee retention within their organizations as only 14 percent had policies in this field (Baquero and Schulte, 2007). As for the technology factors the surveyed organizations were not very familiar with information systems that specifically support knowledge and information sharing. For example prior to 2003 less than 37 percent of the organizations had used any of the following technologies: group/collaboration tools, search engines, document management/taxonomy, and intranet portals. In average about 20 percent of these organizations planned to implement in a future time these technologies. Baquero and Schulte (2007) conclude that their results, from a global perspective, suggest that the level of adoption of KM practices in Colombia's private, public and academic sectors is very low and that not many organizations have implemented KM policies and strategies. Finally, as to management practices among the organizations that have KM practices, the authors report that most of these practices are under the responsibility of the executive management team. Only 23 percent were under the supervision of the Human Resource manager.

Data on KM practices in Peruvian organizations are found in Matzkin (2008) although the analysis is mostly focused on the nonprofit sector. In the research participated 106 managers from Peruvian nonprofit organizations, public organizations, and profit organizations contributing in social development programs. The first impressive result was that the level of KM awareness among managers from public, profit, and nonprofit organizations was only 51.9 percent. In other words, near of 1 out of 2 of the surveyed managers had at that time never heard of KM. Although KM values and cultures haven't been directly addressed in this study, the low level of KM awareness suggests very low levels of explicit KM culture and values in these Peruvians organizations. Nonetheless moderate to upper levels of implicit KM practices were found in public, nonprofit, and profit organizations. The implicit knowledge practices were quantified on six components: (1) the use of strategic management methodologies such as key performance indicators; (2) the existence of internal procedures used to improve management and processes; (3) the existence of systemized practices consisting in keeping a written track of work processes; (4) considering the personnel suggestions to improve processes; (5) the use of professional email to share information; (6) and the organization's e-learning practices. The author suggested that despite the existence of some KM practices, these could not however be coordinated in order to achieve explicit strategies for organizational learning since they remained in the realm of the implicit. Finally, an important structural problem was observed in the surveyed organizations that consisted in high employee turnover which was related to the precariousness of the personnel labor status. Important turnover rates prevent organizations and their employees to profit and share experiences, knowledge, and management practices. In particular, it was found that employees working in bigger organizations had more long term labor contracts than those working in smaller organizations (Matzkin 2008).

In Argentina a survey conducted in 2000 revealed that 83 percent of the surveyed managers knew what KM was about, thus showing a high level of KM awareness (Leclic 2002). Two years after the survey it was found that the majority of firms that had planned to implement a KM program didn't do so mainly for budget restrictions. For Argentina (except the previous study), Chile, Bolivia, and Ecuador no reliable published KM indicators specific to organizations were found.

Taken as a whole, the limited amount of information that is available shows the following facts:(1) medium to upper levels of KM awareness were observed in different South American countries, (2) medium levels of KM practices exist in public and (non)profit organizations; (3) when KM practices exist these remain mainly implicit limiting the foundation of KM mindsets and KM values; (4) structural variables (e.g., labor turnover, organizations size, limited use of technology, budget restriction) constrain KM practices and the development of KM mindsets and values; (5) in the Colombian case, executive management handled the implementation of KM.

4. A practical guideline for exploring KM in South America

The above sections have set a conceptual framework for exploring KM practices in South American organizations. In this section we present a KM process guideline based on that framework. The aim of this guideline is two-fold: first, to set a practical tool that can be used by local managers in their day to day work to develop KM mindsets and strategies similar to what Berrelleza and Matzkin (2009) have achieved for the Peruvian construction sector; secondly to confront the below empirical results to a conceptual framework and model. Our guideline is based on a balanced scorecard architecture. A balance scorecard is a strategic planning and performance management system used to monitor and align business processes with strategy that also includes non financial measures (Kaplan and Norton, 1993) We share Kalpic's and Bernus (2006), Bose and Thomas (2007), and Berrelleza and Matzkin (2009) analysis for whom a business process modeling (i.e., here a balanced scorecard) can be seen as a tool for knowledge management that allows the transformation of informal into formal knowledge which facilitates its externalization and sharing.

The guideline has 4 layers labeled: External factors, Learning and growth, Business processes, Customer satisfaction, and Expected financial results (see Figure 1).

4.1 External factors

This layer (not represented in our diagram) relates to Byounggu's and Heeseok's (2003) external factors that are mediated by industry types. Other socio-cultural factors should be considered such as country´s specificities regarding business management regulations and legal variables (Baker & McKenzie, 2008). For example in most European countries training is regulated by laws that make mandatory organizations to spend a minimal amount of budget and working hours to train their employees. This is not the case in some South American countries. External factors although important remain difficult to quantify but should nevertheless be kept in mind.

4.2 Learning and growth

This layer relates to the above structural factors that act over employee's motivation, job satisfaction, and the organization's internal processes over their human capital. This layer is concerned with the human resource management strategies of the organizations.

Recruiting and training boxes: The organization sends signals about what is important through its recruiting priorities, and promotions. An important aspect of sustainable success has to do with talented people, that's why these boxes are especially important. Recruiting mistakes at this stage have consequences in the following boxes.

Employee satisfaction box: They learn to understand just how much they are worth, and what they can give to the workplace. They become intellectually-stimulated, and emotionally-engaged. They must have a high sense of empowerment in order to be able to make decisions.

Less turnover box: Low turnover keeps your employees longer, they feel more secured, and thereby reduces the loss of intellectual capital from people leaving the company.

4.3 Business processes

This layer focus on core management variables that describe how organizational values and mindsets are implemented in a day to day basis and whether they will favor (or not) the emergence of a knowledge sharing culture in the business units.

Innovation in processes & products box: KM saves money and time by not reinventing the wheel for each new project. In this layer management has to identify different processes that should be improved to increase value and customers' satisfaction.

Knowledge tools box: Increases productivity by making knowledge available more quickly, sharing information using technology and (in)formal communication channels. The existence of documents which describe key processes will help in avoiding mistakes in operation processes.

4.4 Customer satisfaction

This layer relates to internal and external customer satisfaction which is largely dependent on the outcomes of the "business processes" layer. This layer should help companies to identify their specific market segment and to determine core measures that will describe the successful outcomes of a well-formulated and implemented strategy (Bose and Thomas, 2007).

Customer retention: Customers are more demanding than ever, hence relationships with them are now becoming more complex. This specific box will help organizations to determine indicators and metrics that help them to retain customers.

Customer satisfaction box: This box is just a consequence of the previous outcomes of the "business processes" and customer retention.

4.5 Expected financial results

How can we measure the current and future value of knowledge management? This is a question this guideline can help us solve. This layer sets the financial results and standards that the organization wants to achieve leveraging over the different variables of the guideline.

We present a possible path (out of many) that could impact positively in the financial results of organizations.

4.6 Path

In the *learning and growth layer,* the model starts with a correct selection, recruitment, and hiring process. This is the point to begin with, if we don't have the right people, with the right skills in the right place, with the appropriate labor contract, the probability of success will be reduced. The right people must be trained and mentored, and this learning process should be become continuous and endless (Senge, 2006). Then, as the guideline in Figure 1 shows, if companies have well trained people there will be a positive impact in the sense of belonging and in job satisfaction. People usually talk about being part of something larger than themselves, of being connected, of being generative (Senge, 2006). If low turnover rates exist, it means that the company has few leaves and dismissals. The interactions of these variables lead to a virtuous cycle that contributes to the emergence of a learning culture inside the organization. To make this possible an appropriate management style is needed (business process layer). Management practices and values should favor bottom-up communication channels and use appropriate management methodologies that will allow discussing improvements and innovations over processes and products and impact positively in the ROI and ROE of companies. Another expected impact is that this process will impact positively in customer satisfaction and retention and finally in the financial results of the company. This is possible if management values and practices fit the human resource management strategies and vice versa.

This model can be been seen as a chain of cause and effect that may impact directly and positively in the financial results of a company no matter its size and industry type. The failure or success of using this guideline depends in the ability of the company to be aware of changes in its internal and external environments in order to reformulate or adapt the current scorecard and its indicators. By this mean the objective of the model is to show that KM is not just a source of costs or a "romantic" theoretical concept. Three short business cases belonging to South American organizations are presented in the "Results" section.

5. Methodology

Data was collected through an online standardized questionnaire from 88 middle and high level managers attending MBA programs and from the authors' corporate contacts living in 6 South American countries. The questionnaire was inspired from the one used by Matzkin (2008), the above theoretical framework, and formulated in order to explore KM practices in regard of the organizations' structural variables and core management practices. Another aim of the questionnaire was to test the pertinence of the KM guideline presented above by applying it to three different organizations taken from our sample. The questionnaire

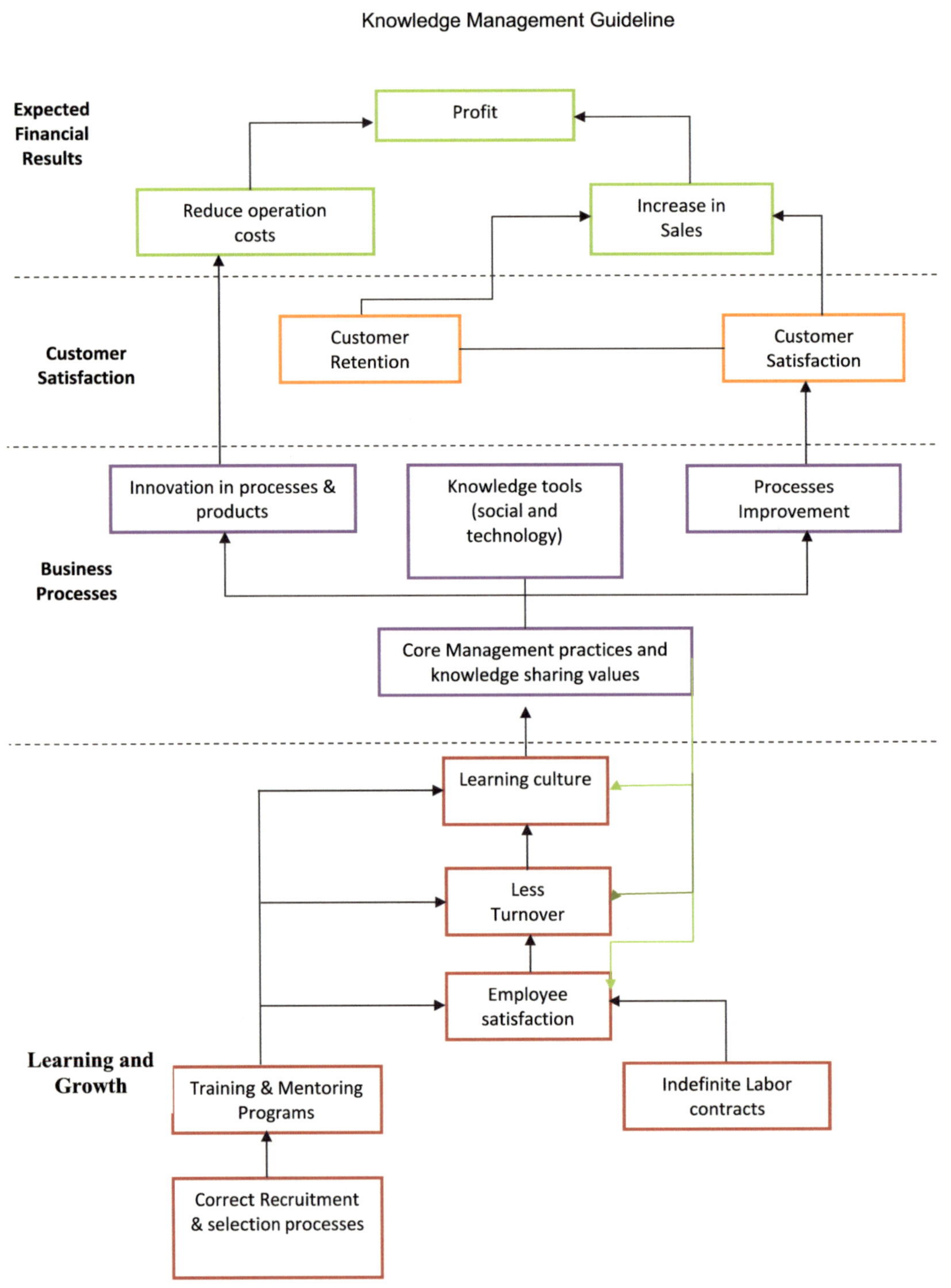

Fig. 1. Knowledge management guideline

included closed questions concerning familiarity with knowledge management, knowledge sharing, use of technology, and managing practices in their organizations. Some questions allowed open text fields that enabled respondents to add qualitative information.

The survey was conducted in August 2011 and the response rate was of 30%, slightly more than what is usually found in research using a survey methodology (e.g., Athanassiou et al., 2002; Corso et al., 2006; Salojärvi et al., 2005, Baquero and Schulte, 2007). 3 questionnaires were rejected as they were returned incomplete or respondents were no more working in South America.

5.1 Sample's descriptive information

Table 1 shows the characteristics of the sample. Most respondent were from Peruvian (55.29%) and Colombian (24.70%) organizations thus limiting meaningful comparisons between countries (see below for a discussion on that point). Another important characteristic of the sample was that most of the surveyed managers worked in large (more than 500 employees) organizations (56.47%). Additionally, Peruvian and Colombian organizations covered all industry types whereas the remaining countries covered only some of them. Finally, more than 88% of the surveyed managers worked in private organizations, about 8% in public ones, and just a small part were from nonprofit organizations (3.53%). In summary, the typical respondent's ID was a manager working for a large profit organization.

			Type of Organization		Size					
Country	N	Non profit	Public	Profit	≤20	≤50	≤100	≤500	> 500	Industry type
Argentina	6	0	0	6	0	1	0	3	2	Energy, Education
Bolivia	2	0	0	2	1	0	0	0	1	Bank, Education
Chile	3	1	1	1	0	0	0	1	2	Telecomunication, Education
Colombia	21	0	0	21	1	3	2	1	14	All types covered
Ecuador	6	0	1	5	0	0	2	1	3	Banking, Telecomunication, Retail
Peru	47	2	5	40	4	3	9	5	26	All types covered
Total	*85*	*3*	*7*	*75*	*6*	*7*	*13*	*11*	*48*	
Total (%)	100	3.53%	8.23%	88.24%	7.06%	8.24%	15.29%	12.94%	56.47%	

Table 1.

Because of the sample's size and its unequal number of respondent per country we decided not to perform country comparisons. However this did not limit the reach of results considering these two facts: in the first place, as presented in the "Knowledge Management in South America" section, Bolivia, Colombia, Ecuador, and Peru are Andean countries with many cultural similarities. In the second place, many of the globalized companies that operate in South America cluster their operations by sub regions. The Andean sub region generally includes Bolivia, Colombia, Peru, Ecuador and sometimes even Chile. Hence, there was an overlap both from a cultural point of view and from a business one. Argentina would be the only exception but not enough data was collected to make a separate analysis.

The following paragraphs analyze KM practices in organizations connected to the structural, core management, and values factors.

6. Results

6.1 Structural, core management, and value variables

Table 2a summarizes results relating to the structural factors of the surveyed organizations. In this dimension one of the key questions was related with the nature of labor contracts of

Table 2a
Structural Variables

Labor Contract		Turnover Perception	
Permament	Period	High	Low
80.00%	20.00%	36.47%	63.53%

Table 2b
Core Management and Values

Training perception			Talent Retention Program		Mentoring and Coaching Programs		Knowledge sharing Values		Bottom-Up Improvements	
Poor	Fair	A plus	Yes	No	Yes	No	Yes	No	Yes	No
32.94%	35.29%	31.76%	25.88%	74.12%	45.10%	54.90%	69.41%	30.59%	70.59%	29.41%

Table 2c
Information Management Variables

KM program		Knowledge Sharing Methods		Intranet		Process Classification Methods		Strategic Management tools	
Yes	No	Yes	No	Yes	No	Yes	No	Yes	No
37.65%	62.35%	57.65%	42.35%	76.47%	23.53%	85.88%	14.12%	58.82%	41.18%

Table 2. a, b, c

the employees. As stated above high turnover rates limit knowledge sharing practices and mindsets as the human resource life cycle is shorter (Eriksen, 2010). Overall data show that 80% of the surveyed organizations offer formal permanent labor contracts to their employees. 20% of the labor contracts are temporary ones, which durations do not exceed six months to a 1 year. This result isn't surprising if we consider that most of respondents work in important multinationals where labor conditions have higher standards compared to what is usually observed in South America. We performed a statistical test in order to check whether the size of the organizations had an effect on labor contracts types but no significant difference was observed $x^2_{(4)} = 3.61 p > .20$.

A complementary variable related to the previous one was the "turnover perception" managers had on their organizations. Considering Table 2a there is a positive descriptive relation between the existence of permanent labor contracts and lower turnover rates as 63.53% of managers perceived a low turnover rate. Here too, the turnover perception didn't differ significantly according to the size of the organizations ($x^2_{(4)} = 1.37 p > .20$). Yet, a third of managers (32.94%) perceived high turnover rates. This latter percentage could possible constrain, not only KM practices, but also have an effect on the perceived organizational justice inside organizations (see "Business cases" section below).

The next results analyze core management practices and KM sharing values existing inside organizations, such as: training perception, talent retention programs, mentoring or coaching programs and knowledge sharing activities. (see Table 2b)

Training strategies are important not only for organizational learning but also for employee's motivation. Although 40% of the surveyed managers ignored the amount of training budget that their organizations spent on an annual basis, 35.92% considered that their organizations had fair interest in training their employee, and up to 31.76% believed that in their organizations there was a very high interest in training. Hence, about two thirds (67.05%) of managers have a neutral or very positive perception regarding training matters. Only a small third of them (32.94%) considered that their organizations showed a low interest in training issues. When comparing the perceptions on training with organization's size once more no significant difference was observed ($x^2_{(8)} = 10.33 p > .10$). However an ad hoc comparison that consisted in contrasting medium sized and big organizations (i.e.; 100 employees and more) versus small organizations (less than 50 employees) was marginally significant ($x^2_{(2)} = 5.84 p = .054$). This tendency is consistent with previous results observed in Peruvian nonprofit organizations (Matzkin, 2008) and with the idea that bigger organizations have more resources to budget training activities compared to smaller ones.

Along with training, talent retention programs contribute to organizational learning (Zhu et al., 2010) and represent a management leverage on employees. An expected good management practice consists in retaining and developing talented workers. Surprisingly for 74.12% of the managers their organizations lacked of such programs. Qualitative data reported by managers indicated that it wasn't uncommon to see good elements quit their jobs as the organization didn't value their skills, training, and knowledge (e.g. many reported quitting after following an MBA program). The remaining 25.88% reported sophisticated talent retention programs managed by the human resource department and team managers. For this variable a size effect was found ($x^2_{(3)} = 8.56 p > .05$; less than 100 employees organizations versus those of more than 100 employees): the bigger the organization, the more it had talent retention programs. This result is consistent with the above one on training where bigger organizations tend to have more training budgets. Nonetheless, the observed low proportion of talent retention programs is a concern since it can turn into another source that might affect the perceived organizational justice of employees. If companies have high turnover rates, they should be worried about keeping their talented people by developing long-term talent strategies in order to keep their intellectual capital inside the company.

Another core management factor relating to training and talent retention was "coaching and mentoring" practices. It was expected that a team or business unit manager would favor this knowledge transmission practice among his subordinates. Descriptive results show that in only 45.10% these knowledge sharing activities exist in the surveyed organizations. As for above, the existence of these practices seem to be related to organization's size, particularly in bigger organizations ($x^2_{(4)} = 13.10\, p < .05$, and $x^2_{(3)} = 12.60\, p < .01$ when comparing less than 100 employees organizations versus those of more than 100 employees).

A final core management question related to the existence of "bottom-up" communication channels favored by managers to collect information in order to generate organizational improvements. 70.59% of the surveyed managers reported the existence of these practices in their organizations. This result can be related to organizational openness to share knowledge and to empower employees in decision making. This view is supported by the fact that 69.41% of the respondent indicated that knowledge sharing values were supported in their organizations.

Altogether these first results on structural variables, management practices, and knowledge sharing values report that the surveyed South American organizations showed medium to upper levels of good practices regarding some of their human resource management policies. For example, the labor contracts they offered to their employees were globally acceptable considering the region's standard, and turnover rates were moderate. Observed structural information appeared to be independent from organization's size. Perceptions over management and values showed more conventional practices. Although perceptions on training and bottom-up communication channels were globally positive, results showed low levels of talent retention programs, mentoring and coaching practices. Therefore it appears that organizations seem not to be linking training, mentoring and talent management into a coherent organizational learning scheme.

6.2 Information and explicit/implicit knowledge management practices

The following analysis focus on information sharing, KM practices, and technology use (see Table 2c).

Firstly, similar to results reported by Baquero and Schulte (2007) for Colombia, Matzkin (2008) for Peru, and Leclic (2002) for Argentina, very few organizations - only 37.65%, have implemented or are considering implementing formal KM programs. Additional qualitative information showed that managers weren't very acquainted with the formal KM programs when these existed inside their organizations. Many of them related them to a variety of training projects, interdisciplinary teams, communities of knowledge, or specific publications. Of interest was to observe that managers considered that KM programs were in priority more useful to improve internal management issues (69.41%) than to improve products and services delivered to their stakeholders. This result is consistent with Matzkin (2008) who reported a similar fact in Peruvian organizations.

Secondly, when we focus on how organizations manage information and knowledge, 57.65% of the managers reported that their organizations made use of methodologies such as focus and quality circles and discussion groups. This result is independent from organization's size and is once more very similar to the one reported by Matzkin (2008) in Peruvian organizations. In the same range of results, only 58.82% of organizations made use of strategic performance management tools as balanced/sales scorecards or Key Performance Indicators. The use of such performance management tools are global indicators of knowledge sharing practices since the pertinent use of these methodologies suppose intensive collaborations between different hierarchical and functional levels inside an organization. In contrast to previous results, 85.88% of the managers responded that their organizations had written documentation of all their processes to help them solve problems, perform projects, and in some cases to facilitate corporate communication. For these variables, organization's size was marginally significant ($x^2_{(4)} = 8.95, p = 0.062$). An ad hoc comparison that contrasted organizations with less than 100 employees with those of 100 and more employees reached significance level ($x^2_{(3)} = 7.50,\ p = 0.05$). This tendency was expected since bigger organizations, because of their size and structure, need more formal procedures to store and spread information efficiently.

Thirdly, when focusing on technology, 76.47% of the surveyed managers reported that their organizations had an intranet to facilitate information sharing. In relation with the previous result, bigger organizations made more use of intranets than smaller ones: ($x^2_{(4)} = 23.8,\ p < .001$). Finally, 67.14% of the organizations have or plan to implement e-learning methodologies (this result isn't shown in Table 2c). For this criterion no significant difference was found according to organizations' size. These results show higher use of technology in organizations compared to what was reported some ago years by Baquero and Schulte (2007).

Overall results indicate low levels of explicit KM practices in South American organizations and are consistent with the levels found by Baquero and Schulte (2007) in Colombia and Matzkin (2008) in Peru. Yet, the existence of implicit knowledge management practices in these organizations should not be underestimated although managers are not always aware they are managing them. The implicit knowledge management practices were measured using an additive model based on the tested components. Composite measure methods have been widely used in knowledge management literature and have shown interesting insights to the research data (e.g., Garcia-Olaverri et al. 2006, Matzkin, 2008, and Salojärvi et al., 2005). The implicit knowledge management index (IKMI) varied from 0 to 1: the higher the score, the higher the level of implicit knowledge management practices. The composite score included seven components and were given similar weights as in Matzkin (2008): (1) talent retention programs; (2) mentoring and coaching programs; (3) Knowledge sharing values; (4) bottom-up communication channels; (5) the use of strategic methodologies similar to the Balanced Scorecard; (6) the existence of systemized practices consisting in keeping a written track of work processes; (7) and the organization's e-learning practices. Results are presented in Figure 2 and show medium levels of implicit knowledge management practices across organizations with IKMI ranging from .37 to .64. IKMI levels seem to increase with the organization's size. However a one way anova didn't show any significant difference when comparing organization's sizes. A Student t test that compared the higher and lower index (.64 Vs. .37) was marginally significant $t_{(12)} = 2{,}14p = .053$ suggesting that size does have a marginal effect on implicit practices but no source of systematic variation was observed. The implications of these results are considered in the "Discussion" section.

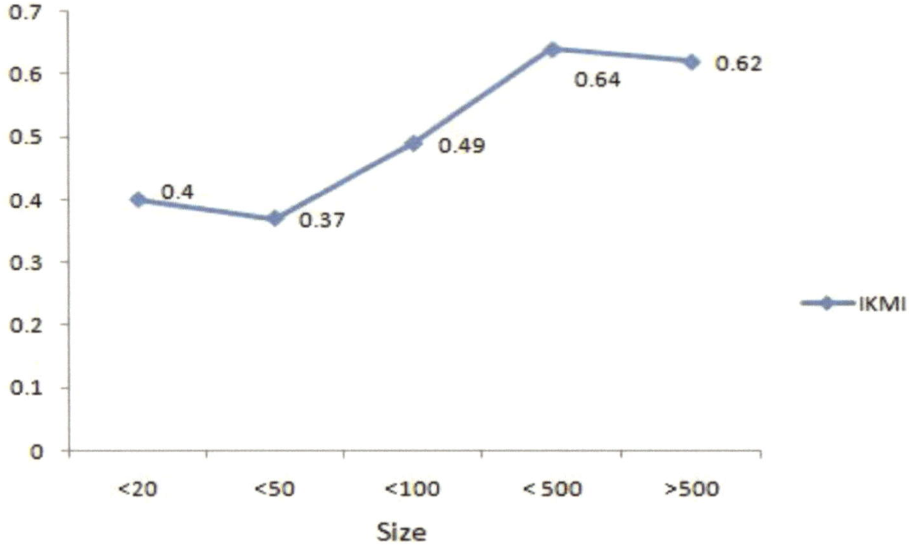

Fig. 2. Levels of IKMI in function of size

6.3 Business cases

In this section three businesses taken from the sample were analyzed through the KM guideline described above (see Figure 1 knowledge management guideline, and Case 1, Case 2, and Case 3 below). These examples illustrate three different situations that show how the interaction between management practices, values, and structural variables lead to different outcomes regarding the knowledge management practices that are observed in these organizations. From a KM perspective, case 1 represents an ideal situation where "leaning and growth" and "core management and values" layers are aligned. Case 2 illustrates the dissociation between management knowledge oriented values with the existing human resource policies applied by the organization. Case 3 represents a more traditional hierarchically managed organization type that has not yet developed many knowledge mindsets. It should be mentioned that the three cases represent successful organizations leaders in their market. An alternative way to make use of this model (not used in the cases below) is to set specific indicators and goals to reach for each box. These two different uses are of course complementary.

Case 1 (Bank)

The company is an important bank of Colombia (more than 500 employees). The "learning and growth" layer shows that important structural variables such as having "permanent labor contracts" and a low "labor turnover" rate interact with "employee's satisfaction" and forms a firm basis for the development of a "learning culture". The manager from that company confirmed that the bank had a high interest in training employees along with mentoring and coaching activities. When analyzing the "business processes" layer, the bank's core management practices and values (bottom-up communication channels, empowerment, performance evaluation, talent retention, methodologies) favor the use of

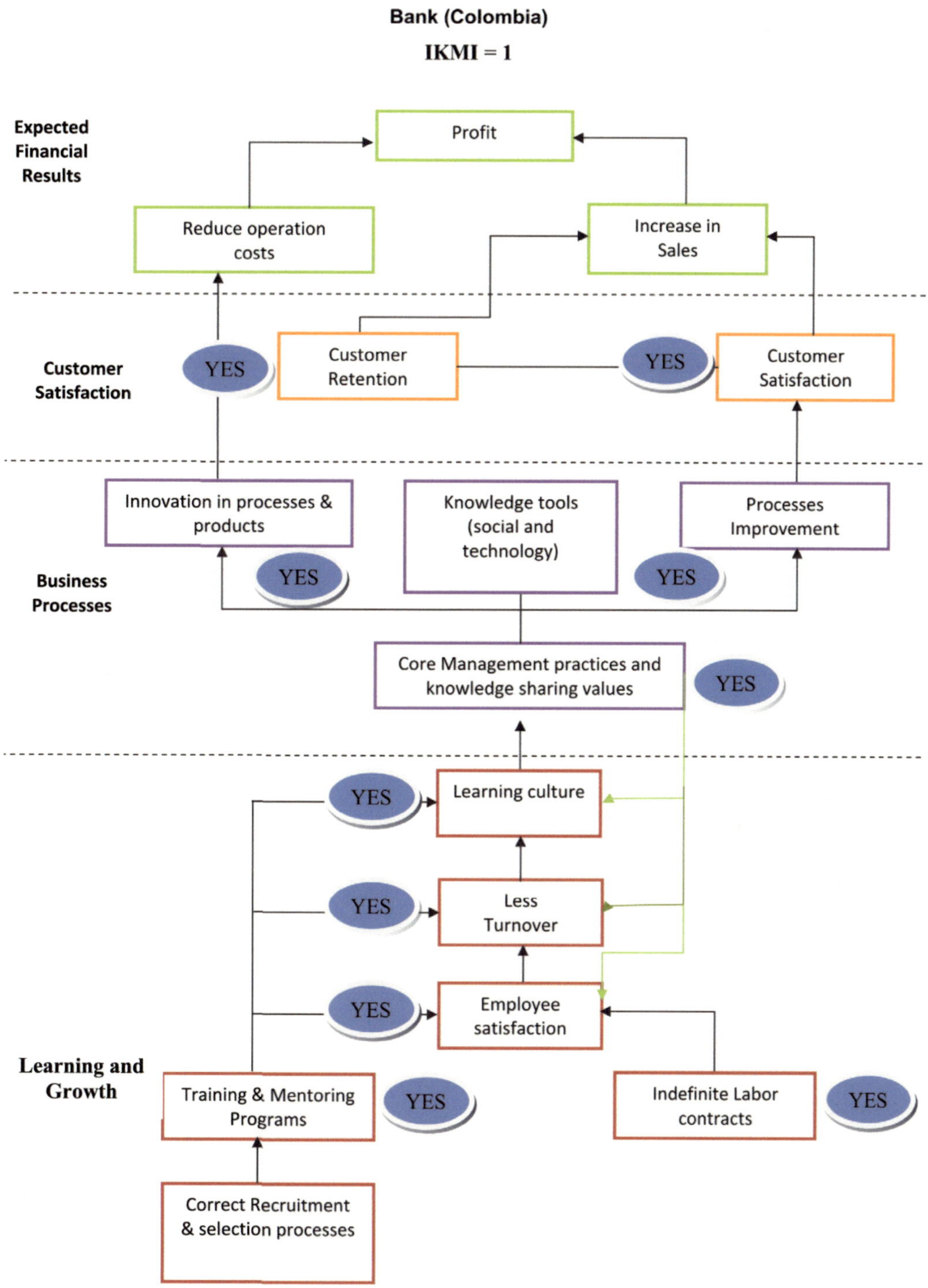
Bank (Colombia)
IKMI = 1
Expected Financial Results
Profit
Reduce operation costs
Increase in Sales
Customer Satisfaction
YES
Customer Retention
YES
Customer Satisfaction
Innovation in processes & products
Knowledge tools (social and technology)
Processes Improvement
Business Processes
YES
YES
Core Management practices and knowledge sharing values
YES
YES
Learning culture
YES
Less Turnover
YES
Employee satisfaction
Learning and Growth
Training & Mentoring Programs
YES
Indefinite Labor contracts
YES
Correct Recruitment & selection processes

Case 1.

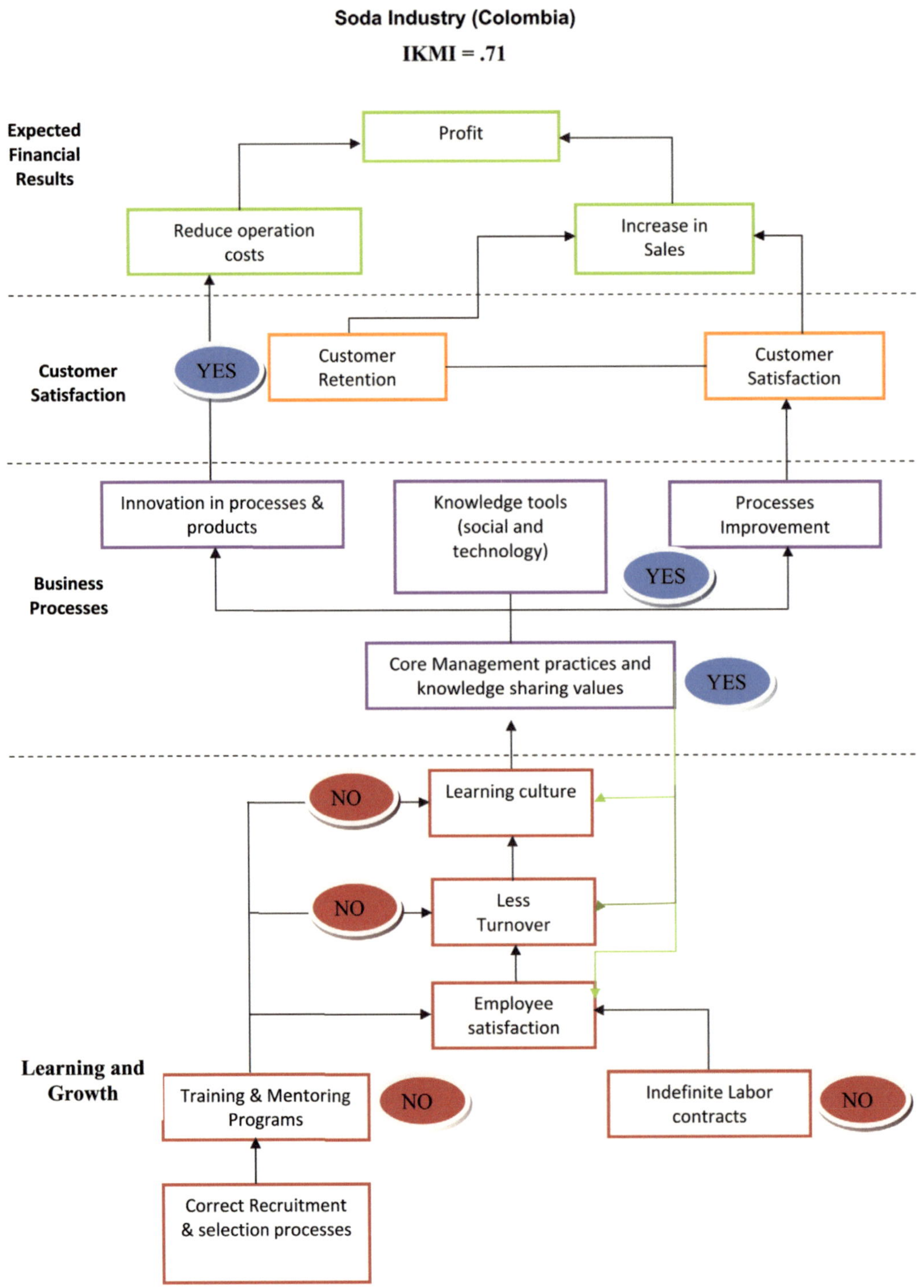
Soda Industry (Colombia)
IKMI = .71
Expected Financial Results
Profit
Reduce operation costs
Increase in Sales
Customer Satisfaction
YES
Customer Retention
Customer Satisfaction
Innovation in processes & products
Knowledge tools (social and technology)
Processes Improvement
Business Processes
YES
Core Management practices and knowledge sharing values
YES
NO
Learning culture
NO
Less Turnover
Employee satisfaction
Learning and Growth
Training & Mentoring Programs
NO
Indefinite Labor contracts
NO
Correct Recruitment & selection processes

Case 2.

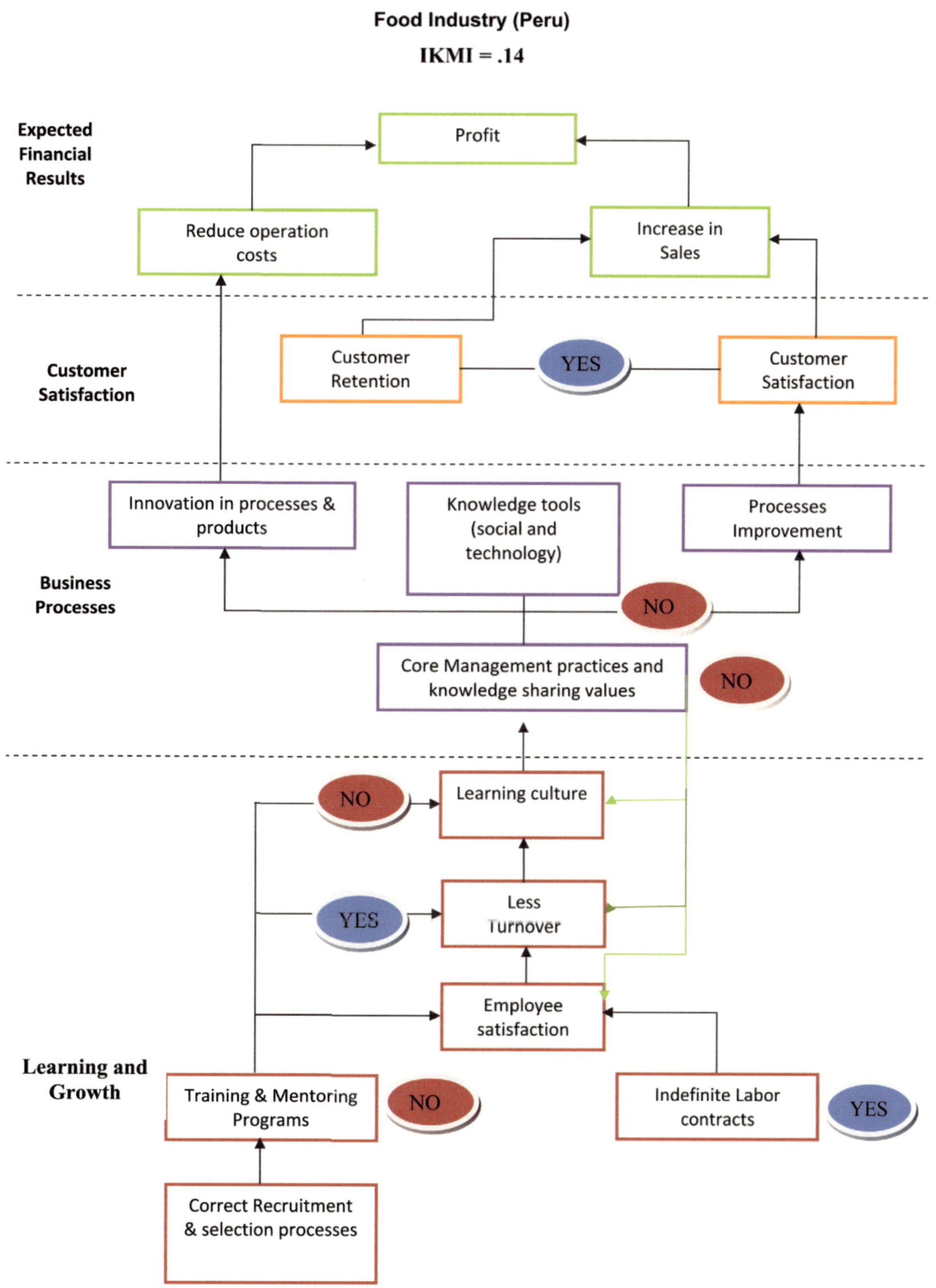
Food Industry (Peru)
IKMI = .14
Expected Financial Results
Profit
Reduce operation costs
Increase in Sales
Customer Satisfaction
Customer Retention
YES
Customer Satisfaction
Innovation in processes & products
Knowledge tools (social and technology)
Processes Improvement
Business Processes
NO
Core Management practices and knowledge sharing values
NO
NO
Learning culture
YES
Less Turnover
Employee satisfaction
Learning and Growth
Training & Mentoring Programs
NO
Indefinite Labor contracts
YES
Correct Recruitment & selection processes

Case 3.

"knowledge tools" and the conditions for improving "business processes and products" on a formal and documented basis with the support of the employees (learning and growth layer). Financial evidence show that bank is leader in its market and was ranked in the top 10 of the 2010 "Great Place to Work" ranking. This case shows how structural, cultural factors, core management and practices interact and support the materialization of a KM culture or at least mindsets. The measured IKMI was of 1.

Case 2 (soda industry)

This is a major company in the Colombian soda market (more than 500 employees). This case is interesting since in one hand, it shows that in the "business processes" layer, the company has appropriate sharing values and management practices. For example, bottom-up communication channels, collaborative working methodologies (e.g. focus groups, quality circles) to solve problems and improve business processes; there is an intranet to share information. On the other hand, the "learning and growth" layer shows that important structural and learning factors are not aligned with management decisions and mindsets. The company has high turnover rates, many non permanent labor contracts, and training isn't a priority. Although no information was available, employee satisfaction is probably affected as is the perceived organizational justice. This is a clear example of dissociation between management, which pushes to create sharing knowledge mindsets in the company, and the reality of the human resources practices that are unable to sustain the conditions to support the emergence of a learning culture. In order to implement efficient KM practices some structural changes seem necessary. In this company, the human resource strategies aren't entirely aligned with the observed management actions and values. This being said, the company still has a dominant market share as it distributes renowned sodas (although the brand owner could decide not to renew the distribution agreement with his Colombian partner). The measured IKMI was of .71

Case 3 (food industry)

The company is one of Peru's giant in the food industry (more than 500 employees). The company presents a traditional business management approach focused on a hierarchical top-down management style. At the "learning and growth" layer the company is concerned by the labor conditions of the employees as permanent labor contracts seem to be the norm and the manager who was surveyed reported a low turnover rate. It is not known whether globally employees experiment job satisfaction but the company shows little concern in training, learning and growth aspects. Moreover, no talent retention program exists. The "business processes" layer shows a management style not apparently concerned in asking employees to participate in the improvement of business processes and products innovation. No explicit sharing knowledge methodologies, values, or mindsets were reported. This hierarchical configuration in the management style constrains the organization's openness and its shift toward a KM culture. External factors as industry type might contribute to this business profile. The measured IKMI was of .14

7. Conclusions

Despite the important limitations of the sample (in size and unequal distribution per country) and the explorative nature of this research, the above results contribute in four ways to the understanding of KM practices in South American organizations and in particular the factors that favor or constrain these practices.

7.1 A global approach

First of all, the present work compiles new data on KM from six South American countries, a region where information and publications are scattered and very sparse. To our knowledge it is the first statistical based research that attempts an integrative approach of KM practices in South American organizations from Andean countries, in addition to Argentina and Chile, settling a reference for further research. Certainly future research on this topic will need larger and more balanced samples and clearly establish what is meant by cultural and other possible differences between the countries. As a matter of fact, to what extent are KM practices modeled by differences existing between South American countries? We believe that the foremost differences between countries do not rely on organizational processes determined by cultural specificities but rather on differences based upon organizations' structural basis (e.g., types of labor contract and working conditions of employees) some of which are imposed by labor and employment Law background that are specific to each country (Baker & McKenzie, 2008). Regarding the diversity in management practices many culture specific research have been done (e.g., Gerhart and Fang, 2005) but it is also true that many multinationals tend to favor their own management culture over the country´s specificities.

7.2 Stability in KM practices in South America

A second contribution was to empirically replicate some results on KM practices in Colombia and Peru reported by Baquero and Schulte (2007) and Matzkin (2008). Four years after their research were published, the present results show that explicit KM practices remain sparse in South American organizations and are limited to big organizations; despite the genuine interest proclaimed by many managers over this matter. Budget reasons are chiefly put forward by managers to explain why KM programs don't take off in the region (Baquero and Schulte, 2007; Leclic, 2002) Perhaps a fundamental reason is that knowledge and innovation aren't in South America important factors of production contrary to what happens in Europe, North America, and is some Asian regions (see Tome, 2011 for an European insight on this subject). In addition to this, external factors such as industry type as other business regulations probably shape the KM practices that are observed (Byounggu and Heeseok, 2003). In relation with the use of technology a majority of organizations whether they are small or big have an intranet and are familiar with e-learning practices. According to the industry type some organizations use sophisticate databases and information management systems. Results we report regarding the use of information technology are slightly higher than those reported at the time by Baquero and Schulte (2007).

Considering overall results, in the past years possibly knowledge sharing mindsets have increased and spread throughout South American organizations though explicit KM practices didn't seem to have evolved in a significant way. Nonetheless moderate levels of implicit knowledge management practices were observed. According to results the levels of practices were marginally higher in bigger organizations. A majority of organizations - but not all, widely use modern management styles that imply some knowledge sharing methodologies (e.g., quality circles, bottom-up communication channels, performance indicators, flat structures, etc.). As shown in the business case N°2, KM practices are much less effective (i.e., not converted into actionable knowledge) if they are not supported by the appropriate management of the human resource (i.e., recruitment, talent retention, labor contracts, etc.). Actual KM practices in South American organizations reflect that most organizations have little awareness (or concern) in seeing and/or seeking the relation between KM and organizational strategy development. We believe an integrative approach in research is necessary in order to obtain a global picture on KM practices in South American organizations. To this global approach, inquiring at a business level is a complementary source of knowledge.

7.3 KM guideline: A diagnosis method

The third and fourth contributions of this research to KM understanding in South American organizations rest upon the proposal of a KM guideline inspired on a balanced scorecard. This guideline is supported by the theoretical framework presented above and puts emphasis on the structural, core management practices, and values that favor or constrain the emergence of knowledge sharing mindsets inside organizations. The three business cases showed that the guideline resulted being a pertinent global diagnosis methodology that can be used to understand KM practices in the organization. Integrated to the guideline, the IKMI composite score gave a general quantification of the organizations implicit KM practices. As a complementary analysis, next step should consider specific quantifiable goals to reach for each of the model's box. Future empirical data on KM practices could generate positive changes to this guideline in its actual form. Furthermore, the implicit knowledge management index should be improved.

7.4 Future research directions

A key issue that was not addressed in this work related to investigate who inside organizations has the responsibility of KM programs, practices, and budget? This information could enlighten the dynamics of the emergence of knowledge sharing mindsets within organizations. Similarly, this line of research could also give more input on the constraints that exist behind the development of KM practices. Complementary to KM, future research could benefit from the study of "organizational unlearning" processes (see Fernandez et al., 2011; Becker, 2005; Holan et al. 2004). Empirical research on this subject could probably generate more hypotheses on the reasons why many South American organizations fail to implement sustainable KM cultures. Finally from a pragmatic perspective, upcoming research will have to dissert and be able to quantify the benefits that KM practices effectively bring to South American organizations; not only on a profit basis but also on employees satisfaction and well being. For this reason comparative research on KM practices that would contrast different regions of the world will undoubtedly generate promising expectations vis-à-vis our global understanding of KM.

8. References

Abdul Hamid, J.; Sulaiman, S. (2011) The effect of personal motivation and organizational support on knowledge sharing behavior of teaching professionals. (Ed.) Huei-Tse Hou, *Knowledge Management*/Book 2 ISBN 979-953-307-571-5

Adams, J.S. (1963) Toward an understanding of inequity. *Journal of abnormal and social psychology*, 67. Pp 422-436

Athanassiou, N.; Crittenden, W.F.; Kelly, L.M. & Marquez, P. (2002) Founder centrality effects on the Mexican family firm's top management group: Firm culture, strategic vision and goals, and firm performance", *Journal of World Business*, Vol.37, N°. 2, pp.139-150

Andriessen, D., G.(2008) Stuff or love? How metaphors direct our efforts to manage knowledge in organizations. *Knowledge Management Research & Practice* 6, 5–12

Baker & McKenzie (2008) Overview of Labor and Employment Law in Latin America" (2008). *Law Firms.* Paper 48

Baquero, T. Schulte, W. (2007). An exploration of knowledge management practices in Colombia. *The journal of information and knowledge management systems* Vol. 37 No. 3, 2007 pp. 368-386

Becker, K. (2005) Individual and organizational unlearning: direction for future research. *International Journal of Organisational Behaviour*, Volume 9(7), 659-670

Berrelleza, M; Matzkin, D (2009) Las cuatro variables a tener en cuenta para administrar con eficacia y de ma-nera sostenible el capital humano de una organización, en un enfoque aplicable a la industria de la construcción. *Inter Managers* Vol.5 N°1, Lima.

Bies, R. J., Moag, J. F. (1986). Interactional justice: Communication criteria of fairness. In R.J. Lewicki, B. H. Sheppard, & M. H. Bazerman (Eds.), *Research on negotiations in organizations* (Vol. 1, pp. 43–55).Greenwich, CT: JAI Press

Bose, S.; Thomas, K. (2007) Applying the balanced scorecard for better performance of intellectual capital. *Journal of Intellectual Capital* 8. 4 : 653-665.

Bouthillier,F.;Shearer, K. (2002) "Understanding knowledge management and information management: the need for an empirical perspective". *Information Research*, Vol. 8 N°. 1, October 2002

Byounggu, C.; Heeseok, L. (2003) An empirical investigation of KM styles and their effect on corporate performance. *Information & Management* 4, 403–417

De Long, D.W.; Fahey, L. (2000) Diagnosing cultural barriers to knowledge management. *Academy of Management Executive* 14(4), 113–127.

Eriksen, B., H. (2010) Organizational learning and employee turnover. Paper presenter at the DRUID 2010 summer conference June 15 - 18, 2010

Fernandez, V.; Enache, M.; Simo, P.; Sallan, J.M. (2011): Organizational forgetting/ unlearning: The dark side of the absorptive capacity (Ed.) Huei-Tse Hou, *Knowledge Management*/Book 2 ISBN 979-953-307-571-5

Ferreira, S. Neto, M. (2005) "Knowledge Management and social learning: exploring the cognitive dimension of development". *Km4dev* Vol. 1 N°3, pp. 4-17

Gelade, G.A. (2003). The impact of human resource management and work climate on organizational performance. *Personnel Psychology, 56*, 383-405

Gerhart, B. & Fang, M. (2005). National culture and human resource management: Assumptions and evidence. *International Journal of Human Resource Management*, 16, 971-986.

Gorey, R. M.; Dobat, D. R., (1996), "Managing in the knowledge era". *The Systems Thinker*, Vol. 7, N°. 8, pp. 1-5.

Holan, M; Phillips, N.; Lawrence, T.B. (2004) Managing organizational forgetting. *MIT Sloan Management Review*. Vol. 45 N° 3, pp 45-51

Kalpic, B.; Bernus, P. (2006) "Business process modeling through the knowledge management perspective". *Journal of Knowledge Management*, Vol. 10 N°. 3, pp. 40-56

Kaplan, R.S.; Norton, D.P. (1993). "Putting the balanced scorecard to work". *Harvard Business Review*, September-October, Vol. 71, N° 5, pp. 134-147

Ko, Dong-Gil; Kirsch, Laurie J.; and King, William R.. 2005. "Antecedents of Knowledge Transfer from Consultants to Clients in Enterprise System Implementations," *MIS Quarterly*, (29: 1)

Leclic, S. (2002): Country focus: Argentina. *Inside knowledge*. Volume 6 issue 4. http://www.ikmagazine.com/xq/asp/sid.0/articleid.151D501A-2599-49EF-A826-0BC787851415/eTitle.Country_focus_Argentina/qx/display.htm

Leventhal, G. S. (1976). The distribution of rewards and resources in groups and organizations. In L. Berkowitz & W. Walster (Eds.), *Advances in experimental social psychology* (Vol. 9, pp. 91–131). New York: Academic Press.

Maier, R.; Hädrich, T. (2006) "Centralized Versus Peer-to-Peer Knowledge Management Systems". *Knowledge and Process Management* Vol. 13 N° 1 pp. 47–61

Matzkin, D.S. (2008) "Knowledge management in the Peruvian non-profit sector", *Journal of Knowledge Management*, Vol. 12 (4) pp.147 - 159

Michel, C.; Heim, E., Herweg,K., Breu, T. (2010)Exploring the effectiveness of development research with a monitoring and learning approach. *Knowledge Management for Development Journal* Vol. 6, No. 2, 105–119

Newell, S.; Huang, J.; Tansley, C. (2006) ERP Implementation: A Knowledge Integration Challenge for the Project Team. *Knowledge and Process Management* Volume 13 Number 4 pp 227–238

Roos, J., Roos, G., Dragonetti, N.C. and Edvinsson, L. (1997), *Intellectual Capital: Navigating the New Business Landscape*. Macmillan Press, London

Ryan, A. M., Schmit, M. J., & Johnson, R. (1996). Attitudes and effectiveness: Examining relations at an organizational level. *Personnel Psychology, 49*, 853-882

Salojärvi, S.; Furu, P.; Sveiby, K.E. (2005) "Knowledge management and growth in Finnish SMEs". Journal *of Knowledge Management*, Vol. 9 N°. 2, pp. 103-122

Senge, P. (2006) *The Fifth Discipline: Strategies and Tools for Building a Learning Organization*. Doubleday/Currency. ISBN 0385517254, 9780385517256

Smith, H.; McKeen, J.; Satyendra, S (2010) Creating the KM mindset: why is it so difficult? *Knowledge Management Research & Practice* . (8), 112–120

Spreitzer, G.M., Kizilos, M.A., & Nason, S.W. (1997). A dimensional analysis of the relationship between psychological empowerment and effectiveness, satisfaction, and strain. *Journal of Management, 25*, 679-704

Toledano O´Farrill, R. (2011): Tacit knowledge in organisations: a socio-constructivist approach to its effective use and appropriation. Ed.) Huei-Tse Hou. Knowledge Management/Book 2 ISBN 979-953-307-571-5

Tome, E. (2011) Knowledge Management: An European Perspective. (Ed.) Huei-Tse Hou, *Knowledge Management*/Book 2 ISBN 979-953-307-571-5

UNDP (2010) International Human Development Indicators http://hdr.undp.org/en/data/profiles/

World Bank statistics for Latin America and Caribbean region (2010) http://data.worldbank.org/region/LAC

Zhu, Valerie.; Sun, Linyan (2010) the Interactive relationship between corporate cultures, leadership Style and knowledge Management. *International Journal of Asian Business and Information Management*, 1(3), 54-68, July-September 2010

7

Learning from Corporate Memory and Best Practices

Nada Matta and Oswaldo Castillo Navetty
Charles Delaunay Institute, Tech-CICO Team, University of Technology of Troyes, Troyes France

1. Introduction

Knowledge management is currently defined as a process of identification, formalization, disseminating and use of knowledge in order to promote creativity and innovation in companies (Grundstein, 2000). This process (Fig. 1) takes into account the transformation and the evolution of tacit to explicit knowledge (Nonaka & Takeushi, 1995) and of individual to collective knowledge.

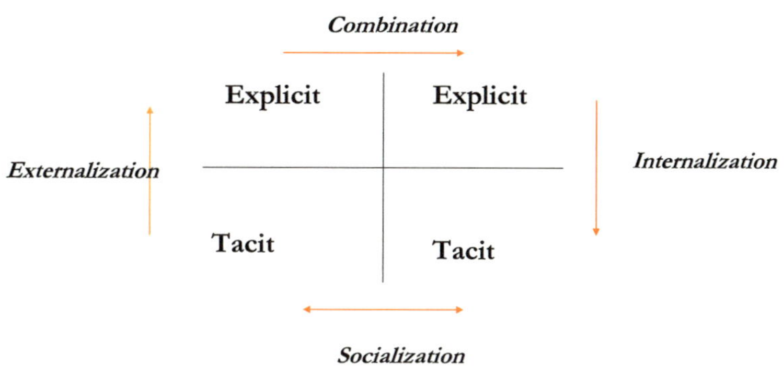

Fig. 1. Knowledge Management (Nonaka & Takeushi, 1995).

Knowledge Engineering (Charlet, 2003), (Aussenac-Gilles et al, 1996) offers a rational framework allowing a representation of knowledge obtained through the experiments (Matta, Zaher, 2008). This technique found a great application in knowledge management and especially to capitalize knowledge (Dieng & Matta, 2002). In fact, the rational representation of knowledge allows their exploitation and their re-use. It is a necessary condition to allow a re-use and a knowledge appropriation. Behaviour laws provide strong semantics to observe as well as an argumentation of this behaviour, ready to be reproduced to solve new problems (Newell, 1982). These techniques provide semantic representation of knowledge that can answer to main objective of knowledge management: knowledge externalization and internalization (Nonaka & Takeushi, 1995). For that, some knowledge management approaches aim at making explicit the problem solving process in an organization. Their techniques are inherited mainly from knowledge engineering. So, we find in these approaches in one hand, models representing tasks, manipulated concepts and

problem solving strategies, and in the other hand, methods to extract and model knowledge. We note for instance MASK (Ermine, 2002), (Dieng et al, 2001) and REX (Malvache & Prieur, 1993) methods. These methods are used mainly to extract expertise knowledge and allow defining corporate memories.
A corporate memory is defined as the « explicit and persistent representation of the knowledge and the information in an organization » (Van Heijst et al, 1997). We can distinguish several types of memories: profession memory, project memory and organization memory. The sharing and the appropriation of the corporate memories are still real blocking points within organizations. The methods of knowledge management are not sufficient to allow an effective appropriation of the knowledge by the actors of the company. However, the objective of knowledge capitalization is indeed sharing and re-use of an experience with the aim of optimizing the process of organizational learning.
Sharing documents, information and experiment without structuring of these information and feed-back analysis as used currently on social network (Wenger, 1998) as support of knowledge sharing, is not sufficient to enhance learning. In fact, the "how" is shared but not the "what". Behaviour laws provide strong semantics to emphasize reason of this behaviour. To enhance learning in an organization, the representation of knowledge has to emphasize the know-what and know-how (Easterby-Smith & Lyles, 2007). In fact, to enhance learning from organization, it is necessary to emphasize when and how activities and especially what and why these activities (Colin & Spender, 1998).
An experiment is done to enhance learning from experience. In fact, we use CSAO (Castillo & Matta, 2005), an approach that combine knowledge engineering and pedagogical techniques and we define a course that push engineering school students to learn knowledge capitalization methods. These students are not familiar to knowledge engineering techniques but they know software engineering approaches (modelling and development).
CSAO approach (Fig. 2) pushes from one side, (by using knowledge engineering techniques) to structure expertise in order to emphasize the process of the activity, the goals and steps done by expert for each activity and concepts manipulated in each step. From another side, it proposes (based on pedagogical principles) to define practical exercises, guided by a framework that help learners to auto-evaluate their progress. CSAO are developed at the beginning to help in knitting learning CSAO (Castillo & Matta, 2005).
The result of our experience is very fruitful, students are able, after succeeded this course to model knowledge in companies. Reports results are more complete and detailed than when they are assisted by a teacher.
We present in this chapter the principle base of the CSAO, by summarizing knowledge engineering techniques and pedagogical bases. Then we present the experience: conditions, process, guides and results. A discussion concludes the chapter by analyzing the relation between these techniques and social network.

2. Appropriation of a profession memory

One of the main motivations for building a memory in a company is the improvement of employees' learning. This learning can be at an individual, group or organizational level (Dieng et al, 2001). By looking at our preliminary experiences of defining a profession memory (explicit representation of an activity in a specific domain (Castillo & Matta, 2005), and more specifically at the learning from such memories, we noticed that the learning from a profession memory is not easy. These memories are generally presented under several points of view (classifications, constraints, processes, problem solving strategies, etc.). The links between these views are put in background because the knowledge formalization shows the nature of the knowledge. Learning and following the learning progress in such a memory can be easy for a knowledge engineer but it is complex for an organization's actor who is specialist on his profession and who wants to learn a know-how formalized by an expert in his domain.

To facilitate the learning from a profession memory, we adapted techniques from educational engineering by modifying the way of building the profession memory, and especially, by showing this memory, to organization's actors in different ways.

3. Educational engineering

According to Paquette (Paquette, 2002), educational engineering or training engineering has to offer principles, procedures and tasks that allow to:

- Define the contents of a training by means of a structural identification of the knowledge and the recounted,
- Realize an educational scenario of the training activities and to define the context of use and the structure of the learning material,
- Define infrastructures, resources and services necessary for distributing lessons and preserving their quality.

So, educational engineering leans on two processes in the heart of the knowledge management (Paquette, 2002), (Rolland, 2000):

- At first the extraction of the knowledge from domain experts or documents;
- Then the acquisition, by the organization actors, of the knowledge by learning;
- The transformation of the information in knowledge by means of the formal on informal activities taking a variety of forms and supports.

Complete training of an operator contains three phases: learning or intensification of the general knowledge; learning of procedures and typical solutions; and training on simulator in "real situations". This last phase is more recognized for operational learning (Rolland, 2000). During this phase, "the operational competence can be developed, and the expertise level is incremented. The student learns here of how to use knowledge learnt previously quickly, deliberately, in any situation and under any degrees of stress and workload". In her work, Kalina Yacef (Yacef, 2003), found the following conclusions, from structuring of the operational training point of view:

- This one has to be made by the practice, in situation of action;
- This practice must be structured so as to respect the development of levels of expertise following the tasks and to be directed to purposes;
- The competence evolve with the practice, it is necessary to take measures of evaluation based on the result of the actions and not on the reasoning follow-up;
- The acquisition of competence is made on one hand by the automation of certain behavior and on the other hand by the development of capacities to solve new problems.

These studies allow us to develop a learning system (Castillo & Matta, 2005). Our particular interest is the construction of a system based on a profession memory. By taking into account the practical knowledge (problem solving) of the training contents, our system becomes a practical learning system.

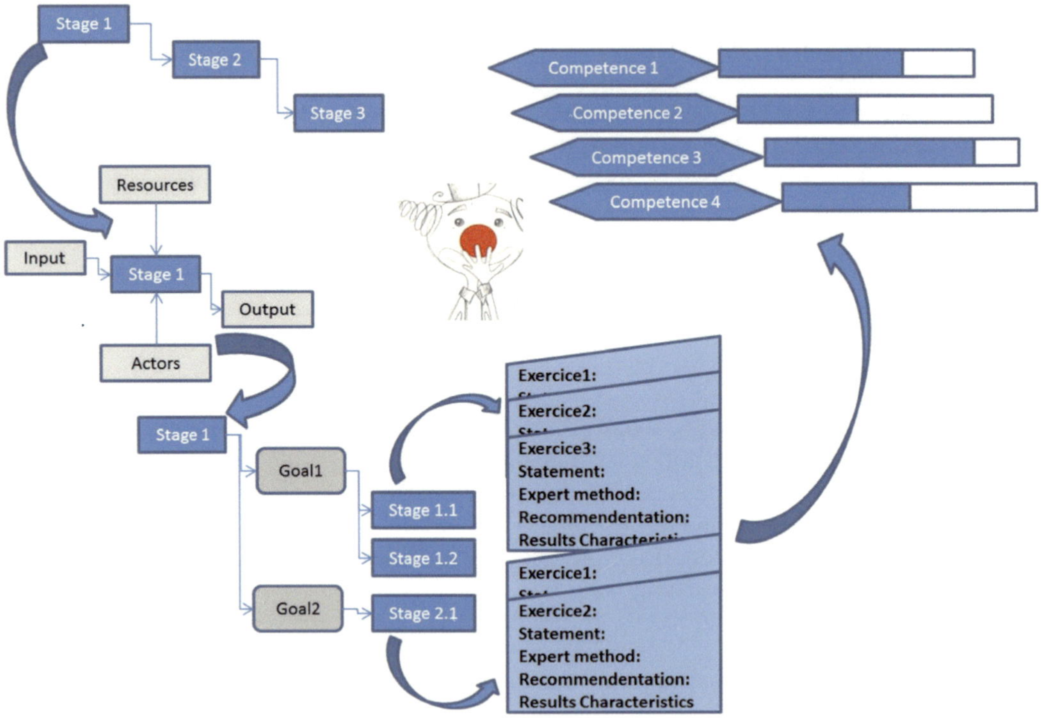

Fig. 2. Progression process illustration of knowledge learning from experience (Castillo & Matta, 2005).

4. CSAO: Proposition of a practical learning system

We thus try to show the difficulties of a domain and how to encounter them. It is for that reason; in our work we feel the need to exploit concepts of knowledge engineering especially the process of knowledge formalization. Indeed, the knowledge engineering techniques allow to emphasis the difficulties of an activity while the educational engineering allows estimating the learning progress levels. We shall base our approaches on the one hand, on some educational engineering evaluation techniques as diagnosis, training approaches and problem solving learning and on the other hand on knowledge engineering techniques to extract and restructure the contents of the training and of the evaluations. The first postulate to be considered is the expert source of the knowledge has to participate as well in the defining of the profession memory as in the definition of some means for knowledge appropriation (Fig. 2).
An activity process is used as a guide of progression of learning. For each stage, is associated Input/output, knowledge type needed to do the step and the role of actors who can do this stage. Then, goals (objectives) and steps are described that show how the expert performs each stage (Fig. 3).
Exercises are also associated to each stage and to all process. A sheet (Fig. 4) guides the learner to do exercises. In each sheet guide, stage objectives, expert problem solving, recommendations and result characteristics are defined by the expert. The learner tries to satisfy the stage objectives. The expert problem solving representation (and especially sub-objectives) guides him in this purpose and show him the goal of techniques used to solve the problem. The recommendations and result characteristics allow learner to evaluate his result.

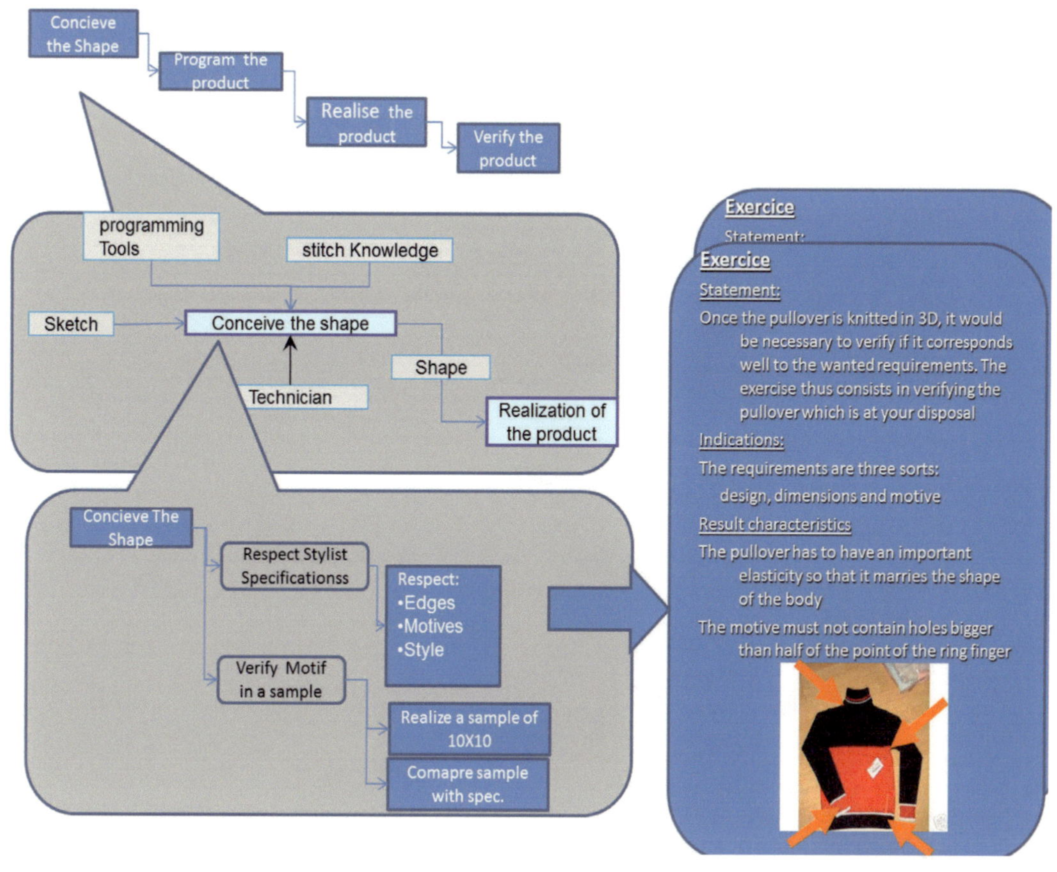

Fig. 3. Organization of the content of expertise (Castillo & Matta, 2005).

5. Experimentation: Application on a course

We use CSAO and especially the guide sheet in order to tackle knowledge engineering learning. In fact, we organize in our university a course on Knowledge Engineering. This course is for software engineering students. They have information about engineering techniques: specification, design, etc, of software and information system. But they do not have any information about knowledge, expertise, knowledge modelling, etc. We also note the difference between Software Engineering method that guides to build a system from an idea, a need and Knowledge Engineering approach that start from an expertise and model it. Even two approaches are belonging to engineering techniques (modelling) but there is a basic difference on the objects and methods used. So, Knowledge Engineering course is new to student and they need practical learning in order to appropriate its techniques, especially that the entire course is only done on 6 months, students do not have time to experiment notions in several applications.

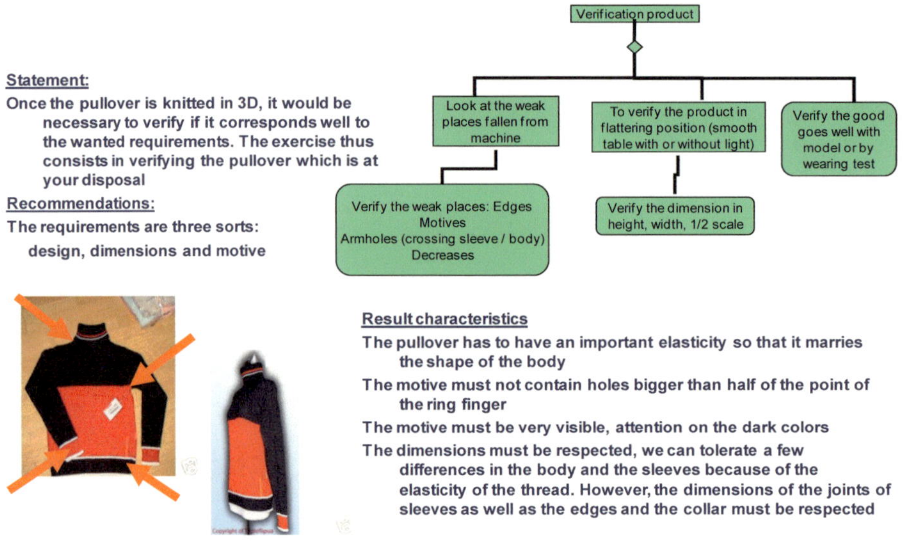

Fig. 4. Exercise sheet guide (Matta, Castillo, 2009).

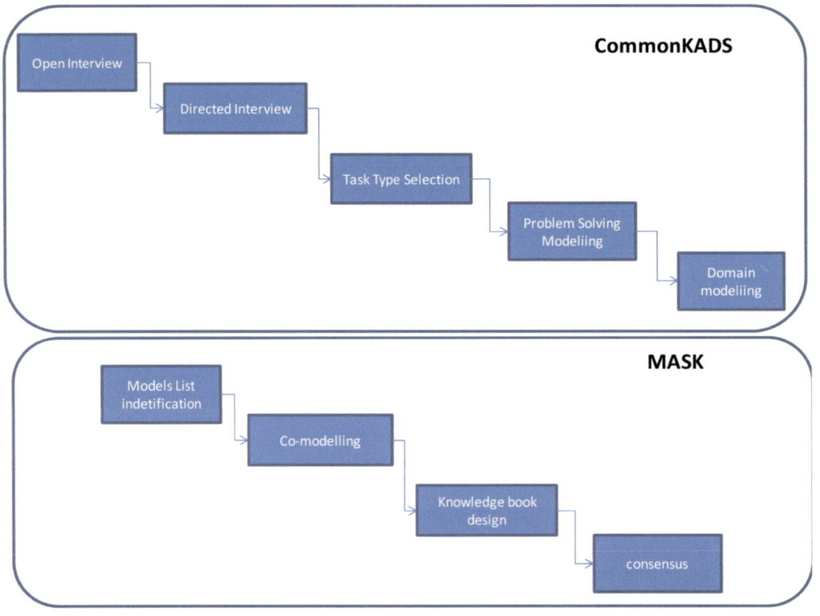

Fig. 5. Projects process: modelling with CommonKADS and with MASK methods.

The course is organized as projects. Students have an access to principles and theory on Knowledge Engineering as reports and recorded courses. These courses are organized as a normal course: Introduction to Knowledge Engineering, Modelling approaches (CommonKADS, etc.), Applications and Implementations (KBS, Knowledge Management, etc.). Students need to apply these techniques in order to learn how to model knowledge. So, two projects are organized for this aim. They have to apply two knowledge engineering approaches CommonKADS (Breuker & Vand de Velde, 1994) and MASK (Ermine, 2002) in real applications. Sheet guides and process are modelled based on an expertise on knowledge engineering applications (12 years on building KBS and knowledge book) (Matta, Castillo, 2009).

5.1 Projects organization

Students are organized on teams. In each team, one student is considered as an expert if he has an expertise (during some years) in an activity (sports, games, etc.). Each team have to produce a report in which the related expertise is modelled using CommonKADS (for the first Project) and using MASK (for the second project). They have 2 months for each project. They follow at first the knowledge engineering process from interview to modelling (Fig. 5). For each phase, they are guided by a sheet guide (Fig. 6) and (Fig. 7). They have to evaluate their intermediate results based on results characteristics defined in sheet guides for each phase. They have also to validate models with the expert. Final results (reports) are then sending to the knowledge engineering expert for final evaluation.

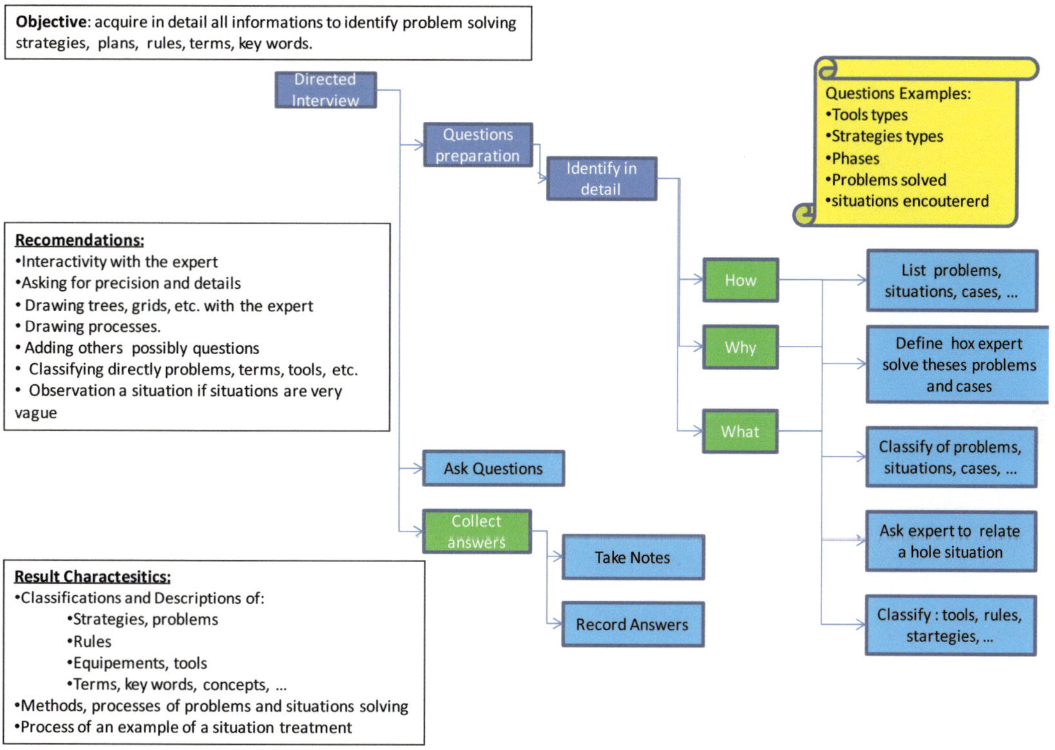

Fig. 6. Sheet Guide for the Phase Directed Interview using CommonKADS method.

5.2 Results

These experiences are done since two years. Each project type has 2 months as delay. Students have to give results as complete reports: models organized as deliverables (Fig. 8): problem solving model (Fig. 9), ontology (Fig. 10)for CommonKADS and a knowledge book with Index, models, comments ... for MASK (Fig. 11).

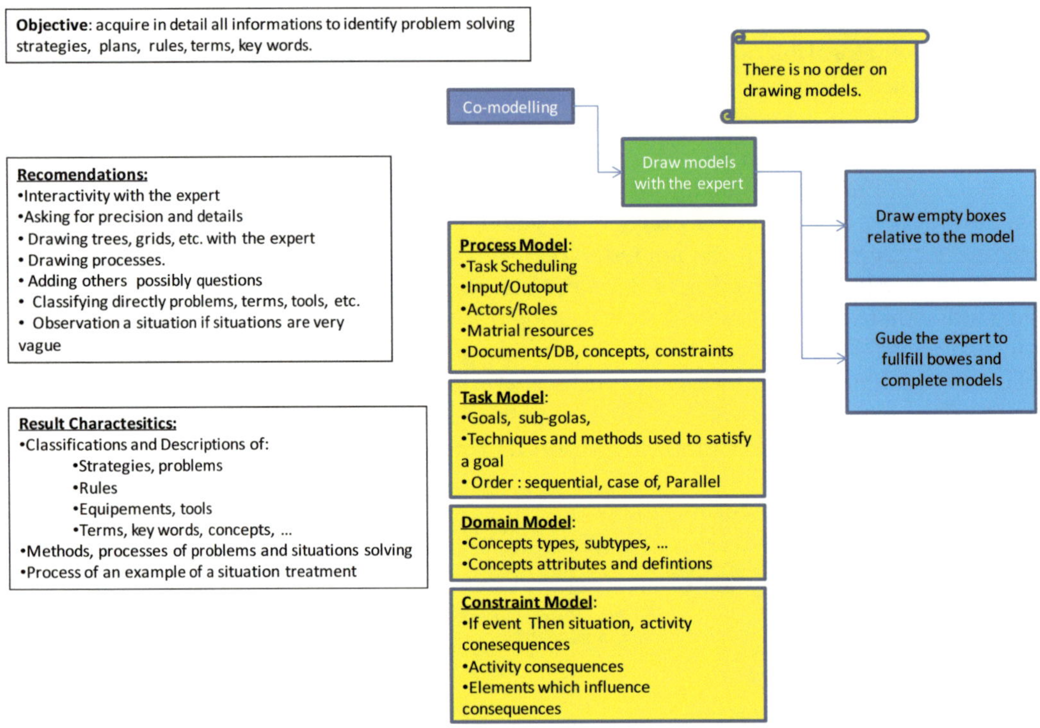

Fig. 7. Sheet Guide for the Phase Co-modelling using MASK method.

Basket Ball Expertise

1. Introduction: Objectives
2. Knowlekdge Acquisition :
    1. Free Interview: Global process model
    2. Directed : Interview :
        1. CLassifications : Ground composition, players types, equipements, attacks strategies, defense strategies, problems, infractions, mistake types
        2. Case models: attack, Screen « Pick & Roll », offensif systme « SHORT », defense activity, playing situation analysis, example of basket game
3. Problem Solving Modelling:
    1. Strategies: defensive, offensive, evaluation, mistake diagnostic, repair
    2. Global Model of problem solving
4. Domain Model:
    1. Types: players, equipements, infrastructures, attack, defense, infraction,s mistakes
    2. Conceptual Graphs: mistakes/infractions, play actions, players equipements
    3. Global Domain model
5. Conclusion

Fig. 8. An example of report Index: modelling of Basket Ball expertise with CommonKADS.

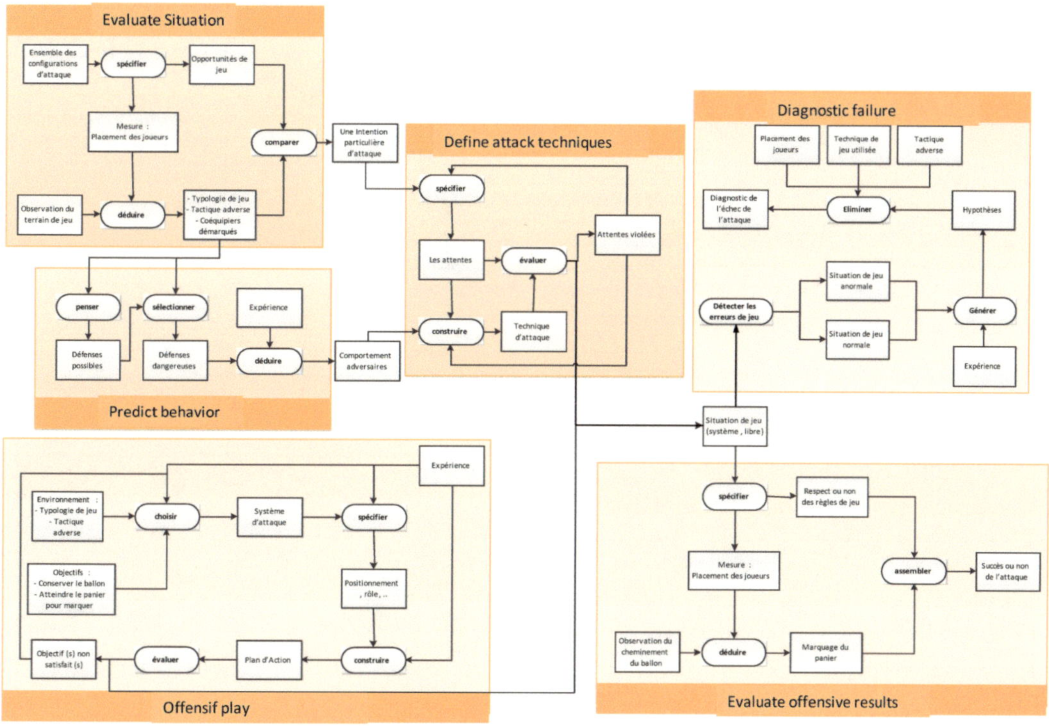

Fig. 9. Example of results (CommonKADS problem Solving model of "basket-ball" expertise).

90% of projects are complete. Students took time to go in details and identify deeply expert's tasks and model them. Their analysis is very good. Models resulted show expert methods and heuristics. They can be used to support learning from studied expertises. In fact, when they are assisted, students model only one case of knowledge. They do not duplicate models. Teacher has to negotiate with them in order to repeat their task and model several examples. When they work by their own selves, they have to satisfy results characteristics specified in sheet guide. So for each type of model, they repeat their task and they model several examples in order to enhance heuristics rules. The "why" and the "what" is emphasized in models. They take time to go deeply and acquire several aspects and not settle for only few aspects of expertise. By repeating their task, learning is in progress. Students go deeper more and more in each modelling task and learn know-how and specially, success key of each task. They can control very well expertise modelling and its complexity.

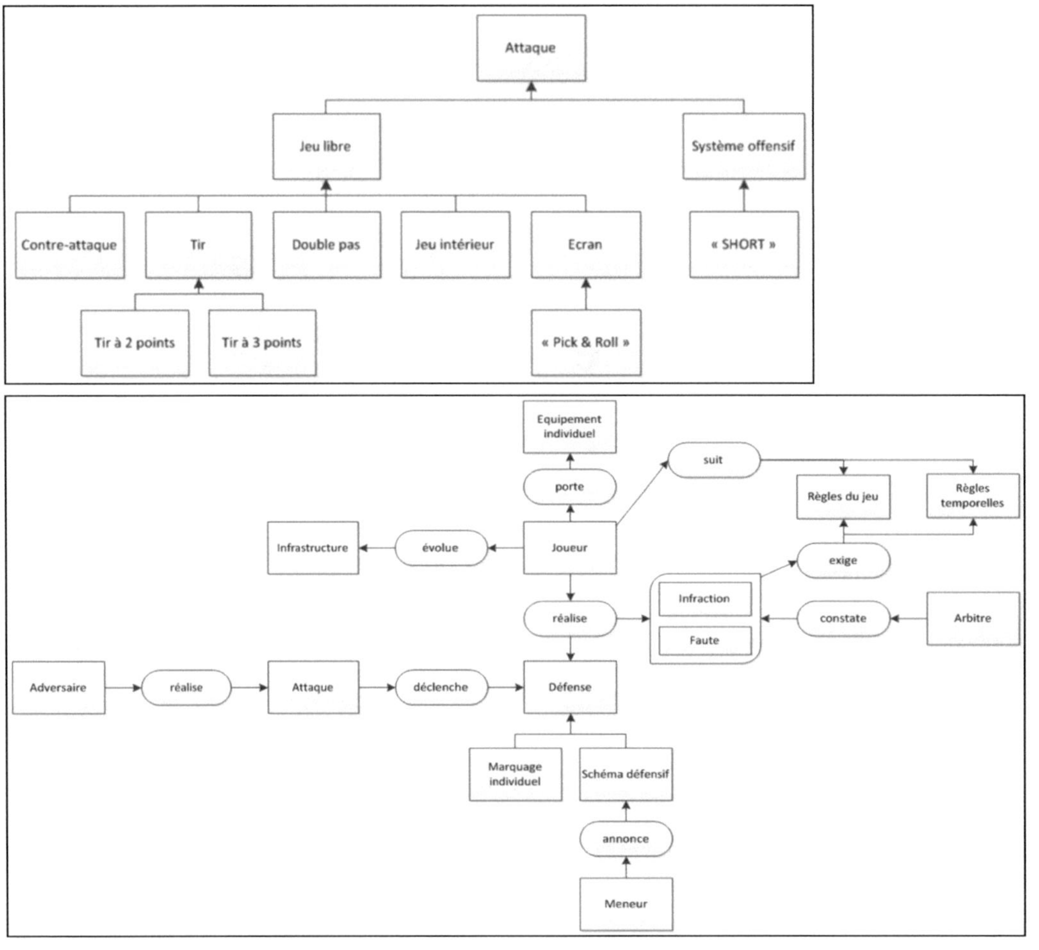

Fig. 10. Example of results (CommonKADS domain model of "basket-ball" expertise).

Each year, an evaluation of the course is done:

- Students appreciate recorded courses but it is not sufficient for them. When they discover these courses, they cannot be able to model expertise. That confirms our idea that only expertise models are not sufficient to enhance learning and internalization. Expert reasoning is at another level than learners. So showing models even with specific guidelines cannot help people to appropriate this knowledge.
- Guidelines sheets are much appreciated and more used than courses. They are guided by these sheets and especially by recommendations and results characteristics. In fact, these elements help them to evaluate their results at each step and to modify them. That is the main reason that the final result was very complete and models are deeply defined.
- Guiding modelling steps by steps make easily the appropriation of the expertise. At the beginning, they are afraid about the complexity of their task: modelling and expertise with its different aspects. But when they followed steps of modelling, they do not feel the complexity. That is a confirmation of the Newell (Newell, 82) theory: complex problem solving has to be decomposed in steps in order to understand it.

- Pushing students to emphasize the "why", and the "what" of the expertises using the "how", is the main reason of the deeply modelling and the success of results.

This course was at the beginning organised as a normal course with a presentation of the theory and assisted projects. The results were not very complete. Students (except some of them) did not go in details and models deeply expertise. We analysed the problem and we identify two main reasons: 1- the difference on reasoning level between the knowledge engineering expert who assist students and students understanding, 2- students do not take time to go deeply and understand knowledge modelling principles. That pushes us to use CSAO in order to enhance learning of knowledge engineering.

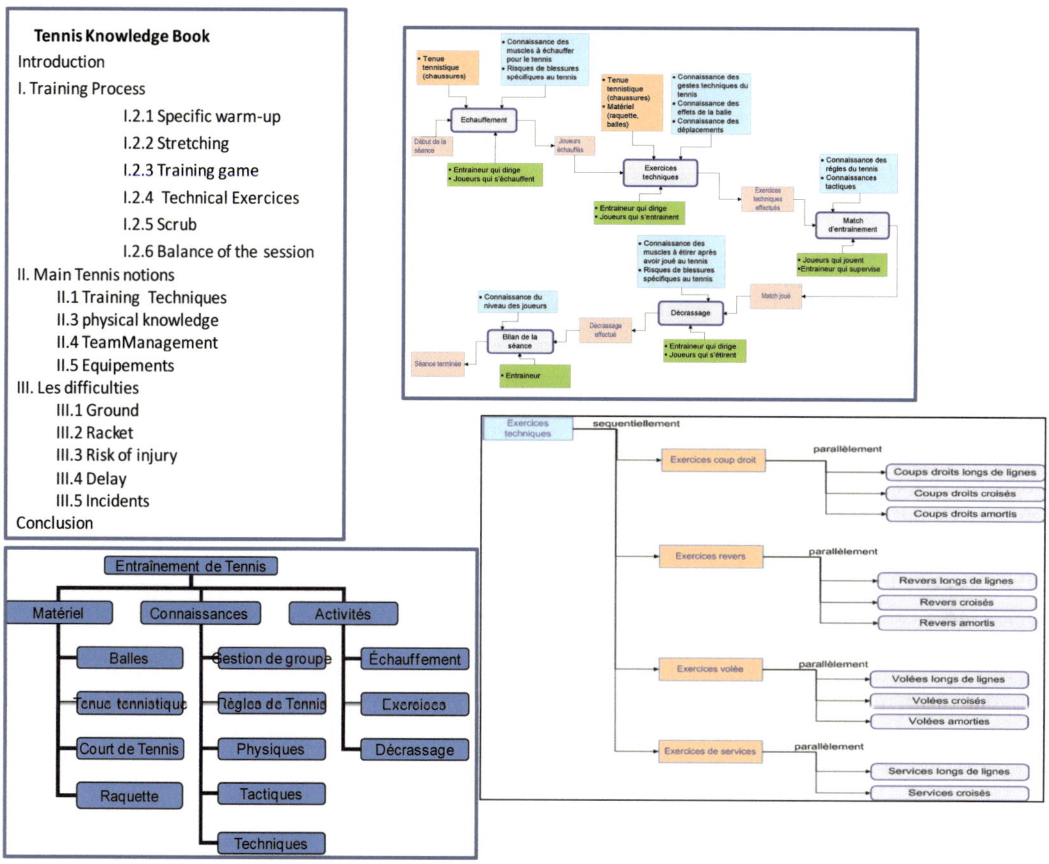

Fig. 11. An example of knowledge Book: Modelling of Tennis expertise with MASK.

6. Conclusion

Knowledge management is a process which enhances as well the knowledge capitalization as the sharing and the appropriation of this knowledge. Several techniques of knowledge capitalization were defined. However, the appropriation of the knowledge remains another subject to be deepened. The phase of appropriation requires a quite particular attention because of its success is going to depend on the efficiency of the organizational learning and thus the performance of the company partially. Otherwise, educational engineering techniques supply devices (teaching equipment, tools of evaluation and process of learning) to assist the appropriation of the knowledge. We studied these techniques to supply a device of appropriation of knowledge formalized in the form of profession memory.

We present in this chapter, an example of the use of the CSAO method to enhance learning of practice knowledge. CSAO is based on two techniques types: knowledge engineering (to structure practice knowledge) and educational engineering (to enhance learning). We show that the use of CSAO is more benefit that a traditional educational techniques, because students are pushed to evaluate their own work and to go deeply on their study and modelling. They have more autonomy and self control on their work that is why their results are more analytic.

We aim at applying CSAO on other type of course: "Enterprise Resources Planning" ... and on professional learning. That helps to complete the approach to tackle other type of evaluation and the progression on learning.

CSAO was defined at the beginning to enhance professional learning in an organization. We plan to apply it in several applications than textile and integrate it in organizational learning tools. For instance, social networks between actors and learners can be a good support to share problems to deal with. At the same time, actors need also several access types to a professional memory as a decision support and not only learning support. They are several techniques studied for this aim (semantic web, CBR, etc.). We study how to integrate these techniques with our learning support CSAO.

Otherwise, professional memory has to be updated and enriched with knowledge emphasizing from new activities. Tagging techniques (Cahier & Zacklad, 2002) have to be integrated with structuring and knowledge representations in order to enhance memory updating.

Other type of knowledge can be produced in cooperative activity. We note specially negotiation, coordination, and organization knowledge. We study how to keep track and represent this type of knowledge in a specific domain: design projects (Matta et al, 2011).

7. References

Aussenac-Gilles, N.; Laublet, P.; Reynaud, C. (1996). Acquisition et Ingénierie des connaissances, Tendances Actuelles, Cepadues Editions, 1996.

Breuker, J.; Van de Velde, W. (1994). *Common-KADS Library for expertise modelling Reusable problem solving components, Frontiers in Artificial Intelligence and Applications*, J. Breuker and W. Van de Velde (EDS), Amsterdam: IOS.Press 1994.

Cahier, J.-P.;Zacklad,M. (2002). Towards a Knowledge-Based Marketplace model (KBM) for cooperation between agents, In Proc. of *COOP'2002* conference, St Raphael, 4-7june 2002, IOS Press.

Castillo, O.; Matta, N. (2005). A practical learning system for the French Textile and Apparel Institute. *GESTS International Transactions on Computer Science*, 1738-6438, December 2005, vol.24, n° 1, p. 8-20.

Colin, E.; Spender J.C. (1998). *Managerial and organizational cognition: Theory Methods and Research*, SAGE, 1998.

Charlet J. (2003). *L'ingénierie des connaissances, Développements, résultats et perspectives pour la gestion des connaissances médicales*, Mémoire d'Habilitation à Diriger des Recherches, université Pierre et Marie Curie, 2003.

Dieng-Kuntz, R. ; Corby, O. ; Gandon, F. ; Giboin, A. ; Golebiowska, J. ; Matta, N. ; Ribière M. (2001). *Méthodes et outils pour la gestion des connaissances*. 2eme edition. Dunod éditeur. 2001.

Dieng-Kuntz, R.; Matta, N. (2002). *Knowledge Management and Organizational Memories*, Kluwer Academic Publishers, 2002.

Easterby-Smith, M.; Lyles, M.A. (2007). Handbook of Organizational Learning and Knowledge Management, Blackwell, 2007.

Ermine J.L. (2002). *La gestion de connaissances*, J.-L. Ermine.- Hermès sciences publications, 2002.

Grundstein M. (2000), From capitalizing on Company Knowledge to Knowledge Management, chapter 12, pp. 261-287, in *Knowledge Management, Classic and Contemporary Works*, Morey D., Maybury M., Thuraisingham B. (Eds), The MIT Press, Cambridge, Massachusetts, 2000.

Malvache, P.; Prieur, P. (1993). Mastering Corporate Experience with the REX Method, Proceedings of ISMICK'93, *International Synopsium on Management of industrial and corporate knowledge*, Compiegne, October, 1993

Matta N.; Zaher L. (2008). Applications of knowledge Engineering for Design, *Methods and Tools for effective Knowledge Life-Cycle Management*, Bernard A., Tichkiewitch S. (Eds), Springer, 2008.

Matta, N.; Castillo, O. (2009). Learning from Profession Knowledge: Application on Knitting, IEEE proceedings of the 5th International Conference on Signal-Image Technology and Internet based Systems, Marakesh, November, 2009.

Matta N.; Ducellier G.; Charlot Y.; Beldjoudi R.; Tribouillas F.; Hibon E. (2011). Traceability of Design Project Knowledge using PLM, In IEEE proceedinds of International Conference on Cooperation Technologies and sciences, Philadelphia, May, 2011.

Nonaka, I.; Takeuchi, H. (1995). *The knowledge-Creating Company: How Japanese Companies Create the Dynamics of Innovation*. Oxford University Press, 1995

Newell A. (1982). The Knowledge level, Artificial Intelligence Journal, 19 (2), 1982.

Paquette, G. (2002). "L'ingénierie pédagogique: pour construire l'apprentissage en réseau", Presses de l'université de Québec, 2002.

Rolland, M. (2000). "Bâtir des formations professionnelles pour adultes", Editions d'Organisations, 2000

Van Heijst, G.; Schreiber, A.; Wielinga, B. (1997). Using Explicit Ontologies in KBS Development. *International Journal of Human Computer Studies*, Vol. 46, 1997.

Wenger, E. (1998). Communities of Practice - Learning as a Social System. *Systems Thinker*, June 1998.

Yacef, K. (2003). "Some thoughts about the synergetic effects of integrating ITS and LMS technologies together to the service of Education". R. Calvo and M. Grandbastien (eds), Proceedings of Towards Intelligent Learning Management Systems, held in conjunction with AIED'03, University of Sydney, Australia, Sydney, 2003.

8

Documents in Knowledge Management Support: A Case Study in a Healthcare Organization

Mauricio B. Almeida and Renato R. Souza
School of Information Science, Federal University of Minas Gerais
School of Applied Mathematics, Getúlio Vargas Foundation, Rio de Janeiro, RJ
Brazil

1. Introduction

Documents are entities of great importance, both in the social context and in the organizational environment. The very ordinariness of the term "document" masks the complexity involved in defining what a document is, and belies their significance in the Knowledge Management scope. This article is intended to focus on the pragmatic dimension to the study of documents with the aim of characterizing them in ontology-based systems. A historical account of the origins of documents is outlined, together with a development of the theory of document acts - a theory which treats of what humans can do with documents. The pragmatic characterization is reached through a template to be followed with the aim of analyzing examples derived from a case of study about medical organizations.

2. Documents in healthcare organizations

Defining Knowledge Management (KM) is no trivial task. The meaning of KM is neither straightforward nor consensual. On the one hand, one can claims that KM is not possible, since knowledge is what the individual knows and involves mental processes, like understanding and learning, which take place in one's mind only. On the other hand, one can consider that KM consists of the set of administrative practices whose objective is to deal with corporate knowledge and which are aimed at providing for business needs. We follow here the latter perspective approaching the knowledge recorded in documents, which are employed in organizational communication processes.

Documents are valuable entities for KM initiatives, once they are pervasive entities in the everyday life, in different sorts of organizations, acting as endpoints of information flows. A wide variety of documents is used in a multitude of fields of human activity, which makes complex the task of seeking systematic approaches to characterize them. In seeking an introductory understanding of the role of documents in KM, we present a fragment of text extracted from a medical standard[1], which illustrates the multiplicity of documents required to carry out an ordinary activity in healthcare organizations:

---

[1] Adapted from HL7 version 3 Standard: Blood, Tissue, Organ; Donation, Release 1, Committee Ballot 2. Retrieved August 22, 2010, from http://www.hl7.org/

"Eve Everywoman arrives at a blood bank collection center and fills out the donor questionnaire including common identifying information: name, gender, etc. Additional information is collected, such as: blood type, recent surgeries, recent illnesses, diagnosed diseases, etc.
Horace Helper verifies that Eve is a new donor and registers her as a candidate in the blood bank system. Nancy Nurse evaluates Eve's donor questionnaire answers and determines that Eve does meet the initial eligibility requirements for blood donation.
At this time, a unique Donation Identification number is assigned, which will distinguish Eve's blood samples and blood products from this donation event throughout the entire process. This blood donation ID has been established as mandatory by International Regulations. Then, Nancy Nurse enters a new blood donation order into the blood bank system.
Nancy Nurse asks Eve to read a blood donation consent form, which informs about the possibilities of adverse events which can follow a donation. Nancy Nurse draws a sample of blood from Eve, which is taken to the blood bank laboratory for hematological tests.
Dr. Boris Bleeder uses the blood bank system to query the lab system for the results of the lab test done on the blood samples. He evaluates the lab results, determines that Eve meets all donation requirements, and asks her to sign the consent letter to continue the donation process.
Nancy Nurse positions Eve and performs the activities associated with the blood donation itself. Nancy Nurse enters all the donation event information into the blood bank system and delivers the labeled and identified whole blood bag to the Blood Bank Laboratory for further testing, analysis and manufacturing."

The text above describes an everyday situation in which a person wanting to donate blood triggers certain procedures in a healthcare organization, more specifically in a blood bank. Throughout the whole process, data are employed to fulfill forms, reports and labels. Further, data are recorded in information systems (e.g. the *blood bank system*) and in documents (e.g. the *donor questionnaire*). From a practical point of view, it is to such recording function that documents primarily serve. Some documents, though, are bearers of additional properties and not merely record data. This is already true for simple documents aforementioned, for example the donor questionnaire, in which a donor sign thus testifying the validity of the information therein provided. Those documents reveal other aspects, insofar as they give rise to new sorts of commitments. Through a document, one can create obligations to others, as in the case of a *blood donation order*; acquit an institution of legal problems, as in the case of a *consent letter*; induce the adoption of certain procedures, as in "[...] *established as mandatory by International Regulations*". Hence, documents exhibit a variety of ethical and legal powers, playing an essential role in many human interactions within organizations.

In this chapter, we argue that KM in healthcare organizations can take advantage of an appropriate characterization of documents according to pragmatic aspects. In order to explore the significance of documents as organizational agents, we build upon the *document acts* approach. Document acts, roughly, concern to *what humans do with documents* in their interpersonal activities into organizations: from signing or stamping them, to depositing them in registries, to using them to grant or withhold permission, and to establish or verify identity (Smith, 2010).

In what follows we outline the importance of such document acts in the organizational environment, seeking to shed new light on two main issues: i) how to reach a pragmatic characterization for documents regarding the effects they cause in the organizational routine; ii) how to identify the role of documents in organizations according to the pragmatic approach. As the main contribution, we develop such template grounded on well-founded theories, providing to the KM practitioner a tool to formally distinguish documents. The investigation takes place within the scope of a KM project underway in a medical organization specialized in hematology and blood transfusion (Almeida et al, 2010). The chapter is organized as follows: following a brief historical account of the origins of document, we describe theories to manage the complex phenomena arising from the usage of documents into everyday life and, eventually, in the organizational environment. After emphasizing the relevance of documents as economic entities, we present a case study in which we provide a template for characterization of documents in a medical institution. Thus, we explain the rationale underlying the template and provide examples of its use in real situations. Finally, we discuss findings and present our conclusions, as well as perspectives for future work.

3. Documents as social and economic entities

In this section we advance the theories capable of enabling a more comprehensive view of the phenomena that take place in organizations from the usage of documents. First, we bring a historical overview about what a document is. We explain documents as social entities, and so as economic entities, seeking a better understanding of the document role in organizational scenarios.

3.1 Prior approaches to define documents: A brief historical account

The Greek word associated with the term *document* is the verb *δοκεῖν*, whose sense is most closely conveyed by the English verbs "to show", "to represent", and "to prove". The Latin term *docere*, "to educate", was derived from this Greek root, with the senses of "explaining something through a narrative" and "proving a fact or a conclusion through logical argumentation". *Docere*, in turn, gave rise to the Latin term *documentum*. The present-day term *document* keeps the sense of "instruction regarding an action with the aim of confirming a fact" (Fernandez & Arroyo, 1982). Taken literally, a document is a kind of example, instance or warning that teaches us something. With this slant, the term document also acquires a deontic-normative connotation, that is, denotes something concerning duties or obligations.

During the nineteenth century, a field of study called *documentation theory* emerged in the face of the rapid increase in the number of scientific publications. This increase was due to the appearance of periodicals in addition to books, as well as of technological fields in addition to natural sciences. Hence, the necessity arose for the continuous publication of articles in periodicals, as scientists had to be kept informed of the latest research; and with this came the need for the analysis of such publications. This analysis came to be known as *documentation*, a word that replaced *bibliography* to nominate the field concerned with the management of documents. The pioneers of this field were Paul Otlet[2] and Suzanne Briet.[3]

A document is also extensively studied in the archival field. *Archival documents* are created or received by a physical or juridical person, that is, a person or a group of persons having the right to act in a legal capacity, in the course of a practical activity to accomplish specific purposes. The primary purpose of archival documents is to serve legal and evidentiary roles in public and private organizations. Their secondary goal is make possible historical and cultural investigation.

---

[2] Paul Marie Ghislain Otlet, Belgian documentalist, 1868 - 1944

[3] Renée-Marie-Hélène-Suzanne Briet, French librarian and historian, 1894 - 1989

Nowadays, a document is defined as: "a written or printed paper that bears the original, official, or legal form of something and can be used to furnish evidence or information" (American Heritage Dictionary, 2000). Such a definition leaves some questions unanswered when applied to documents of the sorts which we have to deal with in current organizations. Schamber (1996), for example, points to questions that arise in the context of the emergent technologies of the late twentieth century: Do linked portions of documents constitute a single document? Does a thread of email messages, or a set of records in a database, constitute a single document? Who owns the intellectual rights to the contents of a set of documents created through collaboration?

It is beyond this chapter goals to discuss the full extent of the complexity of the aforementioned fields of study. Some useful references one might consult to know more about this matter are Buckland (1997) and Schellenberg, (1956).

3.2 Documents as social entities

In this section we advance the theories capable of enabling a more comprehensive view of the phenomena that take place in organizations from the usage of documents. Thus, we first explain how very ordinary obligations are created from the use of human speech through the framework of the speech acts theory. Then we present a unifying view called *document acts*, which creates a bridge between speech acts and documents.

3.2.1 How obligations are created

Since Aristotle, the study of language had been viewed as pertaining only to uses of a language of the statement-making sort. The discovery of speech acts in the 20th century matches the recognition that we can use language to do other things beyond merely describing reality. Thomas Reid[4] and Adolf Reinach[5] are recognizes as responsible by the initial efforts to advance in a theory which explains other uses of language (Smith, 2003).

Reid employed the expression *social acts* to explain uses of language - such as giving promises, issuing warnings, granting forgiveness and so forth - that must be directed to other people. Reinach, in turn, developed a systematic theory of the performative uses of language - that is, the uses which are performances of acts of certain kinds - with emphasis on the act of promising applied to the analysis of legal phenomena (Mulligan, 1987). However, Reinach´s theories remained without influence and the main developments of speech act theory, as we know it nowadays, were first set out by Austin.[6]

Austin realized that some sentences do not describe anything in the world at all, that is, they are neither true nor false. Instead, they seem to enable something to get done, that is, they are performances of acts of certain kinds (Austin, 1962). These sentences are named *performatives*, by contrast with sentences in which something true or false is being stated, which are called *constantives*. The speech acts theory establishes that, in any ordinary language, a speaker performs acts of three different kinds: *locutionary acts*, in which, more than merely uttering sounds, one is speaking the words with the meaning they really have; *illocutionary acts*, in which one is using the words in order to ask a question, give an order, make a promise, and so forth; and *perlocutionary acts*, used so that one can draw someone's attention to something, or to convince someone to do something.

[4] Thomas Reid, Scottish philosopher, 1710 - 1796
[5] Adolf Bernhard Philipp Reinach, German philosopher, 1883 - 1917
[6] John Langshaw Austin, British philosopher of language, 1911 - 1960

Morris (2005) explains that the most important language features depend on the illocutionary acts being performed, rather than on the meaning of words and sentences. Examples of the effectiveness of speech acts are obligations and claims to which promises and orders give rise and the behavior which certain speech acts are intended to bring about. Austin's general speech acts theory was consolidated into a theoretical framework due to Searle[7], in which the dimensions of utterance, meaning and action could be seen as being unified together. The key aspects of Searle's framework are *constitutives rules, institutions* and *collective intentionality* (Smith, 2003).

Searle (1985) makes a distinction between *regulative rules* and *constitutive rules*. The former merely regulate existing forms of behavior, but the latter, in addition to regulate, also create new forms of behavior. Thus, a constitutive rule has the form *x counts as having status y in a context c*, where the y term marks something that has consequences in the form of rewards, penalties, or actions that one is obliged to perform in the future. Constitutive rules made possible, for example, games like chess, football or basketball. Speech acts are performed by uttering expressions in accordance with certain constitutive rules.

The constitutive rules themselves rarely occur alone, but within the scope of a certain rules system. The *institutional facts* are the facts whose existence presupposes the existence of certain systems of constitutive rules called *institutions*. When a speech act is performed, certain institutional facts are created because one treats the world in certain cognitive ways, within certain contexts. There could be *observer-independent features*, such as force, mass, and gravitational attraction; and *observer-relative features*, which could include money, property, marriage, and government. The latter are examples of institutions in Searle's parlance, that is, they are systems of constitutive rules.

The constitutive rules also allow knowing how an utterance can give rise to an obligation for one who makes a promise, insofar as a promise affects people's behavior. Where such rules exist, one can perform certain specified activities and in virtue of that behavior, be interpreted in terms of certain institutional concepts. In principle, this approach had an individualist character; but it could be generalized through the so-called *collective intentionality* – the form by which people engage themselves in collaborative behavior insofar as they share certain kinds of beliefs, desires and intentions.

The notion of collective intentionality distinguishes between *brute facts* (Anscombe, 1963) on the one hand, which are those facts that can exist independently of human intentionality, and *dependent facts* of different sorts. The most important distinction, however, is between *subjective dependent facts*, which depend on individual intentionality, and *social facts*, which depend on collective intentionality. Within this framework, one can explain acting powers, functions, states, properties, relations, organizations and special objects which describe the world but do not pertain to the realm of brute facts.

Within the context put forward in this section, language is believed to be the fundamental social institution because it enables new forms of collective intentionality to exist at ever-higher levels of complexity.

3.2.2 How documents produce action: The document acts

Documents may be thought, roughly, as a set of sentences organized and recorded in some medium. Documents can gather sentences together, which work as means of

[7] John Rogers Searle, American philosopher, 1932 –

communication. We are not concerned here with the semantic meaning of documents though. What interest us here are either the effects that documents might have within certain contexts or the combined effect of a sentences-set, rather than the particular form of communication adopted. Speech acts, as we have seen, produce additional effects in the social environment; through the use of language we can do things with words (Austin, 1962).

Accordingly, we claim that acts produced by documents also generate additional social effects which are worth to be accounted. As documents perdure through time, these effects turn into other ones not directly observable whereas they manifest themselves in other temporal and geographical contexts. The notion of intentionality is the key to clarifying the connection between speech-acts and document-acts. The meaning of the word "intentionality" here must not be confused with the ordinary meaning of the word "intention". Intentionality is the power of minds to be about, to represent, or to stand for things, properties and states of affairs (Jacob, 2010). Intentionality means to be directed towards a goal or a thing.

In order to understand the role of intentionality here, one should consider that, in certain circumstances, documents record information required for performing actions. Such circumstances are associated with the official usage of a document. Following Heining (2005), we claim that such usage can be assessed through *function* and *practices*. The *function* of a document defines it in the context of playing a certain role in a complex action. This complexity is explained in terms of intentional behavior, whereby one segments an action into parts according to steps that display an order of reasoning. To specify the function of a document it is necessary to specify its standard use, the kind of action in which it plays its role. Such general types of action are named *practices*, which are actions reflected in their instances. This means that in order to instantiate a practice, one needs to know how to do it. Ultimately, there are not accidental executions of practices: they are all intentional.

Indeed, documents may function in unorthodox ways, which do not correspond to their real function. But in the context of their official use, documents acquire the capacity to concretize the relevant kinds of human intentionality, to occupy the relevant kinds of positional roles within larger corporate wholes, through which the actions of countless individuals become coordinated (Smith, 2010). At this point, one can notice that document acts, as well as speech acts, correspond to what humans are able to do through an intentional behavior. Speech acts are events existing only in their execution, but documents are objects which perdure through time retaining a history of changes. Thus, they can serve to create new kinds of enduring social and organizational orders, which can in turn allow the human beings involved to create new kinds of value.

A document acts theory is widely inclusive and able to accommodate different types of documents, a variety of media and of documents´ provenance. With a document we can: i) do many things as fill in, sign, stamp, copy, transfer, invalidate, destroy; ii) achieve different goals as create organizations, record deliberations, initiate legal actions and so forth; iii) take actions in different institutional systems to which documents belong as property, law, commerce, trade, credentialing, identification, to mention but a few. Examples of documents acts may be clearly found in so-called economic entities.

3.3 Document as economic entities

When making economic decisions, individuals view the world as composed of economic facts. Tables and chairs, mountains and trees, minerals and rain, dogs and cats – ultimately all real things in the world - remain the same as clearly apprehensible to one as these real things are when he is not acting as an economic agent. Similarly, all phenomena in the world are viewed by the economic agent as constituents of a reality articulated through economic considerations (Zuniga, 1998).

However, there is a difference in how the individual, *qua* economic agent, divides the reality he perceives. He orders things in the world according to their role in the economic conditions which affect his plans. As a result, a thing of natural beauty such as a tree may acquire an economic character if one perceives a causal connection between the tree and his need for a shelter. The most evident example is money: materially, a piece of paper or of metal, but which exerts vast powers over people's life.

The question which arises in this context is what makes any object or thing an economic entity. According to a clarification due to Carl Menger[8], the chief point is that economic entities are not reducible to either beliefs or to some intrinsic property of things. Economic objects, as social phenomena, are the product of beliefs and objective properties of things, some of which are physical facts and others are social facts. Knowledge and beliefs play an important role in social phenomena. For example, a dollar bill is treated as money because of people's beliefs that it is an instance of a universal medium of exchange. Money is not reducible to a physical description of the paper, metal, plastic, or electronic components which comprise the various kinds of money we recognize as money.

One must also consider that people are frequently mistaken in their beliefs. Accordingly, an economic entity is not arbitrarily designated to be an instance of a type because one merely believing it to be so. Although economic judgments are subjective, they are not arbitrary. There are conditions for each economic category in order that the truth or falsity of a belief about an economic entity can be objectively settled. Within the economic realm, Menger (2004) describes some essential aspects of characterizing something as an economic entity:

- Economic good: an economic good exists as such by virtue of putative features that an individual attaches to a thing in relation to a goal the individual has in mind;
- Commodity: a thing is a good or commodity if an agent perceives it to be in direct connection with the fulfillment of a want or need.
- Money: economic entities have to hold the widespread acceptance of a medium as exchange and legal orders which legitimize them;
- Value: to be a value, a good must be characterized as an interested evaluation since the agent perceives a causal connection between the possession of the good and the fulfillment of an end;
- Price: something must be quantifiable according to a numerical magnitude that can be measured exactly and objectively.
- Exchange: consists in the situation which occurs if two individuals contemplate a mutual transfer of commodities such that they assess their needs to be better satisfied with the transfer than it would be the case in the absence of such a transfer;

There are several other relevant initiatives describing elements of social reality. Those who are interested would be wise to refer to the works of Lawson (2008) in economy, of the aforementioned Reinach in law, of Koepsell (2000) in economic rights, and of Pouivet (2010) in forgery, to mention but a few.

[8] Carl Menger, Austrian economist, 1840 - 1921

4. Case study: Pragmatic characterization of documents in a healthcare organization

Entities of the economic world are putative examples of the power retained by documents, in the sense of theories presented thus far. Such power enables documents to leverage people and organizations, as illustrated by economic entities. Within the healthcare segment, documents carry extensible economic, legal and medical entailments. Healthcare institutions possess documents of numerous sorts, including management, regulatory, and technical documents. Indeed, there are uncountable kinds of medical documents, which are complex instances employed for several purposes in healthcare processes (Almeida e Andrade, 2011), such as:

- to support patient care: to remind staff of information, to help in organizing the care process (e.g. care information, clinical decision making, patient demographics);
- to fulfill external obligations: legal requirements, accreditation, reimbursement regulations (e.g. procedure coding), order documentation (e.g. exams, medication), and events (including adverse events, surgeries, sample collections);
- to support administration: in planning, controlling, and refunding the healthcare institution's services (e.g. medication and medical materials, equipment use, procedure coding, diagnostic coding);
- to support quality management: by enabling critical assessment and systematic monitoring of processes (e.g. clinical outcomes);
- to support scientific research: by enabling patient selection and statistical analysis (e.g. possibly relevant clinical information, not yet used in clinical reasoning);
- to support clinical education: by providing information for critical review and case examples (e.g. contextual information about consultation setting).

As a consequence of those multiple uses, medical documents are a aggregate of facts, impressions, measurements and knowledge recording. Classification of these kinds of information is required for automatic processing by computers and for system interoperability. Nevertheless, it is as yet unclear how one is to characterize a document regarding its effects in order to improve the effectiveness of KM initiatives.

In the remainder of this section we step toward a complementary characterization by taking documents from the medical segment as our working material. First, we describe a template for characterizing documents, and then we provide examples of documents of healthcare institutions.

4.1 Template and examples of its use

The first step in developing a template consists in selecting, from the scope of documents under analysis, those that are bearers of document acts. Such selection is made by considering documents which do more than merely record data: in addition to be economic entities, these documents trigger organizational actions. In fact they trigger document acts, which can be assessed by a performativity test for verbs (Morris, 2005). Then, the document act is characterized according three components: the *context*, the *content* and the *force*. The complementary characterization of a document is obtained by describing each of these components as follows.

The *context* concerns conditions of the world in which a document act is manifested. In order to characterize the context of a document, at a minimum the following questions should be considered: who issues the document? Who receives the document? What is pertinent concerning the temporal aspect? What is pertinent concerning the geographical aspect? In addition, other contextual features that contribute to the success of the document act are gathered under the label *possible situations*.

The *content* consists of the proposition underlying the document act, that is, the common element that characterizes the effect of that document, independently of the form in which this element is presented. For example, there is a common element in the sentences "Is the door shut?", "Shut the door!", and "The door is shut". This common element is the proposition that the door is shut, queried in the first sentence, commanded to be made true in the second, and asserted in the third (Green, 2007). In analyzing a document, one can see that such a common element is regarded to its official usage. For example, the underlying proposition of "The debts are paid" could be the content component of different economic documents, namely checks, credit cards, and so forth.

The component named *force* aims to determine the commitments, that is, the organizational relationships established, and the way in which the content is related to the company´s environment. We rely on Searle (1985) to define the components used to describe the force of document acts:

- *Point*: corresponds to the purpose of document acts, namely, whether it is an assertive, a commissive, a directive, a declarative, or an expressive;
- *Degree*: corresponds to the strength of a point, which is defined according to the taxonomy proposed by Searle and Vanderveken (1985);
- *Content conditions*: corresponds to conditions required by the propositional content in order that the document act can be achieved;
- *Preparatory conditions*: states of affairs that an entity must address for the success of the document act.

Once presented the basic issues, we summarize the elements for the characterization into a template where some additional details and examples are added (Fig. 1).

The template is now applied to examples of documents extracted from the healthcare organization use case described at the beginning of this paper. Some documents pertaining to the scope of healthcare institutions can be identified: demographic patient questionnaires, reports of tests, donation orders, consent letter, to mention but a few. The latter two documents were selected because of their capacity to produce effects. Indeed, they are documents inherent to any healthcare organization in which blood donation process takes place, that is, independently of specific characteristics, their purpose is the very activity of blood transfusion. The Figs. 2-a and 2-b depicts the analysis form created according to the proposed list of topics.

The examples just mentioned are typical of management and the effects of documents are not limited to data recording. In the first case, the document commits a set of employees to the execution of tasks: laboratory tests, sample collecting, medical analysis, and so forth. In the second case, the effects may involve legal demands insofar as, in consenting, one declares that knows the procedures and agree that they are suitable.

Other kinds of documents can be included in our analysis, such as: policies, documents of regulatory agencies, documents of trade and professional organizations, legislations, officially recognized classification systems, and standards (Almeida et al, 2010). Examples are specific instances in the healthcare organizations, like the International Society of Blood Transfusion's (ISBT) 128 standard (ISBT 128, 2010), and the Food and Drug Administration's quality requirements for blood donation establishments.

Step	How to execute
Selecting document bearers of document-acts	Identify actions triggered by the document in its official usages Identify economic entities
Describing the context	Identify who issues and who receives the document Identify what are the related temporal and geographical aspects
Defining the content	Identify the underlying proposition of the document Identify the general purpose of the document
Assigning the point	Identify the point according to the content defined. The point can be: • An assertive point, which tells how the world is, for example, predicting. • A commissive point, which commits one to doing something, for example, promising. • A directive point, which tries to get the hearer to do things, for example, ordering. • A declarative point, which changes the world, for example, declaring. • An expressive point, which expresses attitudes, for example, apologizing.
Assigning the degree	Identify the degree according to the point defined, here presented in ascending order: • Assertives: assert > claim > state > deny > > assure > argue > inform > suggest … • Commissives: commit > promise > threaten > accept > consent > refuse > offer … • Directives: direct > request > require > demand > forbid > advice > recommend … • Declaratives: declare > resign > appoint > approve > confirm > endorse > name … • Expressives: apologize > thank > congratulate > complain > protest > greet ...
Assessing content conditions	Identify premises that assure the point and degree feasibility, for example, invoicing can only refer to payments and not to salaries.
Assessing preparatory conditions	Identify premises that assure the success of the point and degree, for example, in placing an order the buyer presupposes that the supplier still sells those products.

Fig. 1. Template for the pragmatic document characterization

Context	**Who issues**	A blood bank clerk
	Who receives	A blood bank nurse
	Temporal aspect	Daily, during blood bank business hours
	Local aspect	Locally, inside the blood bank facility
	Possible worlds	-Purpose: starting a blood donation procedure -Institutional system involved: healthcare -Actions possible on the document: sign, stamp -Role of the agents: clerk and nurse
Content		Donating blood
Force	**Point**	Directive
	Degree	Command
	Content conditions	Donor to fulfill the requirements for donation
	Preparatory conditions	The clerk is authorized to start a donation process

Fig. 2. a. analysis form for the document *blood donation order*

Context	**Who issues**	A candidate to donor
	Who receives	A physician
	Temporal aspect	During the donation procedure
	Local aspect	Locally, inside the blood bank facility
	Possible worlds	-Purpose: consent in medical procedures Institutional system involved: healthcare -Possible actions on the document: sign -Role of the agents: physician and volunteer
Content		Donating blood
Force	**Point**	Commissive
	Degree	Consent
	Content conditions	The donor consents to procedures to be carried out
	Preparatory conditions	The physician is legally able to perform those procedures

Fig. 2. b. analysis form for the document *consent letter*

Context	**Who issues**	International Council for Commonality in Blood Banking Automation (ICCBBA)
	Who receives	Hospitals, blood banks, transfusion services, healthcare services in general
	Temporal aspect	Frequently updated
	Local aspect	Worldwide
	Possible worlds	-Purpose: standardize the terminology for blood in information systems and equipment -Institutional system involved: healthcare -Possible actions on the document: read, suggest -Role of the agents: international non-profit normalization institution; healthcare services
Content		Provide safety for patients submitted to transfusion
Force	**Point**	Directive
	Degree	Recommend
	Content conditions	The healthcare institution should agree with ISBT data structure and terminology
	Preparatory conditions	The ICBBAA gather medical authorities recognized worldwide, as well as lab equipment vendors.

Fig. 3. a. Analysis form for the document *ISBT 128 standard*

In the FDA's document, the point is a directive and the identified is *direct*, which corresponds to the primitive for English directives (Searle & Vanderveken, 1985), exhibiting the higher degree. In the case of ISBT standard, the point is still a directive, but the degree identified is *recommend*. Once the national context is considered (United States), *direct* is more powerful than *recommend*. On the other hand, if considered in the international context, the preparatory conditions are not valid and the force falls. In each context the document receives a different characterization regarding the effect it may provoke. From this analysis, we are able to identify relevant aspects as discussed in the next section.

Context	**Who issues**	Food and Drug Administration (FDA)
	Who receives	Blood banks, transfusion services, and plasmapheresis centers
	Temporal aspect	Determined by law
	Local aspect	Nationwide, United States (U. S.)
	Possible worlds	-Purpose: assist manufacturers of blood components in developing a quality program -Institutional system involved: healthcare -Possible actions on the document: read -Role of the agents: U. S. government authorities; U.S. blood banks and transfusion services
Content		Provide safety for patients submitted to blood transfusion
Force	**Point**	Directives
	Degree	Direct
	Content conditions	The healthcare institution must agree with FDA guidelines
	Preparatory conditions	Institution's authority supported by national laws

Fig. 3. b. Analysis form for the document quality requirements for blood establishments

4.2 Discussion

Since we have presented the template and examples, we now discuss the results, aiming to elucidate the contributions proposed to the field of KM. First, we discuss the effects that some kinds of documents can have on information systems focusing in ontology-based systems, which are intensively employed nowadays in the biomedical field. Then, we discuss the usage of the proposed characterization of documents to classify documents in ontologies. The use of ontologies for KM it is a well-founded topic (Almeida & Barbosa, 2009).

The first topic to be discussed regards to the effects that certain kinds of documents can generate in another contexts. Consider, for example, the ISBT standard mentioned in section 4.1. The ISBT is a worldwide standard which aims to provide safety for patients submitted to blood transfusion. The point assigned to the respective document act is *directive* and the degree is *recommend* (Fig. 3a). Thus, ISBT is a standard that recommends forms of standardizing blood samples around the world, providing a common ground for labeling and automatically processing them.

Despite its worldwide acceptance and use, ISBT lacks the ontological ground that permits information systems to be interoperable. Its data-structure composed by classes, modifiers and attributes (ISBT 128, 2010) can deal with short-term questions of standardization in a federated approach, but it is not grounded on principles that allow interoperability on a large scale among blood manipulation equipment, support decision medical systems, healthcare management systems, and other systems present in healthcare institutions.

While these issues may not be problematic in a limited landscape, they prevent the integration and interoperation of information systems on a large scale. A data-structure organized in such a way contributes to the well-known "data-silo problem", requiring the construction of middleware among systems and preventing expertise reuse along medical institutions. Such a problem is also present in other documents of the medical field, as in the HL7 - a set of standards for electronically defining clinical and administrative data in the healthcare industry - as demonstrated by Vizenor and Smith (2004). These are examples of the utility of the proposed approach in making explicit the effects that a document act can have in another context different from that in which it was created, as illustrated in the information systems realm.

The second topic under discussion involves how the proposed template can be used classify entities in an ontology for documents. One is able to use the template´s characterizations in ontology development once it has been provided some way of formalizing them. This can be done through the establishment of the notions called *strong* and *weak illocutionary commitment* (Searle & Vanderveken, 1985). *Strong commitment* regards to acts that maintain the same conditions - point, preparatory conditions and content conditions - except by their degree, when determining its force. If an act has a stronger degree than the other, the former is required for the latter to occur. Once generalized, this notion is called *strong commitment*. On the other hand, there is a *weak commitment* in the cases where all mentioned conditions are exactly the same, that is, the four parameters are exactly the same.

Such distinctions, obtained through assessing the degree of force, are not propositional but illocutionary regarding their effects. Such notions of strong and weak commitment are pertinent to logical relations of entailment and there are tableaus depicting inferential relations among acts (Vandeveken, 1990). Then, these distinctions allow the formulating of new axioms for an ontology development, providing a useful dimension of analysis once documents acts are identified according to criteria adopted in prior examples.

5. Summary and conclusions

We have presented a proposal towards a complementary dimension to characterize documents. In order to reach the proposed results, we have presented a brief historical account of the origins of the term *document* that identifies some functions of a document in the societal context. Following this line of thought, we have presented developments of the speech acts theory and that of an extension called the document acts theory - a theory to deal with acts raised by the power of documents - showing in what aspects the former can be used to aid the formulation of the latter. We have proposed a template to reach the claimed complementary characterization successfully. Finally, we have discussed the use of the pragmatic characterization in building ontologies and pointed out how one can identify the effects of such characterization on the information systems realm.

We conclude, through our approach summarized in a template, that is possible to recognize a distinct action level embedded into documents by human acts. In identifying this level, one is able to detect other relevant manifestations within an organizational environment. Although defining documents is not trivial undertaking, we advocate that the complementary dimension proposed should be incorporated in a proper analysis of them. For the development of ontologies, this additional consideration may be useful by obtaining well-shaped representations. Moreover, such characterization reveals other facets of documents' power, as shown in the case of medical standards. In looking at the situation from this point of view, one can see how documents accepted worldwide can generate undesirable long-term effects.

Finally, we mention some topics for future work. Among them, there is an investigation aiming to implement illocutionary acts, complementing initiatives that already exist (Auramaki, Lehtinen, & Lytinen, 1988; Vanderveken, 1990). Moreover, we intend to propose a more detailed account of transcription from the speech acts level to the document acts level in order to clarify how different propositions inside the same document can be conciliated.

6. References

Almeida, M.B., Proietti, A.B., Ai, J.; Smith, B. (2011). The Blood Ontology: an ontology in the domain of hematology. Proceedings of the International Conference of Biomedical Ontologies (ICBO), 2011.

Almeida, M.B., Barbosa, R.R. (2009). Ontologies in Knowledge Management support: a study of case. Journal of American Society of Information Science and Technology, 60(10), 2032-2047.

Almeida, M.B., Andrade, A. Q. (2011). Information, reality and epistemology: an ontological take. Proceedings of the Workshop of Ontologies in Biomedicine and Life Sciences (OBML) at Informatik 2011, Berlin.

American Heritage Dictionary of the English Language, (2000). Orlando: Houghton Mifflin Co.

Anscombe, G. E. M. (1963). Intention. New York: Cornell University Press.

Auramaki, E., Lehtinen, E., & Lytinen, K. (1988). A speech act-based Office Modeling Approach. ACM Transactions on Office Information Systems, 6(2), 126-152.

Austin, J. L. (1962). How to do things with words. Oxford: Oxford University Press.

Buckland, M. K. (1997). What is a document? Journal of the American Society of Information Science, 48(9), 804-809.

Fernandez, F. S. & Arroyo, J. M. I. (1982). Reflexiones sobre documento: palabra/objeto. Retrieved March 03, 2009, from http://dialnet.unirioja.es/

Green, M. (2007). Speech Acts. Retrieved June 22, 2010, from http://plato.stanford.edu/entries/speech-acts/

Hennig, B. (2005). Documents: Towards a formal ontology of filling in forms. Retrieved July 02, 2010, from http://www.borishennig.de/texte/2005/doc.pdf

HL7 (2008). HL7 Version 3 Standard: Blood, Tissue, Organ; Donation, Release 1, Committee Ballot 2, January 2008. Retrieved Sept. 04, 2010, from http://www.hl7.org

ISBT128 (2010). ISBT 128: Standard Terminology for Blood, Cellular Therapy, and Tissue Product Descriptions. Retrieved Nov. 04, 2009, from http://www.iccbba.org/standardterminology.pdf

Jacob, P. (2010). Intentionality. Retrieved July 2, 2010. From http://plato.stanford.edu/entries/intentionality/

Koepsell, D. R. (2000).The ontology of cyberspace. Chigaco: Open Court.

Lawson, T. (2008). Ontology and Economics: Tony Lawson and his Critics. London: Routledge.

Mengers, C. (2004). Principles of Economics. Retrieved April 3, 2010, from

http://mises.org/etexts/menger/Mengerprinciples.pdf
Morris, M. (2005). An Introduction to the Philosophy of Language. Cambridge: Cambridge University Press.
Mulligan, K. (1987). Promising and Other Social Acts: Their Constituents and Structure. In K. Mulligan (Ed.), Speech Act and Sachverhalt: Reinach and the Foundations of Realist Phenomenology. Dordrecht: Nijhoff.
Pouivet, R. (2010). The ontology of forgery. Retrieved June 23, 2010, from http://www.interdisciplines.org/artcognition/papers/2
Schamber, L. (1996). What is a document? Rethinking the concept in uneasy times. Journal of the American Society for Information Science. 47(9), 669-671.
Schellenberg, T. R. (1956). Modern archives: principles and techniques. Chicago: University of Chicago Press.
Searle, J. (2000). Mind, Language, and Society: Philosophy in the Real World. New York: Basic Books.
Searle, J. (1985). Expression and Meaning: Studies in the Theory of Speech Acts. Cambridge: Cambridge University Press.
Searle, J. & Vanderveken, D. (1985). Foundations of Illocutionary Logic. Cambridge: Cambridge University Press.
Smith, B. (2003). John Searle. Cambridge: Cambridge University Press.
Smith, B. (2010). Document Acts. Retrieved July 02, 2010, from http://ontology.buffalo.edu/smith/
Smith, B. et al. (2007). The OBO Foundry: coordinated evolution of ontologies to support biomedical data integration. Nature Biotechnology. 25(11), 1251-1255.
Vanderveken, D. (1990). Meaning and Speech Acts, Vol I. Cambridge: Cambridge University Press.
Vizenor, L. & Smith, B. (2004). Speech Acts and Medical Records: The Ontological Nexus. Paper presented at the EuroMISE 2004, Prague, Czech Republic.
Zuniga, G. L. (1998). An ontology of economic objects. American Journal of Economics and Sociology. 58(2), 299-312.

9

An Empirical Study of Knowledge Management in University Libraries in SADC Countries

Priti Jain
Senior Lecturer, Department of Library & Information Studies
University of Botswana, Gaborone
Botswana

1. Introduction

Academic libraries have transformed drastically from MARC and circulation desk to metadata and web information, print collection and inter library loans to online databases and e-resources, quiet areas to learning and knowledge commons, bibliographic instruction to information literacy and life-long learning, information management to knowledge management and so on. Accordingly, the roles of academic librarians have changed radically at both library practitioners and library school educators' levels. They are no more traditional information protectors and managers. Open access, knowledge management, digital scholarship, institutional repositories are all often owned by the libraries and the librarians.

"KM as a fad is dead. But KM as a means for organizations to grow stronger and more productive in a climate of uncertainty is gaining ground" (Knowledge Management Research Centre, 2010). The above phrase caught eye and it is self-explanatory. Indeed KM is no more a fad, but a reality to be productive and a means to gain and sustain a competitive edge over rivals in all areas of life. In this global economy which is knowledge based, economic activities have shifted from people working with their hands to people working with their heads, from tangible resources like steel to intangible resources like knowledge (Davenport 2002 in Boom, & Pimentel, 2009). Academic libraries are no exception to this change. As "Academic libraries are information centers established in support of the mission of their parent institutions to generate knowledge, and people equipped with knowledge in order to serve the society and advance the well-being of mankind" (Raja, Ahmad, Sinha, 2009:701). The main functions of academic libraries are to support the mission and vision of their parent institutions. To fulfill this function academic libraries have to evolve as their parent institutions' mission, vision and information needs change.

Thus, Knowledge management has been recognized as vital by all 21st century information professionals, who have evolved from traditional cataloguer and reference librarians to value adding service providers, teacher librarians and, most recently, knowledge managers. This study was initiated in the above background, with a main purpose to investigate the KM practices in university libraries in SADC countries. Since university libraries are academic libraries, the words university and academic are used interchangeably, but the study is limited to university libraries.

2. The concept of knowledge management

Knowledge is defined as, "The facts, feelings or experiences known by a person or group of people" (In Collins English Dictionary, 2004). According to Drucker (1989) "Knowledge is information that changes something or somebody -either by becoming grounds for action, or by making an individual (or an institution) capable of different or more effective action." There are two types of knowledge; tacit and explicit knowledge. Explicit knowledge is documented and articulated into a formal language; it is rule-based, stored in certain media and easily communicable and shared; for example, organizational databases, web-pages, subject-portals, policies and manuals. Tacit is personal, hard to document and it is knowledge in action used by people to perform their tasks every day. Tacit knowledge has a personal quality, which makes it hard to formalize and communicate. Tacit knowledge is deeply rooted in action, commitment, and involvement in a specific context (Nonaka, 1994:16). Knowledge management is the management of knowledge that is critical to a person to work more efficiently, inclusive of both tacit and explicit knowledge. Let us now look at some more definitions of KM as explicit and tacit knowledge:

KM as Explicit knowledge refers to:	**Source**
Knowledge that can be expressed in words and numbers and can be easily communicated and shared in the form of hard data, scientific formulae, codified procedures or universal principles.	Nonaka and Takeuchi (1995).
KM as tacit knowledge is:	
A mix of fluid experiences, values, contextual information and intuition that provides a structure to evaluate and incorporate new experiences and information. It originates and is applied in the minds of individuals.	Davenport & Prusak (2000)
KM as explicit and tacit knowledge is:	
A process or practice of creating, acquiring, capturing, sharing, and using knowledge, wherever it resides, to enhance learning and performance in organizations.	Skyrme (2001).

Table 1. Definitions of knowledge management

From the above definitions, it is obvious that KM does not consist of only tacit knowledge as indicated in some KM literature. It comprises both tacit and explicit knowledge, which are complementary. KM can be characterized as below:

- KM is a process of several activities; creating, acquiring, capturing, sharing, using and re-using it;
- It includes both explicit and tacit knowledge;
- It is an ongoing activity;
- Information is the building block of KM;
- It is action oriented or application based; and,
- The main drive behind KM is to improve organizational performance.

Thus, KM is "capacity to act" (Sveiby, 1997), and a "justified belief that increases an entity's capacity for effective action" (Nonaka, 1994). It is a "set of tools, techniques, methods, ways of working, even behaviors - that are all designed to help an organization to be more effective" (Collison, 2010), it is "what we do to accomplish our goals faster and more effectively by delivering the right knowledge to right person at the right time and in the right context" (Ugwu & Ezema, 2010:184). In the context of this chapter KM is defined as a purposeful management process to capture, exploit, share and apply both tacit and explicit knowledge for the benefit of the employees, organization and its customers. It is integration of both internal and external knowledge into action and it is an ongoing activity.

To appreciate the concept of KM fully one has to understand the difference between information and knowledge.

2.2 Difference between information and knowledge management

This subject has been debated for more than two decades; there is ample literature surrounding the issue. Despite that there is ambiguity between these two terminologies. Some people can easily distinguish the two, for instance, according to Boom, & Pimentel (2009), "The main difference between knowledge and information is that knowledge is connected to the bearer and information can be disconnected from the bearer". According to McKnight (2007) Knowledge Management is about **people**, how they create, share and use information, whereas Information Management is often associated with the information technology **systems** that help to create, store and share information. However, some people are still inclined to use information and knowledge interchangeably. From the available literature and the author's own understanding the similarities and differences between the two can be identified as below:

Similarities between information and knowledge	
Both are vital for everyone	
Both are multidisciplinary	
Both are organized and disseminated using new technology	
Differences between information and knowledge	
Information	**Knowledge**
Information is more easily identified, organized and disseminated	Identification of knowledge is a complex activity
Information is always visible	Knowledge is not always visible
No analytical skill is required to gain information	To gain knowledge you need some analytical skills
Information is neutral	Knowledge is contextual
Information is a flow of messages	Knowledge is created by that very flow of information anchored in the beliefs
All information is not useful	Knowledge is often useful
Information can be disconnected from the bearer	Knowledge is connected to the bearer
Information is only organized data in a meaningful milieu	Knowledge is predictive and future-oriented
Information Management (IM)	Knowledge Management (KM)
IM emphasizes human involvement in auditing, acquiring, storing, retrieving and disseminating information	KM emphasizes human involvement in capturing, creating, sharing, learning and contextualizing information
IM success depends on the preservation and retrieval of information	KM success depends on collecting distributing and utilization of knowledge
IM is working with objects	KM is working with people
IM treats information as a resource	KM treats knowledge as resource
IM includes only explicit knowledge	KM includes both tacit and explicit knowledge

Sources: Nonaka & Takeuchi (1995:58), Chase (1998), Meadow et al (2000:35), Jain (2007), Boom & Pimentel (2009).

Table 2. Similarities & Differences between Information and Knowledge Management

It is apparent from the above table that there is a substantial difference between information and knowledge. At the same time it cannot be overemphasized that information is the building block of KM. In other words, all knowledge is information, but all information is not knowledge. What is knowledge in one context can be information in another context, thus both are dependent upon the context and purpose which they are used for.

3. Major impetus of KM in academic libraries

KM literature reveals the following major drivers of KM in academic libraries:

Survival factor with increased user demands and competition: Due to other information providers as competitors, libraries face survival problems and must strive to find innovative ways to provide customer service. KM is the most recent and most discussed survival factor for libraries. According to a study carried out by Sarrafzadeh, Martin, & Hazeri (2010), 82.2% LIS professionals regarded KM as a survival factor for libraries to respond to challenges they face in a continuously changing environment. Since KM equips academic libraries with ample amenities to satisfy the incessantly changing library customer needs, it is a survival kit and a strategic tool for academic libraries.

Increased visibility of libraries: Libraries often have a poor image; they are not visible to their parent organization and work in isolation. The ultimate aim of KM is to achieve an organization's mission. Therefore, all parts of an organization (including libraries) must ensure that KM contributes towards the realization of the organizational mission and vision. Adoption of KM could assist library and information professionals in meeting user needs aligned with the organization's strategic goals and objectives. In addition, KM provides libraries with the opportunity to collaborate with other units in their organizations and hence become more integrated into corporate operations and enhance their overall visibility within the organization (Sarrafzadeh, Martin, & Hazeri, 2010). KM endows academic librarians with various platforms to collaborate with academia, such as playing a leading role in electronic and open access publications by providing guidance on copyright issues, and self-archiving published articles in institutional repositories. All these activities improve the visibility of academic libraries.

Academic libraries as knowledge creating organizations: Academic libraries are perceived as knowledge creating organizations, as a system of integrated activities and business processes that work together collaboratively to facilitate accomplishing overall organizational goals (Daneshgar & Parirokh, 2007). Academic libraries are the treasure house of knowledge to cater for the needs of scholars, scientists, technocrats, researchers, students and others who are in the mainstream of higher education (Guru et al, 2009). Librarians are acknowledged as knowledge creators through content management, organization of knowledge, and evaluating the validity and reliability of information obtained from unfamiliar sources (Sinotte, 2004). Librarians bring a set of values that are fundamental to the long-term survival of scholarship. Librarians care about access and understand that some resources may have value to disciplines and time periods beyond their initiation (Case, 2011). Academia stimulates the creation and transmission of knowledge, and academic libraries have played a significant role in supporting such activities (Kim & Abbas, 2010). Thus, academic libraries are knowledge creating and knowledge-based organizations. "Historically, as a basis for collection, organization, storage, and distribution of knowledge and information, libraries represent an important link to the knowledge innovation and management" (Roknuzzaman & Umemoto, 2009:651).

Hence, Debowski (2006) puts emphasis on the need for cultivation of new knowledge competencies through the development of appropriate work-based learning programmes for librarians as early advocates of the knowledge management.

Increased value of knowledge in the knowledge economy: In a study undertaken by Roknuzzaman & Umemoto (2009), knowledge economy was considered to be one of the important drivers for libraries' movement towards KM. The above authors have noted that the value of knowledge has always been central to library practice, but the new knowledge-based economy places its significance more than ever before. Increasingly, governments and funding agencies are recognizing universities as knowledge industries for creating new knowledge and innovation through their research. Hayes (2004) strongly maintains that "A university can be viewed as a knowledge factory creating new knowledge through research and by educating knowledge workers, both of which are essential for the modern economy". Thus, being the knowledge-intensive institutions, some university librarians have adopted KM and have already expanded their existing roles. By utilizing their traditional skills university librarians are playing a crucial role in dissemination and exchange of knowledge among students and teaching staff in order to enhance learning, teaching and research activities. All of this contributes towards a knowledgeable and learned society and knowledge economy.

Need of improved library services and customer satisfaction: Another force for adopting KM in academic libraries is the promotion of existing library practices and better services for clientele (Roknuzzaman & Umemoto, 2009). Due to the rapid advancement in information technology and changing needs of customers, there is an increased need for a more improved approach to library service delivery at the academic libraries. KM enables librarians to capture, store, organize, share and disseminate the right information to the right customer at the right time. Customers are paramount and knowledge about them is important for all organizations; no organization can survive without them. It is customer knowledge around which an organization's services and products are focused. The "availability of sophisticated ICT infrastructure combined with emerging business processes such as various service orientation configurations, constitute major characteristics of many of today's libraries in western universities" (Daneshgar & Bosanquet, 2010:21) and around the world. The two authors classify customer knowledge in academic libraries into (i) knowledge about customers, (ii) knowledge from customers and (iii) knowledge for customers including both explicit and tacit knowledge. It is expected that KM activities will build a greater understanding of customers and their requirements and as these requirements will hopefully lead to the delivery of more appropriate and timely services (Daneshgar & Bosanquet, 2010). Customer knowledge management is central for both improved library services and for high customer satisfaction. Customer feedback informs the provision of library services. Thus, academic libraries are adopting KM to make libraries the centers of customer service. By using the right tools university librarians can empower their customers with the right contents at the right time, in the right format. For instance, using web applications such as Web 2.0 and Web 3.0 libraries can reach users wherever they are and social tools can further improve customer service and overall library services.

To surmount budget constraints: Academic libraries are always constrained with budget declines. As noted by (Roknuzzaman & Umemoto, 2009), many libraries suffer from shrinkage of budget and skilled human resources, two of the important factors for any KM project. KM equips academic libraries with abilities to produce more with less and reduces duplication of efforts, for example, using online reference services, a reference librarian can serve multiple users in one time, which is cost and time effective.

Information explosion: This is the rapidly increasing amount of information and consequently availability of more information/knowledge to everyone. According to the experts, human knowledge is doubling every thirty two hours. Due to this, we are in a state of information overload and decay of existing knowledge, which is continuously replaced with new knowledge. According to Israel (2010), this information explosion affects library users in a variety of ways; it damages health, leads towards bad decision making and creates information anxiety. In the same way, the information explosion confronts university librarians with many challenges; such as, selection and acquisition of library resources, organization of acquired resources, collection development, cataloguing, and reference services. At the same time it enables users to select from a wide range of resources (Israel, 2010), which creates competition. Information explosion and knowledge growth calls for innovative approaches to manage the right knowledge. Since KM emphasises on updating of knowledge regularly in order to remove obsolete information and avail the most updated information, using the KM systems academic librarians can overcome the problem of information explosion to a greater extent.

4. Challenges/barriers to knowledge management in academic libraries

The KM literature (Jain, 2007, Raja, Ahmad, Sinha, 2009, Roknuzzaman & Umemoto, 2009, Guru et al, 2009) reveals the following major impediments to incorporate KM into library practice:

- *Reluctance of library practitioners:* According to (Roknuzzaman & Umemoto, 2009), the response of LIS practitioners to KM is comparatively slow and they are reluctant to incorporate KM into library practice because of their traditional mind set. Some librarians do not take any initiative for positive changes in their libraries.
- *Lack of incentives:* Incentives are the biggest motivators. In the absence of proper incentive plans, academic librarians observe reluctance towards KM activities.
- *Inadequate staff training:* The success of KM projects are dependent on adequate training plans in all the activities of KM process, e.g. training in knowledge capture, organization, dissemination, and use of new technology skills.
- *Insufficient tools and technologies:* This refers to libraries not being well-equipped with KM enabling technologies.
- *Lack of sufficient budget / funds:* Budget is a two-way issue. On one hand, librarians are adopting KM to solve financial problem by producing more with less. On the other hand, due to budgetary constraints libraries are not well-equipped with essential infrastructure for KM, e.g. new technology, training, incentives.
- *Misunderstanding of KM concepts:* Many academic library managers do not understand the concept of KM properly; hence, they are not able to appreciate and support KM project fully.
- *Lack of a centralized policy for KM:* It is the first step in any KM initiative however most academic libraries lack a centralized policy for KM initiatives.
- *Intellectual challenge:* to manage tacit knowledge and pull the relevant information from the overflowing reservoir of information is another big challenge in the academic libraries.
- *Cultural challenge:* Developing the right culture and environment for capturing, sharing and creating knowledge is a limitation to knowledge adoption in academic libraries. Particularly, librarians are not familiar with capturing and sharing tacit knowledge embedded within the experience, talent, and intuition of the library staff.

- *Managing central knowledge repositories:* Increasingly, all organizations are developing institutional repositories for the parent organization. There are difficulties in generating contents for knowledge repositories, especially in the beginning. Mandatory self-archiving policies are found to be a good solution, but wide implementation of such policies is a challenge (Xia, 2009).
- *Digitization of library resources:* Not all academic libraries are well-equipped with the necessary infrastructure, such as, technology, staff expertise in digitization, copyright issues.
- *Lack of collaboration:* The success of any KM project depends on strong collaboration and partnership within and without the library. On an internal basis collaboration is required between senior and junior staff, teaching faculties and students, human resource and IT staff units. External collaboration is strong partnerships with other libraries or allied corporate organizations. Often such collaborations are lacking and this becomes an obstacle to KM success. As observed by Roknuzzaman & Umemoto (2009), generally the junior staff are reluctant to share their knowledge and ideas with their seniors, because they feel that there is no benefit of it. Traditionally librarians were not used to working with IT departments, however due to the emergence of the digital age and knowledge economy today librarians have to work hand-in hand with IT experts.
- *Change management:* Academic librarians often find it difficult change their mind-sets to become knowledge managers from traditional librarians.

In the above background this section now presents the major findings of the preliminary studies.

5. Research findings

This preliminary study was undertaken to investigate the KM practice at the university libraries in SADC countries. The data was collected in July-September 2011.

5.1 Scope & context of the study

SADC (Southern African Development Community) was established in April 1980 by the Governments of nine Southern African countries. Currently SADC has a membership of 15 Member States, namely; Angola, Botswana, Democratic Republic of Congo (DRC), Lesotho, Madagascar, Malawi, Mauritius, Mozambique, Namibia, Seychelles, South Africa, Swaziland, United Republic of Tanzania, Zambia and Zimbabwe (Southern African Development Community, 2011). It was difficult to determine the total number of university libraries in these SADC countries in the absence of availability of information on the internet.

5.2 Research purpose & objectives

As mentioned in the introduction, the main purpose of this study was to explore the KM practice in university libraries in SADC countries. To meet this purpose, the objectives of this study were:

- to discover the understanding of knowledge management concept;
- to ascertain the reasons for practicing knowledge management in university libraries; and,
- to explore the challenges associated with knowledge management practice.

5.3 Methodology

A structured questionnaire was used to carry out the study, including both quantitative and qualitative questions. Reasons for employing this approach were to ensure reliability, time

effectiveness and mutual inclusiveness. A total of thirty (30) questionnaires were delivered electronically, of which only 12 were returned (40% response rate).
The purpose of any sampling is to secure a sample which will represent the characteristics of the entire population. In this study the purposive sampling was used because the aim of the study was to collect data from librarians from each SADC university library. If the director was not available, any staff member could participate in the survey. It was assumed that one questionnaire would represent the whole library and therefore there was no need to repeat the survey with other library staff.
As it was not a large amount of data, data analysis was done by simple frequency count and cross tabulation, comparing responses across demographic variables. The qualitative (open-ended) questions were analyzed separately, by identifying and grouping key responses into themes, after which related/associated themes were further grouped into variables for frequency count.

5.4 The major findings

Out of 12 participating libraries 8 (67%) claimed to be practicing knowledge management (KM) and considered themselves as knowledge managers. The following section presents the major findings.

SADC Countries	No. of Participating Libraries
Botswana	1
Malawi	1
Namibia	1
South Africa	4
Tanzania	2
Zambia	2
Zimbabwe	1

Table 3. Participating Libraries N=12

A systematic way of gathering, organizing, managing, disseminating and use of information & knowledge.
KM refers to collection, processing and dissemination, both published and unpublished and non-documented information emanating from traditions and practices.
KM is the process of codifying what employees know, and sharing that information among employees in order to devise best practices.
The effective management of knowledge to preserve organizational knowledge.
A process of organizing/managing knowledge for easy retrieval, use and retention for future use.
KM is the utilization of existing knowledge and share it.
KM is a process that helps organizations find, select, organize, disseminate and transfer important information and expertise necessary for activities such as problem solving, dynamic learning, strategic planning and decision making.
The ability to manage knowledge.
KM is about the sharing and retaining of knowledge and expertise in the organization. To persuade people to share knowledge, they have to be motivated and provided with the necessary tools.

Table 4. KM defined by the respondents N=12

Reasons	%	No.
To improve library services	100	12
To improve library productivity	92	11
To produce more with less due to dwindling library budget	92	11
To leverage existing knowledge	83	10
To manage information explosion	67	8
To manage rapid knowledge decay	67	8
To make informed decisions	67	8
To establish best practices	50	6
To avoid duplication of efforts	50	6

Table 5. Reasons for practicing KM N=12

Challenges	%	No
Constant budget decline	92	11
Lack of incentives	83	10
Inadequate staff training	83	10
Limited expertise in KM	58	7
Lack of clearly defined guidelines on KM implementation	75	9
Insufficient Technology	67	8
A lack of knowledge sharing culture	58	7
A lack of cooperation among juniors and seniors	42	5
To track the materials from departments is time consuming	33	4

Table 6. Challenges in knowledge management N=12

6. Discussion

This section discusses the major findings of the study based on the three research objectives.

6.1 Understanding the concept of KM

The majority of the participants seemed to understand the concept of KM, which is apparent from Table (4); the KM concept was well-defined by the participants. A similar survey conducted in 2006 showed KM practicing libraries as only 45%, the number has increased to 67%. Therefore, an increase in the number of libraries practicing KM is also an indication that there is a greater understanding of the KM concept. Other optimistic signs were from those who did not practice KM, but completed the questionnaire and preferred to be called information scientists and knowledge custodians rather than simply librarians or information managers. As in general comments, one respondent mentioned, "Today KM is a way forward to 21st Century librarians, but due to resource constraints we are not able to practice it". Yet another added, "This is a good study to evaluate ourselves. KM is a strategic tool to manage the ever-changing library users needs". These developments are in line with what Roknuzzaman & Umemoto (2009) have suggested that library practitioners need to broaden their understanding, change traditional mindset, and to apply a holistic approach of KM system design and library practice focusing on both explicit and tacit knowledge. The following section further puts forward participants' understanding of the KM concept.

6.2 Reasons for practicing knowledge management

The main reasons for KM adoption were identified as; to improve library services and productivity, to produce more with less due to financial constraints, to leverage already existing knowledge, to manage information explosion, to manage rapid knowledge decay, to make informed decisions, to establish best practices, and, to avoid duplication of efforts. Let us now briefly deliberate on each of the above points.

To improve library services and productivity: To improve library services was identified as one of the most important reasons to initiate KM by all the participants (100%), while a majority of 92% acknowledged that they were practicing KM to improve productivity. Indeed KM improves library services as well as library's overall productivity in numerous ways. Library services are improved by providing time and cost-effective, customer-focused and 24 hours library services in a consistent manner. Through KM systems, each customer receives the same answers for similar queries; it would be difficult to monitor consistency of customer services without KM systems. All this leads university libraries towards improved services and productivity. By reducing duplication of efforts and using time and cost-saving information and knowledge management strategies librarians are released to utilize their time in more productive tasks such as research and innovative projects. At the same time library customers can also set up virtual "my library" and various learning spaces for improved library services. Online Reference services such as "Ask a Librarian" service automates responses to many queries by providing customers answers from an established knowledge base.

To produce more with less: This was recognized as another reason to encourage KM in university libraries by 92% of the participants. Certainly KM is a good solution to produce more with less by managing the most relevant information and omitting the irrelevant. It is well-articulated in the KM literature that the budget shortfall is a primary driving force as well as an obstacle for the implementation of KM in academic libraries. Wen (2005) has rightly observed that in recent years, budgets in academic libraries are stagnant at best and declining in general. Academic libraries have felt the pinch from both sides - less budget and more demand, they have sensed the threat of being marginalized by internet-based information services and students and faculty's own information gathering efforts. Hence, it is important for academic libraries to operate more efficiently with reduced financial and/or human resources and produce more with less. Emphasizing the management of most critical and actionable information, KM can support this endeavor. For instance, university libraries may be stocked with irrelevant books and other information materials, which are seldom used. By investing only in relevant information and knowledge the issue of budget decline can be addressed to some extent. Today the focus has changed from "just in case to just in time information".

To leverage already existing knowledge: This was acknowledged as another reason for practicing KM by a majority of 83% participants. Often organizations do not know what knowledge they already have. Owing to this, even the large global corporations are spending money on training and development to gain knowledge that they already have (Goodman & Schieman, 2010). KM leverages the existing knowledge within an organization. Through needs assessment, knowledge mapping and knowledge auditing exercises, hidden organizational knowledge becomes visible and usable. Thus, by practicing KM, organizations can identify and leverage their collective knowledge to compete, including the creation, storage/retrieval, transfer, and application of knowledge (Alavi & Leidner, 2001). Indeed KM is a useful mechanism to leverage existing knowledge.

To manage information explosion: This was observed a significant factor to accept KM by 67% participants. With too much information to digest, a person is unable to locate and make use of the information one needs and this information overload can hinder information usefulness to the individual (Israel, 2010). Information explosion is the negative aspect of knowledge sharing. Increased information sharing leads to increased information explosion and hence academic librarians are increasingly challenged to solve this dilemma of information overload. The situation is worsened due to limited financial resources. KM solves this dilemma of information explosion by managing the right information, to the right people at the right time.

Due to information explosion and overabundance, the main issue now is to recognize, locate and utilize this specialized knowledge and most critical knowledge embedded in organizational databases, processes and routines as a distinct factor of production to increase productivity and competitiveness (Saadan, 2001). KM is one such tool that can help in managing information explosion by managing what is most critical and essential.

To manage rapid knowledge decay: Managing knowledge decay was perceived as a critical factor to adopt KM by 67% of the participants. Due to information and knowledge explosion knowledge is decaying faster than ever before. It is indeed important to practice KM to deal with the rapid knowledge decay to serve the users with the right knowledge at the right time and avoid sifting through decayed and obsolete knowledge. This requires academic librarians to renovate the existing library environment and promote a knowledge-sharing culture by initiating communities of practice, management of best practices, change management, organizational learning, and use of appropriate knowledge-sharing technologies (Roknuzzaman & Umemoto, 2009). KM systems emphasize continuous update and maintenance of knowledge in order to manage rapid knowledge decay.

To make informed decisions: This was perceived as important to adopt KM by 67% of the participants. KM equips each person with informed decision making capability. When people have access to the right information and knowledge, they will definitely be able to make wise decisions.

To establish best practices: This was another reason to take up KM articulated by 50% of the participants. A best practice is "A method or technique that has consistently shown results superior to those achieved with other means, and that is used as a benchmark" (Business Dictionary, 2011). KM is a complex set of processes and procedures, some more successful than others. KM emphasizes the identification of such best practices because tried and tested solutions and practices are always superior over newly introduced ones. Due to long-term experience best practices are time and cost-effective, they provide operational excellence, and enhance performance capabilities to create competitive advantage. They create a learning environment and reduce training needs. However, it has to be noted that no practice is best for everyone and no best practice remains best forever. Academic libraries should continuously look for better best practices.

To reduce duplication of efforts: This was found to be another reason to approve KM by 50% of the participants. Knowledge sharing is one of the most critical components of KM.

Often academic library practitioners are doing similar things in their own divisions in isolation. A good example of such a practice can be a reference service. Individual librarians continue doing their personal research on how to serve their customers, while they could long establish a reference query database and update it regularly on the receipt of a new query and share it. However, with the advance of technology, there are online and virtual reference services, such as Knowledge Base of QuestionPoint, which reduces response time and duplication. Using KM applications duplication of efforts is reduced, training needs are minimized and all services are time and cost-effective.

6.3 Challenges in KM practice

The study identified the major challenges in practicing KM as; constant budget decline, lack of incentives, inadequate staff training, limited expertise, lack of clearly defined guidelines on KM implementation, insufficient technology, and a lack of knowledge sharing culture. A lack of cooperation among juniors and seniors and tracking the materials from departments did not appear to be major challenges. Now the main challenges faced by the knowledge practicing university libraries are discussed.

Unremitting budget decline: This was perceived as a challenge by 92% of the participants. Budget decline features twice, as a reason to adopt KM, as well as a challenge to practice KM. It is a well-known fact that unlike the private or business sector, academic libraries typically do not have extra financial resources to reward staff. Budget has an impact on everything including inadequate tools and technologies, a lack of reward system, poor training plans and a lack of expertise in KM. With a stagnant or dwindling library budget, academic libraries have to increase their operational efficiency in order to meet this challenge. Indeed, when libraries face tight budgets or budget reductions, it is only too natural for the library administration to hesitate to invest in such a Knowledge Management system (Wen, 2005). This calls for an adequate budget for the success of KM implementation.

Incentives & staff motivation: Lack of incentives was yet another critical issue for 83% of the participants in order to motivate library staff for KM especially for knowledge sharing. At the same time it is not an easy feat to motivate staff to contribute and share their knowledge. Some staff may not want to share their knowledge for fear that once their knowledge is shared, they might no longer be valued or deemed indispensable. Some staff may not share their knowledge for free, as there are free riders, who only take for granted others' knowledge but never share their own (Susarla, Liu, & Whinston, 2003). Rewards are good motivators to KM adoption and building organizational trust among librarians. To develop a motivational workforce reward programs should be aligned with human resource development policies to be seen as a vehicle for cultural change. Aharony's (2011) findings established that the more staff received rewards the more they trusted the organization and were ready to collaborate, and they had a more positive attitude toward KM (Constant, Kiesler & Sproull, 1994, Aharony, 2011).

Inadequate staff training & limited expertise: Inadequate staff training was acknowledged as a challenge by 83% and limited expertise by 58% of the participants. Both are important and complementary. For effective application of KM adequate training is vital and insufficient training might lead to limited expertise. According to Townley (2001), training and support for the adoption of new knowledge and behaviors are perhaps the most important and costly part of any knowledge management application. Advocating the need for training need, Lee (2005) emphasizes that as a learning organization, libraries should be allocated annual funding to provide continuing education and staff training to all staff members. Knowledge must be renewed and expanded to prevent it from becoming stagnant. Skills development of staff was considered the first and foremost to create KM culture in academic libraries in Nigeria (Ugwu & Ifeanyi, 2010). Thus, training is vital and staff need to be trained in each aspect of KM, knowledge capturing, storing, retrieval and dissemination and formulation of knowledge strategy. As university libraries play a leading role in today's changing world in generating ideas and advancing societies, they need to be knowledgeable enough in order to cope with the rapid changes and strong competitive environments (Daneshgar & Parirokh, 2007).

A lack of clearly defined guidelines on KM implementation: This was pointed out as a challenge by 75% of the participants and this seems to be a problem world-wide. For example, only twelve (12) UK universities had a Knowledge Management strategy (McKnight, 2007). Establishing principles for KM implementation are fundamental to KM success; which are referred as KM strategies. Formulating a KM strategy should be the first step in any KM initiative. A KM strategy is a plan that describes how an organization will manage its knowledge better for the benefit of the organization, employees and other stakeholders. Based on the real needs and problems in a particular library, a KM strategy should stipulate the overall KM vision aligned with organizational strategic plans including specific objectives, action plans, budget, mentoring and training plans and associated challenges including an evaluation plan to measure the expected outcomes of KM initiatives. An audit of all the information and knowledge systems in an organization can help identify the urgent need for IM and KM strategies (identifying the multiplicity of data sources held in filing cabinets, insecure laptops, hard disks that are not regularly backed-up, in the heads of key staff approaching retirement etc). The audit can also determine the priorities for attention in the information and knowledge management strategies (McKnight, 2007). Thus, clearly defined guidelines are essential to reap the benefits from KM implementation.

Insufficient technology: Inadequate technology was acknowledged as a challenge by 67% of the librarians, while sufficient technology is decisive for KM success. It enables KM initiatives in two ways: by connecting people with contents providing the means for people to capture, discover, organize, store, retrieve and disseminate knowledge/information, and connecting people with people using collaborative software such as electronic communication tools, electronic conferencing tools, collaborative management tools and workflow management systems. A good IT infrastructure is not a sufficient condition for the success of KM but a necessary condition for it (Arora, 2002). Insufficient technology impedes the successful implementation of KM in academic libraries. Lack of sufficient technologies can be attributed to budgetary constraints. Therefore, there is a need for a proper budgetary planning in order to acquire adequate KM enabling technologies for the successful execution of KM project.

A lack of knowledge sharing culture: A lack of knowledge sharing culture was perceived a challenge by 58% of the participants. This is one of the critical factors, and the first cultural roadblock in KM implementation. The finding of this study corroborates with what Parirokh, Daneshgar, & Fattahi (2008) had established in their study that KM and knowledge sharing issue had not been institutionalized in the majority of academic libraries. The above authors have envisaged that the knowledge-sharing capabilities of academic libraries will eventually become one of their major critical success factors, developing a knowledge sharing culture is the backbone of KM success. Academic librarians have to share knowledge with their students, teaching staff and other stakeholders. However, a knowledge sharing culture is more conducive to knowledge creation and enhanced performance and reduces duplication of efforts. There is a range of technologies and tools to share knowledge such as the internet, intranets and extranets, groupware technologies e-mails and Lotus Notes discussion databases, chat rooms, expert-led discussions, web seminars, online meetings, virtual class room sessions, video-conferencing, sharing resources through library consortium. A knowledge sharing culture involves both organization and library staff. Organizational support refers to availability of appropriate KM enablers such as organizational procedures, culture and technological infrastructures. On an individual basis it refers to librarians' personal interests and the degree of enthusiasm for sharing knowledge (Parirokh, Daneshgar, & Fattahi, 2008). This again calls for change management at an organizational as well as an individual level. Organizations need to put in place appropriate incentives and training plans in order to motivate library staff for knowledge sharing and individual staff need change of mindsets to appreciate the benefits of knowledge sharing. Often librarians fail in locating and managing the knowledge potential in the heads of their own people (Selhorst, 2009). Parirokh, Daneshgar, & Fattahi (2008) have suggested numerous activities and strategies that can encourage knowledge sharing among librarians; research projects, training programs, online newsletters, teaching methods, knowledge-sharing policies and strategies, leadership and dedication of time, group discussions, communication channels, formal procedures including publication of manuals for staff and documenting experiences.

7. Conclusion & recommendations

Based on the findings and discussion it can be concluded that the majority of the participating librarians have recognized the importance of KM by distinguishing the reasons and challenges of practicing KM. However, challenges also point out that even after twenty decades, KM still remains a challenge for many university libraries in Africa. According to Yaacob (2010:14), "KM is a challenge to the information professionals and for the fields of librarianship and information science and needs to be taken seriously to leverage the intellectual assets and to facilitate knowledge utilization and creation". In order to achieve this "today's university libraries should assume active roles in becoming knowledge creation organizations and must strive for turning into truly humanistic knowledge societies where constant learning is possible for every librarian." (Daneshgar & Parirokh, 2007:31). Thus, KM is a way forward to survive and thrive for academic libraries/librarians.

To overcome the identified challenges and successful KM implementation in university/academic libraries, the author makes the following recommendations:

- First and foremost, a KM strategy is vital to lay out the background, expected outcomes and resource implications;
- Parent organizations should take KM seriously and allocate sufficient financial resources in order to provide needed KM infrastructures;
- To understand and adapt KM effectively, a rigorous training is essential for academic librarians;
- There should be adequate incentives for academic librarians to motivate them for KM practice and to create a knowledge sharing culture;

- To revitalize the library undertakings there is a need of proactive, self-confident, self-promoting, customer-focused and well-prepared library staff.
- There is a need for a mechanism to measure and monitor the progress and challenges of KM initiatives.

Further research

Based on the findings, there is a need for further research in the following areas:

- A more comprehensive study of Knowledge Management practices in University Libraries in Africa
- Role of incentives in promoting a knowledge sharing culture in academic libraries in Africa
- Customer knowledge Management in academic libraries.

8. References

Aharony, N. (2011). Librarians' Attitudes toward Knowledge Management. *College & Research Libraries,* Pp. 111-126.

Alavi, M. and D.E. Leidner, D.E. (2001). Review: Knowledge Management and Knowledge Management Systems: Conceptual Foundations and Research Issues. *MIS Quarterly,* 25(1): 107-136.

Arora, R. (2002). Implementing KM- a balanced score card approach. *Journal of Knowledge Management,* 6(3): 240-249.

Boom, D & Pimentel, T. (2009). A Framework for implementing knowledge management. Available at: http://www.cclfi.org/files/Knowledge%20Management%202009.pdf (Retrieved on 16 July, 2011).

Business Dictionary. (2011). BudinessDictionary Com Available at: http://www.businessdictionary.com/definition/best-practice.html (Retrieved on 2 July, 2011).

Case, Mary M. (2008). Partners in Knowledge Creation: An Expanded Role for Research Libraries in the Digital Future. *Journal of Library Administration,* 48 (2): 141-156.

Chase, R.L. (1998), Knowledge navigators. Available at: http://www.sla.org/pubs/serial/io/1998/sep98/chase1.html (Retrieved on 16 July, 2011).

Collins English Dictionary. (2004). Glasgow: Harper Collins.

Collison, C. (2010). So, what is Knowledge Management? Available at: http://chriscollison.wordpress.com/2010/05/24/so-what-is-knowledge-management/ (Retrieved on 2 July, 2011).

Constant, D., Kiesler, S. and Sproull, L. (1994). What's Mine Is Ours, or Is It? A Study of Attitudes about Information Sharing. *Information System Research,* 5(4): 400–21.

Daneshgar, F. & Parirokh, M. (2007). A knowledge schema for organisational learning in academic libraries. *Knowledge Management Research & Practice,* 5: 22–33. Available at:

http://faculty.fims.uwo.ca/koziol/781/documents/A%20knowledge%20schema %20for%20organisational.pdf (Retrieved on 9 July, 2011).

Daneshgar, F. and Bosanquet, L. (2010). Organizing Customer Knowledge in Academic Libraries" Electronic Journal of Knowledge Management Volume 8 Issue 1 (pp21 - 32), available at: http://www.ejkm.com/volume8/issue1 (Retrieved on 9 July, 2011).

Davenport, T. H., Prusack, L. (2000). Working Knowledge: How Organizations Manage What They Know. Boston: Harvard Business School Press.

Davenport, T.H. (2002). in Boom, D & Pimentel, T. (2009). A framework for implementing knowledge management. Available at: http://www.cclfi.org/files/Knowledge%20Management%202009.pdf (Retrieved on 30 July, 2011).

Debowski, S. (2006). *Knowledge Management*. John Wiley and Sons, Australia.

Drucker, P. (1989). *The New Realities.* Harper & Row, New York.

Goodman, N. & Schieman, J. (2010). Using knowledge management to leverage training and development initiatives. *Industrial and Commercial Training,* 42 (2): 112 - 115

Guru, B.P.M.C., Gopalaswamy, M., Arun, J. & Padmamma, S. (2009). Academic Library Management in India Challenges and Opportunities. Available at: http://crl.du.ac.in/ical09/papers/index_files/ical-74_245_695_1_RV.pdf (Retrieved on 6 August, 2011).

Hayes, H. (2004). The role of libraries in the knowledge economy. *Serials,* 17 (3): 231-238.

Israel, I.G. (2010). Information explosion and university libraries: Current trends and strategies for intervention. *Chinese Librarianship: an International Electronic Journal.* Available at: http://www.white-clouds.com/iclc/cliej/cl30ifijeh.pdf (Retrieved on 6 August, 2011).

Jain, Priti (2007). An Empirical Study of Knowledge Management in Academic Libraries in East and Southern Africa, *Library Review,* 56(5): 377-392.

Kim, Yong-Mi & Abbas, June (2010). Adoption of Library 2.0 Functionalities by Academic Libraries and Users: A Knowledge Management Perspective. *The Journal of Academic Librarianship,* (36) 3: 211–218.

Knowledge Management Research Center. (2010). 2010 Knowledge Management Conference: Making KM Productive. Available at: http://www.scribd.com/doc/26355818/Hong-Kong-Knowledge-Management-Society-2010-Knowledge-Management-Conference-Making-KM-Productive-30-March-2010 (Retrieved on 3 July, 2011).

Lee, Hwa-Wei. (2005). Knowledge Management and the Role of Libraries. Available at: http://www.ub.edu/bid/19mcknig.htm (Retrieved on 23 July, 2011).

McKnight, S. (2007). A Futuristic View of Knowledge and Information Management. Available at: http://www.white-clouds.com/iclc/cliej/cl19lee.htm (Retrieved on 31 July, 2011).

Meadow, C. T., Boyce, B.R. and Kraft, D.H.(2000). Text information retrieval systems, 2nd ed. San Diego, CA: Academic Press.

Nonaka, I. (1994). A dynamic theory of organizational knowledge creation. *Organization Science*, 5 (1):14-37.

Nonaka, I. and Takeuchi, H. (1995), *The Knowledge Creating Company*. Oxford University Press, New York, NY.

Parirokh, M. Daneshgar,F. & Fattahi, R. (2008). Identifying knowledge-sharing requirements in academic libraries. *Library Review*, 57(2): 107 - 122

Raja, W. Ahmad, Z. & Sinha, A.K. (2009). Knowledge Management and Academic Libraries in IT Era: Problems and Positions. Available at: http://crl.du.ac.in/ical09/papers/index_files/ical-124_198_418_2_RV.pdf (Retrieved on 23 July, 2011).

Roknuzzaman, Md, & Umemoto, K. (2009). How library practitioners view knowledge management in libraries: A qualitative study. *Library Management*, 30(8/9): 643-656

Saadan, K. (2001). Conceptual Framework for the Development of Knowledge Management System in Agricultural Research and Development. Malaysian Agricultural Research and Development Institute (MARDI). Available at: http://my.apan.net/meeting/downloads/nrKnowMv4.pdf (Retrieved on 3 July, 2011).

Sarrafzadeh, M., Martin, B. & Hazeri, A. (2010). Knowledge Management and Its Potential Applicability for Libraries. *Library Management*, 31(3): 198-212.

Selhorst, K. (2009). The power of collective intelligence: Improving customer service with social tools.

Sinotte, M. (2004). Exploration of the field of knowledge management for the library and information professional. *Libri*, 54: 190–198.

Skyrme, D.J. (2001). From Information Management to Knowledge Management: Are You Prepared? Available at: http://www.skyrme.com/pubs/on97full.htm (Retrieved on 23 July, 2011).

Southern African Development Community. (2011). SADC 1980 Years of Progress 2010. Available at: http://www.sadc.int/ (Retrieved on 30 July, 2011).

Susarla, A., Liu, D, & Whinston, A.B. (2003). Peer-to-Peer Enterprise Knowledge Management. In *Handbook on Knowledge Management. Pt. 2: Knowledge Directions*, pp 129-139, Berlin: Springer.

Sveiby, K.E. (1997). *The New Organisational Wealth - Managing and measuring Knowledge-Based Assets*. Berrett-Koehler, San Fransisco.

Townley, C.T. (2001). Knowledge Management and Academic Libraries. *College & Research Libraries*, Pp. 44-55.

Ugwu, C. I. & Ifeanyi J. Ezema (2010). Competencies for successful knowledge management applications in Nigerian academic libraries. *International Journal of Library and Information Science*, 2(9): 184-189.

Yaacob, R.A., Jamaluddin, A. & Jusoff, K. (2010). Knowledge Management and Challenging Roles of Academic Librarians. *Management Science and Engineering*, 4(4): 14-23.

Wen, Shixing. (2005). Implementing Knowledge Management in Academic Libraries: A Pragmatic Approach. Available at: http://www.white-clouds.com/iclc/cliej/cl19wen.htm (Retrieved on 16 July, 2011).

Xia, J. (2009). Library Publishing as a New Model of Scholarly Communication. *Journal of Scholarly Publishing*, 40(4): 370-383. (Retrieved on 16 August, 2011).

10

Organizational Forgetting/Unlearning: The Dark Side of the Absorptive Capacity

Vicenc Fernandez, Jose M Sallan, Pep Simo and Mihaela Enache
Universitat Politècnica de Catalunya
Spain

1. Introduction

During the past twenty years, absorptive capacity has become one of the constructs most widely used in diverse lines of work on the subject of organisational research. Initially, Cohen & Levinthal (1998,1990) defined absorptive capacity as the ability of a company to recognise the value of knowledge from the environment, assimilate it and exploit it for commercial purposes, with its development being a critical factor in obtaining a competitive advantage.

The enormous potential for explanation of the construct (Lane et al., 2002) has led to its use in more than one thousand publications indexed in research lines as organisational learning (Simonin, 1999; Barkema & Vermeulen, 1998), knowledge management (Szulanski, 1996; Ahuja & Katila, 2001), strategic alliances (Lane & Lubatkin, 1998; Lane et al., 2001) and innovation management (Kim & Kogut, 1996; Van den Bosch et al., 1999).

The application of the absorptive capacity in different, important, complex organisational phenomena has given rise to the use of diverse measures which are not clearly seen to converge in the same construct (Zahra & George, 2002). This has led some investigators to try and reconceptualise the construct absorptive capacity (Zahra & George, 2002; Lane et al.; 2002; Van den Bosch et al., 2003; Fernández, 2005; Lane et al., 2006), obtaining similar results which offer a new starting point for conducting research into the construct. These publications propose various lines of research about how to study the construction of a sustainable competitive advantage through possessing absorptive capacity. However, in our opinion, investigating the absorptive capacity of a company is merely a part of this research, for which reason, we postulate that research into the development and maintenance of absorptive capacity is equally important as investigating the causes and circumstances involved in the loss of this capacity.

Based on the above publications, this study establishes a working framework for including organisational forgetting or loss in the study of absorptive capacity and the creation of competitive advantages. Specific reference has been made to the concept of organisational forgetting, loss or unlearning by a small group of academics (Prahalad & Bettis, 1986; Nystrom & Starbuck, 1984; Martin de Holan & Phillips, 2003), in most cases, without it being the main subject of the research. This investigation also uses as a starting point the studies conducted by Martin de Holan & Phillips (2003, 2004) and Fernandez & Sune (2009) investigating how and why organisational forgetting occurs.

The theoretical contribution made by this document is to establish a set of guidelines for research into organisational forgetting/unlearning, in order to lay down a path for creating a solid, consistent basis of knowledge about absorptive capacity.

2. Review of literature

The review of literature is divided into two parts: a compilation of the main advances made in the absorptive capacity construct over the past twenty years and an introduction to organisational unlearning and forgetting processes.

2.1 Absorptive capacity

Acknowledgement of the importance of external flows of knowledge to companies has been a constant phenomenon in innovation processes during the past twenty years (Rigby & Zook, 2002). According to Cohen & Levinthal (1990) "external sources of knowledge are often critical in the innovation process on all organisational levels in which the unity of innovation is defined". With a view to studying the importance of that knowledge, Cohen & Levinthal (1989, 1990) introduced the absorptive capacity construct, which refers to the ability of a company to identify, assimilate and exploit knowledge from external sources for commercial purposes. One of the most important contributions made by Cohen & Levinthal was the integration into a single construct of diverse internal company processes in the creation of sustainable competitive advantages, through knowledge obtained from the environment (Zahra & George, 2002).

The widespread use of absorptive capacity has been studied and investigated on several occasions, as shown in the works of Zahra & George (2002), Lane et al. (2002) and Van den Bosch et al. (2003). These publications describe the importance of absorptive capacity in many different fields, including investment in R&D (Cohen & Levinthal, 1998), basic research activities in companies (Rosenberg, 1990; Dyer & Singh, 1998), strategic management (Lane & Lubatkin, 1998; Nahapiet & Ghosghal, 1998), technological management (Schilling, 1998; Mowery et al., 1996; Prager & Omenn, 1980), international business (Kedia & Bhagat, 1988), cooperation with scientists from outside the company (Cockburn & Henderson, 1998; Zucker et al., 1994, 1998, 2002; Gambardella, 1992), organisational economies (Glass & Saggi, 1998), trust and compatibility between acquired companies (Lane et al., 2001), employee skills (Vinding, 2006) and innovation (Fabrizio, 2009). Nonetheless, the ambiguity and diversity of the definitions used to describe absorptive capacity has given rise to different results and an unstable scientific basis for the construct (Zahra & George, 2002).

Lane et al. (2002) carried out a thematic study on research into the absorptive capacity construct. This study identified three publications that would have reviewed and expanded the original definition of the construct established by Cohen & Levinthal (1990). According to this research, the first academics to do this were Lane & Lubatkin, in 1998. The first noticeable difference in reconstructing the construct was a change in the analysis unit from the organisation to the relationship between two organisations. In the study by Lane & Lubatkin (1998), the notion of relative absorptive capacity is developed and it is proposed that the absorptive capacity of a company (receiver) in relation to another (emitter) depends on three factors: the type of new knowledge offered by the emitting company, the similarity between the compensation practices and organisational structures of the emitting and receiving companies and to what extent the receiving company is familiar with the organisational problems of the emitting company.

Another enlargement to the definition of absorptive capacity was introduced by Van den Bosch et al. (1999), with new aspects related to the company environment being introduced which allowed for the construct to be better understood. According to these authors, the absorptive capacity of a company generates an internal learning process which is later transformed into a new absorptive capacity. This way, feedback is established between the internal learning and the development of the absorptive capacity, which is conditioned by the type of environment in which the company competes.

The following reconceptualisation of the construct results from the research conducted by Zahra & George (2002). It defines absorptive capacity as a set of organisational routines and strategic processes through which companies acquire, assimilate, transform and use knowledge with the aim of creating value. In this case, the definition attempts to give more emphasis to dynamic capacities (Teece et al., 1997) which are oriented at strategic changes and flexibility. The redefinition of the construct by Zahra & George (2002) involves a change in the classic absorptive model formed by the acquisition, assimilation and exploitation dimensions (Cohen & Levinthal; 1990) towards a model to which the knowledge transformation dimension is added. According to the authors, these dimensions can be grouped into two components, depending on the extent to which they contribute to creating a competitive advantage (Zahra & George, 2002): potential absorptive capacity (acquisition and assimilation of knowledge from external sources) and realized absorptive capacity (transformation and exploitation of knowledge from external sources). Adopting a similar approach, Lane et al. (2006) discerned the learning process of exploration, transformation and exploitation, meaning that the classic focus on knowledge exploration processes (Lichtenthaler, 2009) was unable to guarantee the successful marketing of that knowledge without the appropriate knowledge exploitation processes.

	Potential absorptive capacity		Realized absorptive capacity
Phase 1	Acquisition	Phase 3	Transformation
Phase 2	Assimilation	Phase 4	Exploitation

Table 1. Dimensions of absorptive capacity, according to Zahra and George (2002)

In 2005, Fernandez conducted a study in which he analysed a selection of thirty publications on studied absorptive capacity that had caused an important impact on the scientific community. The result of the study was that Fernández was able to identify two limitations in the scientific studies published to date, which should be taken into account in future research into the construct. Firstly, the lack of a consistent, common basis between studies conducted into the construct, despite the fact that abundant literature exists about absorptive capacity (Zahra & George, 2002). This led to the final results of several studies being contradictory (Example: Tsai (2001) and Mowery et al. (1996)). Secondly, most studies are focused on studying absorptive capacity in R+D-intensive environments. Furthermore, very few investigators had studied the construct in relation to types of knowledge other than technological, as was the case of Lyles & Salk (1996). Although some studies emphasise the difficulties of separating the innovation process from absorptive capacity, the study by

Escribano et al. (2009) reveals the moderating effect of absorptive capacity on innovation processes in organisations.

2.2 Forgetting and unlearning of organisational knowledge

The knowledge-based approach (Barney, 1996) proposes that organisational knowledge represents the most critical intangible course in modern organisations (Nissen, 2005) since it is the principal source of sustainable differentiation capable of providing a competitive advantage (Dierickx & Cool, 1989; Lippman & Rumelt, 1982). This type of knowledge may be conceptualised through stocks of knowledge and knowledge or information flows (Dierick & Cool, 1989; DeCarolis & Deeds, 1999) and arises, in part, from some previous studies into the processing of information and organisational design. Since that time, both elements (stocks and flows of knowledge) have been the main topic in a large number of research lines such as the approach based on resources (Barney, 2001), capacities (Eisenhardt & Martin, 2000; Kogut & Zander, 1996), information view of NPD (Ancona & Caldwell, 1992) and organisational learning (Bontis et al., 2002; Huber, 1991).

Stocks of knowledge are described as the accumulation of knowledge assets existing within a company, while knowledge flows represent the streams of knowledge produced between different parts of the company or between external agents and the company which can be assimilated and transformed into stocks of knowledge (DeCarolis & Deeds, 1999). Knowledge flows have been classified based on three criteria:

- horizontal and vertical, i.e., knowledge that flows between units on the same level or between units on different levels within the company (Gupta & Govindarajan, 2000 ; Schulz, 2001),
- internal and external, i.e., knowledge that flows between units from the same company or between different companies (Kyriakopoulos & Ruyter, 2004), and
- incoming and outgoing, i.e., knowledge that flows towards a particular unit or from a particular unit (Gupta & Govindarajan, 2000).

Dierickx & Cool (1989) introduce a different classification of knowledge flows through the "bath-tub" metaphor. Based on this example, the stock of water is indicated by the level of water in the tub, and its level depends on the extra flows of water into the tub (through the tap) and the water lost from it (through a leak). Using this metaphor, Dierickx & Cool (1989) propose that a company's stock of knowledge may be increased through extra flows of knowledge or decreased or be reduced or lost through reduced flows of knowledge or organisational forgetting flows.

As commented above, stocks and flows of knowledge have been considered the main topic of organisational learning during recent decades. In this case, academics have focused their research on how, when and why organisational knowledge is created, acquired and managed. However, the organisational learning process is just part of a whole. According to Martin de Holan & Phillips (2004), the organisational forgetting process is just as important as the organisational learning process in achieving a sustainable competitive advantage. Research into organisational learning must be completed with information about how and under what circumstances companies forget, unlearn or lose organisational knowledge.

Organisational forgetting can be defined as the voluntary or non-voluntary loss of organisational knowledge on any level (Martin de Holan & Phillips, 2003). Although the study of organisational forgetting is a topic of little interest, some investigators have studied it in recent years (including Nystrom & Starbuck (198) and Starbuck (1996)). Nonetheless, most of these studies have dealt with organisational forgetting as a complement to the main subject of the research, or as an important aspect to be considered, but without analysing in any depth the circumstances in which it arises or how it arises. Recently, new research has been published which have attempted to treat organisational forgetting as the main subject (Lei et al., 1999; Martin de Holan & Phillips, 2004), but very few of them do so in an empirical way.

A review of literature shows that organisational forgetting has mainly been investigated from two standpoints (Martin de Holan & Phillips, 2004). Some studies consider organisational forgetting as the previous step to organisational learning. This standpoint proposes that certain routines, rules, tasks, roles, policies, values or strategies must be forgotten in order to acquire and assimilate new organisational knowledge through new routines, rules, tasks, roles, policies, values or strategies. Bateson (2000) postulates that organisational learning may be acquired on three different levels. For each one, Bateson implicitly proposes the need to implement a different organisational forgetting process. According to his research, level-one learning means "forgetting" actions or routines that were executed up to that time, in order to begin learning new actions or routines. Level-two learning involves "forgetting" certain rules, policies or strategies in order to implement a new learning process. Lastly, level-three learning refers to a change in the way of generating interpretations, i.e., a change in the mental model. Similarly, Argyris & Schöen (1974) propose a model comprised of two types of learning, in which an organisational forgetting process implicitly takes place. The first type is single loop learning and coincides with the level one learning of Bateson (2000). The second is known as double loop learning and is equivalent to the type two and three learning processes proposed by Bateson (2000). Regarding organisational forgetting in mental models, Prahalad & Bettis (1986) explain that the dominant logic of an organisation may act like a learning filter or barrier and so certain types of high-level learning require a change (and forgetting) in the organisation's dominant logic.

As opposed to the controlled and voluntary forgetting processes described in the preceding section, other researchers have studies accidental or undesired organisational forgetting (Argote et al., 1990; Dar et al., 1995; Epple et al., 1991). These studies are focused on the deterioration of knowledge in the organisational memory (Olivera, 2000) and in the existing control mechanisms for preventing this. According to Argote (1999), this type of organisational forgetting leads to extremely negative consequences on productivity and competitiveness, for which reason it must be prevented. This is shown explicitly in publications about organisational learning (Martin de Holan & Phillips, 2003), but no detailed studies have been conducted into the causes of accidental organisational forgetting processes.

	New knowledge	Established knowledge
Accidental	Dissipation	Degradation
Intentional	Suspension	Elimination

Table 2. Organisational forgetting modes, according to Martin de Holan & Phillips (2004)

Based on the two standpoints on forgetting set out above, Martin de Holan & Phillips (2004) have developed a theory about organisational forgetting, discussing its role in the dynamics of organisational knowledge within organisations and presenting a general classification of types of organisational forgetting processes. Based on this study, the authors propose a change in the approach of the scientific community to organisational forgetting, converting the classic approach which assumes that forgetting is a simple function, dependent on time and on use, into a much more complex process. Table 2 shows the types of organisational forgetting proposed by Martin de Holan & Phillips (2004), which are based on the two approaches mentioned above.

	Intentional	Unintentional
Codified	Internal innovation Obsolescence of knowledge	External innovation Loss of a knowledge repository
Non-codified	Internal innovation	External innovation Persons who embody the knowledge leave the organisation Low frequency of use

Table 3. Causes of organisational forgetting, according to Fernandez & Sune (2009)

The latest significant contribution to the subject of organisational forgetting and unlearning was made by Fernandez & Sune (2009) who presented a new classification of these processes (see table 3) that is totally compatible with the one proposed by Martin de Holan & Phillips (2004). According to their results, they concluded that forgetting is closely related to innovation. When innovation is internal, the type of forgetting generated will be intentional, since the specific purpose of innovation is to abandon the use of prior knowledge. When innovation is external, the type of forgetting generated will be unintentional. This is the case with a type of innovation that is not managed internally by the unit of analysis, but instead imposed from outside. With respect to unintentional forgetting, it should be highlighted that this involves the unwanted loss of a stock of knowledge by the unit of analysis; in such instances, the aim is to minimise its impact. In addition to innovation, the loss of the knowledge repository and the infrequent use of knowledge are identified as other causes of unintentional forgetting. The nature of the knowledge repository will differ, depending on whether the stock of knowledge is codified (e.g. computer file, written document, etc.) or non-codified (e.g. employees, organisational routines, etc.). The third cause of the unintentional forgetting of non-codified knowledge is its infrequent use.

3. Development of a working framework on organisational forgetting/unlearning

For the purpose of developing a working framework for conducting research into organisational forgetting or loss in studying absorptive capacity, an attempt is made to identify and describe the different organisational elements that could become deteriorated or unlearned which are linked to the absorptive capacity construct, in order to subsequently highlight them and analyse them within their own context.

Convington (1981) classifies the content of organisational memory in terms of the semantic value of the knowledge itself. Among the different classification methods proposed by Convington (1981), the one based on regulatory orientation (descriptive and prescriptive) has been widely accepted and used by the scientific community, as shown by the large number of researchers who have used it during the past decades (Stein, 1995). The content of descriptive organisational memory represents the actual classes that provide frameworks of action with which persons must work, such as technical and scientific knowledge, job descriptions within a company, inputs and outputs and events occurring in organisations (Stein, 1989). Descriptive knowledge is an approximation to the formal knowledge of a discipline as it describes things in the form of rules, abstract concepts and general principles. Descriptive knowledge is usually expressed in formal terms and stored in the organisational memory in the form of physical documents, such as databases and written documents.

The content of prescriptive organisational memory represents the actions that must be carried out to achieve the results expected by the organisation. This type of knowledge is the result of an internal evolution within the organisation, with a view to achieving greater efficiency in its procedures. Prescriptive knowledge is usually much more difficult to codify than descriptive knowledge, and is also not very susceptible to generalisations, unlike what occurs with descriptive knowledge. This type of organisational knowledge (prescriptive) is targeted as more operative issues, and is therefore expressed in the form of policies, strategies, rules, guidelines, etc.

3.1 Descriptive organisational knowledge

Descriptive knowledge is characterised in that it describes objects, situations, theories, technologies and other elements used within an organisation. It is also commonly expressed in formal terms (Stein, 1995). A study on literature written about absorptive capacity (Fernandez, 2005) says that most researchers consider absorptive capacity to be a skill related mainly to the acquisition of technical and scientific knowledge (descriptive knowledge), leaving out other types of descriptive knowledge and prescriptive knowledge.

Continuing with the classification proposed by Martin de Holan & Phillips (2004), descriptive knowledge and more specifically, technical and scientific knowledge, may be subject to organisational forgetting through four channels. Based on the three-dimension absorptive capacity model, the organisational forgetting dissipation mode is related to knowledge acquisition and assimilation processes. Little is known about the causes and conditions in which such losses occur, as they have only been studied indirectly in research into knowledge acquisition and transfer (Martin de Holan & Phillips, 1998). Due to the lack of difficulty in their codification and storage in the form of database or written documents (Nonaka & Takeuchi, 1995; Stein, 1995), the organisational forgetting suspension and elimination modes are processes of little practical interest, since these organisational forgetting modes are characterised in that they are mechanical and easy to put into practice. For similar reasons to the above, descriptive knowledge and more specifically, scientific and technical knowledge that has been correctly assimilated undergoes a very low degree of degradation in organisational memory.

In sum, the organisational forgetting of descriptive knowledge during the processes forming the absorptive capacity construct is of major interest in the acquisition and assimilation phases, due to the dissipation of knowledge. The study of how, why and under what circumstances dissipation takes place in both these processes can be considered as the natural evolution in the study of absorptive capacity carried out up to the present time. This type of research could enable the identification of inefficiencies in the processes integrating the absorptive capacity, thereby improving it.

3.2 Prescriptive organisational knowledge

On the other hand, prescriptive knowledge shows the actions and direction to be followed in order to achieve the results expected by the organisation. Although it maintains formal aspects, prescriptive knowledge is directed more at operating issues.

"When competition is mainly based on knowledge, companies must evolve using the comprehension of their own knowledge and the processes through which knowledge is converted into organisational capacities and the capacity of those organisational capacities is converted into a response to the demands of its environment" (Lane & Lubatkin, 1998). Winter (2000) describes organisational capacity as a high-level routine (or a collection of routines) which, along with their incoming flows, provides company management with a set of potential options or decisions to achieve significant results for a specific type of problem.

3.2.1 Zero-level organisational capacities

From the global perspective of absorptive capacity, the acquisition, assimilation and exploitation of knowledge coming from the environment not only refers to technical and scientific knowledge, but to other types of knowledge which in most cases, are usually more difficult to assimilate and exploit, such as knowledge related to marketing and knowledge about management or leadership techniques (Lane et al., 2001). Unlike technical and scientific knowledge, this type of knowledge is assimilated by the organisation through rules, tasks and guidelines, which, when combined, form zero-level organisational capacities. According to Winter (2003), zero-level organisational capacities are those which enable a company to carry out everyday work on a short-term basis. Collis (1994) proposed that infinite capacity levels may exist in organisations, from the lowest level (level zero) which allows everyday work to be carried out in the company, to capacities of any level that enable the creation, modification or elimination of lower-level capacities. Winter (2003) suggests that in practice, it is only necessary to study the zero and first-level capacities, as the rest are only of interest in the mathematical sense.

Focusing on zero-level organisational capacities, and based on the absorptive capacity approach, prescriptive knowledge is assimilated through organisational rules, guidelines and routines instead of databases or written documents, as in the case of technical and scientific knowledge. The form in which this type of prescriptive knowledge is stored involves new implications in the organisational forgetting process. Prescriptive knowledge, as occurs with descriptive knowledge, may suffer dissipation (organisational forgetting or loss) through the absorptive capacity acquisition and assimilation processes. However, the causes and consequences of that organisational forgetting are usually different, and so the control mechanisms for one type of knowledge and another must be studied using different approaches. A second difference between descriptive and prescriptive knowledge in organisational forgetting emerges with the degradation of knowledge. Given that prescriptive knowledge is assimilated through rules, guidelines and routines, this type of organisational knowledge usually undergoes greater degradation if the adequate control mechanisms are not applied. Prescriptive knowledge is more easily affected by degradation

than descriptive knowledge, as it contains a large portion of tacit knowledge (unlike descriptive knowledge).
Organisational forgetting by elimination, i.e., based on the decision of the company, usually involves many complications, since that knowledge is not in a physical site but in the routines, tasks and guidelines used on a daily basis by employees. Authors such as Greenwood & Hinings (1996), Piderit (2000) and Cox (1997) have indirectly investigated this type of organisational forgetting, through studying organisational change. However, the reasons why the elimination of routines or organisational capacities is more effective in certain situations than in others have not yet been studied in sufficient depth. Regarding the elimination of zero-level capacities, Winter (2003) proposes the existence of first-level capacities, or dynamic capacities that allow a change to be made in lower level capacities, through the creation, modification, adaptation or elimination of zero-level capacities.

3.2.2 First-level or dynamic organisational capacities

According to Teece et al. (1997), a dynamic capacity is the ability of a company to integrate, build and reconfigure internal and external competencies that will allow it to rapidly react to changes taking place in its environment. In other words, dynamic capacities reveal organisational skill in achieving new and innovative forms of obtaining a competitive advantage (Leonard-Barton, 1992). The redefinition of Zahra & George (2002) about absorptive capacity suggests that it is a dynamic capacity which enables the acquisition, assimilation, transformation and exploitation of knowledge in the environment in order to obtain a sustainable competitive advantage. Based on that standpoint, absorptive capacity is a first-level organisational capacity, as it allows certain changes to be made in zero-level capacities, with the objective of achieving an advantage over competitors.
The study conducted by Van den Bosch et al. (1999) shows that a company's absorptive capacity makes it possible to generate internal learning (creation, adaptation, modification or elimination of knowledge and capacities) which subsequently leads to an increase in that company's absorptive capacity. Indirectly, the study postulated that absorptive capacity, a first-level organisational capacity, was able to change zero-level or descriptive knowledge capacities. Based on that perspective, absorptive capacity can also undergo an organisational forgetting process, through the four modes proposed by Martin de Holan & Phillips (2004), but the form and conditions with which this occurs are widely different from those studied to date.
Cohen & Levinthal (1990) and other authors say that absorptive capacity is a sub-product of organisational learning, which gives rise to more efficient learning in the future. According to those authors, and based on the similarity with cognitive structures, the accumulation of absorptive capacity over a specific period permits a more efficient accumulation in the following period, and thus, improved internal learning of descriptive knowledge and of zero-level organisational capacities. Continuing with the explanation given by Cohen & Levinthal (1990) and Van den Bosch et al. (1998), absorptive capacity can be considered a sub-product of learning, for which reason research into the dissipation or suspension of absorptive capacity is difficult to consider. This fact coincides with the small number of empirical studies performed on dynamic capacities, as opposed to the large number of theoretical publications that exists on dynamic capacities. Before initiating organisational forgetting due to dissipation and suspension, the scientific community should study the mechanisms and conditions necessary for the development of absorptive capacity in greater depth.

Despite the fact that the dissipation and suspension of absorptive capacity have not yet been studied, the degradation and elimination of absorptive capacity have been dealt with in various publications (Bettis & Prahalad, 1995; Lei et al., 1999; Nystrom & Starbuck, 1984). According to these studies, the capacity to forget (eliminate, according to the terminology used to date) higher-level organisational capacities is a key factor in the success of an organisation. Enlarging on the simile proposed by Bettis & Prahalad (1986), organisational capacities function like elements that funnel lower-level capacities. For this reason, to adapt to the changes taking place in the environment, companies must be able to eliminate the organisational capacities that prevent them from adapting to the new situation. Depending on how significant the change is, and its extension, it will be necessary to eliminate organisational capacities from one level to another, and it may even be necessary to eliminate or change the deeply-rooted aspects of an organisation, such as its organisational culture or the dominant logic proposed by Prahalad & Bettis (1986). Although the elimination of high-level or dynamic capacities has been discussed in several studies, the manner in which they must be eliminated and under what circumstances it is more convenient to eliminate them has not yet been studied in sufficient depth and with an empirical focus. Another gap exists in this respect in studying organisational forgetting in relation to dynamic capacities and more specifically, absorptive capacity.

Lastly, the degradation of dynamic or first-level capacities has been studied in depth (Prahalad & Hamel, 1990; Hamel & Prahalad, 1994) as the cause of degradation in competitive advantages. The type of environment (Slater, 1996), competitive level (Lei & Slocum, 2005), changes in market needs (Srivastava et al., 2001; Woodruff, 1997), new technologies (Mata et al., 1995), characteristics of the organisation (Lei & Slocum, 2002) and other decisive factors have been studied as causes of degradation of competitive advantages and consequently, of some first-level organisational capacities. For this reason, research into the degradation of dynamic capacities is less attractive than the previous types of organisational forgetting when considering the study of absorptive capacity. Nevertheless, a compilation of those studies and their inclusion within the context of organisational forgetting could permit a better comprehension of the importance of creating control mechanisms to prevent the loss of this type of organisational knowledge.

4. Conclusions

This chapter has attempted to explore organisational forgetting or unlearning through different levels of organisational knowledge related to absorptive capacity, with a view to establishing a working framework on the subject. With this purpose, the type of organisational forgetting proposed by Martin de Holan & Phillips (2004) has been used, comprised of four forgetting modes: dissipation, suspension, degradation and elimination. Similarly, due to the great diversity of organisational knowledge linked to absorptive capacity that exists in any organisation, the classification proposed by Covington (1981) has been used, using categorisation that is based on the regulatory orientation of organisational knowledge. With respect to the type of organisational knowledge, part of the prescriptive knowledge has been segmented into two levels (zero and first level) based on the classification proposed and used by Collis (1994) and Winter (2003) for organisational capacities. From this point on, the existence of research on the type of organisation forgetting for each level of organisational knowledge has been explained, also showing the gaps that the scientific community has not yet discussed, or which have been discussed in insufficient depth. Table 4 shows a summary of the working framework developed.

	Descriptive knowledge	Prescriptive knowledge	
		Zero-level capacities	First-level capacities
Dissipation	XXXX	XX	X
Suspension	XXXX	XX	X
Degradation	X	XXXX	XXXX
Elimination	X	XXXX	XXXX
X: of little academic interest XX: of some academic interest XXXX: of considerable academic interest			

Table 4. Type of organisational forgetting or unlearning process depending on the organisational knowledge related to absorptive capacity

This chapter shows the existence of studies which have dealt with different types of organisational forgetting over the past twenty years, but in most cases, indirectly or without analysing the subject in sufficient depth. Furthermore, the research carried out to date on organisational forgetting has been planned without considering the different types of organisational knowledge existing in an organisation. We consider that this distinction is of supreme importance, since the forms and conditions in which organisational forgetting takes place for each type of knowledge are different, therefore leading to a different approach in each study.

This new working framework aims to clarify the existence of different types of organisational forgetting on different organisational knowledge levels. This framework aims to show the complex nature of organisational forgetting in research and the need to conduct studies in greater depth on the subject, in order to understand how, why and in what conditions organisational forgetting takes place and to investigate the existing mechanisms for controlling it.

4.1 Future research

The purpose of this chapter is not to ensure that research compiles and studies all the existing types of organisational forgetting or unlearning, as each one has its own peculiarities and therefore such research would be well nigh impossible to conduct. However, each organisational forgetting mode on each organisational level may lead to research with very interesting findings in an academic and practical sense. As Martin de Holan & Phillips (2004) suggest, on some occasions, the most important activity in knowledge management is to channel an organisational forgetting process while on others, the main activity is to try and avoid that process, in order to respectively reach or maintain a competitive advantage.

5. References

Ahuja, G. & Katila, R. (2001). Technological acquisitions and the innovation performance of acquiring firms: A longitudinal study. *Strategic Management Journal*, Vol.22, No.3, pp. 197-220, ISSN 0143-2095

Ancona, D. G. & Caldwell, D. F. (1992). Demography and design - predictors of new product team performance. *Organization Science*, Vol.3, No.3, pp. 321-341, ISSN 1047-7039

Argote, L.; Beckman, S. L. & Epple, D. (1990). The Persistence and Transfer of Learning in Industrial Settings. *Management Science*, Vol.36, No.2, pp. 140-154, ISSN 0025-1909

Argote, L. (1999). *Organizational learningcreating, retaining, and transferring knowledge*, Kluwer Academic, ISBN 0792384202, Boston, USA

Argyris, C. & Schöen, D. A. (1974). *Theory in practice*, Jossey-Bass, San Francisco, USA

Barkema, H. G. & Vermeulen, F. (1998). International expansion through start-up or acquisition: A learning perspective. *Academy of Management Journal*, Vol.41, No.1, pp. 7-26, ISSN 0001-4273

Barney, J. B. (1996). The resource-based theory of the firm. *Organization Science*, Vol.7, No.5, pp. 469, ISSN 1047-7039

Barney, J. B. (2001). Is the resource-based "view" a useful perspective for strategic management research? yes. *Academy of Management Review*, Vol.26, No.1, pp. 41-56, ISSN 0363-7425

Bateson, G. (2000). *Steps to an ecology of the mind: Collected essays in anthropology, psychiatry, evolution and epistemology*, University of Chicago Press, ISBN 0226039056, Chicago, USA

Bettis, R. A. & Prahalad, C. K. (1995). The Dominant Logic - Retrospective and Extension. *Strategic Management Journal*, Vol.16, No.1, pp. 5-14, ISSN 0143-2095

Bontis, N.; Crossan, M. M. & Hulland, J. (2002). Managing an organizational learning system by aligning stocks and flows. *Journal of Management Studies*, Vol.39, No.4, pp. 437-469, ISSN 0022-2380

Cockburn, I. M. & Henderson, R. (1998). Absorptive capacity, coauthoring behavior, and the organization of research in drug discovery. *The Journal of Industrial Economics*, Vol.XLVI, No.2, pp. 157–182, ISSN 1467-6451

Cohen, W. M. & Levinthal, D. A. (1989). Innovation and Learning - the 2 Faces of R-And-D. *Economic Journal*, Vol.99, No.397, pp. 569-596, ISSN 1468-0297

Cohen, W. M. & Levinthal, D. A. (1990). Absorptive-Capacity - A New Perspective on Learning and Innovation. *Administrative Science Quarterly*, Vol.35, No.1, pp. 128-152

Collis, D. J. (1994). Research Note - How Valuable Are Organizational Capabilities. *Strategic Management Journal*, Vol.15, pp. 143-152, ISNN 0001-8392

Covington, C. R. (1981). *The presidency as a learning organization: The development of organizational memory within presidential agencies*. University of Illinois at Urbana-Champaign, Illinois, USA

Cox, J. R. W. (1997). Manufacturing the past: Loss and absence in organizational change. *Organization Studies*, Vol.18, No.4, pp. 623-654, ISSN 0170-8406

Darr, E. D.; Argote, L. & Epple, D. (1995). The acquisition, transfer, and depreciation of knowledge in service organizations: Productivity in franchises. *Management Science*, Vol.41, No.11, pp. 1750-1762, ISSN 0025-1909

DeCarolis, D. M. & Deeds, D. L. (1999). The impact of stocks and flows of organizational knowledge on firm performance: An empirical investigation of the biotechnology industry. *Strategic Management Journal*, Vol.20, No.10, pp. 953-968, ISSN 0143-2095

Martin de Holan, P. M. & Phillips, N. (2003). Organizational forgetting. In: *The Blackwell handbook of organizational learning and knowledge management*, M. Easterby-Smith & M. A. Lyles (Eds.), 393-409, USA

Martin de Holan, P. M. & Phillips, N. (2004). Remembrance of things past? The dynamics of organizational forgetting. *Management Science*, Vol.50, No.11, pp. 1603-1613, ISSN 0025-1909

Martin de Holan, P. M.; Phillips, N. & Lawrence, T. B. (2004). Managing organizational forgetting. *Mit Sloan Management Review*, Vol.45, No.2, pp. 45-51, ISSN 1532-9194

Dierickx, I. & Cool, K. (1989). Asset stock accumulation and sustainability of competitive advantage. *Management Science*, Vol.35, No.12, pp. 1504-1511, ISSN 0025-1909

Dyer, J. H. & Singh, H. (1998). The relational view: cooperative strategy and sources of interorganizational competitive advantage. *Academy of Management Review*, Vol.23, No.4, pp. 660, ISSN 0363-7425

Eisenhardt, K. M. & Martin, J. A. (2000). Dynamic capabilities: What are they? *Strategic Management Journal*, Vol.21, No.10-11, pp. 1105-1121, , ISNN 0001-8392

Epple, D.; Argote, L. & Devadas, R. (1991). Organization learning curves: A method for investigating intra-plant transfer of knowledge acquired through learning by doing. *Organization Science*, Vol.2, No.1, pp. 58-70, ISSN 1047-7039

Escribano, A.; Fosfuri, A. & Tribó, J. A. Managing external knowledge flows: The moderating role of absorptive capacity. *Research Policy*, Vol.38, pp. 96–105, ISSN 0048-7333

Fabrizio, K. R. (2009). Absorptive capacity and the search for innovation. *Research Policy*, Vol.38, pp. 255-267, ISSN 0048-7333

Fernández, V. (2005). Remarks about the research of the absorptive capacity construct. *Intangible Capital*, Vol. 10, No.I, pp. 1-9, ISSN 1967-9818

Fernandez, V. & Sune, A. (2009). Organizational Forgetting and its causes: an empirical research. *Journal of Organizational Change Management*, Vol.22, No.6, pp. 620-634, ISSN 0953-4814

Gambardella, A. (1992). Competitive advantages from in-house scientific research: the US pharmaceutical industry in the 1980s. *Research Policy*, Vol.21, pp. 391–407, ISSN 0048-7333

Glass, A. J. & Saggi, K. (1998). International technology transfer and the technology gap. *Journal of Development Economics*, Vol.55, No.2, pp. 369-398, ISSN 0304-3878

Greenwood, R. & Hinings, C. R. (1996). Understanding radical organizational change: Bringing together the old and the new institutionalism. *Academy of Management Review*, Vol.21, No.4, pp. 1022-1054, ISSN 0363-7425

Gupta, A. K. & Govindarajan, V. (2000). Knowledge flows within multinational corporations. *Strategic Management Journal*, Vol.21, No.4, pp. 473-496, ISSN 0143-2095

Hamel, G. & Prahalad, C. K. (1994). *Competing for the future*, Harvard Business School Press, ISBN 0875847161, Boston, USA

Huber, G. P. (1991). Organizational learning: the contributing processes and the literatures. *Organization science*, Vol.2, pp. 88-115, ISSN 1047-7039

Kedia, B. L. & Bhagat, R. S. (1988). Cultural constraints on transfer of technology across nations: Implications for research in intenational and comparative management. *Academy of Management Review*, Vol.13, pp. 559-571, ISSN 0363-7425

Kim, D. J. & Kogut, B. (1996). Technological platforms and diversification. *Organization Science*, Vol.7, No.3, pp. 283-301, ISSN 1047-7039

Kogut, B. & Zander, U. (1996). What firms do? Coordination, Identity and Learning. *Organization Science*, Vol.7, No.5, pp. 502-518, ISSN 1047-7039

Kyriakopoulos, K. & de Ruyter, K. (2004). Knowledge stocks and information flows in new product development. *Journal of Management Studies*, Vol.41, No.8, pp. 1469-1498, ISSN 0022-2380

Lane, P. J.; Koka, B. & Pathak, S. (2002).A thematic analysis and critical assessment of absorptive capacity research. *Proceedings of Academy of Management Meeting*, pp. 1-6, USA, 2002

Lane, P. J. & Lubatkin, M. (1998). Relative absorptive capacity and interorganizational learning. *Strategic Management Journal*, Vol.19, No.5, pp. 461-477, ISSN 0143-2095

Lane, P. J.; Salk, J. E.; & Lyles, M. A. (2001). Absorptive capacity, learning, and performance in international joint ventures. *Strategic Management Journal*, Vol.22, No.12, pp. 1139-1161, ISSN 0143-2095

Lei, D. & Slocum, J. W. (2002). Organization designs to renew competitive advantage. *Organizational Dynamics*, Vol.31, No.1, pp. 1-18, ISSN 0090-2616

Lei, D. & Slocum, J. W. (2005). Strategic and organizational requirements for competitive advantage. *Academy of Management Executive*, Vol.19, No.1, pp. 31-45, ISSN 0896-3789

Lei, D.; Slocum, J. W. & Pitts, R. A. (1999). Designing organizations for competitive advantage: The power of unlearning and learning. *Organizational Dynamics*, Vol.27, No.3, pp. 24-38, ISSN 0090-2616

Leonard-Barton, D. (2006). *Wellsprings of knowledge*, Harvard Business School Press, ISBN 0875846122, Boston, USA

Lichtenthaler, U. (2009). Absorptive capacity, environmental turbulence, and the complementarity of organizational learning processes. *Academy of Management Journal*, Vol.52, No.4, pp. 822-846, ISSN 0001-4273

Lippman, S. A. & Rumelt, R. P. (1982). Uncertain imitability - An analysis of interfirm differences in efficiency under competition. *Bell Journal of Economics*, Vol.13, No.2, pp. 418-438, ISSN 0361-915X

Lyles, M. A. & Salk, J. E. (1996). Knowledge acquisition from foreign parents in international joint ventures: An empirical examination in the Hungarian context. *Journal of International Business Studies*, Vol.27, No.5, pp. 877-903, ISSN 0047-2506

Mata, F. J.; Fuerst, W. L. & Barney, J. B. (1995). Information technology and sustained competitive advantage: A resource-based analysis. *Mis Quarterly*, Vol.19, No.4, pp. 487-505, ISSN 0276-7783

Mowery, D. C.; Oxley, J. E. & Silverman, B. S. (1996). Strategic alliances and interfirm knowledge transfer. *Strategic Management Journal*, Vol.17, pp. 77-91, ISSN 0143-2095

Nahapiet, J. & Ghoshal, S. (1998). Social capital, intellectual capital, and the organizational advantage. *Academy of Management Review*, Vol.23, No.2, pp. 242-266, ISSN 0363-7425

Nissen, M. E. (2005). Dynamic knowledge patterns to inform design: A field study of knowledge stocks and flows in an extreme organization. *Journal of Management Information Systems*, Vol.22, No.3, pp. 225-263, ISSN 0742-1222

Nonaka, I. & Takeuchi, H. (1995). *The knowledge-creating company: how Japanese companies create the dynamics of innovation*, Oxford University Press, New York, USA

Nystrom, P. C. & Starbuck, W. H. (1984). To avoid organizational crises, unlearn. *Organizational dynamics*, Vol.12, No.4, pp. 53-65, ISSN 0090-2616

Olivera, F. (2000). Memory systems in organizations: An empirical investigation of mechanisms for knowledge collection, storage and access. *Journal of Management Studies*, Vol.37, No.6, pp. 811-832, ISSN 0022-2380

Piderit, S. K. (2000). Rethinking resistance and recognizing ambivalence: A multidimensional view of attitudes toward an organizational change. *Academy of Management Review*, Vol.25, No.4, pp. 783-794, ISSN 0363-7425

Prager, D.J. & Omenn, G.S. (1980). Research, innovation, and university-industry link- ages. *Science*, Vol.207, No.4429, pp. 379–384, ISSN 0036-8075

Prahalad, C. K. & Bettis, R. A. (1986). The Dominant Logic - A New Linkage Between Diversity and Performance. *Strategic Management Journal*, Vol.7, No.6, pp. 485-501, ISSN 0143-2095

Prahalad, C. K. & Hamel, G. (1990). The Core Competence of the Corporation. *Harvard Business Review*, Vol.68, No.3, pp. 79-91, ISSN 0017-8012

Rigby, D. & Zook, C. (2002). *Open-market innovation*, Harvard Business Review, Boston, USA

Rosenberg, N. (1990). Why do firms do basic research (with their own money)? *Research Policy*, Vol.19, pp. 165–174, ISSN 0048-7333

Schilling, M. A. (1998). Technological lockout: An integrative model of the economic and strategic factors driving technology success and failure. *Academy of Management Review*, Vol.23, No.2, pp. 267-284, ISSN 0363-7425

Schulz, M. (2001). The uncertain relevance of newness: Organizational learning and knowledge flows. *Academy of Management Journal*, Vol.44, No.4, pp. 661-681, ISSN 0001-4273

Simonin, B. L. (1999). Ambiguity and the process of knowledge transfer in strategic alliances. *Strategic Management Journal*, Vol.20, No.7, pp. 595-623, ISSN 0025-1909

Slater, S. F. (1996). The challenge of sustaining competitive advantage. *Industrial Marketing Management*, Vol.25, No.1, pp. 79-86, ISSN 0019-8501

Srivastava, R. K.; Fahey, L. & Christensen, H. K. (2001). The resource-based view and marketing: The role of market-based assets in gaining competitive advantage. *Journal of Management*, Vol.27, No.6, pp. 777-802, ISSN 0149-2063

Starbuck, W. H. (1996). Unlearning ineffective or obsolete technologies. *International Journal of Technology Management*, Vol.11, No.7-8, pp. 725-737, ISSN 1741-5276

Stein, E. W. (1995). Organizational Memory - Review of Concepts and Recommendations for Management. *International Journal of Information Management*, Vol.15, No.1, pp. 17-32, ISSN 0268-4012

Stein, E. W. (1989). Organizational memory: Socio-Technical framework and empirical research. University of Penssylvania, Philadelphia, USA

Szulanski, G. (1996). Exploring internal stickiness: Impediments to the transfer of best practice within the firm. *Strategic Management Journal*, Vol.17, pp. 27-43, ISSN 0143-2095

Teece, D. J.; Pisano, G. & Shuen, A. (1997). Dynamic capabilities and strategic management. *Strategic Management Journal*, Vol.18, No.7, pp. 509-533, ISSN 0143-2095

Tsai, W. P. (2001). Knowledge transfer in intraorganizational networks: Effects of network position and absorptive capacity on business unit innovation and performance. *Academy of Management Journal*, Vol.44, No.5, pp. 996-1004, ISSN 0001-4273

Van den Bosch, F. A. J.; Van Wijk, R. & Volberda, H. W. (2003). Absorptive capacity: antecedents, models, and outcomes. In: *The Blackwell handbook of organizational learning and knowledge management*, M. Easterby-Smith & M. A. Lyles (Eds.), 278-302, ISBN 0631226729, USA

Van den Bosch, F. A. J.; Volberda, H. W. & de Boer, M. (1999). Coevolution of firm absorptive capacity and knowledge environment: Organizational forms and combinative capabilities. *Organization Science*, Vol.10, No.5, pp. 551-568, ISSN 1047-7039

Vinding, A. L. (2006). Absorptive capacity and innovative performance: a human capital approach. *Economics of Innovation and New Technology*, Vol.15, No.4/5, pp. 507–517, ISSN 1043-8599

Winter, S. G. (2000). The satisficing principle in capability learning. *Strategic Management Journal*, Vol.21, No.10-11, pp. 981-996, ISSN 0143-2095

Winter, S. G. (2003). Understanding dynamic capabilities. *Strategic Management Journal*, Vol.24, No.10, pp. 991-995, ISSN 0143-2095

Woodruff, R. B. (1997). Customer value: The next source for competitive advantage. *Journal of the Academy of Marketing Science*, Vol.25, No.2, pp. 139-153, ISSN 0092-0703

Zahra, S. A. & George, G. (2002). Absorptive capacity: A review, reconceptualization, and extension. *Academy of Management Review*, Vol.27, No.2, pp. 185-203, ISSN 0363-7425

Zucker, L. G.; Darby, M. R. & Armstrong, J. (1994). Intellectual captial and the firm: the technology of geographically localized knowledge spillovers. *NBER Working Paper Number 4946*

Zucker, L. G.; Darby, M. R. & Armstrong, J. S. (2002). Commercializing knowledge: University science, knowledge capture, and firm performance in biotechnology. *Management Science*, Vol.48, No.1, pp. 138–152, ISSN 0025-1909

Zucker, L. G.; Darby, M. R. & Brewer, M. B. (1998). Intellectual human capital and the birth of U.S. biotechnology enterprises. *American Economic Review*, Vol.88, No.1, pp. 290–306, ISSN 0002-8282

11

Informal Learning and Complex Problem Solving of Radiologic Technologists Transitioning to the Workplace

Victoria J. Marsick and Jennifer L. Yates
Teachers College, Columbia University, and Merritt College
United States of America

1. Introduction

Knowledge use can be highly dependent on the judgment of professionals who translate "book knowledge" into practice. Practitioners use judgment and interpretation to create new knowledge suited to local circumstances. Some of this knowledge is unique to individuals, but often local knowledge is valuable if shared with others facing similar challenges. Knowledge use can be difficult under the best of circumstances. Professionals regularly take many human and technical factors into consideration when learning to apply what they know to new circumstances. Much of this learning is informal. It takes place on the job as professionals learn through and from their experience of using what they know to meet the needs of a range of unanticipated circumstances. Organizations can reap dividends when conditions support effective informal learning on the job. The consequences of not doing so can be seen in lost opportunities and ineffectiveness. In some settings, such as healthcare, life or death outcomes can weigh in the balance. In all cases, lost learning diminishes the quantity and quality of knowledge generated and shared, and as such, detracts from the goals of knowledge management.

In this chapter, we address the relationships between informal learning and knowledge creation, sharing and management in organizations. We first explore the social dimensions of knowledge management in relationship to the informal learning literature in order to examine potential links between the two with a focus on how professionals learn and generate new ideas or practices at work. We turn then to the heart of this chapter based on a multiple case study of informal learning and complex problem solving of radiologic technologists. This research provides an in-depth look at knowledge creation and sharing through the lens of informal learning.

2. Linking knowledge management and informal learning

A good deal of learning, especially for professionals, happens organically and informally as people tackle common challenges at work. The proportion of informal-to-formal learning in organizations is estimated at 70-80%, a ratio confirmed by several studies (e.g., Leslie, Aring, & Brand, 2003; Loweinstein & Spletzer, 1999; McCall, Lombardo, & Morrison, 1998). Knowledge management and informal learning are often examined in separate literatures, yet there are important links between them. Conversation, social interaction and collaboration, relationships, and work-based learning practices form the heart of informal workplace learning. These practices are also key to conceptualizations of knowledge creation and sharing that emphasize its social dimensions and a constructivist view of what knowing means.

2.1 Social dimensions of knowledge management

O'Toole (2011) points to two main approaches to knowledge management, one that emphasizes "semantic knowledge retention in the form of databases" and a second that "emphasizes knowledge management as a social communication process" (p. 26). This depiction parallels the frequently cited classification of knowledge as explicit or tacit, although as many authors have also noted, both types of knowledge can sometimes co-exist in any given circumstance. Explicit knowledge is more easily captured and shared via IT databases and communication systems, whereas tacit knowledge is often not fully conscious or understood, and is shared through conversation, storytelling, nonverbal communication, and art or drama or other aesthetic experiences.

Nonaka and Takeuchi (1995) built their understanding of knowledge creation on the importance of converting tacit knowledge to explicit knowledge as a means of creating new knowledge in the workplace. Nonaka and Takeuchi (1995) purported that "tacit knowledge is deeply rooted in an individual's action and experience, as well as in the ideals, values, or emotions he or she embraces" (p. 8). They recognized two dimensions of tacit knowledge, the first being technical knowledge or "know-how" specific to a particular craft, and a cognitive dimension consisting of "schemata, mental models, beliefs, and perceptions so ingrained that we take them for granted) (p. 8). Van Krogh et al. (2000), building on these ideas, emphasized the difference between managing knowledge and knowledge enabling. The latter "depends on an enabling context" which they further define as "a shared space that fosters emerging relationships" that resembles "the Japanese idea of *ba* (or 'place')" which "is connected to …two points: knowledge is dynamic, relational, and based on human action; it depends on the situation and people involved rather than on absolute truth or hard facts" (p. 7). In doing so, they take a constructivist view of knowledge creation, that is, that people make their own meanings in interaction with one another in context. Constructivism is "postmodern" in that its adherents do not believe in an objective truth that is separate from the people who create it. Knowledge, therefore, is constructed and interpreted individually based on a person's history and experience, but knowledge can be shared because social realities often overlap and interact.

Cianciolo, Matthew, Sternberg, and Wagner (2006) describe tacit knowledge as "an adaptive intellectual resource stemming from the active interaction between individuals and their dynamic environment" (p. 617). A trusting environment is essential for this to happen. Building on Nonaka and Takeuchi (1995), Van Krogh et al. (2000) identify five key steps for knowledge creation: sharing tacit knowledge, creating a concept, justifying a concept, building a prototype, and cross-leveling knowledge (p. 9). They note that "managing conversations" is one of only two links that are common to all five steps. "Effective conversations," they continue, "allow for higher creativity; stimulate the sharing of tacit knowledge, concept creation, and justification; are essential for developing a powerful prototype; and lubricate the flow of knowledge across various organizational levels" (Ibid). Conversations take place in relationships and social interaction. Context — in particular a supportive caring *ba,* conducive to trust – affects this kind of knowledge creation and sharing. In organizations, context is influenced by group and organizational structures, practices, climate and culture.

2.2 Informal learning

Similar ideas – constructivism, tacit knowing, meaning making through interaction with others, and the critical importance of context to learning that is highly situated – likewise permeate research and practice focused on informal learning. Informal learning is often defined in contrast to formal learning. It is organic, and typically motivated, directed and sustained by one's own intentions and interests. An online survey by The American Society for Training & Development and the Institute for Corporate Productivity of 1,104 human resources and learning professionals—managers, directors, vice presidents, or C-level officers in large enterprises operating in multiple nations defined informal learning: "as a learning activity that is not easily recognizable as formal training and performance support. Generally speaking, it takes place without a conventional instructor and is employee-controlled in terms of breadth, depth, and timing. It tends to be individualized, limited in scope, and utilized in small chunks" (Paradise, 2008, p. 53).

In 1990, drawing on work by John Dewey, Marsick and Watkins (1990) defined informal and incidental learning by contrasting it with formal instruction. Informal learning is intentional, although often highly tacit. Sometimes it is incidental, that is, an accidental byproduct of another activity. Incidental learning is not intentional, although the originating activity may be. It can be noted or not, recognized in the moment or not, processed through subsequent reflection, or often through less conscious processes involved in adaptive socialization. Conditions that might delimit such learning include ability to reframe one's understanding of a situation, as well as capacity for seeing a situation in complex or nuanced ways. Informal learning is enhanced when people are, and encouraged to be, creative in their thinking and approaches to challenges they face; when they proactively pursue interests and solutions to problems; and when they are able to step back and look at "why" things are as they are and how they can be differently understood. Marsick and Watkins (1990) proposed an enriched problem-solving model of informal learning that was heavily influenced by Argyris and Schon's (1974) double-loop learning, that is, learning that examines underlying assumptions, values and beliefs that influence meaning making. Marsick and Watkins' (1990) model started with deep probing of the situation in order to frame one's understanding of the challenge or problem, followed by identification and consideration of a range of alternatives. Learning typically occurs informally in these early phases, often in experimenting with solutions. A learning review follows action to learn from both intended and unintended consequences, and to plan for a new cycle of framing, experimentation with solutions and learning from results.

This early model emphasized the individual as learner. Marsick and Watkins, in collaboration with Cseh (Cseh et al., 1999), revisited this model based on a study of managers in Eastern Europe that revealed the central role of context to what and how managers learned. Marsick et al. (2009) further revised and expanded their model based on examination of newer scholarship: on implicit and tacit learning theory, emotions and intuition, collaboration and social learning, and the dominant role of context in informal learning. They concluded that while the outlines of their earlier understanding hold, individuals cannot learn without a rich, social climate and that they do so intuitively as well as rationally or consciously:

> Perhaps a better analogy for thinking about informal and incidental learning is an amoeba-like process, multi-dimensional in nature, consisting of iterative cycling back and forth among phases of the process—with frequent forays into conversation, work with other people, and exploitation of a wide array of resources, often Internet-based or technology-driven, that provide new stimuli for further inquiry. Typically, the learning process includes an element of collective learning as work groups struggle together to solve a problem or sail forward to creatively address a new challenge (Marsick et al., 2009, p. 591).

A discussion of professional informal learning is incomplete without mentioning Schön's (1983, 1987) seminal work on reflective practice of professionals. Schön distinguished between reflection-in-action, the insight and adjustment that often occurs intuitively and tacitly based on prior experience and practice; and reflection-on-action, the more conscious look back after doing something that leads to rational examination of what went right or wrong. Schön adapted the idea of a ladder of inference, often used in explaining double-loop learning, to professional learning in practice as the ladder of coaching. He examined the professional learning of architects, musicians, psychologists and others with this framework and showed how much professional learning occurs in action and through interaction with other people and with the materials of the situation as professionals think about the situation in light of their specialized knowledge.

Eraut (2004a) and his colleagues have extensively researched the informal learning of professionals —e.g., teachers, health care and social workers, engineers, accountants. Their studies show that professionals deepen situational awareness and sensitivity to organizational context; develop personal capabilities and learn how to work better in teams; improve role performance (e.g., leadership, supervision, crisis management, and supporting other people's learning); increase task performance capabilities (speed, fluency, skill range and complexity); improve judgment, decision making and problem solving; and gain and apply new theoretical knowledge and resources.

Eraut further deconstructs learning that takes place via "thinking" during professional work, showing that their informal learning takes place when:

- Assessing clients and situations
- Deciding what, if any, action to take
- Pursuing that action, and modifying along the way as needed
- Managing oneself while balancing time, resources, priorities, relationships

Eraut explores the tacit dimension of such learning, noting that sharing of tacit knowledge is a sophisticated process, in which social interaction and context play a prominent role. Through his research, Eraut (2004a) has also identified different "modes" of cognition at play in each of these situations:

- Assessing involves pattern recognition
- Decision-making involves instant, intuitive response
- Overt activity involves routinized action
- Metacognition involves situational awareness

Eraut (2004a) suggests that training and education neglect key steps needed for effective use of knowledge at work, especially pattern recognition and conditions that support testing and expanding knowledge on the job. Individuals, continues Eraut, draw upon accumulated "personal knowledge" in socially situated workplace learning "that enables them to think, interact and perform." Personal knowledge is holistic. It includes non-codified "personalized versions of public codified knowledge ...., everyday knowledge of people and situations, know-how in the form of skills and practices, memories of episodes and events, self-knowledge, attitudes and emotions . . . . it focuses on the use value of knowledge rather than its exchange value in a world increasingly populated by qualifications" (p. 264).

Using this framework, Eraut and colleagues examined learning that occurs during normal working processes to better understand how these capabilities are learned. Four main types of work activity accounted for a high proportion of reported learning in much of their research:

- *Participation in group activities* included teamworking towards a common outcome, and groups set up for a special purpose such as audit, development or review of policy and/or practice, and responding to external changes.
- *Working alongside others* allows people to observe and listen to others at work and to participate in activities, and hence to learn some new practices and new perspectives, to become aware of different kinds of knowledge and expertise, and to gain some sense of other people's tacit knowledge.
- *Tackling challenging tasks* requires on-the-job learning and, if well-supported and successful, leads to increased motivation and confidence.
- *Working with clients* also entails learning (1) about the client, (2) from any novel aspects of each client's problem or request, and (3) from any new ideas that arose from their joint consultation. (Eraut, 2004a, pp. 266-267)

Context plays a big role — the context of one's personal life as well as work and professional practice. Eraut (2004a) emphasized that professional learning at work is fraught with missed opportunities that in part have to do with changing circumstances, personal proclivities, group dynamics, work climate, and availability of resources. He emphasized: "a group climate for learning has to be created, sustained and re-created at regular intervals" and "when mutual learning is low and relationships are dominated by suspicion this has to be a management responsibility" (p. 268).

Marsick, Watkins, Callahan, and Volpe (2009) reviewed 39 qualitative studies of informal and incidental learning strategies. They found that in these cases, learning was integrated with work and daily routines, and triggered by a jolt, challenge, or surprise. Learning strategies involved trial-and-error, reflection in and on action, observation of others, engagement with others at work, and self-directed learning projects. Learning took place through an enriched problem solving cycle, often collaboratively with others. They concluded that studies support the importance of individual motivation, self-reliance and self-direction in setting and reaching goals, and in finding opportunities for learning that aids performance, and their own personal agendas. But the context of organizations — culture, structure, processes, practices — plays a key role in enabling or inhibiting the motivation, time, resources, expectations, and rewards for learning.

Fuller et al. (2003) — who with other colleagues have developed and used a Working as Learning Framework (WALF) to research learning at work over five years in a range of occupations and economic sectors as part of a broader study funded by the Department of Trade and Industry in the U.K. — underscore the situated nature of this kind of learning. Context is critical in their view of informal workplace learning: "We need, therefore, to start from an analysis of the organizational context and work process in order to uncover and unpack what is being learned, how it is being learned and by whom" (p. 5).

2.3 Summary of key ideas vis-à-vis health care professionals

Informal learning in some jobs and some organizations can be highly individualized, for example, when learners are entrepreneurs, independent problem solvers, valued for creativity, or work in contexts where unique solutions are required that do not need to conform to technical or scientific standards. Jobs of health care workers, by contrast, fall somewhere in between highly standardized, routinized work (such as that found in industrial and manufacturing settings) and highly individualized work calling for unique solutions to problems. Their work and learning are guided by a body of scientific knowledge built and tested over time, yet they apply their knowledge in circumstances that can be unique in that each patient brings his or her prior life and medical history, physical characteristics, personality, family / national culture and context to diagnosis and healing. Health care workers, moreover, work collaboratively in teams, so they are also challenged to learn from and with others, often under pressure due to pain and potential life and death consequences.

Literature reviewed on both knowledge management and informal learning shows overlap among some key ideas, especially when examined for relevance to this kind of professional learning on the job in health care settings. To sum up, knowledge management as a social communication process (O'Toole, 2011) takes a constructivist approach that emphasizes meaning making that is highly social and collaborative. Informal learning literature takes a similar stance. Both literatures show that an enabling context is key. Informal learning research shows that learning occurs in organic ways on the job and is integrated with work tasks.

As the study reported in this chapter will show, professionals learn to apply scientific knowledge continuously as they make judgments about new challenges in light of their own personal knowledge and prior experience. Much of their learning, however, depends on social interaction; and that, in turn, is influenced by social and organizational context. Knowledge creation and sharing is often tacit, yet there are opportunities – whether or not taken – to surface and examine tacit knowing both to "train" professionals new to the situation, but also, to take better advantage of collective wisdom that is specific to unique local history and context.

3. Study of radiologic technologists' learning and complex problem solving

Radiologic technology is the art and science of producing medical images of the human body for diagnostic purposes. Technologists work with patients and sophisticated computerized equipment to produce detailed representations of human anatomy, physiology, and pathology. In the performance of their duties, technologists are called upon to solve a variety of problems. Technical aspects of problem solving involve adapting examinations to individual patient needs, and trouble-shooting equipment and computer problems. Providing patient care and managing relationships with coworkers create non-technical and frequently ill-structured problems. The most difficult problems technologists face are complex in nature with technical and non-technical, well- and ill-structured aspects.

Prior to entering the profession, student technologists typically spend two years in a formal educational program learning the basic skills and knowledge essential to clinical practice. This education includes learning in the classroom, simulated laboratory experiences, and clinical experience in a medical imaging department. In the relatively short period of time students spend in a radiography program they learn the theory, facts, and procedures needed to solve well-constructed or instrumental problems. However, this time period is not sufficient for the development of complex problem solving skills. The developmental process for solving ill-structured problems is relatively slow (King & Kitchener, 1994), necessitating a continuation of learning in the workplace. "...the increasing complexity of today's medical field has made it impossible for students to learn all that is needed by graduation" (Trad, 2009, p. 101).

3.1 Research questions and design

A research study conducted by Yates (2011) examined learning and knowledge sharing among radiologic technologists. The researcher, herself a radiologic technologist and radiography education program director, chose to focus on learning that followed postsecondary preparation as new graduates developed the capacity to negotiate the complexities of the workplace. As one research subject noted, "Actual work is quite diverse. It's nothing like what they teach you in school" (Robin). Findings from this study demonstrated that the workplace serves as an advanced practicum for new graduates, where real-life clinical situations help technologists develop a way of knowing that goes beyond the application of instrumental and technical knowledge. Yates sought to understand the nature of difficult problems encountered in clinical practice, to identify specific learning practices leading to the development of professional expertise, and to uncover workplace conditions that supported subjects' learning and enabled problem solving. Study results provide a snapshot of informal learning in a particular healthcare context that is confirmatory to earlier work by Eraut (2004a; 2004b), Marsick and Volpe (1999), Marsick, Volpe, and Watkins (1999), Marsick and Watkins (1990), Nonaka and Takeuchi (1995), O'Toole, (2011), Schön (1983, 1987), and Von Krogh et al. (2000).

The study's purpose was to explore the process of learning and development of skills used in solving complex problems typically encountered on the job. The research questions posed were: (1) How does experience inform radiologic technologists' capacities for solving complex problems encountered in clinical practice? (2) What similarities and differences exist in how radiologic technologists operating at different stages of cognitive development solve complex problems in clinical practice? (3) How do research subjects describe and understand the ways in which their workplace supports or inhibits the development of complex problem solving skills? A case study approach was used, with a volunteer sample of 22 radiologic technologists employed at six hospitals in the West Coast region of the United States of America.

3.2 Research methods

Both qualitative and quantitative data were collected for the study. Qualitative data consisted of (1) in-depth semi-structured interviews with technologists that included discussion of a reconstructed problem and hypothetical problem scenarios; and (2) brief semi-structured interviews conducted with at least one supervisor and/or manager from each of the 6 research sites about workplace factors and culture. Quantitative data were collected only from the technologists and consisted of: (1) a demographic questionnaire; (2) the independently scored Reasoning about Current Issues online assessment based on the Reflective Judgment Model (King & Kitchener, 1994); and (3) hypothetical problem scores derived from the interview data. IRB procedures were followed in collecting data to assure protection of human subjects.

Aggregated data from demographic questionnaires, RCI scores, and hypothetical problem scores were analyzed using SPSS 17.0 for descriptive and analytical statistics. The researcher sought to discover whether any relationships existed among the following study variables: years of experience, educational preparation, age, RCI score, and hypothetical problem scores. Linear correlation was used in bivariate analysis to estimate the Pearson Correlation Coefficient for relevant item pairs using one-tailed test of significance at 0.05. Analytical tests were performed to understand the relationship between the capacity for reflective judgment in the context of the workplace and patient outcomes as assessed using a rubric to analyze hypothetical problems posed to subjects during interviews. Qualitative data were inductively analyzed for themes and categories. Qualitative data were also used to examine results from statistical analyses.

4. Findings from research study

Results of the study provide detailed descriptions of the processes by which subjects learned to translate basic skills and book knowledge into the ability to adapt to atypical clinical situations. Study results included in this chapter focus on early challenges, learning practices technologists used to overcome those challenges, and workplace conditions that supported or inhibited subjects' learning. Pseudonyms are used in reporting all findings.

4.1 Early challenges

A portion of the interviews explored challenges faced by technologists at the beginning of their careers in medical imaging. Subjects were asked to think back to their first work experiences as a radiographer and recall what was most difficult for them. The most prevalent response related to the process of enculturation into a radiology department's ways of work, learning the facility's particular imaging standards, and the unique technical features of the worksite.

Wanda articulated this challenge well:

> Probably knowing the routine. You know, getting my techniques down. Different type of film, different type of cassettes. Just combinations of those kinds of things I guess…if I'm in a brand new place, knowing where everything is…like surgery or ICU… (Wanda)

Another frequently cited challenge involved developing the capacity to adapt radiography examinations to patients' individual needs. Jeffrey and George described their initial difficulties negotiating the complex aspects of the profession that defy formal, structured instruction in education programs.

> When I graduated my x-ray school I was - you know-Merrill's (Frank, Long, & Smith, 2012) by the book. Everything had to be perfect because that's what I was trained. And now [with]…five years as a tech you can kind of see yourself - I guess the word is - taking shortcuts maybe? Finding easier ways to do it - you know, there's not one correct way to do something. As long as you get the right picture. Little tricks of the trade, I guess. Just that and adapting to the hospital's way of doing things. (Jeffrey)
>
> … just being able to adapt to what the patient needed, you know in certain cases. At [X] we didn't have any kids so I didn't have any experience with kids. So then I'm working at outpatient clinics where I'm with kids so it was a little bit tough. You know, just to try and make it easy for them, without hurting them or, you know, causing them pain. And then, you just learn to spend a little extra time explaining it to them or playing with them a little bit before you can start the exam. (George)

Subjects also described difficulties with gaining comfort and competence in the surgical suite, learning to work collaboratively with other team members, and developing the capacity to work independently.

Teresa was challenged by the unique workplace culture she experienced in the operating room.

> I think one of the things I was a little nervous about would be when I'd go to surgery. And when I was working the C-arm in the surgery…they need things done perfect and right the very first time. "No, don't touch this. Don't touch that. Be very careful when you're maneuvering this equipment to make sure that you're not touching anything [in] that sterile field." So there's pressure there. (Teresa)

Kelly's transition from student radiographer to technologist forced her to learn to rely on her own judgment in clinical situations.

> Yeah, I think coming out of school that was probably one of the more challenging things is not always having the tech with me, you know? – to go, "What do you think about this?" You know? So it's like – I'm making my own decisions now. (Kelly)

4.2 Informal learning processes

Subjects were asked to describe specific learning experiences that helped them develop professional expertise. As they articulated their process for learning and discussed how they overcame early challenges, subjects described a variety of informal processes that occurred as they went about their daily activities at work. The sample technologists developed advanced problem solving skills mainly through encounters with actual problems in clinical practice rather than through formal training offered by the employer.

The workplace served as an important context that influenced learning. Technologists in the sample developed professional expertise in a number of ways within the context of the workplace. Challenges and supports offered there served to enable or inhibit subjects' learning. The opportunity to collaborate with a diverse group of peers was the most frequently cited enabler. Availability of resources and access to a helpful, approachable manager were also seen as important for learning and problem solving. Many subjects cited fear of making mistakes as obstructive to learning. Logistical issues such as poorly designed systems, lack of availability of "tools of the trade," communications issues between management and technologists, and obstructive co-workers were the most frequently cited workplace inhibitors.

Learning took place in the context of natural learning communities that fostered learning and knowledge sharing. Findings on radiologic technologists' learning practices support the four main types of work activities identified by Eraut (2004a) as giving rise to learning in the workplace: (a) participation in group activities; (b) working alongside others; (c) tackling challenging tasks; and (d) working with clients (or, in this case patients). Subjects frequently learned through collaboration with more experienced technologists, often through informal mentoring relationships. Learning often took place through reflection on work alone or with peers.

4.2.1 The significance of collaborative workplace relationships

Collaboration and group reflection were important for learning in varying degrees to the overwhelming majority of subjects. Technologists were more likely to seek help from peers for technical rather than non-technical problems. Subjects cited many examples of consulting with peers for help with a difficult problem, solving problems together with co-workers informally on the job and more formally at staff meetings, reflecting on practice with peers, sharing knowledge, and working together as a team.

> You have to talk with other people in order to get things done, in order to get better at it. Definitely a community effort… I talk with a lot of my fellow rad techs. And how they solve their problems, similar to mine. I ask them if they've ever experienced that. And how would they figure it out - or how would they solve it? (Scott)

> …if we have something unusual, whether it's pathology or it's like, a way to take an exam or something like that…we'll share it…."Hey, look what I did. Or look what the machine can do if we do it this way." (George)

…if I recognize that I can't solve the problem, given the first few seconds or the first minute or two, then I'm already thinking, "Who can I pull in to help me solve this?" I have the resources of my MRI tech whose got twenty years experience, my boss who's got twenty-five, thirty years experience, or a co-worker that may look at it from a different vantage point. (Richard)

> I find someone who knows more than me….Is there someone that either had this experience, dealt with this technical side of it, someone I can go to that may be able to help me? If that doesn't work I'll keep searching. (Lynn)

These technologists recognized the diversity of expertise among their peers, tapping these resources when presented with unique workplace challenges.

Carrie described the enabling learning culture created by her supervisor and manager at staff meetings.

> We can bring up anything. We have a monthly meeting and we can bring anything up at our meeting. And they always listen to us and we have changed things from talking about stuff. (Carrie)

For some older subjects who entered the profession prior to the digital age, computers (now ubiquitous in acute care settings) sometimes posed considerable challenges. These technologists relied on more technically adept peers for help with such challenges.

> …there are some peers that are like, right on the target with the computer. It's like their third hand. And they're also on day shift so they get a lot of the extra [training]…And when a new program pops up or when a program has been updated or PM'd - something doesn't jive with what it used to do - they're the people that are…usually the ones that are around during that and will see it first. And they go, "Oh, yeah, yeah, yeah. You just do this, this, and this." (Katherine)

Several technologists described work with particular peers as "seamless":

> …well, sometimes if you have a difficult patient we help each other out in doing the exam. Like one will position the tube, the other one will set the technique…it's weird…you don't really have to talk to each other. You just kind of know what the other one is going to do - and so it's just automatic. (Leigh-Ann)

Working side-by-side with others in trusting relationships facilitated learning and improved efficiency in completing tasks for a number of research subjects.

4.2.2 The importance of mentoring relationships

For the overwhelming majority of research subjects, engaging in mentoring relationships assisted in the transfer of tacit knowledge including enculturation into the imaging department's ways of work, and for learning the "tricks of the trade." Scott and Alex described the roles their mentors played in helping them understand the culture of the worksite as well as the technical "know-how" needed in the development of professional expertise.

> ...yeah, they kind of – told me how things work here and – kind of showed me the ropes, I guess you could say....They really listened to me, listened to my problems and – tried to truthfully figure out a way to help me...(Scott)

> ...there's a tech who's now in special procedures. I think [he] was really instrumental in getting me to see – not just the technical but just kind of the attitude to have. Or the eyes to look through...because he doesn't let things really bother him a whole lot. And he knows how things should be but recognizes how things actually are...He taught me a lot of good habits. I worked with him in surgery a lot. And he always kept the equipment clean and well in repair. He kept his areas organized. And told me how I should behave with the staff in surgery. Because it's a different culture down there – what they expect and how to anticipate what they want. And that was a big help. (Alex)

In most cases, mentoring relationships were informal and spontaneous. Most often, more experienced peers served as mentors. Less often teachers, clinical instructors, supervisors, and radiologists mentored. Effective mentors exhibited the desire to teach, made themselves available to the mentee, were exceptionally competent and patient focused, listened and communicated well, and were kind and empathetic.

> She was amazing. And she had been a tech for, I don't know, eight or ten years...and she was just very – just you know – cool, even-tempered... Just really good at problem solving...she was just on it...at the drop of a dime knew exactly what to do...and she always had really good solutions. And it was really catered towards the patient. It wasn't like "Okay, we're gonna wrench you around because this is the way I know how to do it." It was like, "Oh, well you can't do that? Okay, 'cause I can do this." You know? No problem. (Kelly)

Mentors shared expert knowledge and acted as role models and coaches. They gave mentees time and space to work out problems for themselves, yet were available to help as needed. They worked side-by-side with the mentee as a team, asked questions to encourage critical thinking, and invited questions from the mentee. They also asked mentees to verbalize their thinking and at times tested or challenged the mentee.

> ...they made me think out of the box, you know – It was like, "Here's a walkie-talkie chest. Okay, now here's this next one. Now, how are you gonna do this guy?" Rather than just going "do this, do this, do this." It's like, "Let's see if you can do it. If not, then I'll help you." Yeah, that's it. Made you think rather than just repetition. (George)

> Well, I think he let us do a lot of things on our own, whereas a lot of people would be kind of hovering and always giving their opinion right away, you know. "Oh, wait, what are you doing? You should do it this way." And he just kind of let us work it out...he gave us a lot of space. But he was always there if you had a question, "Oh, can you help me with this?" But he would always let us try and...he'd be like, "Why are you doing that?"...And so we'd have to kind of verbalize what we were doing. "Well, I'm going to – you know – position the plate like this so that when I shoot the cross-table lateral..." (Nicole)

As described by the research subjects, mentors displayed an exceptional capacity for articulating tacit knowledge. They seemed particularly adept in helping mentees develop the mental models needed to apply technical knowlege in innovative ways to unique clinical situations.

4.2.3 Other important learning practices

Other important learning practices included (a) deliberately working through difficult problems; (b) deliberate reflection on practice alone and with peers; (c) on-the-spot experimentation (as described by Schön, 1983; 1987); and (d) repetition of skills. A few technologists mentioned additional learning practices such as (e) observing peers' work; (f) engaging in dialogue with radiologists; (g) reading professional journals and other "trade" publications; and (h) teaching others. All subjects used a combination of practices for learning. The first of these practices was *working through difficult problems*. Learning occurred just in time during everyday clinical practice, frequently involving "complicated" patient exams. Successfully navigating problematic situations helped subjects build confidence and develop competence.

> …for me it was just putting myself in every situation….If there was down time I would go find somebody who was doing something. I would go to the area that I haven't been in in awhile and…see if there was a case going on….Just kind of put yourself in those positions and I would try to be as hands-on as I could. (Kelly)
>
> Like children and trauma situations…you're like "Okay" –but then you do it and you do it right and you're like, "Okay." You know you can do it. (Paula)

Katherine provided a detailed example of how she was able to complete a radiography exam by assessing a patient's emotional needs and working with her, building trust a step at a time to obtain the images needed by the ordering physician to diagnose the patient's medical condition.

> …a couple of weeks ago I was working x-ray and picked up a [requisition] and went up to get the individual in the waiting room…say the last name, they come up, we walk down to take the x-rays, and on her I was doing pelvis, bilateral hips, bilateral knees, and I think an ankle….Well, she was challenging. So I walked her to the room. And I confirmed her name and her birth date and what we'd be doing and she was immediately - even on the way walking like - "Doctors!" and she just went on and on about stuff that I don't even remember all of it because I was really trying to focus her to move forward. And so we got in the room and she was again saying she didn't want to take off her clothes and whatever she had on had to be OK - and she didn't know why I was here - and I was like, "Well this is your choice." She said "Well I'll do whatever." We started with the body part which was furthest away from having to do anything with clothes. I wanted to build up a rapport, get things on a better foot… So we got her on the table, lying down, didn't do anything by the hips, didn't do anything above pelvis even though she had, you know, zippers and whatnot….Went to the foot and heard all about that story….I got like, lots of stories from her….She was talking about not wanting to take off her clothes. I'm - "Okay, how about this? You're all covered. I've got you covered up. What you have is pants on that have metal on them." I said "I've got to take pictures there." I said, Would you mind…if we slide your pants down just a little bit? You don't have to put on a gown, you'll be covered."…so that's how I got through with it. (Katherine)

Teresa described the process of gaining competence and confidence through her experiences working in the surgical department, an area notorious for difficult personalities and a high level of stress.

> Oh well, you've seen it all. And you learn a little bit more about the doctors that you're working with. And the fear of messing up with certain doctors… once that pressure goes away…you're like "Okay, I know this doctor, I know how he likes things done." And

> speaking up for myself… "Okay, that guy can't come in here because he doesn't have [a lead apron] on." And I took my position a little more seriously. It took away some of the pressure because I could tell people what to do. It wasn't just people telling *me* what to do all the time. I could stand up and say "I'm in charge of the radiation here." (Teresa)

Nicole also shared her efforts to "find her voice" in the operating room, negotiating a way to command respect from the more difficult surgeons she worked with in the course of her duties as an imaging professional.

> We're talking about the OR. Yeah I mean like I guess that there's a lot of personalities in here and it's a tense situation so a lot of times we have issues communicating with the physicians, and there's a lot of anger that goes back and forth. And it's hard to know how to – I'm still working out how to…process that. And how to make it…so that I feel comfortable in there. I'm still doing my job, but I'm not being…stepped all over…and it's not every situation but you know… like as far as technically in the OR a lot of the doctors know what they want but don't want to communicate….They want you to anticipate what they want. I've just been trying to be more direct…. I've been trying to make eye contact when I can or just say, "Doctor so-and-so," and address them specifically. Because a lot of times they're – you know – "x-ray, da-da-dah." Like, I'm not a person, I'm x-ray. So I try and [say] "Oh, my name's Nicole." So that maybe they can [realize] that I'm a person…like I'm not just another instrument in the room that they can…throw on the ground. (Nicole)

The second important learning practice was *deliberate reflection on practice – alone or with peers.* Subjects recognized the value of reflection on practice, often describing a process by which they examined the results of their work (the medical images produced during an exam, or a patient's response to their care), made judgments regarding image quality or effectiveness of their actions, and made adjustments accordingly. Some subjects described solitary reflective activities, some described reflecting on work with a peer or group of peers.

Andrew, an exceptionally self-directed learner, described the deliberate process he developed for systematically reflecting on work following his shift.

> Sometimes I would go home after a day and I would think, yeah, there's that one or two x-rays that I think about, you know? Like maybe I should have repeated, you know? And then I would come and look at the report and see if the [radiologists] had anything to say about, you know, "image undiagnostic" or "unsatisfactory image quality" – sometimes that kept me up at night, thinking about those things. Now I've gotten to know the radiologists and their preferences more. I've gotten more comfortable with the equipment – the techniques that I need to know here. Because every machine is different so I've gotten to play with the technique a little bit here. I'm more comfortable with knowing what they consider diagnostic and what they would want repeated. (Andrew)

Leigh-Ann used a combination of reflection-in-action *as* she worked, reflection-on-action *following* her work, and collaboration with a peer to solve a problem.

> "Well, how am I gonna get this view if [the patient] can't do this?" And you're like thinking about it and then – you try it and it doesn't look exactly right. You would ask somebody, "Well, what do you think I could do to make this look better?" (Leigh-Ann)

Jeffrey reflected on the results of his work following an exam. His judgment informed future practice.

> …you're just kind of brainstorming- after the exam. Next time, if I angled [the x-ray tube] to the left or right or up and down, maybe I'd get a better picture… if it's a hard exam or if I had trouble doing it then I'll go back and think about it and "How could I make it easier next time?" (Jeffrey)

Kelly used a process of dialogue to reflect on practice with her peers.

> Even if I know I did something right, I still bounce it off of people because there's always something more that maybe could have been done or that I could have learned…"So then this happened and this happened."…It's more of a conversation for me – to just share the experience and then people will share their thoughts and ideas and whatever…about the experiences they've had and what they've done . (Kelly)

A third important practice was *on-the-spot experimentation.* A number of technologists described a process of on-the-spot experimentation as described by Schön (1983; 1987), utilizing real-time reflection to observe the results of their work and adjust their actions in response to feedback. This process represented an important way of learning to creatively apply theory to practice.

> "Okay, [the patient] can't do this. Then try this." And it's like, "Oh, I got a really crappy radiograph." Or, "The doctor can't see anything there." So that's not the way to do it in this exam. (George)

Alex described a synthesis of learning processes in the development of his practice: application of book knowledge, reflection-in-action, and observation of others' work.

> …sometimes I would think I know how to get a certain projection done because of what I learned from the book. Of course that's one of many ways to get it done. I would be frustrated when that one way didn't work. Well, I spent a lot of time experimenting, trying different ways. Besides what I had observed from other people and deciding for myself what I like. (Alex)

A fourth frequently used practice was *repetition of skills.* Some subjects mentioned repetition of skills as important to their development of professional expertise. This learning practice may seem passive and perhaps less important than the more deliberate practices uncovered. However, in actual clinical experience, repetition does not mean performing the same set of psychomotor skills multiple times in an automated fashion. Each exam represents a different set of problems to be solved due to individual patient conditions and the changing physical environment. Practicing problem solving skills by repetition helps technologists learn to respond to new challenges through innovation.

> I think it's just from repetition, keep doing things and you get used to it. And if I'm not sure how to do something I would ask the senior tech. And they would show me a better way to do it. …at first it was hard to do it a different way. Like if it was a textbook way compared to just doing it from experience. It's just like, I'm not going to get it if I try to do it like that. (Leigh-Ann)

> It's just the longer you're doing it – the more comfortable you feel because you know this is a medium sized patient, or this technique works well for this particular type of situation. (Wanda)

Fifth, in some cases, subjects described *observing peers' work.* Several subjects mentioned observing peers' work as one way of learning problem solving skills. This learning practice on its own is also relatively passive in nature.

> …some of the younger techs have a different way of doing something that – you've only done this way for many years, you know, so – I always like to watch and see…they did that, [and] I'll ask them…"How did you get that one?" And they go, "I do it like this." (Wanda)

As evidenced by the portion of the study focusing on characteristics and behaviors of expert problem solvers, observation of others' work must be followed by experimentation and adjustments in one's own practice if one is to develop professional expertise.

A sixth practice also identified was *engaging in dialogue with radiologists.* Andrew, a relatively inexperienced technologist exhibiting a high score on the problem solving portion of the interview, described the deliberate way in which he engaged in dialogue with a physician for the sole purpose of advancing his own knowledge and professional expertise.

> I remember one time when I first started I went into a radiologist's office and I said, "You know I'm a student. I'm looking to learn. Is it all right if I sit with you for maybe thirty or forty minutes, an hour - and just listen to you dictate?" And he said, "Absolutely." And he pulled up a chair right next to him....And he would dictate and then he would stop in the middle of his dictations and he would point stuff out to me. And say... "This is why it's very important that you get the [costophrenic] angles. Because see this fluid here? If you had clipped that we wouldn't have saw that." And just pointing out every little thing to me. (Andrew)

A few subjects identified a seventh practice: *reading professional journals and other trade publications.* One subject demonstrated a high degree of self-directedness in his description of an application of knowledge found in a professional journal article to clinical practice.

> Like doing cross-table laterals with the hip on a DR [Direct Digital Radiography] wall Bucky. I read an article in a magazine, ASRT [American Society of Radiologic Technologists] magazine, and I tried it there. And I did okay with available time to do it– but one of the other techs on afternoons....I talked to him about it and he showed me how he did it. And you know, it really kind of helped pull things together on how it works here with the room. (Frank)

Finally, occasionally, subjects learned by *teaching others.* Andrew told of another deliberate learning practice he engaged in for the dual purposes of helping others and advancing his own knowledge and skills.

> ...after I graduated I went back to my school and volunteered so I was doing positioning class. So two days out of the week I would go to the labs and I would teach the new students positioning. I would go, starting with the hands all the way up to hips, pelvises - that helped me out a lot, I think...Because I figured if I had six months off and I didn't do anything it would be a little bit harder to get...back into the swing of things. (Andrew)

5. Discussion of study findings

5.1 Imaging departments as communities of practice

Yates' (2011) study subjects used a variety of informal practices to negotiate through and learn from early challenges they faced as new graduates of radiography programs. Subjects' learning occurred within the context of the work environment, through experience with everyday professional activities. The workplace served as the proving ground where technologists developed problem solving skills and professional expertise.

Many of the learning practices described by subjects in this research study involved hands-on experience with difficult problems and often included interacting, collaborating, and reflecting on practice with peers and other members of the health care team. Caring professional relationships enabled learning and problem solving for the overwhelming majority of subjects. These relationships served to facilitate the transfer of explicit as well as tacit knowledge among technologists within imaging departments.

Von Krogh, et al. (2000) emphasize the importance of a culture of caring for enabling knowledge creation.

Knowledge enabling includes facilitating relationships and conversations as well as sharing local knowledge across an organization or beyond geographic and cultural borders. At a deeper level, however, it relies on a new sense of emotional knowledge and care in the organization, one that highlights how people treat each other and encourages creativity-even playfulness. (p. 4)

Mentoring and collaboration, along with experimentation and reflection-on-action, helped subjects develop independent problem solving skills and the capacity for application of technical know-how to new clinical challenges. As described by subjects, medical imaging departments accessed for this study meet the criteria for communities of practice, defined as "groups of people who informally come together to exchange knowledge and experience in a shared domain of interest" (Cianciolo, et al., 2006, p. 623). Von Krogh, et al. (2000) use the term *microcommunities of knowledge* to describe "the small groups within an organization whose members share what they know as well as common values and goals" (p. 5). Cianciolo et al. maintain that communities of practice assist in the process of making tacit knowledge explicit and passing it on to new members. They emphasize the informal and spontaneous nature of communities of practice, in which members self-select for the purpose of developing capability and exchanging knowledge rather than completing a specific task. The communities of practice, or microcommunities of knowledge described by participants in this research sudy were not formalized or externally imposed; they arose spontaneously through daily interactions among members of the health care team as they went about their normal work activites.

Through participation in their respective communities of practice, research subjects were supported and challenged as they learned informally through experience in the workplace. A workplace culture that encourages collaboration and mentoring, allows time and space for reflection both alone and with peers, and provides a wide range of experience enhances informal learning and the development of complex problem solving skills in radiologic technologists.

5.2 Situating the study in the literature of informal learning

Marsick and Volpe (1999) assert that social interaction enhances informal learning, advocating for the design of work processes that maximize opportunities for sharing ideas and collaborating. Wenger (1998) argues "we cannot become human by ourselves" (p. 146) rather, all that we are as humans is based on our relationships and interactions in a social context. Brookfield (1987) views peer support as essential to developing critical thinking skills and emphasizes interpersonal relationships as a context for learning. Schein (1993) states that, "In dialogue, the whole group is the object of learning, and the members share the potential excitement of discovering, collectively, ideas that individually none of them might have ever thought of" (p. 44). In most cases, study subjects seemed to benefit from the diverse perspectives of peers with varying degrees of experience and problem solving capacities.

Raelin (2008) applies Social Learning Theory to work-based learning in the statement "…learners are active observers. In fact, people often learn behavior from observing others before performing the behavior themselves" (pp. 74-75). He asserts that in observing the performance of others, individuals make mental models or conceptual maps to assist them in trying out a skill for themselves.

Due to the nature of clinical practice, tackling challenging tasks usually involved working through difficult patient examinations alone or with another technologist. Marsick and

Volpe (1999), in a review of informal learning studies, reinforced this finding and noted: "Throughout the history of productive organizations, most workplace learning has been left in the hands of employees and has been gained through informal methods and through trial and error" (p. 2).

Davis (2009) substantiates the importance of learning events triggered by encounters with patients in the course of normal practice as one way medical professionals improve knowledge and skills. Schön (1987) begs the question "...how are practitioners to learn wisdom except by reflection on practice dilemmas that call for it?" Marsick and Volpe (1999) assert the importance of learning that occurs "'just in time,' as people face a challenge, problem, or unanticipated need" (p. 4). The value of this type of learning was recognized by many subjects.

Raelin (2008) defines reflection as "the ability to uncover and make explicit to oneself what one has planned, achieved, or observed" (p. 74). Vernon's (1999) study of informal learning and teamwork revealed the importance of reflection as a strategy for learning to be an effective team member:

> ...only reflection allowed participants to form judgments about what was learned and to make decisions about current, future, and alternative applications of what was learned. They also used reflection to assess both the process and the outcomes of their learning experiences and of their interpersonal and trial-and-error experimentation. (Vernon, 1999, p. 35)

Some professionals in this study treated problems they encountered as a mix of what they already knew and new variations that required the ability to reflect-in-action, engaging in a process of real-time inquiry and on-the-spot experimentation (Schön, 1987). This process describes how technologists manipulate equipment and work with patients in a manner that is dynamic yet routine, utilizing tacit knowledge. When patient conditions or equipment problems present complications, the technologist executes "on-line anticipation and adjustment...continuous detection and correction of error," (p. 26) also known as "knowing-in-action." The technologist varies her routine by testing solutions and creatively solving problems in real-time to obtain diagnostic images of the patient's anatomy.

Marsick and Volpe (1999) observed that informal learning 1) is integrated with work and daily routines; 2) is often triggered by an internal or external jolt; 3) is haphazard and influenced by chance; 4) is an inductive process of reflection and action; and 5) is linked to the learning of others. Its value is often directly related to timing; people learn best in response to problems of immediate concern. Organizations can enhance informal learning by attending to specific factors: "Organizations...have to design jobs, work practices, and work relationhsips in such a way that people can talk with one another, collaboratively solve problems, and generally seek responses to challenges that they have identified, even if this does not fit into a preset work schedule" (Marsick & Volpe, 1999, p. 5).

Recent research on expertise and expert performance emphasizes the importance of communities of practice in the development of professional expertise. The central belief of communities of practice, based on work by Argyris (1993) and Wenger (1998) is that "because most of the relevant know-how that distinguishes different levels of expertise is acquired through experience, methods that stimulate the process of thinking about what one is doing and why, and talking about it with others, will facilitate the development of expertise (Cianciolo, et al., 2006, p. 623)."

Cianciolo et al. (2006) recognize a positive relationship between tacit knowledge acquisition and practical intelligence. They define practical intelligence as "the ability to acquire tacit knowledge from everyday experience and to apply this knowledge to handling everyday practical problems in which the information necessary to determine a solution strategy is often incomplete (p. 616)"

Unlike general intelligence which tends to remain relatively stable throughout the lifespan, practical intelligence "is viewed as developing with effort and experience" (Cianciolo et al., 2008, p. 617). Practical knowledge is also seen as distinct from personality and motivation "because it characterizes a person's use of his experiences for learning and performance and not, in particular, his drive to succeed…" (Cianciolo et al., p. 617). Practical knowledge is domain-specific; in other words, context matters. In a review of recent research, Cianciolo et al. (2006) connect high scores on measures of tacit knowledge with higher levels of performance. There seems to be an intimate connection between the acquisition of tacit knowledge, practical intelligence, and professional expertise.

Cianciolo et al. (2006) maintain that communities of practice assist in the process of making tacit knowledge explicit and passing it on to new members. They emphasize the informal and spontaneous nature of communities of practice, in which members self-select for the purpose of developing capability and exchanging knowledge rather than completing a specific task. The communities of practice described by participants in this research sudy were not formalized or externally imposed; they arose spontaneously through daily interactions among members of the health care team as they went about their normal work activites.

5.3 Implications for "managing" and "enabling" informal learning and knowledge creation/sharing of technical knowledge in health care professionals such as radiologic technologists

Considered in light of the above, this study has implications for managers who assist technologists in developing advanced problem solving skills. Development – and knowledge creation/sharing – happen best when learners engage in real-life dilemmas in the context of everyday work activities. Providing appropriate workplace supports helps new graduates negotiate uncertain aspects of professional practice and assures that "seasoned" technologists continue to learn. As they learn, they appropriate knowledge resident in the community and organization, and potentially, they can contribute new knowledge as they discover and share new ways of doing things.

Research on informal learning (Marsick & Volpe, 1999) and the development of professional expertise (Cianciolo, et al., 2006) has identified ways for managers to facilitate learning that may also support knowledge enabling through conversations (Van Krogh et al., 2000). Yates draws conclusions about how this can best happen based on her study and these authors' work. The practices she recommends include:

1. Allow time and space for reflection on practice
2. Create opportunities for collaboration and group problem solving
3. Support mentoring relationships
4. Foster a safe atmosphere where technologists may learn from mistakes
5. Allow technologists to pursue solutions to self-identified challenges arising out of normal work activities
6. Encourage technologists to participate in policy-making and decisions affecting their work processes

Supporting technologists in these ways helps to create learning and knowledge sharing microcommunities within medical imaging departments. One application idea is to devote a portion of staff meetings to developing technologists' problem solving skills. Technologists could anonymously submit brief descriptions of difficult problems encountered in practice. Managers could then present the problems to staff for a brainstorming activity. Utilizing small groups rather than one large group is suggested for this activity as people tend to feel safer sharing ideas and participating with only one or two others. A large group debrief could then conclude the activity so that ideas could be shared with everyone. This activity presents opportunities for technologists to learn from the collective problem solving skills of the group.

Managers may find that inviting technologists to participate in decisions and policy-making in matters affecting their work processes could potentially improve the quality of work, enhance technologists' learning, and promote the conversion of personally held knowing to publicly shared and tested knowledge. Participation may also have a positive effect on job satisfaction, productivity, and patient satisfaction. Managers are reminded that inviting participation is different from soliciting input.

Those involved in the design of physical space may also consider its effect on learning. A large centralized work area easily accessed from adjacent exam rooms may facilitate collaboration and group problem solving among technologists. Isolation of workspaces may discourage interaction and make it difficult for technologists to obtain immediate assistance in case of an emergency.

Managers may foster workplace conditions that enable a path toward professional expertise by supporting informal learning and knowledge creation / sharing in the workplace. It is important to note that informal learning was already being supported to varying degrees in the research sites at the time of data collection. By attending to learning and knowledge sharing in a more intentional manner, imaging managers can help to transform medical imaging departments into learning communities. "Such a community includes learning, not only as a matter of course in the history of its practice, but at the very core of its enterprise" (Wenger, 1998, pp. 214-215). Some components of learning communities may be formalized. However a caveat is that the effectiveness of these strategies may depend on "spontaneity, self-selection, or self-interest" (Marsick & Volpe, 1999, p. 8). Formal intervention could potentially negate their efficacy.

6. Conclusions

6.1 Relationships between informal learning and knowledge creation, sharing, and management

In this section, we look more broadly at what this study of radiologic technologists might mean for informal learning and knowledge creation, sharing and management. As emphasized in the beginning of this chapter, Nonaka and Takeuchi (1995) highlighted ways that tacit and explicit knowledge interact. Van Krogh et al. (2000) further emphasized differences between knowledge management and knowledge enabling. Knowledge is to be mined to advance a business's bottom line by improving productivity, innovation, and products or services that improve profit. As knowledge is created in the workplace, Van Krogh et al. (2000) emphasize that "new concepts must be justified according to organizational values, a knowledge vision, a business strategy, costs, return on investments, and so on. Through justification, unacceptable and unattractive concepts will be screened out" (pp. 130-131). Knowledge, therefore, is selectively created based on the organization's determination of what is profitable.

We suggest that knowledge creation and management for professionals in health care settings utilizes a different – co-equal and collaborative – process for determining what is or is not justified, acceptable or attractive. We turn to informal learning research among professionals for understanding why and how such knowledge creation differs even though there are parallels with work that has been done in the private sector to advance organizational goals. Professionals such as the radiologic technologists in this study also advance organizational goals, but additional benchmarks are used as well as criteria for successful knowledge creation and management. Knowledge is created and passed on via the profession to varying degrees depending on local conditions that enable or inhibit learning. Higher education programs could better prepare professionals by engaging students in learning practices known to facilitate knowledge creation and transfer of knowledge in the workplace. Collaborative partnerships between the two entities could enhance the process of turning locally created knowledge into useful "lessons learned" to be passed on to new as well as experienced practitioners. As importantly, knowledge created and shared may be valued locally for its own sake by the technologists themselves who are self motivated to develop their own expertise; and by the teams of colleagues who are individually and collectively motivated by the knowledge they acquire or deepen in their own pursuit of excellence.

Informal learning research helps to understand the mechanisms and value add for individuals who pursue knowledge and expertise development to meet personal and professional needs irrespective of what the organization demands. This research shows that much of the judgment and experimentation involved in adjusting knowledge and skills to best meet task needs is contextual and not highly explicit. For informal learning in technical professions, Eraut (2004a) suggests that "…tacit knowledge is more likely to be used for generating hypotheses or possible sources of action, which are then checked against other evidence or discussed with other people" (p. 253). Knowledge sharing among colleagues and through relationships often involves conversations, as Van Krough et al. (2000) also emphasize. But the goal for making tacit knowledge explicit and sharing it with colleagues can be both improved performance and the satisfaction of building one's own expertise and that of colleagues who have created a social and organizational climate where everyone gains through knowledge sharing.

6.2 Implications for knowledge-based systems in organizations

What implications does this study have for the role of knowledge-based systems that enable organizations to stay competitive, plan for the future and innovate? Knowledge creation and management strategies are not one-size-fit-all. They too are highly contextual. Knowledge managers and enablers need to carefully diagnose the context to best understand what most matters for success. They need support from the hierarchy to which they report to make changes to practices that can improve the climate and culture for effective knowledge sharing and learning. Some questions they might ask include:

- What mix of database management and social meaning making is key to success in that context?
- How motivated and adept are professionals at informal learning and knowledge sharing?
- In what ways is the social climate supportive of knowledge sharing?
- Do managers have the skills to facilitate learning and conversations that support knowledge sharing?

- Is time managed in such a way that professionals can reflect in and on action, and are encouraged and rewarded when they do so and share their expertise?
- To what extent is work organized so that it is normal and desirable to stop and ask questions when challenges arise?
- Are meetings and other formal gatherings designed to encourage open sharing and problem solving without blame?
- Who are the multiple stakeholders who screen, vet, and build knowledge in the organization and profession? What is their role, and how can it be clarified and enhanced to catalyze knowledge sharing?
- How can informal learning be enhanced in ways that better support, and take advantage, of knowledge technology?

This study has identified many ways that this occurs for radiologic technologists that are consistent with prior research on professional informal learning. Many of these studies have emphasized what individuals can best do to maximize their own learning. Yates' study adds insight into the social and organizational context that is critical in supporting individual informal learning and knowledge sharing. Health care institutions may not be able to control for the motivation and personal skills that individuals bring to work, but they can do much to affect climate and help managers who wish to enhance learning and knowledge sharing.

6.3 Limitations affecting our recommendations

Finally, limitations affect our recommendations because of the type of data and research designs of studies we have reviewed and examined in drawing conclusions. For example, Yates'(2011) study utilized a multiple case study approach, focusing deeply on the workplace experiences of a relatively small number of radiologic technologists. Qualitative data included in-depth interviews including discussion of reconstructed and hypothetical problems. Therefore, a limitation of the study relates to the self-reporting of subjects regarding learning processes used and invented solutions to the hypothetical problems. The researcher's direct observation of subjects solving actual problems at work might have more accurately assessed ability; however time constraints and patient privacy rules made this method impractical.

As many scholars attest, informal and incidental learning are challenging to research. Informal learning is highly tacit (almost intuitive, sometimes semi-conscious, and not explicitly articulated) and not easy, therefore, to observe behaviorally. Incidental learning is often unconscious until tapped. It is difficult to disentangle work and informal or incidental learning. It is not always clear how much of an outcome can be linked primarily to a particular informal or incidental learning experience. Many studies of informal learning, as well, are case studies, each of which uses a slightly different theoretical base for research. Many studies are qualitative and thus rely on perception and self-report. Many of these studies examine isolated critical incidents. Eraut (2004a) seeks to correct this focus on isolated points in times by conceptualizing informal learning from experience as holistic, and by drawing upon actors' full experience and capabilities as they interact with others and co-construct meaning at work.

Studies currently undertaken by Fuller et al. (2003) take a big step toward providing solid evidence for a systemic view of informal and incidental learning at work based on purposeful sampling of a wide range of businesses, large and small based on a common

Work as Learning Framework that they evolved over time based on literature review and research. Another promising approach is that developed by Skule (2004). "Rather than trying to measure learning directly" which is difficult because of its very nature, he sought "to identify the factors most conducive to informal learning at work" by conceptualizing the learning environment in the workplace." Skule began his research by interviewing 4-8 workers, managers or stewards for occupational groups in each of 11 different private and public sector enterprises in Norway, followed by a survey of 1300 employees in private sector and 200 public sector employees in Norway. Skule developed a measure of the learning intensity of work based on three factors:

- "Subjective judgement of how learning intensive/educational the job is"
- "Length of job-specific learning required to master the job"
- Durability of acquired skills, measured by how long it is possible to be away from work, and still remain professionally updated." (p. 10)

Further research that would test our thinking might involve mixed methods research of a sampling of health care professionals in a variety of contexts that utilize a common framework and take place over time that integrates insights culled from both informal learning research and knowledge creation, sharing, and management. It would be interesting to discover whether the learning processes identified in Yates' study of radiologic technologists are relevant to other types of healthcare professionals as well as for workers in other domains.

7. References

Akroyd, D. & Wold, B. (1996). Critical thinking: A method for program evaluation. *Radiologic Science and Education,* Vol. 3, No. 1, (April, 1996), pp. 6-15.

Argyris, C. & Schön, D. (1974). *Theory in Practice: Increasing Professional Effectiveness,* Jossey-Bass, ISBN 0-87589-230-2, San Francisco, CA.

Brookfield, S. D. (1987). *Developing Critical Thinkers: Challenging Adults to Explore Alternative Ways of Thinking and Acting,* Jossey-Bass, ISBN 1-55542-356-6, San Francisco, CA.

Cianciolo, A. T., Matthew, C., Sternberg, R. J., & Wagner, R. K. (2006). Tacit knowledge, practical intelligence, and expertise, In: *The Cambridge Handbook of Expertise and Expert Performance,* K. A. Ericsson, N. Charness, P. J. Feltovich, & R. R. Hoffman (Eds.), pp. 613-632, Cambridge University Press, ISBN 978-0-521-60081-1, New York, New York.

Cseh, M., Watkins, K. E., & Marsick, V. J. (1999). Re-conceptualizing Marsick and Watkins' model of informal and incidental learning in the workplace, In: *1999 Proceedings of the Academy of HRD,* K. P. Kuchinke (Ed.), pp. 349-355, Academy of Human Resource Development, Baton Rouge, LA.

Davis, D. A. (2009). How to help professionals maintain and improve their knowledge and skills: Triangulating best practices in medicine, In: *Development of Professional Expertise,* K. A. Ericsson (Ed.), pp. 180-202, Cambridge University Press, ISBN 9780521740081, Cambridge, MA.

Eraut, M. (2004a). Informal learning in the workplace. *Studies in Continuing Education,* Vol 26, No.2, pp. 247 -273.

Eraut, M. (2004b). Practice-based evidence, In: *Evidence-based Practice in Education*, G. Thomas & R. Pring (Eds.), pp. 91-101, Open University Press, ISBN 9780335213344, Maidenhead, U.K.

Frank, E. D., Long, B. W., & Smith, B. J. (2012). *Merrill's Atlas of Radiographic Positioning and Procedures.* Elsevier Mosby, ISBN 978-0-323-07321-9, St. Louis, MO.

King, P. M. & Kitchener, K. S. (1994). *Developing Reflective Judgment*, Jossey-Bass, ISBN 1-55542-629-8, San Francisco, CA.

Kolb, D. (1984). *Experiential Learning: Experience as the Source of Learning and Development.* Prentice Hall, ISBN 0-13-295261-0, Engelwood Cliffs, NJ.

Leslie, B., Aring, M. K., & Brand, B. (2003). Informal learning: The new frontier of employee and organizational development. *Economic Development Review,* Vol. 14, No. 4, pp 12-18.

Lowenstein, M. A. & Spletzer, J. R. (1999). Informal training: A review of existing data and some new evidence. *Research in Labor Economics,* Vol. 18, pp. 402-438.

Marsick, V. J., & Volpe, M. (1999). The nature of and need for informal learning. In: *Informal Learning on the Job, Advances in Human Developing Resources,* Vol. 1, No. 3, V. J. Marsick & M. Volpe (Eds.), pp. 1-9, Barrett-Koehler and the Academy of Human Resource Development, ISBN 1-59376-023-7, San Francisco, CA.

Marsick, V. J., Volpe, M., & Watkins, K. E. (1999). Theory and practice of informal learning in the knowledge era, In: *Informal Learning on the Job, Advances in Human Developing Resources,* Vol. 1, No. 3, V. J. Marsick & M. Volpe (Eds.), pp 80-95, Barrett-Koehler and the Academy of Human Resource Development, ISBN 1-59376-023-7, San Francisco, CA.

Marsick, V. J. & Watkins, K. E. (1990). *Informal and Incidental Learning in the Workplace,* Routledge, ISBN 0-415-03141-9, London, U.K.

Marsick, V. J., Watkins, K. E., Callahan, M. W., & Volpe, M. (2009). Informal and incidental learning in the workplace, In: *Handbook of Research on Adult Learning and Development,* M. C. Smith with N. DeFrates-Densch (Eds.), pp. 570-600, Routledge, ISBN 0-203-88788-3, New York, New York.

McCall, M., Lombardo, M. M., & Morrison, A. M. (1988). *Lessons of Experience: How Successful Executives Develop on the Job.* Lexington Books, The Free Press, Simon & Schuster, ISBN 0-669-18095-5, New York, New York.

Nonaka, I. & Takeuchi, H. (1995). *The knowledge-creating Company: How Japanese Companies Create the Dynamics of Innovation*, ISBN 0-19-509269-4, Oxford University Press, New York, New York.

O'Toole, P. (2011). *How organizations remember: Retaining knowledge through organizational action,* Springer, ISBN 978-1-4419-7523-2, New York, Dordrecht, Heidelberg, London.

Paradise, A. (2008, July). Informal learning: Overlooked or overhyped? *T+D*, pp. 52-53.

Raelin, J. A. (2008). *Work-based Learning: Bridging Knowledge and Action,* Jossey-Bass, ISBN 978-0-470-18256-7, San Francisco, CA.

Schön, D. A. (1983). *The reflective practitioner: How professionals think in action.* Basic Books, ISBN 0-465-06878-2, New York, NY.

Schön, D. A. (1987). *Educating the reflective practitioner: Toward a new design for teaching and learning in the professions.* Jossey-Bass, ISBN 9781-55542-220-9, San Francisco, CA.

Schein, E. H. (1993). On dialogue, culture, and organizational learning. *Organizational Dynamics, Vol. 22, No. 2*,(1993, Autumn), pp. 40-51.

Skule, S. (2004). Learning conditions at work: A framework to understand and assess informal learning in the workplace, *International Journal of Training and Development*, Vol. 8, No. 1, pp. 8-20.

Trad, M. L. (2009). Mentoring radiation therapy students: A review and survey. *Radiation Therapist.* Vol. 18, No. 2, pp. 101-108.

Von Krogh, G., Ichijo, K., & Nonaka, I. (2000). *Enabling Knowledge Creation: How to Unlock the Mystery of Tacit Knowledge and Release the Power of Innovation.* Oxford University Press, ISBN 978-0-19-512616-7, Oxford & New York.

Vernon, S. (1999). Learning to be an effective team member, In: *Informal Learning on the Job, Advances in Human Developing Resources*, Vol. 1, No. 3, V. J. Marsick & M. Volpe (Eds.), pp 33-41, Barrett-Koehler and the Academy of Human Resource Development, ISBN 1-59376-023-7, San Francisco, CA.

Vygotsky, L. S. (1978). *Mind in society: The Development of Higher Psychological Processes.* Harvard University Press, ISBN 0-674-57629-2, Cambridge, MA.

Wenger, E. (1998). *Communities of Practice: Learning, Meaning, and Identity,* Cambridge University Press, ISBN 0-521-66363-6, New York, New York.

Yates, J. (2011). *Complex problem solving in radiologic technology: Understanding the roles of experience, reflective judgment, and workplace culture.* Unpublished doctoral dissertation, Teachers College, Columbia University.

12

Applying Social Media in Collaborative Brainstorming and Creation of Common Understanding Between Independent Organizations

Erno Salmela and Ari Happonen
Lappeenranta University of Technology
Finland

1. Introduction

This report is based on an experiment performed within the Johto (Innovative management of the supplier network and ICT systems) and Kiima (New business by strategic SME network) research projects funded by Tekes (the Finnish Funding Agency for Technology and Innovation). The experiment looked into the suitability of social media for content production and brainstorming work between organizations. According to Knight et al. (2008), the groups using web tools have showed an improvement in cohesion, but not as great an improvement as that found in face to face groups. They however suggest that web tools are valuable options to organizations that pursue benefits through virtual groups.

The organizations which participated in the experiment were research institutes/ niversities, consultants, service providers, and industrial companies. Almost all of these participants had some kind of linkage to the machinery industry. However, most of the participated organizations did not have any mutual business connections in the real world, but quite many of them knew each other through above-mentioned Tekes projects. In practice, we were dealing with an open innovation environment, which refers to a model of innovation in which firms draw on research and development that lies outside their own boundaries (Chesbrough, 2003). There were very heterogeneous group of organizations and people in this experiment. Grinyer (2000) writes that heterogeneous group (different personality types, backgrounds, training and education) can have positive effect on creativity and innovativeness. Furthermore, informal communication (such as social media mainly is) is considered to be one major factor to stimulate creativity in teams (Sundgren et al., 2005). As such, an aim of our study was to explore social media from the creativity (brainstorming) view of point in the independent company network.

The topic in the social media experiment was: "how to manage an idea process" (stages of the process, performance indicators, and incentives). The chosen topic was a new issue for many of the participant organizations, which is why a research oriented (exploratory) approach, seemed to be a good starting point for the experiment. In research network, the primary target of collaboration is the creation of new knowledge, while the research activities are carried out by every partner without a leading company (Magnusson and Nilsson, 2003). The experiment was performed during a two week period in the autumn 2010 and the web-based Yammer service (www.yammer.com) was used as a tool.

Before starting working with Yammer, the facilitator (a researcher who worked in the Johto and Kiima projects) looked into the backgrounds of utilizing social media in business operations. This happened by participating in seminars that dealt with the topic (e.g. the Finnish National Innovation Forum, 2010) and by exploring earlier scientific articles. This was done to acquire initial information (e.g. good practices and encountered challenges) of using social media in a networked business environment, and how social media is connected to knowledge management.

According to the earlier studies, the integration of networking into knowledge management generates different kind of benefits. Firstly, knowledge networks allow the firms to improve the access, the transfer and the integration of knowledge. Secondly, they are more able in generating knowledge than a single firm. Finally, knowledge networks enable companies to increase competencies to share common tacit knowledge. (Belussi and Arcangeli, 1998; Lorenzoni and Lipparini, 1999). Therefore, the knowledge management system moves from a single company point of view toward a network point of view (Canzano and Grimaldi, 2004). According to Sawhney and Prandelli (2000), the common inter-organizational understanding can be enhanced through collective learning. Simatupang et al. (2002) mention that through collective learning, the understanding of big picture can be improved.

Activating people to produce content in social media seems to be challenging like the following use rates indicate: active users 1 per cent, respondents/commentators 10 per cents, and followers/absentees 89 percents of all users (Charles, 2006). A representative in a seminar stated that in one progressive ICT company the corresponding percentages were 2, 16, 82, although a lot of effort was allocated for facilitating the content work. On the basis of the aforementioned relative portions it seems that the portion of passive participants is substantial. The facilitator of the Yammer experiment decided that these general ratios should be challenged in the Yammer experiment. In practice, it was estimated that a significant amount of work would be required to increase the portion of active users first to "sell" the experiment and later to facilitate the content work. This corresponds to view of Shahriza et al. (2005) who write that use of communication technology tool must be accompanied by proper training, sufficient technical support, and active facilitation. Especially active facilitation was seen important in Yammer work, because the good management of social interactions help to achieve common goals (Chen et al., 2008). Training and technical support were not considered as important because the Yammer tool was extremely easy to use.

When using social media, it is essential to get people to commit themselves to it. According to Breeding (2009), a commitment of resources ensures a steady stream of interesting content over a sustained period. This is important because when using social media it is important to keep the content up to date (Dymi, 2010). One of our seminar sources emphasized that the commitment should happen face to face or, at least, by phone – not by e-mail. The facilitator of the Yammer experiment utilized this perspective by striving to commit as many people as possible to the experiment by describing its objectives face to face or by phone. On the other hand, the aim was to find out what significance it has on the participation and content production activity if the introduction is made only by e-mail.

Committing people to the Yammer experiment was beforehand seen as challenging, because the facilitator could not use traditional management methods as people participated in the experiment from different organizations. For example, Crawford (2001) writes that enforcement can be a mean to promote the active utilization of electronic communication tools. This kind of management was impossible in our Yammer work because of above-mentioned reason. Another challenge was how to find the common issue which gets people from different organizations interested. As a result of these challenges, the facilitator estimated that first the focus has to be on selecting a topic which interests different parties. Secondly, the participants should be managed especially through motivation.

One representative in a seminar emphasized that agreeing on objectives, intermediary objectives and schedules is important in any work performed in social media. This point of view supports the opinion of Phillips and Phillips (1993) that the content learning process must have a well-defined beginning, middle and end. Furthermore, the shared goals for the group serve as a bonding mechanism that helps different partners to combine resources and facilitate the communication (e.g. exchange of ideas) and achievement of common understanding (Tsai and Ghoshal, 1998; Inkepen and Tsang, 2005). One speaker in a seminar who had operated a lot with social media stated that although their own business offers social media consulting services, it took them a year before they learned to utilize social media properly. In addition, the individual in question emphasized that technology is not the problem when applying social media. Instead, the problems are caused because the aims of using social media are insufficiently discussed. In addition, the same person stated that transparency is a good way to get people to produce content in the agreed schedule. One way is to display who has delivered the agreed content on the agreed schedule to all participants of the social media service. In this situation, it can be said that community pressure guides people to produce content on time. On the basis of this viewpoint, the facilitator made beforehand a rough plan of the Yammer experiment including objectives and schedules and, in addition, decided to utilize extensive transparency in the experiment.

All of the above presented viewpoints were based on utilizing social media either inside a company or in operations between partners. This differs significantly from our Yammer experiment, in which most of the organizations did not co-operate in the real world. This was, as estimated beforehand, one of the most interesting challenges in our experiment: how to get people who are "strangers" to each other to participate and actively produce content together? Furthermore, the experiment was dominated by a special situation since the participating organizations did not have a concrete goal, from the viewpoint of their own organizations, for the Yammer work. Instead, the experiment had two exploratory goals - on one hand to get more information on managing an idea generation process and, on the other hand, to gain experiences on using social media in business operations among independent organizations.

2.Experiences of the Yammer experiment

This chapter presents the main stages of the Yammer experiment - preparatory work, registering stage, use/working stage as well as the content created in the experiment on a rough level.

2.1 Preparatory work

Before starting the experiment, the facilitator made a rough plan on how to proceed during the next two weeks and what results would be pursued from the experiment. As it is mentioned earlier, the initial stage of the development process, managing an idea process, was chosen as a content topic in the experiment. This choice was influenced the fact that it was found out both in the Johto and Kiima projects that there seems to be development needs in this process in studied companies.

In the preliminary plan, the first Yammer week was reserved for general discussion on the idea process management. Performance indicators and incentives of the idea process were chosen as the more specific content topic. The aim was to contemplate them during the second Yammer week with the help of brainstorming. The goal of the brainstorming was to gain such good process descriptions as well as indicator and incentive ideas that some of the companies participating in the Yammer work would become inspired to refine them further for their own practical operations after the Yammer period. However, the content of the second Yammer week was left somewhat unplanned, since the purpose was to ask the users after the first week which contents they would especially like to concentrate on during the second week.

Before starting working with Yammer, the facilitator had reserved time for producing preliminary contents, so that the invited persons would have interesting conversation openers when they arrived at the Yammer for the first time. In addition, content was requested from four other researchers that participated in Yammer work. The goal was to receive two conversation openers from each researcher in advance (altogether eight openers) before sending invitations to the other Yammer participants. There were altogether only two openers (plus two from the facilitator), which was a disappointment to the facilitator - *"what might be the enthusiasm of corporate representatives towards the matter if even the ´inner circle´, the researchers, do not produce the requested content"*. This was, from the point of view of continuation of the experiment, the first critical point. At this stage, the facilitator even pondered whether it would be worthwhile giving up the experiment altogether - a so called surrender point 1.

The facilitator presented the objectives, schedules and principles of the experiment beforehand to 13 persons face to face, four persons by phone and 15 persons by e-mail. This introduction took place about two weeks prior to starting the use period, so that it would be possible for people to reserve time for the Yammer work in advance. For two individuals interested in the matter (they were included in the previously mentioned 15 persons who received the introduction via e-mail), the Yammer experiment was presented when it was already underway. Thus, the experiment was presented to 32 individuals, all of whom received an invitation to Yammer. Facebook was familiar to the majority of them from leisure time, but for professional purposes social media had been rarely utilized. In fact, Yammer was chosen as the tool for this experiment due to the resemblance of its user interface to Facebook. Thus, it was estimated that Yammer would be easily adopted by the users, so the success of the experiment would not, at any rate, depend on the user friendliness of the application.

2.2 Registering stage

Altogether 25 persons from 14 different organizations registered to Yammer: 10 companies, three universities/research institutions, and Tekes. In the context of the introduction, the facilitator inquired after the people's interest in joining the project of producing Yammer content. At the same time the facilitator additionally estimated the interest of the people towards the matter on the basis of their "body language". Naturally when using e-mail, this was not possible to observe and only two from the invited persons announced that they are interested the Yammer experiment. On the basis of the number of invitees and estimated level of enthusiasm, the presenter set a goal for the number of registered users. The set objectives were that 10 of the 13 persons whom had received the introduction face to face would be registered and, respectively, two out of four who had been introduced by phone and five out of 15 who had been introduced by e-mail would be registered. Thus, the goal was 17 registered users in all. The actualised number (25) clearly exceeded this goal. From those who had received face to face introduction, 11 persons registered, and from those who had received introduction by phone, three registered, so in these the realizations corresponded well to the objectives. Instead, the registration rate of those who received the introduction by e-mail was a positive surprise, since 11 out of 15 registered. On this basis it would then seem that interest towards working with social media can be awakened also via e-mail.

It is also interesting to observe the accumulation of registered users during the two week use period. Within two days after sending the invitation, 13 persons had registered into Yammer. Ten out of these individuals registered already on the first day. After this, the facilitator sent three notifications every two days for the unregistered persons. To lure new users the notifications included extracts of contents (most interesting topics) that had been discussed in Yammer so far. Furthermore, information on forthcoming Yammer work was attached to the e-mail. After the first notification, three more registered within two days. After the second notification, five more registered within three days and, after the third notification, four more users were gained. Thus, in the beginning of the second week all 25 registered users were involved. Based on these results, the e-mail notification was reasonable to do. However, what must be noted here is that from time to time Yammer sent automatic messages to those invited who were not yet registered. When asked afterwards, at least two persons had registered to Yammer because they wanted to get rid of the constant registering requests sent by Yammer. Figure 1 views the development of the number of users during the Yammer experiment. In addition, the image shows the e-mail notification dates for unregistered users.

Based on the registration rate, people seemed to be interested in this experiment. This is also supported by the comments received from users. The following are a few examples:

> *"It will be interesting to see how this works and what kind of content there will be. Also the functionality of the technique is interesting."*

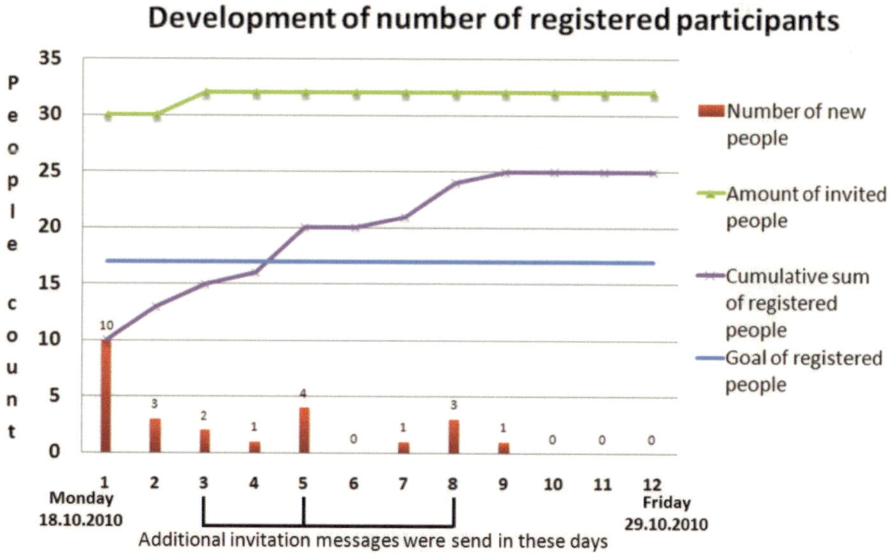

Fig. 1. The development of the number of registered users on Yammer

"When I received an invitation, interest towards this type of experiment arouse instantly. If the strengths of this are utilized properly, this is in some way in the middle of face-to-face communication and anonymous communication. Naturally one also wants something to be reserved for the employer. I am sure that with this group of people we can create something which can be used to once more further refine matters that are actually productive in practice."

"I've got three main incentives for this. First, to find with this group a couple of good ideas on indicators and incentives which can be further refined to receive a new production model for the practice of the Finnish industry. Second, to gain information on how social media could be utilized in the development work of the Finnish industry of small and medium sized enterprises. Third, to find people who think alike and with whom I could co-operate even more in the future."

On the basis of the previous comments, gaining experiences of the suitability of social media in business operations seemed to be as important for users as the discussed topic.

2.3 Working stage

This chapter focuses on the experiences gained during the Yammer work period which lasted for two weeks. As mentioned earlier, the first week concentrated on the more general matter in creating a common understanding of the management of an idea process, whereas in the second week the purpose was to handle more specific topics. In the rough plan, the possible theme of the second week was indicators and incentives of an idea process, but the actual theme choice was, however, a collective decision. After the first half of the first week, an enquiry was realized in Yammer about which contents the participants especially wanted to concentrate on during the second week. Table 1 presents the results of this enquiry.

What issues would you like to be handled in Yammer during the second week?	Portion of the respondents
General issues related to constant improvement and innovation	7.5 %
Good indicator and incentive practices to be found	23 %
Concrete indicators and incentives for development	62 %
Something else	7.5 %

Table 1. Enquiry of subject matters handled during the second week

Altogether 13 answers were ultimately received for this enquiry. Discussing concrete indicators and incentives received the most support, so it was chosen as the main theme for the second week. Good indicator and incentive practices were regarded interesting, as well, so they were also decided to be covered during the second week. This enquiry was additionally used as an indicator of the users' activity level. After publishing the enquiry, only five people out of the 25 registered users answered it within 1.5 days. The small share of respondents frustrated the facilitator – *"I wonder if this Yammer business is worth continuing, since people don't even answer a simple enquiry, in which we decide on the focus points of working for the second week."* Another possible surrender point, but the choice was to continue. By notifying about the enquiry by e-mail and raising the enquiry as the top point of the Yammer user interface, considerably more answers were received within the following 1.5 days – *"13 answers is an OK level"*.

The outcome of the first Yammer week is well illustrated in the summary published by the facilitator to the Yammer users:

> *"First of all, there are 19 registered users. Altogether 32 individuals were invited and nearly half of them received a notification only by e-mail. I am very satisfied with this interest towards the matter. It's difficult to evaluate how much the active users follow the contents since there are no statistics available. Instead, there is more specific information on the more important matter, namely content production. There are nearly 200 comments in all. I was going for a somewhat more balanced content production, since the content production was pretty much in the hands of a couple of fellows. Towards the end of the week the direction was, however, for the better, which meant that more opinions were becoming visible. Hopefully the same continues next week, as well, because it enriches the contents.*
>
> *The content sprawled very much this first week, but I do not consider it as a bad thing at all. This is because it improves the formation of an overall picture, which is what this thing is all about. In the coming week we will then go into those two topics more specifically, namely concrete indicators and incentives as well as good indicator and incentive practices to be found.*
>
> *I wish everyone a good weekend and let's continue on Monday. Although I'm sure some nerds will come by during the weekend, as well ☺... now it seems there are 20 of us, so welcome, Harri."*

When measured by the number of comments, a little more content was created in Yammer during the first than the second week. The main reason for this was that during the second week the focus moved from a more general discussion of the topic to a more specific topic. A brainstorm was organized in Yammer in order to generate ideas on indicators and incentives. The results of this brainstorm are viewed next.

2.3.1 Experiences of the brainstorm performed in Yammer

For the brainstorm, the facilitator made a briefing and distributed it to all persons invited to Yammer. Together with the briefing, the following "motivational e-mail" was sent to the users:

> *"During the second week of Yammer, a web brainstorm will be held on the indicators and incentives of an idea process. During the first week, Yammer worked pretty much as a traditional network teaching environment with interactive features. This network teaching environment matter can be a completely new thing for a part of you, but when inspected from a wider perspective it is not a revolutionary thing, as there has been plenty of similar experiments abroad and in Finland. This brainstorm, however, is a big deal – especially as the object of inquiry is a very complex matter and there are not a lot of prior practical experiences anywhere. It is clear that for this to succeed a lot more active input is needed from this group than there was during the first week. In this brainstorm we have the opportunity to disprove the assumption that it is easier not to participate in a brainstorm online than in a traditional face-to-face meeting. At the same time, it has been said that ideas that are considered and written down calmly are better than ideas "tossed around" in a traditional meeting. Let us, then, prove this assumption right!"*

The users were asked to return their ideas within two days to the facilitator's e-mail. This was done in order to prevent "copying" other people's ideas, which would have been possible if the users had published their ideas directly into Yammer. After receiving the ideas, the facilitator published them as such at once in Yammer. There were 5 idea packages received by the deadline - surrender point number 3. No giving up - "at this stage, it is not worthwhile to stop". However, teeth were grit and the facilitator sent a somewhat provocative e-mail (a part of this below) to the users who had not yet returned their ideas.

> *"25 registered users – five idea packages received; the same activity relation others have reached with social media. Should we, then, be satisfied to reach the same level of activity than everyone else? Perhaps, but personally I am a little bit disappointed, since I had a strong belief that this group can do considerably more and I still believe it. I am especially annoyed on behalf of the few*

fellows who have properly invested in the idea generation. Let us take this day as extra time for pondering ideas and then we'll see where we stand. We are not, in fact, far from the situation where we can proudly present together what we have accomplished. But this requires one more final push."

After this e-mail, one idea package more was received, so altogether six individuals participated in the brainstorm. Beforehand, the facilitator had set the participation of eight individuals in the brainstorm as an objective, so this was not quite reached. However, the facilitator included some ideas which came forward in the first week's Yammer discussions to the results of the brainstorm. As a result, the ideas of four more users were gained, so altogether the ideas of ten users were visible in the results of the brainstorm. The received ideas ranged very much with regard to their refinement grade – from a couple of quickly scratched ideas all the way to complete indicator and incentive concepts. The facilitator asked the participants of the brainstorm how much time they had spent working on their ideas, and it ranged remarkably - from 15 minutes to 3.5 hours.

From the ideas born in the brainstorm, five were taken to be further refined in Yammer – on one hand, the individual ideas which were most recurrent and, on the other hand, the most unique, were chosen to be further refined. There was altogether 2.5 days for refining and commenting on the ideas. Related to the refinement of the ideas, 25 comments from five individuals were received. This fell considerably short of the goal set by the facilitator, since the objective was to get at least 50 comments from ten different users. The activity of the users in refining ideas was very much equivalent to the level of the more general conversation held in Yammer during the first week.

In connection with the brainstorm, a small competition was organized between the users in which the creator of the best idea would be awarded with a bottle of wine or a restaurant gift certificate. This was not believed to have a strong motivating influence on creating ideas, but rather it was seen as an extra spice appropriate to the subject matter. The name of the producer of the best idea was announced to the users in Yammer as well as by e-mail. In addition, the name of the producer was mentioned in the meeting of the Kiima steering group, which caused applause to the rewarded person. A small matter, but surely especially the latter acknowledgement felt good to the winner. In addition, the red wine was reputedly excellent – *"long and good aftertaste is the best quality of this wine"*☺.

2.3.2 User activity in the Yammer work

In Chapter 2.2 it was presented that interest towards the Yammer experiment was measured with the registration rate. The facilitator had an advance presumption that an interest in the matter is not yet enough for users to actively follow the content or especially to produce content. For content production, both strong commitment and real enthusiasm are needed both towards the subject matter and toward writing online. Commitment was a challenge in this experiment, since the network community comprised of different organizations, which meant that the facilitator could not demand anyone to invest in the matter. In addition, people had different interests towards the experiment, so there was no clear common goal. It was not an easy matter to manage the researchers, either (see surrender point 1 presented in Chapter 2.1).

In the experiment, a free version of Yammer, which contained quite few use report options, was used. Two important reports could, however, be found related to the actions of the users. First, Yammer automatically produced report data of the overall number of comments as well as the number of comments of each registered user, which described the user-specific content production activity. Naturally the facilitator and also other users saw also all the new comments published in the service. Secondly, people who had signed in could be seen in Yammer constantly. On this basis, the facilitator could evaluate the number of users who had signed in. However, compiled reports could not be retrieved on how often the users were signed in and how they used the service (e.g. how often they signed in or how much they read the contents produced by others).

User activity was measured on two main levels: the level of following conversation and the level of content production. As mentioned above, there were no accurate statistics available on the users' visits and how actively they followed conversations in Yammer. Findings suggest that the number of people signed in at the same time varied during day time between six and 13 individuals. The names of those who had signed in could be seen in Yammer, so information on who were the most active individuals could be gained, as well. Although it seemed that three individuals had Yammer open the whole time, since they were signed in during the evenings, as well. According to the findings of the facilitator, some of the registered users were present in Yammer only a few times or a few of them perhaps not even once. The facilitator estimated that there were altogether 7–10 users (about 30–40 per cent of the 25 registered users). Afterwards received user feedback proved this estimation to be right

Information about the content production in Yammer was obtained well. In every published comment, the name of the writer of the comment was automatically visible, so it was easy to identify the writer of each comment. In addition, Yammer made a notification of each new comment separately with a red font in the upper part of the page, so the publication of new contents could be seen fast. It would also have been possible to have each new comment sent to the users' e-mail, but this was thought to be a too frequent notification interval. Instead, a summary of new contents to be sent at the end of each day to the users' e-mails was chosen. During the two weeks, contents were published by 15 individuals (60 per cent of all registered users), who produced altogether 350 comments. Figure 2 shows the content production activity of different users measured by the number of messages as well as the cumulative growth in the number of messages per user.

Three of the most active users produced approximately 75 per cent of the comments, four of the most active about 85 per cent, and eight of the most active about 95 per cent. The minimum objective set in advance was that 4–5 individuals would produce 80 per cent of the contents, so this objective was nearly reached. By the middle of the first week, two of the most active users (another of them was the facilitator) had produced about 80 per cent of the contents, after which the facilitator tried with different activation methods (e.g. by asking questions) to increase the activity of others. This was somewhat successful, but still it seemed to be quite difficult, since seeing these people face to face was not possible during the working period. Among the most active content producers (8 individuals with the minimum of 5 comments), for seven people out of eight the Yammer experiment was introduced face to face or by phone and for only one by e-mail. It would therefore seem that the introduction method of the Yammer experiment had an influence in the content production activity. Instead, the method did not seem to have much significance on the registration rate, as stated in Chapter 2.2.

There were altogether 30 conversation openings in Yammer. However, this is not essential information, since inside the conversation paths the discussion covered many different topics, which is typical for an online discussion. For this reason, no conclusions can be made of the importance of the topic/discussion opening in question on the basis of the number of comments in individual conversation paths. In any case, the facilitator opened new conversation paths for the most interesting comments which deviated most from the original topic and which had been published inside the existing conversation paths. In the Yammer experiment, the facilitator opened 20 conversation paths out of 30.

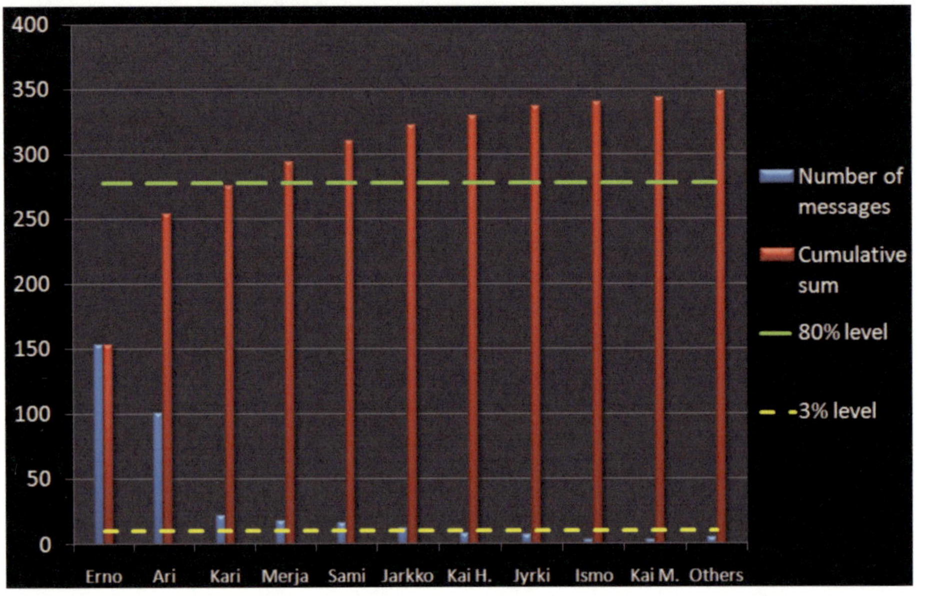

Fig. 2. The number of messages per user and cumulative number of messages

When we compare the user activity of this experiment to other experiments of social media in business operations, this was a successful experiment. In Chapter 1 it was told that when applied in business operations, there are typically 1 per cent active users, 10 per cent answerers/commentators, and 89 per cent followers/absentees in social media. In our Yammer experiment the corresponding percentages were: 8 per cent (2 users who published content every day), 24 per cent (6 users who were signed in approximately every other day and produced at least 5 comments in Yammer), and 68 per cent (17 users who produced less than 5 comments; roughly half of these 17 users were absentees). These percentages are not directly comparable to the previously presented typical percentages, since the grounds for measurement are not specifically known. Regardless, they are certainly indicative. In absolute terms, the numbers of active users in our Yammer experiment are not very flattering, either. At the same time, as a point of comparison we must keep in mind that everyone is not equally vocal in face to face meetings, either.

2.4 The content produced in Yammer

At the end of the Yammer work, the content was moved into Word and, as a result, a total of 67 pages were gathered. In the free version of Yammer, the content had to be manually pasted into Word which was quite laborious - especially when the layout of the content had to be cleaned so that the format would be as readable as possible. Also "copy pasting" took time because, in addition to opening different conversation paths, the longest messages had to be opened individually so that they were completely visible. In chargeable Yammer versions, the content can be exported into a file. In addition, indicator and incentive ideas were created in the brainstorm performed in Yammer and these were published by the users in separate documents instead of Yammer. These created about 30 pages of additional content. Therefore, altogether about 100 pages of contents were produced as a result of two weeks of Yammer work. The volume of content production was not measured on the basis of the amount of writing (number of characters or words) per user, but that would be one measurement possibility.

The quality of the content is naturally more important than the quantity, but also considerably more difficult to measure, since the quality is a very personal attribute; different people appreciate different things. This was true also among the Yammer users, since the users had different expectations and interests towards the Yammer work. Qualitative measuring was performed in practice so that, after the experiment, the users were asked about their views on the content. The following is a compilation of some of the received feedback. What is noteworthy in the feedback is that it is not necessarily targeted at the actual topic which was discussed, but also at the possibilities of working online in general.

> *"From the point of view of a scientist, it came to mind that this very easily created a ready, transcribed interview material, the kind of which makers of qualitative research normally gather by interviews, recordings and then by transcribing it to a written format and, finally, by analyzing it. Now those first three stages were created at the same time. Now systematic methods of content analysis of qualitative research could be used for the material, as well.*
>
> *"This is an extremely good content package. If we would now imagine a situation in which a larger group has a corresponding discussion in order to develop some part of business life or otherwise, the whole conversation would be saved. This kind of a capture of a conversation is not practically possible with e-mail communication or in any other way."*
>
> *"When considering the time span, other work load of the individuals, and the voluntary nature of the participation, I would say that the end result of the experiment is much better than I believe anyone expected."*

The quality of the content created in the Yammer work can also be verified by the fact that the indicator and incentive ideas created in brainstorming evoked active conversation when they were tested a couple weeks after the Yammer experiment in a small group work organized in connection with a meeting of the Kiima project's steering group. At the time of writing of this report it seems likely that the ideas that were created will be refined even further with a few company networks. This shows that the conversation held in Yammer was current with regard to the needs of the companies and that it produced useful information for business purposes. At the same time, it is also interesting to see whether the organizations which participated in the experiment become enthusiastic about utilizing social media in the future in some way also in their own internal operations or partner network. Furthermore, the Yammer work was a starting point for one new research project that deals with idea process management in company networks.

3. Facilitator´s views on the Yammer experiment

Some of the facilitator's experiences of the Yammer experiment were already presented in Chapter 2, e.g. in the form of the three surrender points, but let us consider this in more detail in this chapter, since the facilitator seems to have an important role in the application of social media. The facilitator and one research partner used altogether about 150 hours for the Yammer experiment. This consisted of preparatory work (familiarizing oneself with tools, making a rough plan, introducing the experiment to companies, and production of preliminary contents), facilitating the Yammer discussion and content production in Yammer, and writing reports (content report and this use experience report). The time used was distributed as follows between the aforementioned stages: preparatory work 20 per cent, facilitating the Yammer discussion and content production 40 per cent, and reporting 40 per cent. The effort was, therefore, significant, which explains the occasional inclination to surrender - especially when user activity was not quite at the desired level. The following is a presentation of the facilitator's views in the aforementioned main stages of the experiment.

3.1 Preparatory work

The preparatory work made by the facilitator was an important part of the Yammer experiment. Without thorough preparation the experiment would not even have been worth doing. The preparation undoubtedly had a significant influence firstly on the fact that so many of the invited users registered into Yammer and, in general, on the fact that there were so many individuals who wanted an invite. Setting the content theme, objectives and schedule beforehand was important since this made "selling" the experiment to companies considerably easier. Preliminary planning also helped during the Yammer work period - everyone knew, at least to an extent, what they were doing, although according to the feedback received after the experiment people did have some mixed opinions of the exactness of the content definition. Let us return to this subject in Chapter 4.

3.2 Facilitation and content production

The main role of the facilitator during the Yammer work period was first and foremost to activate discussion or to get as many users as possible to produce good content. The facilitator strived to do this in different ways (e.g. e-mail notifications, highlighting the most interesting issues, setting tasks, votes, asking questions, and provocation). Visible advantage was, indeed, gained from this activation work, so it was definitely necessary work. Although it did take quite a lot of working time - *"the expectations of the fruits of the activation work were higher than what was achieved"*.

The role of the facilitator was, in addition to the actual facilitation, to be very much also involved in content production. This was not in the line with the common view about the facilitator´s role: a facilitator concentrates on process while the participants are familiar with the content (Phillips and Phillips, 1993). Before starting the working period, the facilitator decided to concentrate on guiding the content production and to slow down his own content production. However, this turned out to be too difficult when the subject was interesting - *"there was something to say to nearly all comments of other users"*. During the working period, the facilitator put on the brakes on content production a couple of times, but in these instances the conversation seemed to be stopping almost completely, which was not a good thing, either. At the end of the second week, the facilitator got a bit tired, as well, and did not have the energy to bring all thoughts forth in Yammer, although the facilitator would have had something to say - *"the principle of reciprocity, meaning that if you give something, you should more or less get an equal amount back"*. The users did not give similar comments on whether one reason for the small amount of content production could have been that users did not want to share their own knowledge of the subject matter with others. According to the facilitator's evaluation, this may have been possible with regard to a few persons at most. In any case, this was undoubtedly not the most important reason for the small content production activity. Let us return to the other reasons in Chapter 4. The Yammer work period did not fulfill the facilitator's expectations with regard to the activity of the users, which is why the facilitator was somewhat disappointed after the period. The following moods illustrate the facilitator's feelings immediately after the Yammer work period:

> *"Psychologically facilitation online was considerably harder than in face to face meetings. There were, indeed, three points in which I would have liked to call off the game."*
>
> *"I will never do this again... or not in at least five years."*
>
> *"In social media, we cannot properly see others' reactions to the matter and we do not even know who are actually present, although their names could be seen in the list. When facilitating or writing the content, many times I had a feeling of standing in an empty room talking to the walls."*

New user comments were practically the only thing that gave the facilitator information about the users' reactions, which is very little, since on average there were only about 20 user comments per day, excluding the facilitator's own comments. At the same time, the Yammer work also included some content floods. One of the active content producers said that these were enjoyable moments:

> *"From time to time the same kind of enthusiasm could be detected as in the best face to face meetings. The comments streamed in such a pace that one did not have the time to finish writing one's own."*

Immediately after the work period, the facilitator found it very difficult to evaluate the value of the Yammer experiment, since there was quite little feedback during the experiment and after it. Feedback was requested by e-mail from all registered users immediately after the Yammer work period. In retrospect, it might have been worthwhile to organize a round of phone calls with the users after the experiment, so that information on the users' views could have been better received. However, 1–2 months after the working period the facilitator has discussed the matter with about ten users either face to face or by phone. Their feedback has been "cautiously" positive. On the basis of the feedback received, the feelings of the facilitator were eventually positive, which means that the experiment was worth doing. At the time of writing this, the following idea illustrates the facilitator's feelings well: *"Perhaps I will facilitate a similar thing again already after a year... why not even after a couple of months with a smaller group."*

3.3 Reporting

Originally, no reports were planned of the Yammer experiment, but when the experiment had ended, reporting the results was seen as necessary since both the content created in Yammer and the use experiences gained on utilizing social media were seen as useful also for others than those involved in the experiment. The content report can be utilized in the future as an information source for idea process and innovation management (in fact the report was one source for earlier mentioned new research project). Furthermore, as to the power of social media, one can notice just by eying the report what a large amount of information was in the end created during two weeks by 15 content producers. The present use experience report is useful to companies also in the sense that as they start their own application of social media, this report provides analyzed background data of important issues to be considered, so that the worst pitfalls can possibly be avoided.

4. The opportunities and challenges of social media

This chapter views the opportunities, benefits and challenges of applying social media in communication among different companies on the basis of the Yammer experiences.

4.1 Opportunities and benefits

In our Yammer experiment, no actual, specific development work was conducted, but a group of organizations discussed together the development opportunities related to the chosen theme. The organizations who participated in the experiment had different interests towards the experiment. For a part of the participating organizations, the management of an idea process was a genuinely current topic, and practical actions have already been taken in this area. For some of the organizations the matter was new, so the representatives of these organizations were mostly searching for further information on the topic. For some of the persons involved in the experiment, the topic in itself was not the most important thing, but they were more interested in the application opportunities of social media. Therefore, it can be said that the experiment included quite a dispersed group of representatives, which was not necessarily the best possible setting. Basically, a similar experiment could have been made separately for the three aforementioned segments, in which case the interests would have been more coherent inside the groups. Thus, it could be said that organizational aspect is an essential part of working with social media.

As there were no prior business connections between the companies and due to the aforementioned differences in interests, there could not, in practice, have been a concrete development target in the Yammer work. At the same time, the topic of the experiment was new to most, as well, so there was not really any basis for practical development. Therefore, the goal of the experiment was first and foremost to increase the participants' understanding of managing an idea process as well as to find the most important factors which should be taken into consideration in developing an idea management process. Thus, this was very much like a research approach to the topic or, in other words, a foundation was created for practical development work in the future. For this type of work, social media seem to be suited very well. With the help of social media people can, for instance, quickly spread information on good practices in different companies and networks and, thus, gain new ideas for their own organization. On another hand, it could be necessary to arrange face to face meetings along side with work in social media. Shahriza et al. (2005) mention that high performance is associated with the utilization of both face to face and virtual communication for group work; effectiveness and performance cannot be ascertained solely by looking at either face to face communication or ICT exclusively. According to them, the face to face meetings may be more effective when all members are available and when the tasks are highly ambiguous.

To succeed in social media working, it is important to carefully define the subject at hand. The topic of this Yammer experiment may have been too wide and challenging for an online discussion, which possibly had an influence also on the users' content production activity. The following user comment illustrates this: "*In addition to the incompatibility of schedules and other hurry, the greatest obstacle for participation was the extent and vagueness of the theme. It was hard for me to create an idea process for a situation which kind of works anytime, for anyone, and for any organization. Of course there are and should be generic models, but in this instance I experienced it as challenging which meant that my head was completely empty.*"

This comment is related to the previously mentioned organization matter, meaning that the user group was probably too diverse with regard to interests. Discussing issues on a general level is typically related to the research approach used in this experiment. Case-specific sessions could also have been organized in Yammer (e.g. developing an idea process for one company or for its network), but beforehand the facilitator estimated that this would not be sensible with a group that included numerous independent organizations. Instead, after the experiment the facilitator suggested a possibility to start developing a detailed idea process with a smaller group, for instance by applying Yammer, if there is a company interested in this matter. Hopefully this kind of an experiment will be made. It is quite possible, since 4-5 individuals who participated in the Yammer experiment stated that they are interested in the matter (not only when it comes to developing an idea process, but also developing any other interesting topics). This kind of small group size appears to be quite suitable for actual development work. This corresponds to Grinyer´s (2000) view that the effectiveness of a communication declines as the size of the group increases

When it comes to defining the topic, it can be said that the topic had, in fact, been quite specifically defined beforehand (process stages, indicators, and incentives of an idea process). However, it became very quickly obvious in the conversations that there was need for discussing the topic from a wider perspective; the participants wanted to discuss, for instance, the innovation culture as well as the differences in continuous improvement, incremental innovation and radical innovation. The majority of users wanted, therefore, to understand the backgrounds of the matter, which is typical when the issue is new. At this point, the facilitator did not want to return the conversation back to the topic defined in advance since there was clearly a need for an increase in the general understanding of innovation operations.

During the second week, a brainstorm as well as refinement of the created ideas was tried out in Yammer. The test did not exactly provide an answer on how well social media are suited for brainstorming. However, some users did produce good ideas, and they have been further refined with companies, so the brainstorm was useful in any case. The majority of users did not produce any ideas, though. It was possibly easier not to participate in a brainstorm in Yammer than in face to face meetings.

Based on Yammer experiment, utilizing social media seems to have at least the following benefits compared to face to face meetings:

- getting such people together "at the same table" whom it would not be possible to bring together otherwise; thus, it is possible to gain knowledge outside the inner circle (corresponds real-life open seminars)
- ideas are usually refined when they are written down
- the discussion is documented in one location
- "quiet" persons can bring their thoughts out in the open better

Social media will undoubtedly become an integral part of the operations of companies, but even with this we need to learn in stages. The facilitator has experiences which go back ten years on discussion group experiments conducted in individual companies. These experiments failed completely at the time because not enough people were involved. On the basis of the Yammer experiment, the development compared to that time has been considerable since 25 out of the 32 people who were invited from different organizations participated voluntarily in Yammer. As the learning processes are constantly becoming faster, in five years social media will probably be natural communication methods also in business. By that time perhaps all 32 invited individuals will register and 20 of them will participate in the discussion actively. However, before that there is work to be done. First, it is good to experiment what social media are all about. For that, a Yammer experiment like the present one surely gave some foundation, but the next step could be to consider how social media could be utilized in one's own operations. After this, do not postpone the experiment – after all, this matter requires learning and gathering experiences like any other.

4.2 Challenges and obstacles

The Yammer experiment revealed that there are numerous challenges and obstacles in applying social media among organizations and online writing in general. On the basis of the feedback, lack of time was the most essential limitation especially when it came to content production. The facilitator and his research partner were in practice the only ones who had reserved sufficient time for Yammer work in advance (at least a couple of hours each day), even though others also knew of the timing of the discussion already a couple weeks in advance. Either they did not consider the matter to be especially important or the time needed for a profound participation surprised the users. This is well illustrated in the following user comments:

> "*It must be stated that as interesting as these topics were, following them and commenting on them takes some time... it is so damn busy at work at the moment.*"
>
> "*I was on a sick day, so I grabbed the computer and spent the day in Yammer. At work I have not been possibility to take part in it at all.*"
>
> "*At the moment, both work and my own time are at such a challenging point that I have not had much chance to get involved in this Yammer after the first week. With the help of sufficiently early scheduling, matters could be organized so that one could participate more in this sort of thing.*"
>
> "*It is difficult to follow this during the work day. It is irritating. I'll try to participate today...*"

In addition to lack of time, the Table 2 introduces challenges and obstacles in applying social media were detected on the basis of the Yammer experiment.

Less than ideal organization; the group had too varied interests
People do not want to repeat the same contents (when there was not time to read contents of other users)
The written comments leave a mark (self-censorship)
Content production is slow
Everyone's writing skills are not the same
A person who is good verbally can think that the online environment puts a damper on the atmosphere since his own characteristics do not come out
The environment in which one is writing can be challenging (e.g. open office)
Negative prejudice towards online communication
A written text does not depict emotions which is an essential part of communication

Table 2. Observed challenges and obstacles of social media based on Yammer experiment

5. Summary

25 participants from 14 different organizations participated in the social media experiment. The topic of the discussion was the idea process management, which seems to be a current topic for companies. Because the topic was a new matter for the participant organizations, the choice of a research method in the Yammer experiment. According to study the chosen method and application of social media seemed to be a good approach in order to increase common understanding between the independent participants. On the other hand, the study did not exactly provide an answer on how well social media tools are suited for brainstorming. Further research is needed on how social media can be applied to

brainstorming. In addition to the chosen topic, the organizations were at least as interested in gaining experiences of applying social media technologies in their business operations. To respond this knowledge need, the utilized free version of the web-based Yammer tool turned out to be a very good and easy-to-use tool.

The success of the experiment was measured with the registration rate of the invited individuals, content production activity as well as the quality of the content created in the experiment. The registration rate was a positive surprise since 80 per cent of the invitees registered into Yammer. This showed that people were interested in the experiment. However, the activity of the content producers was quite low, which reveals a lack of real commitment towards the experiment. The four most active content producers produced about 85 per cent of the contents when measured by the number of comments. In practice, the biggest reason for the lack of content production was lack of time: the users had not wanted or known how to reserve sufficient time for the experiment in advance. At the same time, the user group had quite varied interests which probably weakened the motivation for content production. This seems to be in line with the observation of Walker and Ellis (2000) and Studt (2004) that having shared goals is an essential aspect in development and innovation work. Furthermore, a lack of knowledge towards the discussed theme was one reason for small content production activity. In any case, the activity figures surpassed many other experiments with social media as 8 per cent of the users were active content producers and 24 per cent were commentators in the Yammer experiment (compare to corresponding 1 and 10 per cent mentioned by Charles, 2006).

The quality of the created content was evaluated on the basis of user feedback and it was mainly evaluated as good. In addition, a good indicator of the quality of the content is that a part of the content created in the Yammer work has later been refined with the companies, the goal being to develop management practices of the idea process. Furthermore, the created content was utilized as source information for a new research project.

Resources had been sufficiently reserved for the facilitation, which was clearly an important part for the success of the experiment. Both the registration rate and content production activity would have certainly been considerably lower without careful facilitation. Facilitation was needed in the preparatory work (e.g. planning of experiment and getting users to commit to the experiment), guiding the content work, and post-treatment (e.g. taking care of necessary further actions and reporting).

To summarize, social media are suited for communication between independent organizations but at the moment we seem to be at the early stages of learning curve when it comes to it. In the coming years, social media will be natural communication tool also in business, which is important in order to reach a critical, content-producing user mass. The following comment from a user of the Yammer experiment illustrates the possibilities of social media well: "*For social media, there is clearly a new type of a void to be filled in business. This is not about replacing the current process, but about a new process.*

6. References

Belussi, F. and Arcangeli, F. 1998, A typology of networks: flexible and evolutionary firms, Research Policy, Vol. 27, pp. 415-428.

Breeding, M. 2009, Social Networking Strategies for Professionals, The systems librarian, October. pp. 29-31.

Canzano, D. and Grimaldi, M. 2004, Knowledge Management and Collaborations: Knowledge Strategy and Processes in the Knowledge Networks, Proceedings of I-KNOW '04 Graz, Austria, June 30 - July 2, 2004.

Charles, A. 2006, What is the 1% rule?, The Guardian, Thursday 20 July.

Chen, M.-H., Chang, Y.-C. and Hung, S.-C. 2008, Social capital and creativity in R&D project teams, R&D Management, Vol. 38, No. 1, pp. 21-34.

Chesbrough, H.W. 2003, The era of open innovation, MIT Sloan Management Review, Vol. 44, No. 3, pp. 34-41.

Crawford, C.M. 2001, Developing webs of significance through communications: appropriate interactive activities for distributed learning environments, Campus-Wide Information Systems, Vol. 18 No. 2, pp. 68-72.

Dymi, A. 2010, Servicers Use Social Media To Create New Opportunity, National Mortgage News, May 17.

Grinyer, P.H. 2000, A cognitive approach to group strategic decision taking: A discussion of evolved practice in the light of received research results. Journal of the Operational Research Society, Vol. 51, pp. 21-35.

Inkepen A.C. and Tsang, E.W.K. 2005, Social capital, networks, and knowledge transfer, Agademy of Management Review, Vol. 30, pp. 146-165.

Knight, M.B., Pearson,J.M. and Hunsinger, D.S. 2008, The Role of Media Richness in Information Technology Supported Communication inGroup Cohesion, Agreeability, and Performance, Journal of Organizational and End User Computing, Vol. 20, No. 4, pp. 23-44.

Lorenzoni, G. and Lipparini, A.. 1999, The Leveraging of Interfirm Relationships as a Distinctive Organizational Capability: A longitudinal study, Strategic Management Journal, Vol. 20, No. 4, pp. 317-338.

Magnusson, J. and Nilsson, A. 2003, To Facilitate Or Intervene – A Study of Knowledge Management Practice in SME Networks", Journal of Knowledge Management Practice, Vol. 4. http://www.tlainc.com/articl48.htm, read September 15. 2011.

Phillips, L.D. and Phillips, M.C. 1993. Facilitated work groups - Theory and practice, Journal of the Operational Research Society, Vol. 44, pp. 533-549.

Sawhney, M. and Prandelli, E. 2000, Communities of creation: managing distributed innovation in turbulent markets, California Management Review, Vol. 42, No. 4, pp. 24-54.

Shahriza, N., Karim, A. and Heckman, R. Group communication media choice and the use of information and communication technology to support learning: a case study, Campus-Wide Information Systems, Vol. 22, No. 1, 2005, pp. 28-42.

Simatupang, T.M., Wright, A.C. and Sridharan, R. 2002, The knowledge of coordination for supply chain integration, Business Process Management Journal, Vol. 8, No. 3, pp. 289-308.

Studt, T. 2004, The 10 rules of technology transfer, R&D Magazine, Vol. 46, No. 2, pp. 36-38.

Sundgren, M., Dimenaes, E., Gustafson, J.E. and Selart, M. 2005, Drivers of organizational creativity: a path model of creative climate in pharmaceutical R&D, R&D Management, Vol. 35, pp. 59-374.

Tsai, W. and Ghoshal, S. 1998, Social capital and value creation: the role of intrafirm networks. Academy of Management Journal, Vol. 41, pp. 464-476.

Walker, A. and Ellis, H. 2000, Technology transfer: strategy, management, process and inhibiting factors, International Journal of Innovation Management, Vol. 4, No. 1, pp. 97-122.

13

Knowledge Management Through the TQM in the Metrology Area

Alejandro Barragán-Ocaña[1,2], M. Ángeles Olvera-Treviño[2], M. Gerson Urbina-Pérez[1], Darío Calderón-Álvarez[1] and J. Julio Nares-Hernández[1]
[1]*Autonomous University of the State of Mexico*
[2]*National Autonomous University of Mexico*
Mexico

1. Introduction

Knowledge Management (KM) is continually used in various economic and social sectors as scientific, technological, educational, industrial and organizational. Its understanding and use help us to ensure the generation, exchange and application of knowledge under many specific contexts, which contribute to the learning and the cognitive development of all its stakeholders.

Particularly, it is a way to manage the knowledge is represented by Total Quality Management (TQM) within organizations. TQM has allowed companies and institutions to identify and establish their processes, to define and document their operations and to standardize their procedures to ensure customer satisfaction. It has been possible thanks to the transformation and arrangement from tacit to explicit knowledge that is generated within the organization by all stakeholders in the organization. In addition to that, it promotes the communication with the costumer, the realization of measurements, their analysis, and the continuous improvement and innovation of processes and products.

In this sense, measurements and their control represent a way to verify the compliance with the requirements and their possible deviations that arise during the implementation process. However, they also provide a mechanism for continuing improvement and innovation as they allow us to establish actions to improve the effectiveness of the system itself based on this information. Thus, a fundamental science for the proper development of measurements, specifically in the scientific and technical areas, is represented by the metrology that helps us to guarantee the quality of measurements and therefore, customer satisfaction.

The main objective of this work is to provide explanatory elements through an empirical study that enables us to understand how TQM through metrology is a valuable tool for KM within technical environments for promoting standardization, learning and continuous improvement, which even in some cases, these have been linked to several innovative products or processes. Specifically, we approach the case of the contribution that TQM has had from testing and calibration laboratories.

2. Knowledge management and TQM

There is a consensus on the importance knowledge and innovations have as a competitive difference so as to encourage the success of a company (Johannessen *et al*, 1999). According to Lundvall (2006) the knowledge economy is found to be based on two premises: the intensive use of knowledge and the speed with which it becomes obsolete. Based on the previous, individuals and organizations are forced to develop new never-ending learning abilities that allow them to face such challenges.

Helander *et al* (2010) point out that learning is a valuable asset and a vital factor for production and it is therefore, defined as a mix of experience, values and information, which under a specific context, constitute a reference framework so as to evaluate and incorporate new experiences and information that can be expressed and content in data bases, documents, organizational routines, processes, practices and norms (Davenport & Prusak, 2000). Similarly, Dalkir (2005) defines knowledge as a fundamental way of knowledge often supported by experience, values and opinions.

In that sense, Polanyi (1966) classifies knowledge into two categories, tacit knowledge and explicit knowledge. The first one makes reference to personal knowledge, which has the characteristics of being hard to articulate, communicate or reproduce and, it is often related to specific situations. Explicit knowledge instead, can be transmitted or communicated through formal or systematic language. Nowadays, there has been a change from knowledge production based on the old scientific paradigm characterized by the predominance of theory, experimentation, disciplinarity and autonomy of scientists and institutions (mode 1), to a more active generation of it by means of transdisciplinarity, specificity, accountability and their social distribution (mode 2)(Nowotny *et al*, 2003).

In the contributions done by Polanyi, Nonaka & Takeuchi (1995), we find that they describe in their knowledge creation model the following four ways of conversion: 1.- From tacit to tacit (socialization), understood as harmonized knowledge; 2.- From tacit to explicit (exteriorization), represented by conceptual knowledge; 3.- From explicit to explicit (combination), symbolized as systematic knowledge; and 4.- From explicit to tacit (internalization), carried out through operational knowledge.

This knowledge dynamic proposed by the previously mentioned authors has become one of the basic principles in the understanding and correct operation of the KM. In that way, Knowledge Management is considered as a discipline that has the goal to generate, use and share the knowledge existing in spaces and organizations so as to fulfill the individuals' needs and the organizations and communities' development (Barragán, 2009).

Among the main benefits from implementing the KM, the following can be highlighted: it generates synergies among all the organization members, it accelerates the market's innovation and development, and it improves the quality of processes and reduces costs and risks involved in the organization's processes (Mohd *et al*, 2010). In that way, innovation is an element that helps us improve yielding, solve problems, add value to processes and products and, create competitive advantages within the organizations[1]. Therefore, KM and human capital represent essential elements in developing business, understanding them as sources of innovation and renovation (Gloet & Terziovski, 2004).

Kaynak (2003) points out how TQM represents an integral management philosophy that contributes to the continuous improvement in all organization's functions. On the other hand, Kalpič & Bernus (2006) discuss the existence of elements such as 1.- The organization that learns; 2.- Re-engineering of processes in business; 3.- Shaping businesses processes; 4.- Quality administration; and 5.- Movements in businesses'

---

[1] Edquist (2001) explains how innovations in an organization can be generated in technology and organizational processes; as well as in products (goods and services).

intelligence that represent the base through which, the KM allows building organizations based in knowledge. In that sense, Osayawe & McAndrew (2005) show how the TQM promotes creating an environment that favors innovation, creativity and taking risks for the satisfaction of clients' needs by solving problems through the incorporation of managers, employees and clients, who make use of quality control within the organization. In such a way, within the KM environment we can find the TQM is characterized for being an operative area giving support to the KM processes and the creation of organizational knowledge, while greatly influencing the management thinking and practice inside public and private sectors (Johannsen, 2000).

On the other hand, Mukherjee *et al* (1998) declare that TQM processes affect the way people create new knowledge and also determine efficiency within the organization. In the study on the evaluation of quality improvement projects carried out by these authors, they observed two things: the first one makes reference to the role conceptual and operative learning play in the achievement of goals, the development of new technology knowledge and the change in personnel's attention; the second thing observed is that such process of combining both learning types makes coding and diffusion of this knowledge easier. Likewise, Colurcio (2009) argues how the TQM helps on the creation and exchange of knowledge by means of establishing quality principles and methodologies, as these allow generating the necessary conditions for the development of a modern and successful company.

3. Quality multidimensionality

One of the terms we approach in this research refers to quality multidimensionality. In this sense, Prajogo & Sohal (2004) point out that it is divided into two parts: mechanic and organic. The first one is focused to the total quality control in aspects such as processes, requirements, productivity, and efficiency, among many others. Meanwhile, the organic or dynamic part is more oriented towards the development of elements that encourage the necessary conditions to carry out innovations. For example, in their research work, Prajogo & Sohal (2001) have provided evidence about the existence of a strong link between the TQM and innovation. For that purpose, they have described several cases where many companies, through the use of a wide variety of quality tools, have achieved to encourage managing the innovation from implementing TQM practices such as quality culture, learning organization, customer-driven organization and continuous improvement. Among these cases, very important companies can be highlighted, such as: D2D, Rover Group, IBM (UK) Ltd, 3M, Ford, AT&T, Cadillac, Hewlett Packard, Rank Xerox, Exxon Chemical, and Kodak Ltd.

Retaking the previous argument and also based on the theoretical review of literature on the subject, we propose the design of a Knowledge Management model through the use of TQM practices. Under a quality multidimensionality focus and, with an orientation towards testing and calibration laboratories we try to better understand the way in which KM is carried out in the quality and metrology area. Such Knowledge Management model represents a proposal to encourage the KM through the use of implicit elements in the TQM, in the mechanic part as well as the organic one.

For the construction of the model, a wide bibliographic and journalistic research oriented to identifying and analyzing elements used in the TQM practice was carried out. Finding a great amount of them was achieved as it can be seen in table 1.

No.	Author (s)	Year	Elements
1	Havely, A.	2003	The author exposes the possible improvement benefits testing and calibration laboratories could obtain from being accredited by the ISO 17025 norm, among which there can be highlighted : 1.- Improvement of professionalism and abilities, planning, implementation, measurement processes, equipment documentation and maintenance; 2.- Organizational learning through preventive measures and information sources, internal and external; 3.- Inter-laboratory testing; and 4.- Improvement of client satisfaction by means of identifying his needs.
2	Benoliel, J.M.	1999	In his work, he establishes that despite the implementation process of a quality assurance in a laboratory is long and expensive, it has benefits such as: 1.- Improvement of internal organization through processes optimization (procedures formalization and application); 2.- Detection and correction of mistakes; 3.- Demonstration of work abilities; and 4.- Image improvement and handling clients' complaints. Besides developing points that contribute to the implementation of a quality system and organizational improvement such as planning, management responsibility, training, documentation, quality manual, procedures (administrative and technical), development of proof methods, validation of analytic methods and auditing.
			In his study, the author describes how laboratories must fulfill with requirements for certification matters, for technical and management reasons, such as : 1.- Ethic requirements; 2.- Organizational and management procedures; 3.- Clear standards for subcontract in terms of outsourcing (tests) ; 4.- Assurance of quality when acquiring supplies and services ; 5.- Focus on the client, which can make contact and feedback with client better; 6.- Control of unsatisfying work ; 7.- Relevant technical and quality information registry; 8.- Regular internal auditing ; 9.- Periodic review from management; 10.- Qualified and trained personnel; 11.- Facilities

3	Cortez, L.	1999	to assure testing performance; 12.- Calibration testing and methods adequately selected, studied and validated; 13.- To have with the necessary equipment appropriately selected, operated, with periodic, calibrated and verified maintenance; 14.- Guarantee of traceability in measurements; 15.- Well defined sampling procedures; 16.- Well established sampling methods and sample handling; 17.- Quality assurance of testing and calibrations through a quality control system; and 18.- Findings report in a clear, objective and exact way.
4	Cronin, L.B.	1997	He states that the National Accreditation of Measurement and Sampling (NAMAS) points out that the accreditation requirements laboratories must know are oriented to: 1.- Organization, 2.- Auditing and quality revision; 3.- Equipment, methods and procedures; 4.- Handling of testing samples and, attention to complaints and anomalies; 5.- Uncertainty of measurements and handling of traceability; 6.- Quality system; 7.- Personnel; 8.- Environmental conditions; 9.- Registry; 10.- Subcontracts and acquisitions; and 11.- Calibration reports and certificates.
5	Lin, C. & Wu, C.	2005	In their work, they carry out an analysis on how the ISO 9000 norm contributes to knowledge management. In that sense, the authors express that according to the results obtained from interviews carried out with managers, they agree that quality information (document management, messages communication, administrative assistance and quality improvement) and infrastructure (information technology, organization, corporate culture and human resources) represent useful elements to facilitate the Knowledge Management.
			The arguments in this study are in favor of the integration of quality management practices with processes oriented to the creation of knowledge. In their proposal, Linderman *et al* relate client satisfaction, continuous improvement and the vision of the system to the four categories of the knowledge creation

6	Linderman, K. *et al.*	2004	process of Nonaka y Takeuchi. Where some aspects can be highlighted, such as: 1.- Client satisfaction (contact with client, attention mechanisms, complaint management, client analysis, feedback, client's voice, satisfaction and continuous monitoring); 2.- Continuous improvement (equipments, development groups, ideas creation, data analysis, processes control and statistical analysis); and 3.- System's vision (multifunctional orientation, systemic perspective, matrix organization, multifunctional teams, holistic vision and strategic alignment).
7	Molina, M.M. ; Lloréns-Montes, J. & Ruiz-Moreno, A.	2007	Within this research, the relationship between quality management practices and knowledge transference is explained. The authors point out that quality management practices such as cooperation from suppliers, team work, autonomy, process control and cooperation from clients, promote knowledge transference.
8	Ooi, K.B.	2009	Ooi describes how the bond between the TQM principles and organizational knowledge management is related to leadership, strategic planning, focus on client, process management, human resources management, information and its analysis; which through acquisition, dissemination and application of knowledge help to understand its behavior.

Table 1. Review of some examples on the benefits and requirements for the implementation of the TQM's elements.

Once this information was extracted, broken down and analyzed from their respective bibliographic and journalistic sources in order to simplify, the elements found were divided and summarized into two groups (mechanic and organic) and assigned to different categories elaborated for each one of them. In the case of the TQM's mechanic part, the elements were concentrated in the following four areas: 1.- Documentation; 2.- Processes; 3.- Testing and methods; and 4.- Infrastructure (see Table 2).

In the case of the organic or dynamic part of the TQM, the categories were the following: 1.- Continuous improvement; 2.- Focus on client; 3.- Cooperation; and 4.- Information and analysis (see Table 3).

Once the appropriate categories and elements are defined for each one, the model proposed integrates the eight categories and the different elements derived from them. The fundamental idea lies on the fact that it is possible to carry out the KM from the TQM, under the quality multidimensionality concept. In the first part of the model it can be appreciated how it is possible to achieve different requirements of standardizing processes through the TQM's mechanic part, due to the implementation of elements included in the four proposed categories. Combination and internalization of knowledge favor this type of activities as they represent a more systematic and operational knowledge manner (see Figure 1).

No.	Category	Elements
1	**Documentation**	1.- Planning; 2.- Quality manual; 3.- Ethic and legal requirements; 4.- Registry; and 5.- Results report in a clear and exact form.
2	**Processes**	1.- Organization; 2.- Measuring; 3.- Improvement of professionalism; 4.-Optimization; 5.- Formalization of processes; 6.- Technical ability and training; 7.- Definition of organizational, technical and administrative procedures; 8.- Auditing; 9.- Guidelines for subcontracted employment; 10.- Quality assurance in the acquisition of supplies; 11.- Communication management; y 12.- Human resources management.
3	**Testing and methods**	1.- Inter-laboratory testing; 2.- Development of testing methods; 3.- Validation of analytical methods; 4.- Correctly established testing and calibration methods; 5.- Guarantee of the traceability and uncertainty estimation of measurements; and 6.- Well defined methods of sampling and handling of samples.
4	**Infrastructure**	1.- Equipments maintenance; 2.- To have the necessary equipment, carefully selected and validated; and 3.- Adequate and controlled environmental conditions.

Table 2. Main KM elements identified through TQM's mechanic part.

No.	Category	Elements
1	**Continuous improvement**	1.- Organizational learning; 2.- Preventive actions; 3.- Detection and correction of mistakes; 4.- Processes control; and 5.- Leadership.
2	**Focus on client**	1.- Client satisfaction, 2.- Identification of needs; 3.- More contact with him; 4.- Feedback; 5.- Attention mechanisms; 6.- Service to complaints; 7.- Customer service; and 8.- Voice of client.
3	**Cooperation**	1.- Work teams; 2.- Development groups; 3.- Creation of ideas; 4.- Cooperation from providers and clients; 5.- Team work; and 6.-Autonomy.
4	**Information and analysis**	1.- Analysis of information sources; 2.- Continuous monitoring; and 3.- Data analysis.

Table 3. Main KM elements identified through the TQM's organic part.

In the second part of the model, we can observe how the organic or dynamic part, as well as the set categories, are oriented to encourage continuous improvement and in some cases, innovation. This could be explained by the creation of knowledge obtained from the socialization and externalization of it. They are principles that are based on the interaction of groups or people and on the reflection and discussion of tacit knowledge for the creation of conceptual knowledge. The model will be validated and supported through the research of bibliographic and journalistic literature; as well as verifying the categories and elements proposed from a case study, specifically in the context of the metrology area.

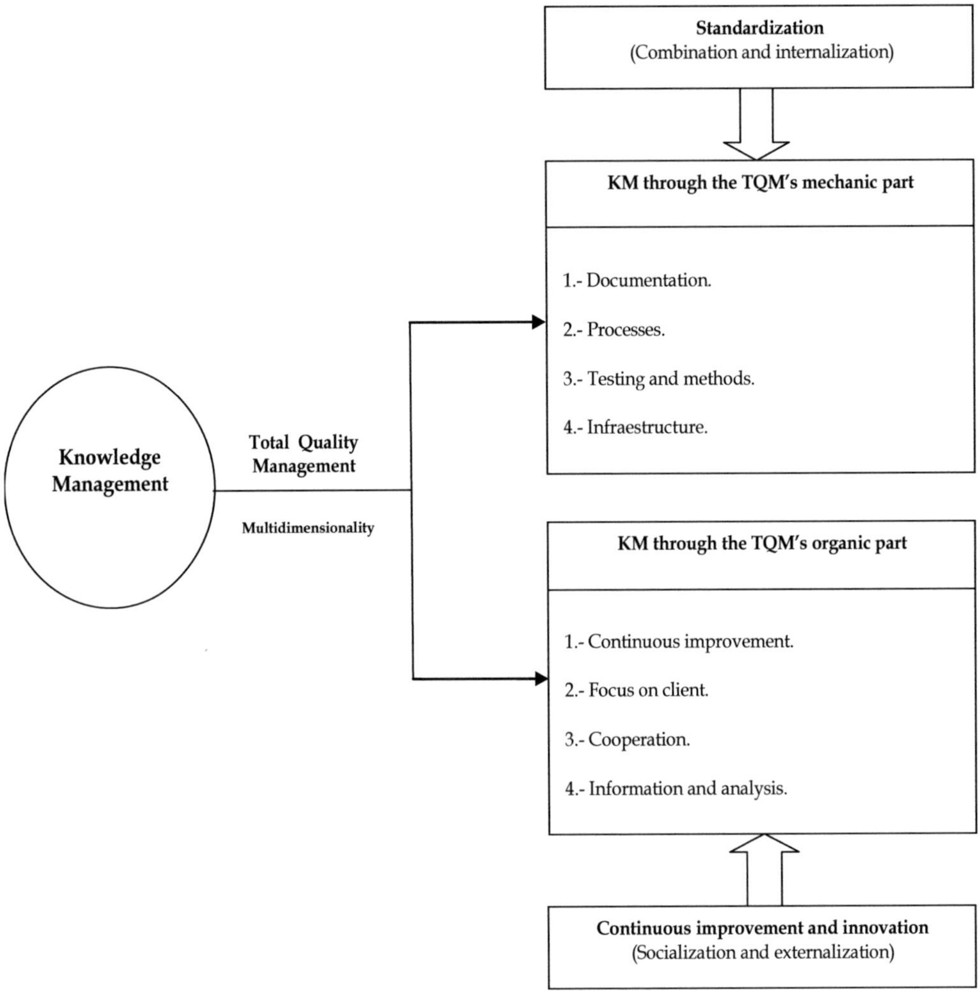

Source: Own creation based on Prajogo & Sohal (2004) and Nonaka & Takeuchi (1995).

Fig. 1. KM model based on the TQM.

4. Metrology in quality

Metrology is defined as the science of measuring and its application (JCGM, 2008). Its use helps to guarantee the quality of measuring and therefore, to improve the several processes where it takes part. Dybkaer (1994) explains that quality in a service laboratory must be shown from two viewpoints. The first one is directed to: a) Identifying the user's needs; b) Selecting measuring procedures; c) Establishing a measuring system of reference to guarantee measuring traceability; d) Having reference materials; and e) Developing competency testing. The second one makes reference to including Good Laboratory Practices and the ISO 9000 certification as competition factors. Cortez (1999) speaks about the importance of setting a distinction between the certification and the accreditation for a laboratory, as the first one makes reference to the evaluation on the quality system's requirements, while the second one not only covers such aspect, but it also evaluates the laboratory's technical competency. In that way, the certification processes as well as the ones of accreditation are applied in testing and calibration laboratories, certification of quality and environmental systems, products certification, personnel and inspection.

The role service laboratories play is mainly focused on contributing in the activities at analytic laboratories, as it is important for them to have valid methods to demonstrate their grade and competency (Taverniers *et al*, 2004). In the certification part, specifically in ISO 9000, this norm provides us with a structure of quality systems for its design, development, production, setup and services, which are related to the TQM's principles (Sun, 2000). In the accreditation part, the main demands when talking about the 17025 norm are focused towards validation of methods, estimate of uncertainty, determining traceability, calibration, reference materials and standards and, assuring quality in testing and results from calibration (Fischbach, 2001).

Although the greatest initiative to implement the quality assurance has come from the industry sector, Groboth (1999) affirms its introduction has been necessary in other service areas; for example, in testing laboratories. This is the reason why once these laboratories go for the accreditation, as in the case of ISO 17025, they can obtain different benefits such as assuring the laboratory's performance, minimizing the risk of obtaining not very reliable results, a reduction on extra testing, an additional financial load and delays on the process; as well as international acceptance and increase on the laboratory's efficiency and efficacy that help trust and satisfaction of clients to increase (Szewieczeka *et al*, 2009).

5. Research methodology

From reviewing the theoretical frame, the research methodology proposal for verification and analysis of the model will be the case study. It has been described by Yin (1981) and Eisenhardt (1989) as a methodology that allows the understanding of dynamics in particular environments. The case studies dealt with can be multiple or simple, with different levels of analysis and variety in methods. Besides, they can be combined among them, as in the case of interviews, files, questionnaires, and observation to obtain quantitative and qualitative evidence. An advantage of this methodology is that it does not require control over the events analyzed and it is focused on the study of contemporary phenomena (Yin, 2003). In that sense, the instrument used to gather information from the case study was to structure a questionnaire, which will be given to the selected calibration laboratory members, along with *in situ* observation. Such tool was previously validated by three university professors through the methodology proposed by Haladyna (2004) to evaluate and in some cases, to modify the pertinence, clarity, design and induction of questions. Therefore, achieving a questionnaire of 14 questions divided into the three following sections: a) Laboratory's general description; b) KM through the TQM's mechanic part; and c) KM through the TQM's organic part, giving the option to integrate other elements not included in the questionnaire, which the interviewee thought to be relevant for the operation of sections b and c.

6. Analysis of the case study

The case study is located in the Metrology Laboratory (calibration) of the Faculty of Chemistry at the National Autonomous University of Mexico, attaché to the Department of Physics and

Theoretical Chemistry. The laboratory started working over 10 years ago, rendering calibration services to analytic laboratories in the UNAM, companies and external laboratories (private); as well as to students who are required to do a social service, thesis or professional and research stays. Nowadays, it has accreditation from the Mexican Accreditation Entity (EMA) in the areas of temperature, mass and volume according to the NMX-EC-17025-IMNC-2006 norm and, the certification on human resources formation process with a metrological orientation according to the NMX-CC-ISO-9001-IMNC-2008 norm.

In order to carry out the study, a questionnaire was applied to the members of the Metrology Laboratory. In the first part, a general description of the laboratory was tackled for contextualization. Among the elements of interest in this section, we can highlight the mission, vision and laboratory's policy of quality, which are mainly aligned to the satisfaction of the metrological needs of their clients, development of scientific projects, creation of professionals and researchers and, integrating the laboratory as part of the traceability chain of measures within the country (see Table 4).

No.	Area	Description
1	**Mission**	*To support the different productive sectors in the satisfaction of their metrological needs through the development of scientific and/or technological projects, to strengthen formation of their professionals, researchers and professors; as well as to give testing laboratory service and to take part in the traceability chain of the country as an accredited calibration laboratory. All of our activities are linked to the needs in the society, as they generate and renew knowledge in the area and favorably have an impact on the development of Mexico.*
2	**Vision**	*To increase the leadership of the Metrology Unit (UM) in the national and international domains through holding on to accreditations, consolidating metrological areas where the laboratory is accredited, increasing the calibration intervals of calibrating magnitudes in each area and testing methods; besides updating and diffusing metrology knowledge in the Faculty of Chemistry and advising the industry on the metrological applications.*
3	**Policy of quality**	*To generate academic activities focused on the contribution to the formation of professionals, researchers and university professors who are helpful in the society with honesty and academic excellence, with foundation on the University Legislation and in the NMX-CC-9001-IMNC-2008. To provide testing and calibration services according to the service norms and following the NMX-EC-17025-IMNC-2008 guidelines, which fulfill and exceed the requirements from internal and external users. We compromise ourselves to give a quality sustained follow-up, in compliance with Mexican norms, to assure the personnel related to the testing and calibration activities have the technical capacity; as well as within the creation of human resources, and that they become familiar with quality documentation and implementation of policies and procedures at their workplace. We also compromise ourselves to a constant improvement.*

Table 4. Mission, vision and policy of quality of the Metrology Laboratory of the Faculty of Chemistry at the UNAM.

No.	Category	Insertion of elements
1	Documentation	1.- ***Planning:*** through the design of social service projects, support on getting the university degree and extension of metrological culture.
		2.- ***Quality manual:*** demanded as part of the laboratory operations.
		3.- ***Ethical and legal requirements:*** the manual of quality is based on ethic and legal requirements. For example, there is a confidentiality agreement for all the activities carried out at the UM.
		4.- ***Registry:*** through filling out the work blog and the blogs related to the whole Quality System of the UM.
		5.- ***Result report of results in a clear and exact form:*** calibration reports are filled in according to the SNC (National Calibration System).
2	Processes	1.- ***Organization:*** the activities carried out are planned, structured and organized in a collective manner for the optimization of functions.
		2.- ***Measuring:*** there are efficiency and efficacy measurements in each process.
		3.- ***Improvement of professionalism:*** through training and timely fulfillment of tasks assigned.
		4.- ***Technical ability and training:*** the continuous and updated training is looked for, collegial work is also carried out.
		5.- ***Definition of organizational, technical and administrative procedures:*** all the activities are carried out according to the SOP (Standard Operation Procedure) by technical and administrative personnel.
		6.- ***Auditing:*** the system includes internal and external audits to contribute to the continuous improvement.
		7.- ***Communication management:*** there is an internal meeting program.
		8.- ***Human resources management:*** there are well defined profiles and functions for each activity.
3	Testing and methods	1.- ***Inter-laboratory testing:*** people take part in them to confirm the technical capacity.
		2.- ***Validation of analytical methods:*** as part of the measuring quality assurance program, validation of methods must be carried out when they are modified somehow.
		3.- ***Correctly established testing and calibration methods:*** the methods are established based on the guidelines laboratories from the National Calibration System (SNC) work.
		4.- ***Guarantee of traceability and uncertainty estimation of measurements:*** there are measuring patterns outlined in the National Metrology Center (CENAM), according to the established in the SNC and it carried out the estimation of uncertainty in measurements.
		5.- ***Well-defined methods of sampling and handling of samples:*** it has the manuals and procedures.
4	Infrastructure	1.- ***Equipments maintenance:*** there is a calibration program of measuring patterns.
		2.- ***To have the necessary equipment, carefully selected and validated:*** When getting new equipment, it is selected according to the method's specific needs and the pertaining validation is carried out.
		3.- ***Adequate and controlled environmental conditions:*** there are working areas that are environmentally adequate for each one of the metrological areas.

Table 5. Verification of elements proposed in the mechanic part of the KM-TQM Model.

The second part of the questionnaire is dedicated to verifying and explaining the elements proposed for the mechanic part of the KM-TQM Model. The points identified within the functioning of the laboratory included most of them, because of the fulfillment of requisites demanded in the accreditation under the ISO 17025 norm and its certification in ISO 9000 norm. Therefore, it was possible to observe the fulfillment of most of the elements contained in the model for each one of the specified categories, which has favored standardization of processes at the laboratory (see Table 5).

No.	Category	Insertion of elements
1	**Continuous improvement**	***1.- Organizational learning:*** it is carried out through team work and internal meetings.
		2.- Preventive actions: it is carried out with continuous supervision of technical and administrative work.
		3.- Detection and correction of mistakes: it is executed through continuous supervision and internal and external auditing.
		4.- Process control: with the quality assurance for measurements through statistical control.
		5.- Leadership: it is given in the proposal and development of projects.
2	**Focus on client**	***1.- Client satisfaction:*** an initial interview when hiring a service and a final application of a survey are given to the client.
		2.- Identification of needs: it is carried out during the interview with the client and in the service application, the scope and length of it are agreed.
		3.- Feedback: when delivering the calibration report, doubts are solved or suggestions are given.
		4.- Attention mechanisms: in person, by telephone and through an email.
		5.- Service to complaints: through the user's voice.
		6.- Voice of client: for all the calibration services and to the training process on human resources.
3	**Cooperation**	***1.- Work teams:*** a collegial work is carried out with other academic groups.
		2.- Team work: work meetings within the UM.
		3.-Autonomy: full compromise and responsibility of each person responsible of an area.
4	**Information and analysis**	***1.- Analysis of information sources:*** periodic review of guidelines given by the EMA and the CENAM.
		2.- Continuous monitoring: Given in the established processes.

Table 6. Verification of elements proposed in the organic part of the KM-TQM Model.

In the third part of the questionnaire, the proposed elements were also verified and explained for the organic part of the KM-TQM Model. The items identified in this section were also abundant; although, the amount was less than in the mechanic part of the model. The previous shows an important step forward of this section. However, it shows the need to look in depth in the development of activities that favor the KM through the elements proposed so as to favor the continuous improvement and innovation (see Table 6).

7. Conclusions

This research represents an exploratory study on the potential the Total Quality Management has in the development and operation of the Knowledge Management within technical environments, in order to optimize standardization processes, promote learning, continuous improvement and innovation.

Among the main findings, we can highlight the large presence of elements proposed in the mechanic part of the model within the case study, due to the laboratory's fulfillment of demanded items for its certification and accreditation in the ISO 9000 and ISO 17025 norms respectively. This has favored the standardization of its processes and it has encouraged the creation of more systematic and operational knowledge. In the other hand, although in the organic part of the model, the elements identified were less, an important effort can be observed which is oriented to the continuous improvement based on preventive actions and a focus on the client that even in some cases, has lead the laboratory to create small incremental innovations within its administrative processes. In other situations, these have developed within its technical processes due to the collegial work with other academic groups and personnel of the laboratory itself.

From the study carried out, a clear relationship can be distinguished between development and operation of the KM, and the improvement on performance and organizational competitiveness from TQM's elements. However, the future research lines must be focused on a more detailed study of proposed groups, their categories and the elements contained in each one of them; besides carrying out a quantitative study that allows extrapolating these results in a larger number of cases.

8. Acknowledgment

To the Autonomous University of the State of Mexico and to the Mexican Council for Science and Technology for the resources given for the publication of this work, through the projects 3066/2011 new applications with waste materials (Handbook) and the 3072/2011 determination of the fluence profile in the thermal column of the Triga Mark III reactor. And for the SNI-CONACYT grant.

9. References

Barragán Ocaña, A. (2009). An Approach to Taxonomy of Knowledge Management Models. *Intangible Capital*, Vol. 5, No. 1, pp. 65-101 (In Spanish).

Benoliel, J. M. (1999). Step-by-Step Implementation of a Quality System in the Laboratory. *Trends in Analytical Chemistry*, Vol. 18, Nos. 9+10, pp. 632-638.

Colurcio, M. (2009). TQM : a Knowledge Enabler? *The TQM Magazine*, Vol. 21, No. 3, pp. 236-248.

Cortez, L. (1999). The Implementation of Accreditation in a Chemical Laboratory. *Trends in Analytical Chemistry*, Vol. 18, Nos. 9+10, pp. 638-643.

Cronin, L.B. (1997). Measurement Accreditation. *Engineering Science and Education Journal*, Vol. 6, No. 1, pp. 9-16.

Dalkir, K. (2005). *Knowledge Management in Theory and Practice*. Elsevier Butterworth Heinemann, United States of America.

Davenport, T., & Prusak, L. (2000). *Working Knowledge: How Organization Manage What They Know*. Harvard Business School Press, Boston.

Dybkaer, R. (1994). Quality Assurance, Accreditation, and Certification : Needs and Possibilities. *Clinical Chemestry*, Vol. 40, No. 7, pp. 1416-1420.

Edquist, C. (2001). *The Systems of Innovation Approach and Innovation Policy: An Account of the State of the Art*. Draft.

Eisenhardt Kathleen, M. (1989). Building Theories from Case Study Research. *Academy of Management Review*, Vol. 14, No. 4, 532-550 pp.

Fischbach, R. (2001). Metrological Demands of ISO 17025 on Testing Laboratories. *Accreditation and Quality Assurance*, Vol. 6, No. 1, pp. 41.

Gloet, M. & Terziovski, M. (2004). Exploring the Relationship between Knowledge Management Practices and Innovation Performance. *Journal of manufacturing Technology Management*, Vol. 15, No. 5, pp. 402-409.

Groboth, G. (1999). Quality Assurance in Testing Laboratories. *Journal of Thermal Analysis and Calorimetry*, Vol. 56, No. 3, pp. 1405-1412.

Haladyna, T.M. (2004). *Developing and Validating Multiple-Choise Test Items*. L. Erlbaum Associates, Mahwah, N.J.

Halevy, A. (2003). The Benefits Calibration and Testing Laboratories may Gain from ISO/ IEC 17025 Accreditation. *Accreditation and Quality Assurance*, Vol.8, No.6, pp. 286-290.

Helander, N.; Kukko, M. & Pasi, V. (2010). Cutting Costs and Marking Profits through Knowledge Management, In. *Knowledge Management*, P. Virtanen & N. Helander (Ed), 1-13, India.

JCGM. (September 2008). *International Vocabulary of Metrology-Basic and General Concepts and Associated Terms (VIM)*. 3rd Edition, JCGM, Available from http://www.bipm.org/vim

Johannessen, J-A. ; Bjørn, O. & Olaisen, J. (1999). Aspects of Innovation Tehory Based on Knowledge-Management. International Journal of Information Management, Vol. 19, No. 2, pp. 121-139.

Johannsen, C.G. (2000). Total Quality Management in a Knowledge Management Perspective. *Journal of Documentation*, Vol. 56, No. 1, pp. 42-54.

Kalpič, B. & Bernus, P. (2006). Bussines Process Modelling through the Knowledge Management Perspective. *Journal of Knowledge Management*, Vol.10, No.3, pp. 40-56.

Kaynak, H. (2003). The Relationship between Total Quality Management Practices and their Effects on Firm Performance. *Journal of Operations Management*, Vol. 21, No. 4, pp. 405-435.

Lin, C. & Wu, C. (2005). Mamaging Knowledge Contributed by ISO 9001 :2000. *International Journal of Quality & Reliability Management*, Vol. 22, No. 9, pp. 968-985.

Linderman, K. *et al* (2004). Integrating Quality Management Practices with Knowledge Creation Processes. *Journal of Operations Management*, Vol. 22, No. 6, pp.589-607.

Lundvall, B-Å. (2006). *Knowledge Management in the Learning Economy*. DRUID Working Paper No. 06-6.

Molina, M.M. ; Lloréns-Montes, J. & Ruiz-Moreno, A. (2007). Relationship between Quality Management Practices and Knowledge Transfer. *Journal of Operations Management*, Vol. 25, No. 3, pp. 682-701.

Mohd Nor, M.N.; Abdullah, R., Azmi Murad, M.A. & HasanSelamat, M. (2010). Managing Knowledge in Collaborative Software Maintenance Enviroment, In. *Knowledge Management*, P. Virtanen & N. Helander (Ed), 1-13, India.

Mukherjee, S. ; Lapre, M.A. & Van Wassenhove, L.N. (1998). Kowledge Driven Quality Improvement. *Management Sciences*, Vol. 44, No.11, pp. S35-S49.

Nonaka, I. & Takeuchi, H. (1995). *The Knowledge-creating Company: How Japanese Companies Create the Dynamics of Innovation*. Oxford University Press, New York.

Nowotny, H.; Scott, P. & Gibbons,M. (2003). Introduction: ´Mode 2´ Re-visited: The New Production of Knowledge. *Minerva*, Vol. 41, No. 3, pp.179-194.

Ooi, K.B. (2009). TQM and Knowledge Management : Literature Review and Proposed Framework. *African Journal of Business Management*, Vol. 3, No. 11, pp. 633-643.

Osayawe Ehigie, B. & McAndrew, E.B. (2005). Innovation, Diffusion and Adoption of Total Quality Management (TQM). *Management Decision*, Vol. 43, No. 6, pp. 925-940.

Polanyi M. (1966). *The Tacit Dimension*. Doubleday & Company, United Sates of America.

Prajogo, D. & Sohal, A. (2001). TQM and Innovation : A Literature Review and Research Framework. *Technovation*, Vol. 21, No. 9, pp. 539-558.

Prajogo, D. & Sohal, A. (2004). The Multidimensionality of TQM Practices in Determinig Quality Innovation Performance-An Empirical Examination. *Technovation*, Vol. 24, No. 6, pp, 443-453.

Sun, H. (2000). Total Quality Management, ISO 9000 Certification and Performance Improvement. *International Journal of Quality &Reliability Management*, Vol. 17, No. 2, pp. 168-179.

Szewieczeka, D. ; Karkoszkaa, T. & Zajacb, A. (2009). Analysis of the Clients' Satisfaction in the Accredited Laboratory. *Journal of Achivements in Materials and Manufacturing Engineering*, Vol. 35, No. 1, pp. 95-102.

Taverniers, I.; De Loose, M. & Van Bockstaele, E. (2004). Trends in Quality in the Analytical Laboratory. II. Analytical Method Validation and Quality Assurance. *Trends in Analytical Chemistry*, Vol. 23, No. 8, pp. 535-552.

Yin, R. (1981). The Case Study Crisis : Some Answers. *Administrative Science Quaartely*, Vol. 26, No. 1, pp. 58-65.

Yin, R.K. (2003). *Case Study Research: Desing and Methods*. 3° Edition, Applied Social Research Methods, Series Volume 5, SAGE publications, United States of America.

14

Real Time Knowledge Management: Providing the Knowledge Just-In-Time

Moria Levy
Bar-Ilan University
Israel

1. Introduction

Defining the target of the research and describing the structure of the paper

Knowledge workers are one of the most important assets to be managed. More employees in all organizations are becoming knowledge workers; workers that their knowledge is meaningful to their success. Productivity of these people is likely to be the center of managing people (Drucker, 1999).

Knowledge Management deals with the productivity of the knowledge worker. Real-Time Knowledge Management is a subset of Knowledge Management focusing on knowledge that has to serve the knowledge worker in real time. The aim of this research is to investigate Knowledge Management in conditions of real time needs. The research assumption is that, non standard KM Solutions will be adapted for real time needs.

The research took place between the years 2010-2011. As Knowledge Management is a developing discipline, it is believed that the timing of the research has affected its results. Some Knowledge Management Solutions demonstrated were rather new (especially in the Healthcare Services Sector) and did not exist three years before-hand. In five years, namely 2015 and further, the results may differ again.

The article is built in the following structure:

Firstly, Real-Time Knowledge Management is defined and described. It is assumed that real time requires suited solutions, but these situations cannot be researched as one group, but rather divided into subsets, derived by the expertise level of the knowledge workers. As it is assumed that the expertise level of the role of the knowledge worker should affect the usage of Knowledge Management Systems, the expertise level of the knowledge workers should be taken into consideration. The next paragraph enlarges the discussion regarding the expertise dimension, and how different levels of expertise roles may use specific Knowledge Management Solutions. Based on these two factors, regular versus Real-Time Knowledge Management, and various KM expertise levels, the scope of the research is defined and the research methodology is explained.

For each role, defined as a Real-Time Knowledge worker role, and representing a different level of expertise, the reviewed Knowledge Management Solutions are reviewed, as learned both from literature, and from the field research conducted. This is repeated for each role in the scope of the research: Service Centers, Banks and Medical Physicians. Next, typical

standards KM Solutions are reviewed, enabling the comparison between the different KM Real-Time roles and Non-Real time roles.
The research method chosen was ground theory. Based on the findings, a theory and triggered architecture are suggested. The research is concluded specifying theoretical and business implications, and pointing out directions for further research.

2. Real time knowledge management

Defining what Real Time knowledge Management Is. Synonyms clarifying the need for unique solutions in real time environments
Knowledge workers, as any other type of workers, operate in an environment where spare time is always scarce. However, there is a difference between an Engineer sitting behind his or her desk, and trying to decide how to design a new electric circle, and a Doctor, who is speaking with a patient, as well as deciding as to what check-ups to send that particular patient.
Gartner defines the real time enterprise as "getting the right information to the right people, at the right time" (Gartner, Inc. 2002). This definition is exactly the definition suggested by Kerschberg and Jeong (2005) for Just-In-Time Knowledge Management: "the concept of Just-In-Time Knowledge Management is appealing in that, the goal is to provide the right information, to the right people, at the right time- just in time- so they can take action based on that information".
Malhorta (2005), based on Lindorff, Lindquist, Margulius, Meyer, Siegele and Stewart, add to this definition: "without latency or delay".
Reviewing various sources, the two terms, "Real-Time Knowledge Management" and "Just-In-Time Knowledge Management" are used by researchers alternately. Davenport and Glaser (2002) prefer the term "just-in-time", while Slawy and Majchrzak (2004) and Mellor Gilhardi (1997) choose to use the term "real- time", etc. Some researchers focus on delivering the knowledge in real- time/ just- in- time (i.e. Davenport and Glaser), without examining how critical is it to the specific user, while others (i.e. Kerschberg and Jeong) focus on the specific role where the just-in- time / real- time, is required do to the type of interface between the employee and the customer.
In this research, the term "real- time" was arbitrary chosen, and the focus resides on those employees, who have to decide and give answers here and now. These situations of Real-Time Knowledge Management differ from other job situations, as the employee has to respond to a person sitting in front of him, or speaking with him on the phone, waiting for a professional answer on the spot. Under these circumstances, the research aims to examine what types of Knowledge Management solutions will suit, enabling the employee to best perform at his/her job.

3. The expertise dimension

Explaining how different KM roles vary in the level of expertise. And how the roles in research reflect different the different levels
Examining the real time factor by itself is not sufficient. The usage of Knowledge Management Systems differ not only by the time one may have before making a decision, rather it may depend on the need for the system assistance. This factor representing the need of level was examined by comparing different groups of employees: on one side of the

scale stand the Call Center Representatives, who are knowledge intermediates; they are hired with no specific knowledge, trained for several weeks, and their turnover is about a year. On the other side, are the Physicians- Doctors, who studied for at least seven years, and in most cases they stay in their profession for a lifetime. In between are front line Bankers and Nurses. All the above, operate in conditions where the information based on a decision, has to be provided in real time. The research's assumption is that, this different level of self knowledge, and therefore the different level of need for the knowledge, will affect the Knowledge Management Solutions provided for the different roles.

4. Research scope

Describing the different KM roles examined and what types of knowledge workers theses people represent

The research examines the Knowledge Management Solution for real time needs by examining the following knowledge worker groups. The expertise level is based on average years of learning and job typical turnover:

Knowledge Workers' Group	Real Time Type Of Work	Expertise Level
Physicians (Doctors)	Real Time	Very High
Nurses	Real Time	Medium-High
Front Bankers (Investment Consultants, Tellers)	Real Time	Medium-High
Call center representatives	Real Time	Low
Back Office Employees (Engineers, etc.)	Non Real Time	Varying

Table 1. Researched roles

Note: All Real-Time Knowledge workers are in charge also for Non-Real-Time processes. For example, a Physician is in charge of checking results of patients' check-ups, in order to decide whether to pro-actively recommend a meeting with a patient. The research focuses only on the real time processes of theses knowledge workers. In addition, the research focuses only on the usage of knowledge in real time situations, and not on the creation of new knowledge in these situations.

5. Research methodology

Describing the research methodology chosen for this research and why the specific methodology was chosen

The research described in this paper, is based on the ground theory methodology.

The research questions the way Knowledge Management is implemented, for roles that are heavily based on real-time situations.

In order to fully understand the issue and suggest an effective architecture for future businesses dealing with real time roles, a ground theory (Glaser & Strauss) qualitative research was conducted. Two methods were used for collecting the data: surveying organizations that include heavily based Real-Time Knowledge Management roles; and, reviewing the literature regarding published articles, describing Real-Time or Just- In- Time Knowledge Management researches.

The data was coded, sorted and categorized. The categorization into groups was the key, for explaining why different types of Knowledge Management Solutions were demonstrated for real time situations. Categorizing real time roles by level of expertise of the people filling in these roles, gave the base for the ground theory, enabling the suggestion of a theory and hence, an architecture for real time business roles.

Hereby, are the details of the data sources described with its categorization.

a. Survey Data Sources: A survey conducted in Israel that questioned Knowledge Managers in charge of providing KM Solutions for Real-Time oriented roles. 14 cases were examined, representing the largest organizations of each type in the country:

Organization Type	Business Role	# Organizations Surveyed
Government	Call Center Representatives	1
Car Industry Services	Call Center Representatives	1
Telecommunications	Call Center Representatives	3
Banks	Account Bankers (Tellers)	2
Banks	Investment Consultants	2
Healthcare Services	Physicians (Doctors)	2
Healthcare Services	Nurses Contact Center Representatives	2
Healthcare Services	Administrative Contact Center Representatives	1
Total		14 cases

Table 2. Surveyed organizations

b. Literature Data Sources: A literature review, learning what KM Real-Time (and KM Just-In-Time) articles exist, and what solutions do these describe. The literature examined, represents worldwide knowledge reported cases. The following articles were analyzed:

Article	Organizations Type Described	Business Roles Described
Knowledge Management For Call Centers	(General)	Call Center Representatives
Contact Center knowledge Management	(General)	Call Center Representatives
The Application Of knowledge Management At Call Centers	(General)	Call Center Representatives
A Simulation Approach To Restructuring Call Centers	Utilities	Call Center Representatives (Tech Support For A Wide Range Of Products And Services)
Knowledge Management At Call Centers	Car Industry Services	Call Center Representatives
Critical Issues In Research On Real Time knowledge Management At Enterprises	(General) Hardware	(General) Call Center Representatives- Customer Support

Eyes Wide Shut? Querying The Depth Of Call Center Learning	(General) Insurance	Call Center Representatives
Getting to "Real-Time" knowledge Management: From knowledge Management To knowledge Generation	Utilities	Consultants
Knowledge Management At Malaysian Banks: A New Paradigm	Banks	(General)
Accelerating Customer-Oriented Banking With knowledge Management	Banks	Front Line (Branches And Sale Offices)
Knowledge Management In Banking Industries: Uses And Opportunities	Banks	(General)
Evaluating The Efficacy Of knowledge Management Towards-Healthcare Enterprise Modeling	Healthcare Services	(General)
Knowledge Management In Evidence-Based Medical Practice: Does The Patient Matter?	Healthcare Services	Physicians (Doctors)
Look Before You Leap: Learning From The Experience Of A Flagging KM Initiative At A Healthcare Organization In Asia	Healthcare Services	Physicians (Doctors) Nurses
Just-In-Time Delivery Comes To knowledge Management	Healthcare Services	Physicians (Doctors)
Total		15 articles

Table 3. Reviewed articles

The following paragraphs describe the Knowledge Management Solutions, demonstrated for the three main real time business roles: Call Center Representatives at Service Centers, Front-Line Bankers; and Physicians. These three roles are heavily based on real-time situations. In order to understand the uniqueness of their solutions, where exist; a preceding paragraph describes typical Knowledge Management Solutions for other business roles, where the work is not real- time oriented.

6. KM solutions for non-real time KM roles

Describing typical KM solutions for other KM roles. Describing access to knowledge

Knowledge Management Solutions existed from 1995, serving various types of knowledge workers. As knowledge workers differ, one from another, there is no one system that fits all (Davenport, 2005). Among the different KM Solutions known and described, there are Portals, Communities of Practice, Expert Locators, Social Networks, Blogs, Document Systems, Web Content Management Systems, Wiki's etc. Yet, with regards to 2011, it has been learned from articles as well as interviews of organizations in Israel, that there are two common used Knowledge Management Systems, more popularly used than others. These consist of Portals (Intranets) and Document Repositories (whether as a Network Drive, a Website including Documents, or a Formal ECM System). All other types of Knowledge Management Systems do exist, yet, in most cases, do not serve as the main solution. The Document Repositories, most naturally, handle Documents. The Portals, mainly handle documents, as well, added with some lists (Bulletin Boards, Contacts, Discussions Groups, etc.). Most knowledge workers, when accessing some Knowledge Management System, retrieve a document.

7. KM for call center representatives at service centers

Describing KM solutions for Call Center Representatives at Service Centers based both on the literature and on the analyzed cases. Describing access to knowledge in real-time scenarios

"Call Centers are high-pressure work environments characterized by constant routine, scripting, computer-based monitoring, and intensive performance targets." (Houlihan, 2000). This is true, both for Call Centers, as well as for other types of Service Centers. The representatives at these organizations work mainly in real-time situations, where they are required to pass information to a customer as fast and yet professionally as possible. At these Service Centers, and specifically in the Cellular Sector, one of the first and largest sectors that has built Service Centers, employees pass organizational information to customers, through representatives that did not create the knowledge themselves. This type of knowledge workers can be referred to as knowledge intermediates; they do not possess the knowledge, rather, they transfer it from the organization to the customers.

It should also be noted, that expertise level of these knowledge workers is not too high: They do not need specific pre academic education in order to qualify for the job. The training is provided on site, and usually its duration is two to three weeks.

Davenport, in his book "Thinking for a living" (2005) refers to Call Center Representatives and the applications that they use, as knowledge workers. "The applications for Call Centers include Customer Relationship Management tools, tools for scripting conversations with customers, knowledge tools for solving customer problems, and tools for capturing customer feedback" (Davenport, 2005, p. 106).

Knowledge retrieval is performed either by a scripting system, or some other type of tool "knowledge tool for solving customer problems" which is not described in detail, and therefore may be understood in several ways.

The findings from the data sources, articles, as well as interviews, conclude the same results: Medium and Large Service Centers are automated. The representatives use unique application systems: The information and knowledge are structured, and displayed as knowledge items. The knowledge items are structured, and each group of items share the same structure. This, as opposed to documents, which are described as the main knowledge item for non-real time workers, and where the majority of the documents are designed in free format. The research also investigated the nature of these knowledge items. In the interviews, the knowledge solutions were quested as to knowledge items nature: Where are they stored, how are they designed and how are they accessed? The findings teach that the knowledge items are stored in unique knowledge bases, named "Contact Center Applications" or "Knowledge Management Applications". The systems resemble Web Content Management Systems as they are organized for handling structured knowledge items, and are suited for the vertical Service Center's specific needs. There are two typical ways to display the knowledge: One is by using scenarios, also named scripts, guiding the representative what to ask, say, or in some cases, how to act. This type of knowledge item is mentioned by Davenport (2005) where he describes the British Telecom Call Center case study. The second way is by knowledge items structured in sets of fields, while each representative decides what subset of fields, and hence, what information to use in each case. The issue how to organize the knowledge items is important, as it affects the response time of the Call Center Representative.

In most interviewed organizations, a mixture of the two methods was found, rather the balance (how many scripts, how many structured fields) varied from organization to organization as follows (data displayed in percentages):

Organization	A	B	C	D	E
Structured Fields	70	90	60	70	80
Scripts	30	10	40	30	20

Table 4. Structuring methods usage

Speaking with the knowledge Managers in charge, no one answer was agreed upon whether scripts are preferred or structured fields. In one organization (90:10 in favor of fields) it was stated that scripts are better, and they are changing now in order to add more scripts. In some other organization it was stated that the representatives prefer information displayed as fields, leaving them the independence to decide in what order to access the information. Another organization stated it holds both, scripts for new representatives, and structure fields for the others.

As to the large quantities of representatives at Call Centers, and as to the high effect, as stated, of the knowledge organization on the ability to respond efficiently, most interviewed organizations, and surely all in the Cellular Sector, continually work on improving the Knowledge Trees (Menus) and refining functionality of the search engine adding facilities to effectively find the requested knowledge as simple and fast as possible. These organizations hold unique teams, in charge of writing, preparing and structuring the knowledge properly.

All interviewed organizations were satisfied with having a unique KM System.

It can be concluded, that for this role, the Knowledge Management System, is unique and planned, focused on its real- time business role orientation.

8. KM for front line bankers

Describing KM Solutions for banking investment consultants based both on the literature and on the analyzed cases. Describing access to knowledge in real-time scenarios

Front Line Bankers may be defined as employees, working in the Banking Sector, who serve the customers of the bank. Thus, as opposed to Back Line Bankers who provide services within the bank to other employees, but not mainly directly to the end customer holding an account at the bank.

Analyzing the data sources for this sector was not trivial. Not all articles distinguished what type of knowledge worker at the bank the described Knowledge Management systems are serving. Part of the articles were therefore not taken into consideration, and the only researchers analyzed, were those who explicitly explained whom the target users were, mentioning Front Line Bankers or Real Time/ Just-In- Time needs.

Knowledge Management Solutions described in researches, included mainly Document Systems (Libraries, Maps Pointing to Documents, etc.) and Intranets (some being part of communities of practice).

The interviews held, distinguished among the Front Line Bankers, two types of knowledge workers: Investment Consultants and Account Managers (Tellers). These two types are front line knowledge workers, who both need pre-academic education, in order to qualify for the job. Yet, the Investment Consultant has more years of experience, and the job requires higher levels of training.

The largest two banks in Israel were interviewed, resulting in the following results:

Both banks have built highly invested Knowledge Management Solutions for Investment Consultants. Yet, these all fall into the category of Portals/Intranets.
For Account Managers, the two banks offered different solutions: One bank offered an Intranet. Yet, the second has realized that in order to make these front line knowledge workers more effective, a well structured knowledge base is required. They have launched, six months before the interview took place, Knowledge Management System, based on structured knowledge items, mainly structured as scenarios, accompanied by documents and structured fields. Their users were very satisfied with the change that eased knowledge usage. Special care was put into improving accessibility and easing the account find the relevant knowledge item, both through routine work on the menus (knowledge Trees) as well as on investing in purchasing an advanced search engine. This KM Solution, resembling Knowledge Management Solutions demonstrated at Call Centers, is unique and was not experienced in other medium to large banks in Israel. It should be noted that the need is emerging. Also, a third medium to large sized bank interviewed on this specific issue only, did state that the Front Line Bankers do have direct lines to the Call Center Representatives that use such a system, and they use them to answer customer query and quicken response.
Additionally, the bank that offered the structured Knowledge Management System, was in its last stages of implementing another system for all bankers, where when right clicking a term, in all systems, a window would pop-up with initial most relevant knowledge for that term. The knowledge presented was structured.
The conclusion is that in most cases, these Real-Time Knowledge workers work with the same Knowledge Management systems, as the typical Non-Real-Time Knowledge worker. There are some cases, in which unique systems that resemble the structured knowledge bases were built to ease and quicken response, yet it is not clear if these are and will be an exception, or do they forecast a new trend to be common in the future.

9. KM for medical physicians

Describing KM solutions for medical physicians based both on the literature and on the analyzed cases. Describing access to knowledge in real-time scenarios
Davenport and Glaser describe the context in which Medical Physicians work: "Dr...has a big problem, one common to all Physicians. There is so much knowledge available about the work, that he cannot possibly absorb it all. He needs to know something about almost 10,000 different diseases and syndromes, 3,000 medications, 1,100 laboratory tests, and many of the 400,000 articles…" (Davenport & Glaser, 2002). Medical Physicians may be viewed as extreme knowledge workers in terms of education, experience, information and knowledge relevant to the job, and importance of the decisions taken: Initial learning includes at least seven years of education and additional years of expertise; the relevant knowledge bases that can help them perform in their job, are huge and grow every year; and, the importance of making the right decisions is critical. Furthermore, as Medical Physicians are Real-Time Knowledge workers, they have to make many of their decisions fast, while they are in interaction with a patient.
Several articles were reviewed in order to learn what Knowledge Management Solutions are offered to the Medical Physicians: Cheah and Abidi describe a Healthcare Enterprise organizational memory knowledge base, which is divided into sub-knowledge bases. These, enable access to protocols (Policies and Procedures) separately for every unit. Types of units may include, for example, Outpatient Department, Emergency Unit, Dental Clinic, etc. Additionally, a general knowledgebase includes Medical Procedures/Treatments and Best

Practices (Cheah & Abidi, 1999). This type of KM Solution is based on documents, and represented via Intranets, Helpdesks, Workflow, Groupware, Document Management, etc. Interrelations exist between the sub-knowledgebase, in means of updating one, as triggered for others being updated.

A similar KM Solution, yet less described into details is presented by Chua and Goh, regarding a case study of a Healthcare Organization. The solution was designed, as in our interest, for Real-Time Knowledge workers (Doctors and qualified Healthcare Professionals) based as a Web System (Intranet).

Another example of KM Solution for making clinical decisions is described by Boateng and is based on evidence-based medical practice. Yet, this solution is also based, as the former described ones, on a search in the knowledgebase for relevant articles, hence, based on documents (Boateng, 2010).

Davenport and Glaser describe a different type of KM Solution for Medical Physicians. While the Medical Physicians log on into their operational systems and work within the patient's record, the KM System operates in the background. When ordering a drug for example, the system checks if there may be any allergic reactions to any other medications prescribed. Recommendations are offered also in cases of ordering tests, based on the recorded systems. This type of KM Solution is based on business rules, which are a unique type of structured knowledge items. "The power of (this type) of knowledge-based order entry, referral, computerized medical-record, and event-detection systems is that they operate in real-time." (Davenport & Glaser, 2002).

In Israel, interviews were conducted at the two largest Healthcare Service providers in the country. In both cases, the knowledge was embedded into the operational systems: In one organization, a business rule system was implemented, as described in Davenport and Glaser. It should be noted that this system was implemented already for two years, replacing a former KM Solution based only on an Intranet; at the other organization, the knowledge embedding solution enabled quick access to drugs and tests knowledge bases directly from the user's record, directing the doctor directly to the drug or test in context, when right clicking the term. The solution was new and yet tested as a pilot (implemented for a few months). Initial responses were positive.

It should be noted that these two solutions are similar, yet different; they both embed the knowledge into the operational system, yet while the first solution presented works in "push" mode, the second is "pull" oriented.

For Non Real Time Knowledge Management roles, the usage of business rule systems, as well as other embedded Knowledge Management Systems in operational systems can be found, yet is rather rare.

The conclusion withdrawn is that this sector is probably experiencing a change as toward the preferred solution for Real-Time Knowledge Management. From Intranets and Document Management Systems, which are stand alone Knowledge Management Systems based on documents, the organizations are moving towards embedded Knowledge Management Systems, offering their knowledge workers Just-In-Time recommendations, based on structured knowledge items in pull or push mode.

10. Summarized findings

Summarizing findings across sectors and business roles

In the research, it was found that Real-Time Knowledge workers do use KM Systems. Findings suggest that only in the Call Center Sector, KM unique systems are the default; yet all types of real-time roles have been found to experience real- time unique KM Systems, and have found it useful, wherever implemented, and there is a positive trend of enlarging these systems over time.

Even though unique KM Systems are typical for some roles more than others, based on the self knowledge of the type of the knowledge worker holding the position, all roles do benefit from the unique systems when provided, and do use it on real-time situations. Wherever previous non-unique KM Systems did exist, organizations were satisfied with the change. No organization was found to withdraw a unique KM System after built, returning back to an Intranet or Documenting System.

It should also be noted, that similar types of Real-Time unique systems were found across the different roles.

11. Suggested architecture

Suggesting architecture for providing KM solutions for real-time oriented roles and for other real-time scenarios. Emphasizing on accessibility of the KM solution

Based on the research, a theory is suggested: All Real-Time Knowledge workers can benefit from working with unique KM Systems, and should work with such systems.

As KM unique real time systems were found to be more costly, in terms of content processing and maintenance, and the main criterion defining where to prior investing in building these systems is cost-effectiveness; i.e. where the organization benefits more.

Typical examples of these may include: hold less knowledge workers for the job, as in the case of Call Representatives; benefit from less errors in decisions, like in the case of Physicians; benefit from more professional response to customer queries etc.

In order to suggest a suitable recommendation, the Real Time KM System has to be defined.

A Real-Time KM System is a KM System that benefits from eased accessibility, both externally and internally, as described below:

External Accessibility- Easing the path of the user to the knowledge item.

Internal Accessibility- Easing the readability and hence the understanding of the knowledge, once it was reached.

(Levy, 2009)

Real- Time KM Systems differ from regular KM Systems, in the following ways:

Topic	Real-Time KM System	Non-Real-Time Typical KM System
Entity Managed	Knowledge Item	Document
Structuring Level	High	Low
Accessibility Level	High / Embedded	Varying / Mainly Stand-Alone

Table 5. Real-Time KM Systems' attributes

External Accessibility can be achieved in a few ways:

a. "Pushing" the knowledge to the Real-Time Knowledge worker, while he/she uses an Operational IT System.
b. Easing the "pull" of the knowledge by enabling access using right click, or any similar technique.
c. Enabling direct access to the knowledge items through search engines and fine tuned menus (Knowledge Trees).

External Accessibility can be demonstrated in the following figure:

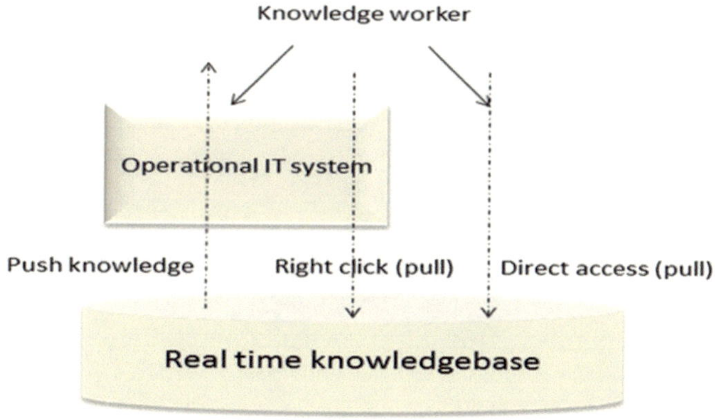

Fig. 1. External knowledge access

Note: Dealing with External Accessibility itself is not unique to the Real-Time KM Systems. However, more care and emphasis were found for real time roles, improving both the hierarchical navigation through the Knowledge Trees (mainly manually) and the search mechanism (mostly automatically- improving the software involved). In Non-Real-Time oriented roles, only few usages of business rules and other push mode mechanisms were found.

KM found Practices:

- Wherever operational IT systems exist, it is preferred to use theses to serve as the interface to the real time knowledge.
- Access, and especially pull oriented access, should be enabled through several access channels, wherever possible.

Internal Accessibility can be achieved by using structured knowledge items, rather than documents. Three types of knowledge items can be used:

a. Business Rules: Short "bottom-lines" advising the knowledge worker what to do. Usable when relevant: knowledge is clear, short and precise.
b. Structured Fields; may be embedded in sub-groups.
   Usable when the body of knowledge is larger, enabling the knowledge worker to decide what specific knowledge is more suitable for the specific case; usable also when there is no one unique answer, the knowledge serving decision support.

Demonstration:

Fig. 2. Internal knowledge access- structured fields

c. Scripts
   Usable for new users; Usable when there is a known workflow for the knowledge decision.

Demonstration:

Fig. 3. Internal knowledge access- scripts

KM found practices:

- Simplicity is most important for easing understanding and usage of content. There is no clear answer to the question whether short (as in structured items) or lengthy (as in scripts) is more simple, and the decision is to be taken in each organization as to its context, striving to maximize simplicity.
- The employees in charge of writing the context may be part of each professional unit in charge of the content, or in a centralized unit. It was found that defining the internal structure and writing the knowledge items is a profession, and it is preferred to organize these technical writers as one centralized unit.

Organizations should strive to design for its Real-Time Knowledge workers KM Systems, including improved external and internal accessibility, in one or more of the defined types above. It has not be proven that Real-Time Knowledge workers will not use and benefit from other types of KM Systems, yet, it has been found that organizations that turned to using these types of unique KM Systems, were satisfied with the change and none wanted to return to classical KM Systems (as Intranets or Document Systems) even though these systems are expensive to build and expensive to maintain.

12. Conclusions

Drawing possible conclusions as to the need of unique KM solutions for real-time scenarios.

The conclusions from the research suggest:

Unique KM Systems were found in usage, serving Real-Time Oriented Knowledge workers. Different real time role types were found to use these systems in different levels, and in typical ways, yet unique KM Systems were in use of all examined role types.

It is recommended to integrate all the various solution types found in usage of the different roles and to implement unique KM Solutions, based on these, for real- time roles in the organization. These solutions will be unique in the way they ease both external access and internal access to the knowledge worker. Organizations should prioritize implementation of these solutions, as they are more expensive to implement. Thus, should be performed, prioritizing roles where knowledge is more in need (as for lower level expertise knowledge workers; scenarios in which the organization considers the decisions to be more critical; etc.).

13. Further research

Clarifying limitations of the conclusions. Suggesting possible future research that may clarify the open issues

The conclusions from the research are limited three fold:
First, the research's scope was mainly based on three sectors of Real-Time Oriented users. It is recommended to further investigate on other sectors as well, validating the findings and theory based on these findings.
Additionally, the scope was limited in the amount of organizations examined. Literature was learned where existed; deepened interviews were performed for each sector in a limited set of the leading ones in each organization. The conclusions may be validated by examining additional organizations worldwide.
And finally, while the research took place, a change was viewed. It is recommended to re-analyze the Real-Time KM topic again within several years learning, if indeed more organizations follow and design unique KM Systems as viewed during the change, and as recommended by this research.

14. Implications for organizations

What can organizations learn from this research?
Organizations have been adopting KM Systems for over a decade. These systems started from very simple ones and are developing over the years, both due to technological new opportunities, as well of fitting specific business needs.
This research enlightened Real-Time Oriented needs, and do suggests designing and building specific unique KM Systems for the Real-Time role types. Furthermore, the research points out what components such systems should include, putting the focus on improved External Accessibility (as in the push mode of business rules), and on Internal Accessibility (whether templates, scenarios or bottom lines). Organizations should not settle only for such types of solutions for Service Support Centers. The default nowadays, rather strive for supporting such solutions to all types of Real-Time Oriented roles, prioritizing where to start, as to the level of criticality of the knowledge required by the knowledge worker in order to perform best. Managers, with the assistance of KM Managers, should initiate the topic and lead these changes in the organization.

15. Summary

Summarizing the research and its conclusions
Knowledge Management is a popular researched discipline. Real-Time Knowledge Management, also termed Just-In-Time Knowledge Management, is a sub-topic less researched. This research raised the question whether Real-Time Oriented knowledge workers need a different type of KM System. The research was based both on analysis of previous researches regarding KM Systems, as well as interviews at Israeli organizations. Three types of Real-Time roles were examined representing different types of knowledge workers, each with a different level of expertise. Analyzing the current situation and the viewed changes in past few years, an integrated solution was purposed for all various real type needs, prioritizing its implementation as no organization can build all systems at once. Real-Time KM Systems have learned to be of a unique type, with improved care as to external accessibility, and with different representation of the knowledge as knowledge items, enabling the internal accessibility as well.
It is believed that these Real-Time KM Systems will be more popular over time, and will develop as to the suggested architecture. Better accessibility in this case is not about saving time. As the resource of time is scarce in real time scenarios, the KM System is, in many

cases, the differentiator between using the system or not using it at all. This fundamental point, organizations do understand.
Real-Time KM Systems serve as a business differentiator.

16. References

Boateng W. (2010). Knowledge Management in Evidence-Based Medical Practice: Does the Patient Matter?, *Electronic Journal of Knowledge Management*, vol. 8 iss. 3, pp. 281-292.

Cheah Y.N. & Abidi S.S.R (1999). *Evaluating the Efficacy of Knowledge Management towards Healthcare Enterprise Modelling*, int. joint conference on artificial intelligence IJCAI'99, Stockholm, 1999.

Chua A.Y.K.& Goh D.H.(2008). Look before you leap: Learning from the experience of a flagging KM initiative at a healthcare organization in Asia, *Aslib proceedings: New Information Perspectives*, vol. 60 no. 4, 2008, pp. 335-348.

Davenport T.H. (2005). *Thinking for a Living*, Harvard Business School Publishing, Boston, Massachusetts, USA, 2005.

Davenport T.H. & Glaser J. (2002). Just in time delivery comes to knowledge management, *Harvard Business Review*, July 2002.

Drucker, P.F. (1999). *Management Challenges for the 21st century*, HarperCollins Publishers, Inc.: New York, NY.

Hafizi M.A. & Nor A. (2006).Knowledge management in Malaysian banks: a new paradigm, *Journal of Knowledge Management*, vol. 7 no.2 2006.

Houlihan M. (2000). Eyes wide shut? Querying the depth of call centre learning, *Journal of European Industrial Training*, 24/2//3/4, pp. 228-240.

Gartner, Inc. (2002), *The real time enterprise*, retrieved from http://rte.gartner.com/

Glaser B.G. & Strauss A. (1967). *The Discovery of Grounded Theory: strategies for qualitative Research*, Barney G. Glaser and Fraces Strauss (2009).

Jayasundara & Chaminda C. (2008). Knowledge management in banking industries: uses and opportunities, *Journal of the University Librarians Association of Sri Lanka*, vol. 12 2008.

Kerschberg L. & Jeonf H. (2005). Just-in-Time Knowledge Management, keynote in *Third Conference on Professional Knowledge Management*, Kaiserslautern Germany 2005.

Lam K. & Law R.S.M. (2004). A simulation approach to restructuring call centers, *Business Process Management Journal*, vol. 10, no. 4 2004, pp. 481-494.

Levy M. (2009). Leveraging Knowledge understanding in Documents. *Electronic Journal of Knowledge Management Practice*, 7(3).

Malhorta Y. (2005). Integrating knowledge management technologies in organizational business processes: getting real time enterprises to deliver real business performance, *Journal of Knowledge Management*, vol. 9 no.1 2005, pp. 7-28.

Mellor Ghilardi F.J. (1997). Getting to real time knowledge management: from knowledge management ro knowledge generation, Medford, vol. 21, iss. 5 1997, pp 99-101.

Rasooli P. (2006). *Knowledge management in call centers*, Master Thesis, Department of Business Administration and Social Sciences, Lulea University of Technology, 2006.

Realcom (2009). *Accelerating customer-oriented banking with knowledge management*. Retrieved from http://www.realcom.co.jp/en/case_studies.html on Sep. 22, 2009.

Roertson J. (2008). *Knowledge management for call centres*,

Slawy O.A. & Majchrzak A. (2004). Critical issues in research on real tome knowledge management in enterprises, *Journal of Knowledge Management*, vol. 8 no. 4 2004, pp. 21-37.